Fourth Edition

Assessment in Special Education

A PRACTICAL APPROACH

Roger Pierangelo
Long Island University

George A. Giuliani
Hofstra University

PEARSON

Boston   Columbus   Indianapolis   New York   San Francisco   Upper Saddle River
Amsterdam   Cape Town   Dubai   London   Madrid   Milan   Munich   Paris   Montréal   Toronto
Delhi   Mexico City   São Paulo   Sydney   Hong Kong   Seoul   Singapore   Taipei   Tokyo

Vice President and Editorial Director: Jeffery
    W. Johnston
Executive Editor: Ann Castel Davis
Editorial Assistant: Penny Burleson
Vice President, Director of Marketing: Margaret
    Waples
Marketing Manager: Joanna Sabella
Senior Managing Editor: Pamela D. Bennett
Project Manager: Sheryl Langner
Production Manager: Laura Messerly

Senior Art Director: Jayne Conte
Cover Designer: Suzanne Behnke
Cover Art: Fotosearch
Full-Service Project Management: Jyotsna Rishi,
    Element LLC
Composition: Element LLC
Printer/Binder: Courier/Westford
Cover Printer: Courier/Westford
Text Font: Times LT Std 10/12

Credits and acknowledgments for material borrowed from other sources and reproduced, with permission, in this textbook appear on the appropriate page within the text.

Every effort has been made to provide accurate and current Internet information in this book. However, the Internet and information posted on it are constantly changing, so it is inevitable that some of the Internet addresses listed in this textbook will change.

Library of Congress Cataloging-in-Publication Data
Pierangelo, Roger.
    Assessment in special education : a practical approach / Roger
Pierangelo, George A. Giuliani.—4th ed.
        p. cm.
    Includes index.
    ISBN-13: 978-0-13-261326-2
    ISBN-10: 0-13-261326-3
    1. Children with disabilities—Education—United States.   2. Disability evaluation—United States.
    3. Educational tests and measurements—United States.   4. Special education—United States.
    I. Giuliani, George A. II. Title.
    LC4031.P483 2013
    371.90973—dc23
                            2011033705

10 9 8 7 6 5 4 3 2 1

ISBN 13: 978-0-13-261326-2
ISBN 10:   0-13-261326-3

This book is dedicated to my wife, Jackie, and my two children, Jacqueline and Scott, who provide me with the love and purpose for undertaking projects that I hope will enhance the lives of others. Their lovely presence in my life is a blessing. I also dedicate this book to my parents, who provided me with the secure and loving foundation from which to grow; my sister, Carol, who has always made me smile and laugh; and my brother-in-law, George, who has always been a very positive guiding light in my professional journey.

—R. P.

This book is dedicated to my wife, Anita, and our two children, Collin and Brittany, who give me the greatest life imaginable. The long hours and many years it took to finish this book would never have been possible without the support of my loving wife. Her constant encouragement, understanding, and love provided me with the strength I needed to accomplish my goals. I thank her with all my heart. I also dedicate this book to my parents, who have given me so much support and guidance throughout my life. Their words of encouragement and guidance have made my professional journey a very rewarding and successful experience.

—G. G.

ABOUT THE AUTHORS

DR. ROGER PIERANGELO

Dr. Roger Pierangelo is an associate professor in the Department of Special Education and Literacy at Long Island University. He has been an administrator of special education programs, served for 18 years as a permanent member of Committees on Special Education, has over 30 years of experience in the public school system as a general education classroom teacher and school psychologist, and serves as a consultant to numerous private and public schools, as well as PTA and Special Education PTA groups.

Dr. Pierangelo has also been an evaluator for the New York State Office of Vocational and Rehabilitative Services and a director of a private clinic. He is a New York State–licensed clinical psychologist, a certified school psychologist, and a board-certified diplomate fellow in student and adolescent psychology and forensic psychology.

Dr. Pierangelo is the executive director of the National Association of Special Education Teachers (NASET) and an executive director of the American Academy of Special Education Professionals (AASEP). He is also vice president of the National Association of Parents with Children in Special Education (NAPCSE).

Dr. Pierangelo earned his BS from St. John's University, MS from Queens College, professional diploma from Queens College, PhD from Yeshiva University, and diplomate fellow in student and adolescent psychology and forensic psychology from the International College of Professional Psychology.

Dr. Pierangelo is a member of the American Psychological Association, New York State Psychological Association, Nassau County Psychological Association, New York State Union of Teachers, and Phi Delta Kappa. Dr. Pierangelo is the author of multiple books in the field of special education, including two coauthored with Dr. Giuliani from Pearson Education titled *Transition Services in Special Education: A Practical Approach* and *Learning Disabilities: A Practical Approach to Foundations, Assessment, Diagnosis, and Teaching.*

DR. GEORGE GIULIANI

Dr. George Giuliani is a full-time associate professor at Hofstra University's School of Education, Health and Human Services and the assistant chairperson of the Counseling, Research, Special Education and Rehabilitation (CRSR) Department. He is also a special professor at Hofstra University's School of Law where he teaches special education law.

Dr. Giuliani earned his BA from the College of the Holy Cross, MS from St. John's University, JD from City University of New York School of Law, and MA and PsyD from Rutgers University. He earned board certification as a diplomate fellow in advanced child and adolescent psychology, board certification as a diplomate fellow in forensic sciences from the International College of Professional Psychology, and board certification in special education from the American Academy of Special Education Professionals.

Dr. Giuliani is a member of the American Psychological Association, Education Law Association, New York State Psychological Association, American Bar Association, Suffolk County Psychological Association, Psi Chi, American Association of University Professors, and the Council for Exceptional Children.

Dr. Giuliani is the executive director of The National Association of Special Education Teachers, executive director of the American Academy of Special Education Professionals, and president of the National Association of Parents with Children in Special Education. He has been a consultant for school districts and early childhood agencies, and has provided numerous workshops for parents, teachers, and other professionals on a variety of special education and psychological topics.

Dr. Giuliani is the author of multiple books in the field of special education, including two coauthored with Dr. Pierangelo from Pearson Education titled *Transition Services in Special Education: A Practical Approach* and *Learning Disabilities: A Practical Approach to Foundations, Assessment, Diagnosis, and Teaching.*

PREFACE

Assessment in Special Education: A Practical Approach, Fourth Edition, continues to represent a new and unique direction in college textbooks. This book is the result of several years of marketing analysis and experience. The format for this text is based on your needs as a student to have a practical, user-friendly, useful, and clearly understood textbook that also can be used as a reference once you enter the workplace. In our market research with undergraduate and graduate students, we found that

- 91 percent of those interviewed felt that most college texts were very difficult to read
- 87 percent found them difficult to understand
- 74 percent felt that most texts contained irrelevant and useless charts and tables
- 93 percent indicated that they could not see using the book as a practical reference tool after the course was over
- 71 percent felt that the formats were overwhelming
- 98 percent felt that most texts contained too much theory and not enough "practical information"
- 90 percent normally sold back their textbooks at the end of the semester because they had no practical value and would "just sit on a shelf"

We have tried to provide you with a "real-world story" or process for the area of assessment that has a beginning, a middle, and an end. Many assessment texts we have reviewed have approximately 15 or more chapters that are not connected, but rather offer students separate pieces that never show clearly the overall process in a straight line. In this text, we provide you with the practical tools necessary to understand the process of assessment in schools and to learn how to "put it all together."

Graduates of most assessment courses understand what constitutes validity and reliability, a description of the tests most often used in assessment, legal issues, and basic statistical terminology. Our textbook not only covers these areas, but it also focuses on the practical application of assessment in schools with discussions of interpreting results, diagnosing a suspected disability, writing a professional report, making recommendations from the data, presenting results to parents, and attending the eligibility committee meetings. From our market research, this is where our book is unique.

Other practical features of this text include the following:

- Content that reflects IDEA 2004
- Combined coverage of formal and informal assessment
- Thorough discussion of all the most up-to-date tests used in school systems
- Opportunities to take test data and learn their practical application in both writing and recommendations
- Practical approaches to parent–teacher conferences and the sensitivity required in discussing test results with parents
- A step-by-step approach from identification of a high-risk child to placement
- Comprehensive coverage of the latest tests and evaluation procedures for all areas of exceptionality
- An emphasis on the application of information to meet the individual, often unique, requirements of students with special needs

- Coverage of assessment that spans infancy and preschool age through high school and into adulthood
- An overall practical focus to balance out the strong grounding in theory so necessary for understanding exceptionality
- Information about assessment vehicles, both formal and informal, to help you make informed decisions about which technique or tool is best with which students
- Numerous teaching–learning aids
- Samples of actual assessment, evaluation, and procedure forms utilized in school systems

After reading this textbook, you should have a thorough understanding of the assessment process in special education from start to finish. Assessment in special education is a step-by-step approach, and the goal of this text is to give you all the tools necessary to understand what really happens in the assessment process.

NEW TO THIS EDITION

Besides the features addressed above, *Assessment in Special Education: A Practical Approach,* Fourth Edition, has many new features. These include:

- Latest updated information regarding the major principles of assessment under IDEA 2004
- Greater coverage of curriculum based assessment (CBA) and curriculum based measurement (CBM)
- Updated references in all chapters covering the most current research in the field of assessment
- Comprehensive coverage of how RTI plays a significant role in the assessment of a child for a suspected disability
- Analysis of the most current, valid, reliable, and popular intelligence, academic achievement, behavioral, perceptual, speech and language, early childhood, hearing, and physical and occupational therapy assessment measures
- Comprehensive coverage of functional behavioral assessments (FBA) and behavioral intervention plans (BIP)
- Latest information of eligibility in special education and how the assessment process dictates classification
- Updated academic evaluation report writing section, with more samples to review
- Detailed information on IEP development and requirements under IDEA 2004

ACKNOWLEDGMENTS

In the course of writing this book, we have encountered many outstanding and professional sites. It has been our experience that those resources have contributed and continue to contribute enormous information, support, guidance, and education to parents, students, and professionals in the area of special education. Although we have accessed many worthwhile sites, we would especially like to thank and acknowledge the National Dissemination Center for Children and Youth with Disabilities (NICHCY) and the National Clearinghouse for Bilingual Education (NCBE).

Dr. Roger Pierangelo extends thanks to the following: the faculty, administration, and staff in the Department of Graduate Special Education and Literacy at Long Island University; the students and parents of the Herricks Public Schools he has worked with and known over the past 28 years; the late Bill Smyth, a truly gifted and "extraordinary ordinary" man; Helen Firestone, for her influence on his career and tireless support of him; and Ollie Simmons, for her friendship, loyalty, and great personality.

Dr. George Giuliani extends sincere thanks to all of his colleagues at Hofstra University in the School of Education, Health and Human Services. Dr. Giuliani would also like to thank the following: his brother, Roger, and sister, Claudia; mother-in-law, Ursula Jenkeleit; sisters-in-law Karen and Cindy; brothers-in-law Robert and Bob—all of whom have provided encouragement and reinforcement in all of his personal and professional endeavors.

We would like to thank Penny Burleson, our editorial assistant, for always helping us attain any materials or information necessary to complete this textbook, and Ann Davis, our editor, whose outstanding guidance, support, and words of encouragement made writing this book a very worthwhile and enjoyable experience.

We would also like to thank the following reviewers: Patricia Barber, SUNY–Geneseo; Maryann Dudzinski, Valparaiso University; Karen Sealander, Northern Arizona University; Kristin Stang, California State University, Fullerton; and Kelly Stout, University of Utah.

CONTENTS

FOUNDATIONAL CONCEPTS IN ASSESSMENT IN SPECIAL EDUCATION

Welcome to the world of assessment in special education. We hope that you enjoy this book and find it very practical and user friendly. This book is divided into two parts. Part I (Chapters 1 through 5) presents an overview of the most important concepts, laws, statistics, and terms you need to know to understand the assessment process. Part II (Chapters 6 through 19) then takes you step by step through the assessment process as it happens every day in schools.

Chapter 1 presents you with an overview of key terms and definitions used in assessment in special education. We then discuss an overview of legal issues in assessment. First, you will learn about the most important historical cases in special education. Following these cases, we will discuss current federal legislation and how it influences children, parents, and special educators involved in the assessment process.

The chapter then continues with addressing what constitutes assessment, the professionals involved in the assessment process, and the various children with disabilities you may come in contact with in special education. We then present you with a brief, general overview of the different methods of assessment. Finally, you will learn about parental involvement in the assessment process.

Chapter 2 focuses on various methods of assessment used in special education. This chapter presents an overview of both formal (norm-referenced tests) and informal assessment (criterion referenced tests, portfolios, curriculum-based assessment, dynamic assessment, and many others). Following a discussion of these methods, you will learn about the decision-making process involved in selecting the appropriate instrument for evaluating students.

Chapter 3 is an overview of the most basic statistical concepts you need to survive the special education process. To fully understand assessment, you must first become familiar with statistics. Statistics are very important in special education, and we will guide you down a very methodical and comfortable road to teach you these concepts.

Chapter 4 addresses concerns about validity and reliability. You will learn that a test needs to be both valid (assessing what it is supposed to measure) and reliable (consistent) to be useful. This chapter also addresses all the different types of validity and reliability so that you will have a strong working knowledge of when a test is most suitable to use.

Finally, in **Chapter 5,** we present basic scoring terminology used every day in assessment. These terms are very important in scoring and analyzing the results of the various measures you will use in the assessment process.

After reading the first five chapters you will be ready for Part II of this text, which will lead you through a practical, step-by-step process involved in assessing children with special needs.

1 INTRODUCTION TO ASSESSMENT

Key Terms

Americans with Disabilities Act
Analysis
Assessment
Assessment approach
Autism
Collection
Consent for evaluation
Deaf–blindness
Deafness
Determination
Developmental delay
Due process
Education of All Handicapped Children Act (EHA)
Education of the Handicapped Act Amendments of 1986
Eligibility and diagnosis

Emotional disturbance
Evaluation
Family Education Rights and Privacy Act
Fourteenth Amendment
Hearing impairment
Impairment
Individualized education program (IEP)
Individuals with Disabilities Education Improvement Act
Informed consent
Instructional planning
Least restrictive environment (LRE)
Mental retardation
Multiple disabilities

Native language
No Child Left Behind Act
Nondiscriminatory assessment
Orthopedic impairment
Other health impairment
Reauthorization
Recommendation
Section 504 of the Vocational Rehabilitation Act
Specific learning disability
Speech or language
Transition services
Traumatic brain injury
Visual impairment
Vocational Education Act of 1984 (Perkins Act)
Zero reject

Chapter Objectives

This chapter presents a general overview of assessment. After reading this chapter, you should be able to do the following:

▊ Define assessment

▊ Understand the purpose of assessment

▊ Understand the basic problems with respect to discrimination in special education

▊ Understand the landmark court cases and federal legislation in special education

▊ Know the various federal legislation pertaining to special education and individuals with disabilities:

   Section 504 of the Vocational Rehabilitation Act

   P.L. 93-380: The Family Education Rights and Privacy Act

   P.L. 94-142: The Education of All Handicapped Children Act

   P.L. 98-524: The Vocational Education Act of 1984—the Perkins Act

   P.L. 99-457: Education of the Handicapped Act Amendments of 1986

P.L. 101-336: The Americans with Disabilities Act

P.L. 101-476: The Individuals with Disabilities Education Act (IDEA)

P.L. 105-17: The Individuals with Disabilities Education Act of 1997

P.L. 107-110: No Child Left Behind Act of 2001

P.L. 108-446: The Individuals with Disabilities Education Improvement Act of 2004

▪ Understand the role of state and federal government in establishing and implementing laws pertaining to special education

▪ Know the professionals involved in the assessment process

▪ List and define the classifications in special education as defined under the Individuals with Disabilities Education Improvement Act of 2004 (IDEA 2004)

▪ Know the three most common ways students are identified for the assessment process

▪ Have a general working knowledge of parental consent in the assessment process

▪ Know the various components of a thorough assessment

OVERVIEW OF ASSESSMENT

Judy is in serious danger of failing fourth grade again. She appears to have difficulty following directions, completing assignments on time, progressing in reading and spelling, and interacting with her peers. Her teacher believes that Judy may have a learning disability and has made a referral to the district's Committee on Special Education.

Benjamin has cerebral palsy and uses a wheelchair. He has recently moved into the community and enrolled in the local high school. His parents are concerned that Benjamin is not developing the mobility and daily living skills that he needs now and in the future. They request that the new school system evaluate Benjamin to identify his special needs.

Carlos has become severely withdrawn in the last year. His grades have been declining steadily, he is starting to skip school, and when the teacher calls on him in class, he responds rudely or not at all. The teacher is worried that Carlos may have an emotional disorder. She makes a referral to the special education department.

Although these children are different from each other in very many ways, they may also share something in common. Each may be a student who has a disability that will require special education services in the school setting. Before decisions may be made about what those special education services will be, each child requires an evaluation conducted by specially trained educational personnel, which may include a school psychologist, a speech–language pathologist, special education and regular education teachers, social workers, and, when appropriate, medical personnel. This is true for any child suspected of having a disability.

Assessment in special education is a process that involves collecting information about a student for the purpose of making decisions (Salvia & Ysseldyke, 2007). It involves gathering information about a student's strengths and needs in all areas of concern (Friend & Bursuck, 2006). According to Taylor (2009), assessment "refers to the gathering of relevant information to help an individual make decisions. The educational and psychological assessment of exceptional students, specifically, involves the collection of information that is relevant in making decisions regarding appropriate goals and objectives, teaching strategies, and program placement" (p. 3).

Assessment is a major focal point in education today. The term **assessment approach** describes the way information is collected for making an educational decision (Cohen & Spenciner, 2007). Assessment includes many formal and informal methods of evaluating student progress and behavior (Overton, 2009). Clearly, gathering information about a student using a variety of techniques and information sources should shed considerable light on strengths and needs, the nature of a suspected disability and its effect on educational performance, and realistic and appropriate instructional goals and objectives.

The professional involved in special education in today's schools plays a very critical role in the overall education of students with all types of disabilities. A comprehensive assessment completed by school professionals may address any aspect of a student's educational functioning (Pierangelo & Giuliani, 2009). The special educator's position is unique, in that he or she can play many different roles in the educational environment. Whatever their role, special educators encounter a variety of situations that require practical decisions and relevant suggestions. No matter which type of professional you become in the field of special education, it is always necessary to fully understand the assessment process and to be able to clearly communicate vital information to professionals, parents, and students.

The importance of assessment should never be underestimated. In special education, you will work with many professionals from different fields. You are part of a team, often referred to as a multidisciplinary team (see Chapter 8), that tries to determine whether a disability is present in a student (Cohen & Spenciner, 2011). The team's role is crucial because it helps determine the extent and direction of a child's personal journey through the special education experience (Pierangelo & Giuliani, 2009). Consequently, the skills needed to offer a child the most global, accurate, and practical evaluation should be fully understood. The development of these skills should include a good working knowledge of the following components of the assessment process in order to determine the presence of a suspected disability (National Information Center for Children and Youths with Disabilities, 2000):

- *Collection:* The process of tracing and gathering information from the many sources of background information on a child such as school records, observation, parent intakes, and teacher reports
- *Analysis:* The processing and understanding of patterns in a child's educational, social, developmental, environmental, medical, and emotional history
- *Evaluation:* The evaluation of a child's academic, intellectual, psychological, emotional, perceptual, language, cognitive, and medical development in order to determine areas of strength and weakness
- *Determination:* The determination of the presence of a suspected disability using knowledge of the criteria that constitute each category
- *Recommendation:* The recommendations concerning educational placement and program that need to be made to the school, teachers, and parents

PURPOSE OF ASSESSMENT

Assessment takes place when students experience difficulty meeting the demands of the general education curriculum and are referred for consideration for special education services (McLoughlin & Lewis, 2008). As will be discussed in great detail throughout this book, following a referral for a suspected disability of a child and with written parental or guardian permission, an individual mul-tidisciplinary and comprehensive assessment is conducted. This means that formal tests, observa-tions, and numerous assessments will be given. The results help to determine if special education is needed and whether factors unrelated to disabilities are affecting a child's school performance.

Assessment should be an active, ongoing process that has a clearly specified purpose (Taylor, 2009). Assessment results provide information useful for determining or modifying a child's program, if necessary. The decisions that use assessment information are varied and complex, and they occur in and out of classrooms (Salvia & Ysseldyke, 2007). Assessment plays a critical role in the determination of six important decisions (National Information Center for Children and Youths with Disabilities, 2000):

- Evaluation decisions: Information collected in the assessment process can provide detailed information of a student's strengths, weaknesses, and overall progress.
- Diagnostic decisions: Information collected in the assessment process can provide detailed information of the specific nature of the student's problems or disability.
- Eligibility decisions: Information collected in the assessment process can provide detailed information on whether a child is eligible for special education services.
- IEP development decisions: Information collected in the assessment process can provide detailed information so that an individualized education program (IEP) may be developed.
- Educational placement decisions: Information collected in the assessment process can pro-vide detailed information so that appropriate decisions may be made about the child's educational placement.
- Instructional planning decisions: Information collected in the assessment process is critical in planning instruction appropriate to the child's special social, academic, physical, and management needs.

LANDMARK COURT CASES IN SPECIAL EDUCATION

The first federal laws designed to assist individuals with disabilities date back to the early days of the nation. In 1798, the Fifth Congress passed the first federal law concerned with the care of per-sons with disabilities (National Information Center for Children and Youth with Disabilities, 1996). This law authorized the Maine Hospital Service to provide medical services to seamen with disabili-ties or those who were sick. By 1912, this entity had become known as the Public Health Service. However, prior to World War II, there were relatively few federal laws authorizing special benefits for persons with disabilities. Those that existed were intended to address the needs of war veterans with service-connected disabilities. This meant that, for most of our nation's history, schools were allowed to exclude—and often did exclude—certain children, especially those with disabilities.

In 1948, only 12 percent of all children with disabilities received some form of special edu-cation. By the early 1950s, special education services and programs were available in school dis-tricts, but often undesirable results occurred. For example, students in special classes were consid-ered unable to perform academic tasks. Consequently, they went to special schools or classes that focused on learning manual skills such as weaving and bead stringing. Although programs existed, it was clear that discrimination was still as strong as ever for those with disabilities in schools.

Legislation and court cases to prevent discrimination in education first came to notice in 1954 with the famous case *Brown v. Board of Education of Topeka, Kansas*. In *Brown*, the U.S. Supreme Court ruled that it was illegal practice under the Fourteenth Amendment of the U.S. Constitution to arbitrarily discriminate against any group of people. The Court then applied this principle to the schooling of children, holding that a separate education for African American students is not an equal education. In its famous ruling, separate but equal would no longer be accepted (347 U.S. 483).

Brown set the precedent for future discrimination cases in education. People with disabilities were recognized as another group whose rights had been violated because of arbitrary discrimination. For children, the discrimination occurred because they were denied access to schools due to their disabilities. Using *Brown* as their legal precedent, students with disabilities claimed that their segregation and exclusion from school violated their opportunity for an equal education under the **Fourteenth Amendment** of the U.S. Constitution—the Equal Protection Clause. If *Brown* prohibited segregation by race, then schools should not be able to segregate or otherwise discriminate by ability and disability.

In the 1960s, parents began to advocate for better educational opportunities for their children. Around the same time, many authorities began to agree that segregated special classes were not the most appropriate educational setting for many students with disabilities. By the end of the 1960s, landmark court cases set the stage for enactment of federal laws to protect the rights of children with disabilities and their parents. Some of the most significant court cases in special education, in their order of occurrence, include:

HOBSON v. HANSEN (1967).   In *Hobson v. Hansen*, a U.S. district court declared that the District of Columbia school system's tracking system was invalid. However, special classes were allowed, provided that testing procedures were rigorous and that retesting was frequent (Sattler, 2008).

DIANA v. STATE BOARD OF EDUCATION (1970).   In *Diana v. State Board of Education*, California was mandated by the court to correct bias in assessment procedures used with Chinese American and Mexican American students. *Diana* had three very important holdings that would later influence the enactment of federal special education laws:

1. If a student's primary language was not English, the student had to be tested in both English and his or her primary language.
2. Culturally unfair items had to be eliminated from all tests used in the assessment process.
3. If intelligence tests were to be used in the assessment process, they had to be developed to reflect Mexican American culture (*Diana v. State Board of Education*, C-70: 37RFT, N.D. Cal., 1970).

PARC v. COMMONWEALTH OF PENNSYLVANIA (1972).   A U.S. federal court in Pennsylvania ratified a consent agreement ensuring that schools may not exclude students who have been classified with mental retardation. Also, the court mandated that all students must be provided with a free public education. Both of these holdings would play a fundamental role in the enactment of future federal special education laws (*PARC v. Commonwealth of Pennsylvania*, 343 F. Supp. 279, E.D. PA 1972).

WYATT v. STICKNEY (1972).   In Alabama, a federal court ruled that mentally retarded children in state institutions had a constitutional right to treatment (*Wyatt v. Stickney*, 344 F. Supp. 387, M.D. Ala 1972).

GUADALUPE v. TEMPE ELEMENTARY SCHOOL (1972).   In Arizona, a U.S. district court agreed to a stipulated agreement that children could not be placed in educable mentally retarded classes unless they scored lower than two standard deviations below the population mean on an approved IQ test administered in the child's own language. *Guadalupe v. Tempe Elementary School* also stipulated that other assessment procedures must be used in addition to intelligence tests, and that parental permission must be obtained for such placements (Sattler, 2008).

MILLS v. BOARD OF EDUCATION OF DISTRICT OF COLUMBIA (1972).   This case set forth future guidelines for federal legislation, including the rights of students with disabilities to have access to a free public education, due process protection, and a mandated requirement to provide special education services regardless of the school district's financial capability (*Mills v. Board of Education of District of Columbia*, 348 Supp. 866, CD. DC 1972; contempt proceedings, EHLR 551:643 CD. DC 1980).

PASE (PARENTS IN ACTION ON SPECIAL EDUCATION) v. JOSEPH P. HANNON (1980).   In this case regarding bias in IQ testing, the judge (Judge Grady in Illinois) found that on the IQ tests he examined, only 9 of the 488 test questions were racially biased. Consequently, IQ tests were found not to be discriminatory. Furthermore, Judge Grady indicated that clinical judgment also plays a large role in interpreting IQ test results. He stated: "There is no evidence in this record that such misassessments as do occur are the result of racial bias in test items or in any aspect of the assessment process currently in use in the Chicago public school system." Therefore, the decision in PASE resolved some of the controversy about the use of IQ tests for special education classification. As a result, the use of intelligence tests was acceptable in psychoeducational assessment as long as they followed all other procedural safeguards under federal law (*PASE v. Joseph P. Hannon*, No. 74 C 3586 N.D. Ill. 1980).

LUKE S. AND HANS S. v. NIX ET AL. (1982).   In the state of Louisiana, all evaluations had to be completed within a 60-day time period. The plaintiffs in this case argued that thousands of students were not being appropriately evaluated within this time period. The court ruled in favor of the plaintiffs and informed the state of Louisiana that greater prereferral assessment should be done before a referral is made (*Luke S. and Hans S. v. Nix et al,* cited in Taylor, 2009, p. 9).

BOARD OF EDUCATION OF HENDRICK HUDSON SCHOOL DISTRICT v. ROWLEY (1982).   The parents of Amy Rowley, a deaf student with minimal residual hearing and excellent lip-reading skills, sought the services of a full-time interpreter in her regular classes. Amy had been provided with an FM trainer (a teacher of the deaf) for 1 hour per day and speech training for 3 hours per week. Even though Amy was missing about half of what was being discussed in class, she was very well adjusted, was performing better than the average child in the class, and was advancing easily from grade to grade.

Based on these facts, the U.S. Supreme Court determined in *Board of Education of Hendrick Hudson School District v. Rowley* that Amy was receiving an "appropriate" education without the sign interpreter. In reaching this opinion, the Court concluded that the obligation to provide an appropriate education does not mean a school must provide the "best" education or one designed to "maximize" a student's potential. However, the program must be based on the student's unique individual needs and be designed to enable the student to benefit from an education. In other words, the student must be making progress (Hager, 1999, p. 5).

JOSE P. v. AMBACH (1983).   Plaintiffs filed suit against New York City, complaining about the inappropriate delivery of services. The plaintiffs argued that many students in special education were not receiving services in an appropriate time frame. The court ruled in favor of the plaintiffs and stated that from the time of referral to evaluation a maximum of 30 days can elapse. The court informed the defendants that all evaluations must be "timely evaluations" (Taylor, 2009, p. 10).

LARRY P. v. RILES (1984). In this California case, using IQ tests as the assessment measure for placing African American students in special education as mentally retarded was found to be discriminatory. Schools in California were mandated by the court to reduce the disproportionate representation of African American students in special education. In *Larry P. v. Riles*, the court determined that IQ tests were discriminatory against African Americans in three ways:

1. IQ tests actually measure achievement rather than ability. Because African Americans throughout their educational history have been denied equal educational opportunities through schools segregated by race, they will inevitably have achievement scores lower than the norms and thus be discriminated against in testing.
2. IQ tests rest on the plausible but unproven assumption that intelligence is distributed in the population in accordance with a normal statistical curve (bell-shaped), and thus the tests are artificial tools to rank individuals.
3. IQ tests lead to the classification of more African American students than white students in dead-end classes for students with mild to moderate disabilities [(No. C-71-2270 RFP (1979) and No. 80-4027 DC No. C-71-2270 in the U.S. Court of Appeals for the Ninth Circuit (1984)].

GEORGIA STATE CONFERENCE OF BRANCHES OF NAACP v. STATE OF GEORGIA (1984). In *Georgia State Conference of Branches of NAACP v. State of Georgia,* a U.S. court of appeals ruled that African American children schooled in the state of Georgia were not being discriminated against solely because there was a disproportionate number of them in classes for low achievers. The court explained that there was no evidence of differential treatment of African American and other students. Overrepresentation of African American children in classes for the mentally retarded by itself was not sufficient to prove discrimination (Sattler, 2008).

DANIEL R. R. v. STATE BOARD OF EDUCATION (1989). *Daniel R. R.* is one of the crucial cases opening the door to increased inclusion of children with disabilities in regular education classes. The court noted that Congress showed a strong preference favoring mainstreaming— that is, educating the student in the regular education classroom with supports. Ironically, the court determined that it was not appropriate to include the child in this case in full-time regular education. However, the court's analysis of the least restrictive environment requirement, especially its interpretation of what is meant by providing supplementary aids and services in the regular classroom, has been followed by a number of other courts (Hager, 1999, p. 6).

In determining whether it is appropriate to place a student with disabilities in regular education, the student need not be expected to learn at the same rate as the other students in the class. In other words, part of the required supplementary aids and services must be the modification of the regular education curriculum for the student, when needed. The court in *Daniel R. R. v. State Board of Education* noted, however, that the school need not modify the program "beyond recognition." Also, in looking at whether it is "appropriate" for the child to be in regular education—in other words, whether the student can benefit educationally from regular class placement—the school must consider the broader educational benefit of contact with nondisabled students, such as opportunities for modeling appropriate behavior and socialization (Hager, 1999, p. 6).

GERSTMEYER v. HOWARD COUNTY PUBLIC SCHOOLS (1994).   Although Howard School District had been told that a child needed an evaluation before entering the first grade, the evaluation was not done prior to the child's entering the first grade. The parents sent their child to private school and the evaluation was only done 6 months after the initial referral. The parents sued the district for the costs of private schooling and tutoring caused by the delay. In *Gerstmeyer v. Howard County Public Schools*, the court ruled in favor of the parents and made Howard School District reimburse them for all associated costs (Taylor, 2009, p. 10).

THE HISTORY OF FEDERAL LEGISLATION FOR INDIVIDUALS WITH DISABILITIES

As a result of numerous historical court cases, federal legislation for individuals with disabilities began to develop in the early 1970s. This section discusses relevant federal legislation that has made a significant impact on the health, welfare, safety, and educational rights of these individuals (in the order in which the legislation was enacted).

Section 504 of the Vocational Rehabilitation Act

Section 504 of the **Vocational Rehabilitation Act** is a civil rights law enacted in 1973. It was created to prevent discrimination against all individuals with disabilities in programs that receive federal funds. For children of school age, Section 504 ensures students of equal opportunity to participate in all school activities (Council of Educators for Students with Disabilities, 2007). Section 504 plays a very important role in assessment, especially for students who do not meet the criteria to be classified for special education. Some students not eligible for services in special education may be entitled to receive accommodations under Section 504 to help them in school. For example, a child with attention deficit disorder (ADD) may meet the criteria for special accommodations under 504, because even though attention deficit disorder is not a classification covered under federal law, under Section 504, students with ADD can receive special assistance. Other students who may be helped under Section 504 would be those with asthma, allergies, arthritis, or diabetes, to name just a few (U.S. Department of Health and Human Services, 2006).

The Family Education Rights and Privacy Act—P.L. 93-380

The **Family Education Rights and Privacy Act (FERPA)**, often referred to as the Buckley Amendment, gives parents of students under the age of 18, and students age 18 and over, the right to examine records kept in the student's personal file (Cohen & Spenciner, 2011). FERPA was passed in 1974 to cover all students, even those in postsecondary education, and includes the following major provisions:

- Parents and eligible students have the right to inspect and review the student's education records.
- Schools must have written permission from the parent or eligible student before releasing any information from a student's records.
- Parents and eligible students have the right to have the records explained and interpreted by school officials.

- School officials may not destroy any education records if there is an outstanding request to inspect and review them.
- Parents and eligible students who believe that information in the education records is inaccurate or misleading may request that the records be amended. The parents or eligible students must be advised if the school decides that the records should not be amended, and they have the right to a hearing.

Finally, FERPA mandates that each school district must give parents of students in attendance, or students age 18 or over, an annual notice to inform them of their rights under this law, including the right of parents or eligible students to file a complaint with the U.S. Department of Education.

The Education of All Handicapped Children Act (EHA)—P.L. 94-142

Because of the victories that were being won for students with disabilities in the early 1970s, parents and student advocates began to lobby Congress for federal laws and money that would ensure that students with disabilities received an education that would meet their needs. In 1975, the stage was clearly set for a national special education law. Years of exclusion, segregation, and denial of basic educational opportunities to students with disabilities and their families set an imperative for a civil rights law guaranteeing these students access to the education system (Heward, 2009).

Despite the advances being made in providing services to students with disabilities, in 1975 Congress found that

- Over 1.75 million children with disabilities were being excluded entirely from receiving a public education solely on the basis of their condition.
- Over 4 million of the estimated 8 million children with disabilities in this country were not receiving the appropriate educational services they needed and were entitled to receive.
- Many other children with disabilities were still being placed in inappropriate educational settings because their disabilities were undetected or because of a violation of their individual rights.
- Because of the lack of adequate services within the public school system, families were often forced to find services outside the public school system, often at great distance from their residences and at their own expense.
- State and local educational agencies have a responsibility to provide education for all children with disabilities.
- It is in the national interest that the federal government assist state and local efforts to provide programs to meet the educational needs of children with disabilities in order to ensure equal protection of the law.

Congress, recognizing the necessity of special education for children with disabilities and concerned about the widespread discrimination, enacted into federal law the **Education of All Handicapped Children Act (EHA)**, P.L. 94-142. Public Law 94-142 set forth federal procedural safeguards for children with disabilities and their parents (Gargiulo, 2008). This law outlined the entire foundation on which current special education practices rest and the basis for our current federal law in special education, the Individuals with Disabilities Education Improvement Act (IDEA 2004).

The Carl D. Perkins Vocational and Technical Education Act (The Perkins Act)—P.L. 105-332

The **Vocational Education Act** of 1984, often referred to as the Carl D. Perkins Act or the **Perkins Act**, authorizes federal funds to support vocational education programs. One goal of the Perkins Act is to improve the access of either those who have been underserved in the past or those who have greater-than-average educational needs. Under the act, "special populations" include those who have a disability, are disadvantaged, or have limited English proficiency. This law is particularly important because it requires that vocational education be provided for students with disabilities (U.S. Department of Education, 2011).

The law states that individuals who are members of special populations (including individuals with disabilities) must be provided with equal access to recruitment, enrollment, and placement activities in vocational education. In addition, these individuals must be provided with equal access to the full range of vocational education programs available to others, including occupationally specific courses of study, cooperative education, apprenticeship programs, and, to the extent practical, comprehensive guidance and counseling services. Under the law, vocational educational planning should be coordinated among public agencies, including vocational education, special education, and the state vocational rehabilitation agencies. The provision of vocational education to youth with disabilities should be monitored to ensure that such education is consistent with objectives stated in the student's IEP.

Education of the Handicapped Act Amendments of 1986—P.L. 99-457

In 1983, Congress amended the Education of All Handicapped Children Act to expand incentives for preschool special education programs, early intervention, and transition programs. All programs under EHA became the responsibility of the Office of Special Education Programs (OSEP).

In 1986, Public Law 99-457, **Education of the Handicapped Act Amendments of 1986**, was passed, amending P.L. 94-142 and requiring the states to provide a free and appropriate public education to children with disabilities ages 3 through 5. The regulations that governed school-age children were then made applicable to the assessment of preschool children. In addition, a new part (Part H) was added to the law, establishing incentives for serving infants and toddlers with special needs.

The Americans with Disabilities Act—P.L. 101-336

In July 1990, President George H. W. Bush signed into law Public Law 101-336—the **Americans with Disabilities Act (ADA)**. He said, "Let the shameful walls of exclusion finally come tumbling down." Senator Tom Harkin, the chief sponsor of the act, spoke of this law as the "emancipation proclamation" for people with disabilities. This civil rights law is based on Section 504 of the Vocational Rehabilitation Act of 1973, but it further extends the rights of individuals with disabilities. It protects all individuals with disabilities from discrimination and requires most employers to make reasonable accommodations for them (Office for Civil Rights, 2006).

The ADA plays a very important role in transitional services for students with disabilities. It also figures significantly in making sure that all school buildings are accessible to people with disabilities. For example, if your school is not accessible for wheelchairs, does not have emergency exits for all, or does not have ramps, this would be a violation of the ADA.

The Individuals with Disabilities Education Improvement Act (IDEA 2004; discussed later in this chapter) and ADA differ in certain important areas, including the following:

- IDEA 2004 benefits only those who are between certain ages (birth to 21 years). By contrast, ADA benefits all people with disabilities, without regard to their age.
- IDEA 2004 benefits only those people in school. By contrast, ADA benefits people who are employed or who use a wide range of public and private services.
- IDEA 2004 provides money to state and local agencies to help educate students with disabilities, defining the rights and services afforded by law. By contrast, ADA prohibits discrimination, but does not provide money to help anyone comply with it.

Regardless of their differences, IDEA 2004 and ADA work together. IDEA 2004 helps state and local education agencies create services to educate students with disabilities, and ADA protects students against discrimination when they are not in school.

The Individuals with Disabilities Education Act—P.L. 101-476

In 1990, the reauthorization of P.L. 94-142 was enacted and became Public Law 101-476. **Reauthorization** is simply the act of amending and renewing a law. Public Law 101-476 is widely known as **IDEA (Individuals with Disabilities Education Act)**. Under IDEA, most of the mandates under 94-142 remained intact (Heward, 2009). However, some of IDEA's most important revisions and additions included the following:

- Adding significantly to the provisions for very young children with disabilities and for students preparing to leave secondary school
- Adding two new categories in special education: autism and traumatic brain injury
- Removing the term *handicapped* from the law and substituting the preferred term, *disability*
- Mandating **transition services** no later than 16 years of age
- Requiring further public comment on defining attention deficit disorder in the law
- Stating that states can be sued in federal courts for violating the laws

IDEA requires a timely, comprehensive, multidisciplinary evaluation, including assessment activities related to the child and the child's play. For infants and toddlers (birth to 2 years of age), a new program was established to help states develop and implement programs for early intervention services.

The Individuals with Disabilities Education Act of 1997 (IDEA '97)—P.L. 105-17

IDEA was amended to P.L. 105-17 on June 4, 1997, and is now often referred to as **IDEA '97**. Some of the changes made were substantial, whereas others fine-tuned processes already in place for schools and parents to follow in planning and providing special education and related services for children with special needs (Venn, 1999). IDEA '97:

- strengthened the least restrictive environment mandate
- strengthened parents' roles further
- added related services to the types of services to be provided for transition services
- strengthened the obligations of other agencies to provide services to students while they are still in school
- emphasized assistive technology

- expanded the number of members of the IEP team
- gave school authorities several options in disciplining a student with a disability
- changed Part H, serving young children, to Part C
- granted the right to receive the related services necessary to benefit from special education instruction

IDEA '97 and Section 504 of the Vocational Rehabilitation Act of 1973 strengthened each other in important areas. For example, they both:

- Called for school systems to carry out a systematic search for every child with a disability in need of a public education
- Mandated a free and appropriate public education (FAPE) regardless of the nature and severity of an individual's disability
- Made it clear that education and related services must be provided at no cost to parents
- Had similar requirements to ensure that testing and evaluation of a child's needs are not based on a single testing instrument
- Emphasized the importance of educating children and youth with disabilities with their nondisabled peers to the maximum extent appropriate (National Information Center for Children and Youth with Disabilities, 1996)

No Child Left Behind Act of 2001 (NCLB)—P.L. 107-110

The **No Child Left Behind Act** of 2001 was designed to improve student achievement and change the culture of U.S. schools. President George W. Bush describes this law as the "cornerstone of my administration." Clearly, our children are our future, and, as President Bush expressed, "Too many of our neediest children are being left behind." With passage of NCLB, Congress reauthorized the Elementary and Secondary Education Act (ESEA)—the principal federal law affecting education from kindergarten through high school. In amending ESEA, the new law represents a sweeping overhaul of federal efforts to support elementary and secondary education in the United States. It is built on four commonsense pillars: accountability for results, an emphasis on doing what works based on scientific research, expanded parental options, and expanded local control and flexibility.

The Individuals with Disabilities Education Improvement Act of 2004—P.L. 108-446

On December 3, 2004, the **Individuals with Disabilities Education Improvement Act of 2004 (IDEA 2004)** was enacted into law as Public Law 108-446. The statute, as passed by Congress and signed by President George W. Bush, reauthorized and made significant changes to the Individuals with Disabilities Education Act. IDEA 2004 is intended to help students with disabilities achieve to high standards—by promoting accountability for results, enhancing parent/ guardian involvement, and using proven practices and materials. Also, it provides more flexibility and reduces paperwork burdens for teachers, states, and local school districts.

Enactment of this law provided an opportunity to consider improvements in the current regulations that would strengthen the federal effort to ensure every student with a disability has available a free and appropriate public education that is of high quality and is designed to achieve the high standards reflected in the Elementary and Secondary Education Act of 1965, as amended by the No Child Left Behind Act of 2001 (NCLB) and its implementing regulations.

The major principles of IDEA 2004 are (Gargiulo, 2008; Friend, 2008; Heward, 2009):

- *Before any evaluations, testing, and placement can be done, there must be parental informed consent*. The definition of **informed consent** is as follows:
  - The parent has been fully informed of all information relevant to the activity for which consent is sought, in the family's native language, or other mode of communication.
  - The parent understands and agrees in writing to the activity for which consent is sought, and the consent describes that activity and lists the records (if any) that will be released and to whom.
  - The parent understands that the consent is voluntary and may be revoked at any time.
- *All students in special education must be placed in the least restrictive environment:* Students with disabilities need to be placed in the environment that is best suited for their educational needs or, as it was termed, the **least restrictive environment (LRE)**. Under federal law, schools must, to the maximum extent possible, ensure that individuals with disabilities, including individuals in public and private institutions or other care facilities, are educated with individuals without disabilities. Also, special classes and separate schooling are to be used only when the nature or severity of the disability is such that education in regular classes with the use of supplementary aids and services cannot be satisfactorily achieved. The settings for placement and service delivery are envisioned to fall on a continuum of least restrictive to most restrictive.
- *All students in special education must have an individualized education program (IEP):* All students in special education are required to have an **individualized education program (IEP)** designed to meet their needs. The IEP includes both short-term and long-term goals, along with how and where services will be provided (see Chapter 19 for a comprehensive discussion of the components of an IEP).
- *The evaluation for placement in special education must be nondiscriminatory:* Under federal law, the following requirements must be adhered to for an evaluation to be considered a nondiscriminatory assessment:
  1. All instruments used to evaluate a student for determination of a disability should be free from bias.
  2. When considering eligibility for special education, the evaluation must be done by a multidisciplinary team.
  3. All testing materials and procedures used for the purposes of evaluation and placement of children with disabilities must be selected and administered so as not to be racially or culturally discriminatory.
  4. All tests and other evaluation materials must be validated for the specific purpose for which they are used.
  5. Tests and other evaluation materials must be administered by trained personnel in conformance with the instructions provided by their producer.
  6. No single procedure can be used as the sole criterion for determining an appropriate educational program for a child.
- *The individual is assessed in all areas related to the suspected disability:* This includes, where appropriate, health, vision, hearing, social and emotional status, general intelligence, academic performance, communicative status, and motor abilities.
- *Tests must be given and reports must be written in the native language:* When doing an assessment, all tests must be given in the child's **native language**, and all reports must be written in the parent's native language.

- *Parents are entitled to due process:* All students and their parents are afforded **due process**. This means that if a conflict or disagreement ensues concerning a student's eligibility for special education placement or services, no changes can be made until the issue has been settled by an impartial hearing.
- *Zero reject for all students:* **Zero reject** means that all students have the right to a public school education and cannot be excluded because of a disability. Students are entitled to a free and appropriate public school education regardless of the extent of the disability. Also, it is the responsibility of each state to find children who may need and be entitled to special education services.

State Laws Relating to Students with Disabilities

How states implement the requirements of federal laws is covered by the primary and basic source of law for the nation—the United States Constitution. Federal laws passed by Congress must be based on the provisions of the Constitution. State constitutions and laws may go beyond what is provided in the federal law, as long as there is no conflict between them, and as long as state laws do not address areas reserved to the federal government, such as providing for the nation's defense. The major constitutional provisions that are important to children and youth with disabilities are (1) those that provide for the spending of money to protect the general welfare and (2) the Fourteenth Amendment, which provides that no state shall "deprive any person of life, liberty, or property, without the due process of law nor deny equal protection of the laws." It is important to remember that there is no constitutional provision requiring the federal government to provide education for its citizens. The Tenth Amendment to the Constitution states that "powers not delegated to the United States by the Constitution, nor prohibited by it to the States, are reserved to the States." Therefore, all states have provided for public education, by either state constitution or state law, or both. States are required under the due process and equal protection clauses of the Fourteenth Amendment to provide education on an equal basis and to provide due process before denying equal educational programming.

Most laws providing for public education are generally state and local rather than federal. Although some educational programs are highly regulated by the federal government, education is, for the most part, a state function. It is important to remember that most federal laws and regulations that provide for educational programming establish minimum standards that states must follow for the delivery of services and programs in order to receive federal funds. Quite often, federal laws give flexibility to the states in implementing the programs or services established with federal funds. Laws and regulations regarding civil rights, on the other hand, are much more firm and concrete. As future special educators, it is therefore essential that you become familiar with your state laws and regulations. It is important to remember that laws provide a framework for policy, and regulations provide the specific requirements for implementing the policy. Where there are differences, inconsistencies, or ambiguities in interpretation or in implementation, the judicial system is responsible for resolving these disputes. Often, court decisions lead to changes in the law or in regulations. It is important to note that laws are not made in a vacuum. Often, laws are made at one level of government in response to developments in other arenas. State and federal law are frequently interactive in this process. The development of special education law is an excellent example. It is likely that interaction among the various branches of government (legislative, executive, and judicial) at both the federal and state levels in the development of special education law and laws protecting the civil rights of individuals with disabilities will continue for some time.

INDIVIDUALS INVOLVED IN THE ASSESSMENT PROCESS

Under the Individuals with Disabilities Education Improvement Act (IDEA 2004) an evaluation of a child with a suspected disability must be made by a multidisciplinary team or groups of persons including at least one teacher or specialist with knowledge in the area of the suspected disability. These professionals must use a variety of assessment tools and strategies to gather relevant functional and developmental information, including information provided by the parent that will assist in determining whether a child has a disability as defined under federal law (Cohen & Spenciner, 2011). The members of the multidisciplinary team often include the following (Pierangelo & Giuliani, 2009):

- General education teacher
- School psychologist
- Special education evaluator
- Special education teacher
- Speech and language clinician
- Medical personnel (when appropriate)
- Social workers
- School/guidance counselor
- Parents
- School nurse
- Occupational and physical therapists

The roles that each of these people play in the assessment process are discussed thoroughly in Chapter 8.

CLASSIFICATIONS UNDER IDEA 2004

IDEA 2004 lists separate categories of disabilities under which children may be eligible for special education and related services. Children are eligible to receive special education services and supports if they meet the eligibility requirements for at least one of the disabling conditions listed in P.L. 108-446 and it is determined that they are in need of special education services (Gargiulo, 2008).

According to IDEA 2004, Sec. 602(3)(A), a child with a disability is a child

1. with mental retardation, hearing impairments (including deafness), speech or language impairments, visual impairments, serious emotional disturbance, orthopedic impairments, autism, traumatic brain injury, other health impairments, or specific learning disability; and
2. who, by reason thereof, needs special education and related services

The definitions of the 13 disabling conditions under IDEA 2004 are listed below:

Autism: A developmental disability significantly affecting verbal and nonverbal communication and social interaction, generally evident before age 3, that adversely affects a child's educational performance. Other characteristics often associated with autism are engagement in repetitive activities and stereotyped movements, resistance to environmental change or change in daily routines, and unusual responses to sensory experiences. The term does not apply if a child's educational performance is adversely affected because the child has an emotional disturbance.

Deaf–blindness: Concomitant hearing and visual impairments, the combination of which causes such severe communication and other developmental and educational problems that they cannot be accommodated in special education programs solely for children with deafness or children with blindness.

Developmental delay: For children ages 3 through 9, a state and local education agency (LEA) may choose to include as an eligible "child with a disability" a child who is experiencing developmental delays in one or more of the following areas:
- physical development
- cognitive development
- communication development
- social or emotional development
- adaptive development

It must also be determined that, because of the developmental delays, the child needs special education and related services. Developmental delays are defined by the state and must be measured by appropriate diagnostic instruments and procedures.

Emotional disturbance: A condition exhibiting one or more of the following characteristics over a long period of time and to a marked degree that adversely affects a child's educational performance:
- An inability to learn that cannot be explained by intellectual, sensory, or health factors
- An inability to build or maintain satisfactory interpersonal relationships with peers and teachers
- Inappropriate types of behaviors or feelings under normal circumstances
- A general pervasive mood of unhappiness or depression
- A tendency to develop physical symptoms or fears associated with personal or school problems

The term includes schizophrenia. The term does not apply to children who are socially maladjusted, unless it is determined that they have an emotional disturbance.

Hearing impairment: An impairment in hearing, whether permanent or fluctuating, that adversely affects a child's performance but that is not included under the definition of deafness in this section. (**Deafness:** A hearing impairment so severe that the child is impaired in processing linguistic information through hearing, with or without amplification, that adversely affects a child's educational performance.)

Mental retardation: Significantly subaverage general intellectual functioning, existing concurrently with deficits in adaptive behavior and manifested during the developmental period, that adversely affects a child's performance.

Multiple disabilities: Concomitant impairments (such as mental retardation–orthopedic impairment) the combination of which causes such severe educational problems that the problems cannot be accommodated in special education programs solely for one of the impairments. The term does not include deaf–blindness.

Orthopedic impairment: A severe orthopedic impairment that adversely affects a child's educational performance. The term includes impairments caused by congenital anomaly (e.g., clubfoot, absence of some member), impairments caused by disease (e.g., poliomyelitis, bone tuberculosis), and impairments from other causes (e.g., cerebral palsy, amputations, and fractures or burns that cause contractures).

Other health impairment: Having limited strength, vitality, or alertness due to chronic or acute health problems, such as a heart condition, tuberculosis, rheumatic fever, nephritis, asthma, sickle cell anemia, hemophilia, epilepsy, lead poisoning, leukemia, or diabetes, that adversely affects a child's educational performance.

Specific learning disability: A disorder in one or more of the basic psychological processes involved in understanding or using language, spoken or written, which may manifest itself in the imperfect ability to listen, think, speak, read, write, spell, or do mathematical calculations. The term includes conditions such as perceptual disabilities, brain injury, minimal brain dysfunction, dyslexia, and developmental aphasia; it does not include a learning problem that is primarily the result of visual, hearing, or motor disabilities; of mental retardation; of emotional disturbance; or of environmental, cultural, or economic disadvantage. Under IDEA 2004, when determining whether a child has a specific disability, a local education agency shall not be required to take into consideration whether a child has a severe discrepancy between achievement and intellectual ability.

Speech or language impairment: A communication disorder such as stuttering, impaired articulation, a language impairment, or a voice impairment that adversely affects a child's educational performance.

Traumatic brain injury: An acquired injury to the brain caused by an external physical force, resulting in total or partial functional disability or psychosocial impairment or both, and that adversely affects a child's educational performance. The term applies to open or closed head injuries resulting in impairments in one or more areas, such as cognition; language; memory; attention; reasoning; abstract thinking; judgment; problem solving; sensory, perceptual, and motor abilities; psychosocial behavior; physical functions; information processing; and speech. The term does not apply to brain injuries that are congenital or degenerative or to brain injuries induced by birth trauma.

Visual impairment: An impairment in vision that, even with correction, adversely affects a child's educational performance. The term includes both partial and total sight blindness.

HOW STUDENTS ARE IDENTIFIED FOR ASSESSMENT

There are normally three ways a student may be identified for assessment of a suspected disability (Pierangelo & Giuliani, 2009):

1. *School personnel may suspect the presence of a learning or behavior problem and ask the student's parents for permission to evaluate the student individually.* This may have resulted from a student scoring far below his or her peers on some type of screening measure and thereby alerting the school to the possibility of a problem.
2. *The student's classroom teacher may identify certain symptoms in a child within the classroom that seem to indicate the presence of some problem.* For example, the student's work is below expectations for his or her grade or age, or the student's behavior is so disruptive that he or she is unable to learn. Further, attempts at intervention strategies suggested by professional staff members have met with little or no success.
3. *The student's parents may call or write the school or the director of special education and request that their child be evaluated.* The parents may feel that the child is not progressing as expected or may notice particular problems in how their child learns. When parents note a problem and request an evaluation, the school must follow through on the assessment process. This is the parents' legal right.

PARENTAL CONSENT AND THE ASSESSMENT PROCESS

To protect the legal rights of parents and their children, IDEA 2004 (sec. 300.300) mandates that a school must obtain written permission before any school evaluation for a suspected disability is undertaken. Request for **consent for evaluation** should not be misinterpreted as a decision that a child has a disability. Rather, it is a means of ensuring that parents have both full knowledge of school actions and involvement in the decision-making process. It is important that parents fully understand the reasons for an individual evaluation so that they feel comfortable with the decisions they must make. This process of parents' rights is discussed in great detail in Chapter 8.

COMPONENTS OF A COMPREHENSIVE ASSESSMENT

An evaluation for special education should always be conducted on an individual basis. When completed, it is a comprehensive assessment of the child's abilities. Under IDEA (sec. 614(2)(B)), no single measure or assessment is used as the sole criterion for determining an appropriate educational program for a child. Further, the child must be assessed in all areas related to the suspected disability, including, where appropriate, health, vision, hearing, social and emotional status, general intelligence, academic performance, communicative status, and motor abilities. In light of these mandates, a comprehensive assessment should normally include many of the following:

- An individual psychological evaluation including general intelligence, instructional needs, learning strengths and weaknesses, and social–emotional dynamics
- A thorough social history based on interviews with parents and student
- A thorough academic history with interviews or reports from past teachers
- A physical examination including specific assessments that relate to vision, hearing, and health
- A classroom observation of the student in the current educational setting
- An appropriate educational evaluation specifically pinpointing the areas of deficit or suspected disability including, but not limited to, educational achievement, academic needs, learning strengths and weaknesses, and vocational assessments
- A functional behavioral assessment to describe the relationship between a skill or performance problem and variables that contribute to its occurrence
- The purpose of a functional behavioral assessment is to gather broad and specific information in order to better understand the reasons for the student's problem behavior
- A bilingual assessment for students with limited English proficiency
- Auditory and visual discrimination tests
- Assessment of classroom performance
- Speech and language evaluations, when appropriate
- Physical and/or occupational evaluations, when indicated
- Interviewing the student and significant others in the student's life
- Examining school records and past evaluation results
- Using information from checklists completed by parents, teachers, or the student
- Evaluating curriculum requirements and options
- Evaluating the student's type and rate of learning during trial teaching periods
- Evaluating which skills have been and have not been mastered, and in what order unmastered skills need to be taught
- Collecting ratings on teacher attitude toward students with disabilities, peer acceptance, and classroom climate

This information can be gathered in a variety of ways. These may include, but are not limited to norm-referenced tests, informal assessment, criterion-referenced tests, standards-referenced tests, ecological assessment, curriculum-based assessment, curriculum-based measurement, dynamic assessment, portfolio assessment, authentic/naturalistic/performance-based assessment, task analysis, outcome-based assessment, and learning styles assessment (Pierangelo & Giuliani, 2009). All of these are discussed in detail in Chapter 2 of this textbook.

CONCLUSION

Assessment is a complex process that needs to be conducted by a multidisciplinary team of trained professionals and involves both formal and informal methods of collecting information about the student. Although the team may choose to administer a series of tests to the student, by law assessment must involve much more than standardized tests. Interviews of all key participants in the student's education and observations of student behaviors in the classroom or in other sites should be included as well. To develop a comprehensive picture of the student and to develop practical intervention strategies to address that student's special needs, the team must ask questions and use assessment techniques that will help them determine the factors that are facilitating—and interfering with—the child's learning.

It is also important that assessment be an ongoing process. As you will see as you read through this book, the process begins even before the student is referred for formal evaluation; his or her teacher or parent may have noticed that some aspect of the student's performance or behavior is below expectations and, so, requests an official assessment. After eligibility has been established and the IEP developed for the student, assessment should continue, through teacher-made tests, through ongoing behavioral assessment, or through other methods. This allows teachers and parents to monitor the student's progress toward the goals and objectives stated in his or her IEP. Thus, assessment should not end when the eligibility decision is made or the IEP is developed; it has continuing value in contributing to the daily, weekly, and monthly instructional decision making that accompanies the provision of special education and related services.

A thorough and comprehensive assessment can greatly enhance a child's educational experience. The assessment process has many steps and needs to be appropriately done. Furthermore, no one individual makes all of the decisions for a child's classification; it is done by a multidisciplinary team. As future special educators, it is your professional responsibility to understand the laws, steps, and various assessment measures and procedures used in the special education process so that when you enter the school systems, you can have a significant and positive impact on all those with whom you are involved in special education.

Vocabulary

Americans with Disabilities Act (ADA): Federal antidiscrimination legislation for people with disabilities enacted in 1990.

Analysis: The processing and understanding of patterns in a child's educational, social, developmental, environmental, medical, and emotional history.

Assessment approach: The way information is collected for making an educational decision.

Assessment: A process that involves collecting information about a student for the purpose of making decisions.

Autism: A developmental disability significantly affecting verbal and nonverbal communication and social interaction, generally evident before age 3.

Board of Education of Hendrick Hudson School District v. Rowley: In *Rowley*, the U.S. Supreme Court concluded that the obligation to provide an appropriate education does not mean a school must provide the best education or one designed to maximize a student's potential.

Brown v. Board of Education of Topeka, Kansas: In *Brown*, the U.S. Supreme Court ruled that it was illegal under the Fourteenth Amendment of the U.S. Constitution to arbitrarily discriminate against any group of people.

Collection: The process of tracing and gathering information from the many sources of background information on a child, such as school records, observation, parent intakes, and teacher reports.

Consent for evaluation: A means of ensuring that parents have both full knowledge of school actions and involvement in the decision-making process.

Daniel R. R. v. State Board of Education: One of the important cases that opened the door to increased inclusion of children with disabilities in regular education classes.

Deaf–blindness: Simultaneous hearing and visual impairments.

Deafness: A hearing impairment so severe that the child is impaired in processing linguistic information, with or without amplification.

Determination: The determination of the presence of a suspected disability using knowledge of the criteria that constitute each category.

Developmental delay: Experiencing delay in one or more of the following areas: physical development, cognitive development, communication.

Diana v. State Board of Education: In this case, California was mandated by the court to correct bias in assessment procedures used with Chinese American and Mexican American students.

Due process: The right to an impartial hearing if parents do not agree with the decisions made about their child in the assessment process.

Education of All Handicapped Children Act (EHA):   The federal law that set forth procedural safeguards for children with disabilities and their parents.

Education of the Handicapped Act Amendments of 1986:   Amended P.L. 94-142, requiring states to provide a free and appropriate public education to children with disabilities ages 3 through 5.

Eligibility and diagnosis: The determination by assessment whether a child is eligible for special

education services and what classification the child will receive.

Emotional disturbance: A disability whereby a child of typical intelligence has difficulty, over time and to a marked degree, with various emotional and behavioral issues.

Evaluation: The evaluation of a child's academic, intellectual, psychological, emotional, perceptual, language, cognitive, and medical development in order to determine areas of strength and weakness.

Family Education Rights and Privacy Act (FERPA):   The federal law that gives parents and eligible students the right to examine the student's personal file.

Fourteenth Amendment: The equal protection clause of the U.S. Constitution, which states that all people must have equal protection under the law.

Georgia State Conference of Branches of NAACP v. State of Georgia: A U.S. court of appeals ruled that overrepresentation of African American children in classes for the mentally retarded by itself was not sufficient to prove discrimination.

Gerstmeyer v. Howard County Public Schools: Here, the court ruled that when a school district delays an evaluation for 6 months, parents can sue for costs associated with the delay and be reimbursed for all associated costs.

Guadalupe v. Tempe Elementary School: In Arizona, a U.S. district court agreed to a stipulated agreement that children could not be placed in educable mentally retarded classes unless they scored lower than two standard deviations below the population mean on an approved IQ test administered in the child's own language.

Hearing impairment: An impairment in hearing, whether permanent or fluctuating.

Hobson v. Hansen: A U.S. district court declared that the District of Columbia's school system's tracking system was invalid.

IDEA (Individuals with Disabilities Education Act):   Federal law requiring a timely, comprehensive, multidisciplinary evaluation.

IDEA '97 (Individuals with Disabilities Education Act of 1997):   Federal law that strengthened parents' roles and the least restrictive environment mandate.

IDEA 2004 (Individuals with Disabilities Education Improvement Act):   The federal law that guarantees a "free and appropriate education," including special education and related service programming, to all children and youth with disabilities who require it. IDEA 2004 also ensures that the rights of children and youth with disabilities and their parents or guardians are protected (e.g., fairness, appropriateness, and due process in decision making about providing special education and related services to children and youth with disabilities).

Individualized education program (IEP): The document that sets forth the short-term and long-term goals of each child who is classified in special education.

Informed consent: The rights of parents to know exactly what will happen to their children in the process of assessment.

Instructional planning: One of the primary purposes of assessment whereby a plan is developed that is appropriate for a child in special education. The plan should focus on social, academic, physical, and management needs.

Jose P. v. Ambach: The court in this case ruled that evaluations in or for special education services must be "timely evaluations."

Larry P. v. Riles: In this California case, using IQ tests as the assessment measure for placing African American students in special education as mentally retarded was found to be discriminatory.

Least restrictive environment (LRE): The idea that all children with disabilities should be educated in an environment that is least restrictive, ensuring to the extent possible that they will receive their education with children without disabilities.

Luke S. and Han S. v. Nix et al.: A Louisiana court case in which the court ruled that greater pre-referral assessment should be done before a referral is made.

Mental retardation: Significantly subaverage general intellectual functioning existing concurrently with deficits in adaptive behavior.

Mills v. Board of Education of District of Columbia: This case set forth future guidelines for federal legislation, including the rights of students to have access to a free public education, due process protection, and a mandated requirement to receive special education services regardless of the school district's financial capability.

Multiple disabilities: The manifestation of two or more disabilities (such as mental retardation and blindness), the combination of which requires special accommodation for maximal learning.

Native language: The language that is the primary language for the child and/or his or her parents.

No Child Left Behind Act (NCLB): With passage of No Child Left Behind, Congress reauthorized the Elementary and Secondary Education Act (ESEA). In amending ESEA, the new law represents a sweeping overhaul of federal efforts to support elementary and secondary education in the United States. It is built on four commonsense pillars: accountability for results, an emphasis on doing what works based on scientific research, expanded parental options, and expanded local control and flexibility.

Nondiscriminatory assessment: Objective and fair testing practices and procedures for all children.

Orthopedic impairment: Physical disabilities including congenital impairments, impairments caused by disease, and impairments from other causes.

Other health impairment: Having limited strength, vitality, or alertness due to chronic or acute health problems (e.g., diabetes, asthma, hypoglycemia, attention deficit disorder).

PARC v. Commonwealth of Pennsylvania: In this case, a U.S. federal court in Pennsylvania ratified a consent agreement ensuring that schools may not exclude students who have been classified with mental retardation.

PASE v. Joseph P. Hannon: Here, the court found that the use of intelligence tests was acceptable in psychoeducational assessment as long as schools followed all other procedural safeguards under federal law.

Reauthorization: The act of amending and renewing a law.

Recommendation: The recommendations concerning educational placement and programs that need to be made to the school, teachers, and parents.

Section 504 of the Vocational Rehabilitation Act: A civil rights law created to prevent discrimination against all individuals with disabilities in programs that receive federal funds, as do all public schools.

Specific learning disability: A disorder in one or more of the basic psychological processes involved in understanding or in using language, spoken or written, which may manifest itself in an imperfect ability to listen, think, speak, read, write, spell, or do mathematical calculations.

Speech or language impairment: A communication disorder such as stuttering, impaired articulation, a language impairment, or a voice impairment.

Transition services: Services and programs to help students in special education make the transition from high school to college or vocational career.

Traumatic brain injury: An acquired injury to the brain caused by an external physical force, resulting in total or partial functional disability or psychosocial impairment or both.

Visual impairment: An impairment in vision (including blindness) that, even with correction, adversely affects a child's educational performance.

Vocational Education Act of 1984 (Perkins Act):   Law authorizing federal funds to support vocational education programs.

Wyatt v. Stickney: In Alabama, a federal court ruled that mentally retarded children in state institutions had a constitutional right to treatment.

Zero reject: All students have the right to a public school education and cannot be excluded because of a disability.

METHODS OF ASSESSMENT AND TESTING CONSIDERATIONS

Key Terms

Authentic/naturalistic/
   performance-based assessment
Basal
Ceiling
Content-referenced tests
Criterion
Criterion-referenced tests (CRTs)
Curriculum-based assessment
   (CBA)
Curriculum-based measurement
   (CBM)

Dynamic assessment
Ecological assessment
Informal reading
   inventory (IRI)
Informal tests
Learning styles assessment
Limitations of testing
Norm group
Norm-referenced
   tests (NRT)
Outcome-based assessment

Portfolio
Portfolio assessment
Showcase portfolio
Standardization
Standardized tests
Standards-referenced tests
Task analysis
Teacher portfolio or record
   keeping
Working portfolio

Chapter Objectives

The focus of this chapter is to discuss various formal versus informal methods of assessment. After reading this chapter you should understand the following:

- Norm-referenced tests
- Intended purposes of norm-referenced tests
- Standardization
- Concerns with standardized testing
- Criterion-referenced tests
- Standards-referenced tests
- Ecological assessment
- Curriculum-based assessment (CBA)
- Curriculum-based measurement (CBM)
- Dynamic assessment
- Portfolio assessment
- Authentic/naturalistic/performance-based assessment
- Task analysis
- Outcome-based assessment
- Learning styles assessment

■ Selecting an appropriate instrument
■ Selection of test content
■ Test interpretation
■ Limitations of testing

ASSESSMENT AND TESTING CONSIDERATIONS

The ways that children and adolescents can be evaluated for special education vary from individual to individual. The assessment method needs to be determined on a case-by-case basis. However, to obtain the most valid and accurate picture of a student's strengths and weaknesses, a comprehensive measure of assessment involves using both formal and informal methods of assessment.

Formal and informal are not technical psychometric terms; therefore, there are no uniformly accepted definitions. **Formal tests** assume a single set of expectations for all students and come with prescribed criteria for scoring and interpretation. **Informal tests** are used here to indicate techniques that can easily be incorporated into classroom routines and learning activities. Informal assessment techniques can be used at any time without interfering with instructional time. Their results are indicative of the student's performance on the skill or subject of interest. Unlike standardized tests, they are not intended to provide a comparison to a broader group beyond the students in the local project or to predict future performance (McLoughlin & Lewis, 2008).

This is not to say that informal assessment is casual or lacking in rigor. Informal assessment requires a clear understanding of the levels of ability the students bring with them. Only then may assessment activities be selected that students can attempt reasonably. Informal assessment seeks to identify the strengths and needs of individual students without regard to grade or age norms.

Scores on **norm-referenced tests (NRT)** are not interpreted according to an absolute standard or criterion (e.g., 8 out of 10 correct) but rather according to how the student's performance compares with that of a particular group of individuals (Salvia & Ysseldyke, 2007). For this comparison to be meaningful, a valid comparison group—called a *norm group*—must be defined. A **norm group** is a large number of children who are representative of all the children in that age group. Such a group can be obtained by selecting a group of children who have the characteristics of children across the United States—that is, a certain percentage must be from each gender, from various ethnic backgrounds (e.g., Caucasian, African American, American Indian, Asian, Hispanic), from each geographic area (e.g., Southeast, Midwest), and from each socioeconomic class.

By having all types of children take the test, the test publisher can provide information about how various types of children perform on the test. (This information—the types of students comprising the norm group and how each type performed on the test—is generally given in the manuals that accompany the test.) The school will compare the scores of the child being evaluated to the scores obtained by the norm group (Taylor, 2009). This helps evaluators determine whether the child is performing at a level typical for, below, or above that expected for children of a given ethnicity, socioeconomic status, age, or grade.

Thus, before making assumptions about a child's abilities based on test results, it is important to know something about the group to which the child is being compared—particularly whether the student is being compared to children who are similar in ethnicity, socioeconomic status, and so on. The more unlike the child the norm group is, the less valuable the results of testing will generally be. This is an area in which standardized testing has fallen under considerable criticism. Often, test administrators do not use the norm group information appropriately, or there may not be children in the norm group similar to the child being tested. Furthermore, many tests were originally developed some time ago, and the norm groups reported in the test manual are not similar at all to the children being tested today.

Norm-referenced tests include basal and ceiling levels, which are used to prevent the examiner from having to administer all of the items with each test. A **basal** is the "starting point." It represents the level of mastery of a task below which the student would correctly answer all items on a test. All of the items prior to the basal are not given to the student. These items are considered already correct. For example, on an IQ test, the examiner may start with question 14 because of the age of the child. That is the basal. Here, the student starts with credit given for the first 13 questions (Overton, 2006).

Once the basal is determined, the examiner will administer all items until the student reaches a ceiling. The **ceiling** is the point at which the student has reached the predetermined number of errors, and therefore, testing is stopped because it is assumed that the student will continue to get the answers wrong. The ceiling is the "ending point." It represents the level of mastery of a task above which the student would incorrectly answer all future items on a test. For example, if on a spelling test a child got numbers 15 to 24 wrong, and the ceiling is 10 incorrect in a row, this means that the examiner would stop administering spelling words to the child because the ceiling has been obtained (Cohen & Spenciner, 2011).

Intended Purposes of Norm-Referenced Tests

Norm-referenced tests compare a person's score against the scores of a group of people who have already taken the same exam, called the *norming group*. When you see scores in the paper that report a school's scores as a percentage—"the Lincoln school ranked at the 49th percentile"—or when you see your child's score reported that way—"Jamal scored at the 63rd percentile"—the test is usually a norm-referenced test. Norm-referenced tests are designed to "rank order" test takers—that is, to compare students' scores. A commercial norm-referenced test does not compare all the students who take the test in a given year. Instead, test makers select a sample from the target student population (say, ninth graders). The test is "normed" on this sample, which is supposed to fairly represent the entire target population (all ninth graders in the nation). Students' scores are then reported in relation to the scores of this norming group. To make comparing easier, test makers create exams in which the results end up looking at least somewhat like a bell-shaped curve (the normal curve; see Chapter 3). Test makers make the test so that most students will score near the middle, and only a few will score low (the left side of the curve) or high (the right side of the curve).

The major reason for using norm-referenced tests is to classify students. NRTs are designed to highlight achievement differences between and among students to produce a dependable rank order of students across a continuum of achievement from high achievers to low achievers. School systems might want to classify students in this way so that they can be properly placed in remedial or gifted programs. These types of tests are also used to help teachers select students for different ability level reading or mathematics instructional groups.

Tests are normed using a national sample of students. Because norming a test is such an elaborate and expensive process, the norms are typically used by test publishers for 7 years. All students who take the test during that 7-year period have their scores compared to the original norm group.

Standardization

All norm-referenced tests include standardized procedures. **Standardization** refers to structuring test materials, administration procedures, scoring methods, and techniques for interpreting results (Venn, 2007). **Standardized tests** have detailed procedures for administration, timing, scoring, and interpretation procedures that must be followed precisely to obtain valid and reliable results. Standardized tests are very much a part of the education scene. Most of us have taken many such tests in our lifetime. A wide variety of standardized tests is available to assess different skill areas. In the field of special education, these include intelligence tests; math, reading, spelling, and writing tests; perceptual tests; and many others. The fact is, standardized tests are a tremendous source of information when assessing a child (McLoughlin & Lewis, 2009).

Concerns with Standardized Testing

Criticisms of standardized tests seem to have grown in proportion to the frequency with which, and the purposes for which, they are used (Pierangelo & Giuliani, 2009). Districts now administer such tests at every grade level, define success or failure of programs in terms of test scores, and even link teacher and administrator salaries and job security to student performance on standardized tests.

Three areas of criticism in regard to standardized tests are content, item format, and item bias. Standardized tests are designed to provide the best match possible to the perceived "typical" curriculum at a specific grade level. However, for programs such as a bilingual education that are built on objectives unique to the needs of their students, many of the items on a standardized test may not measure the objectives or content of that program. Thus a standardized test may have low content validity (see Chapter 4) for specific bilingual education programs. In such a situation, the test might not be sensitive to actual student progress. Consequently, the program, as measured by this test, would appear to be ineffective.

Standardized achievement tests generally rely heavily on multiple-choice items. This item format allows for greater content coverage as well as objective and efficient scoring. However, the response required by the format is recognition of the correct answer. This type of response does not necessarily match the type of responses students regularly make in the classroom, for example, the production or synthesis of information. If students are not used to responding within the structure imposed by the item format, their test performance may suffer. On the other hand, students may recognize the correct form when it is presented as a discrete item in a test format, but fail to use that form correctly in communication contexts. In this case, a standardized test may make the student appear more proficient than performance would suggest.

Further, some tests have been criticized for including items that are biased against certain kinds of students (e.g., ethnic minority, limited English proficient, rural, inner-city). The basis for this criticism is that the items reflect the language, culture, and/or learning style of the middle-class majority. Although test companies have attempted to write culture-free items, the removal of questions from a meaningful context has proved problematic for minority students (Navarete et al., 1990).

Thus, there are strong arguments in favor of educators considering the use of alternative forms of assessment to supplement standardized test information. These alternate assessments should be timely, not time-consuming, truly representative of the curriculum, and tangibly meaningful to the teacher and student. Techniques of informal assessment have the potential to meet these criteria as well as programmatic requirements for formative and summative evaluations.

Validity and reliability are not exclusive properties of formal, norm-referenced tests. Informal techniques are valid if they measure the skills and knowledge imparted by the project; they are reliable if they measure consistently and accurately.

According to Hart (1994, cited in Taylor, 2009) important criticisms of standardized testing include the following:

- Too much value placed on recall and rote learning at the expense of understanding and reflection
- Misleading impression given that a single right answer exists for almost every problem or question
- Students turned into passive learners who need only recognize, not construct, answers and solutions
- Teachers forced to focus more on what can be easily tested than on what is important for students to learn
- Content and skill development trivialized by reducing whatever is taught to a fill-in-the-bubble format (p. 127)

To best prepare students for standardized achievement tests, teachers usually devote much time to teaching the information found on the standardized tests. This is particularly true if the standardized tests are also used to measure an educator's teaching ability. With curriculum specialists and educational policy makers alike calling for more attention to higher-level skills, these tests may be driving classroom practice in the opposite direction.

INFORMAL ASSESSMENT

Criterion-Referenced Tests

Many educators and members of the public fail to grasp the distinctions between criterion-referenced and norm-referenced testing. It is common to hear the two types of testing referred to as if they serve the same purposes or shared the same characteristics. Much confusion can be eliminated if the basic differences are understood. Whereas norm-referenced tests ascertain the rank of students, **criterion-referenced tests (CRTs)** report how well students are doing relative to a predetermined performance level on a specified set of educational goals or outcomes included in the school, district, or state curriculum.

Educators or policy makers may use a CRT to see how well students have learned the knowledge and skills they are expected to have mastered. This information may be used as one piece of information to determine how well the student is learning the desired curriculum and how well the school is teaching that curriculum.

CRTs are scored according to a standard, or **criterion**, that the teacher, school, or test publisher decides represents an acceptable level of mastery. An example of a criterion-referenced test might be a teacher-made spelling test containing 20 words to be spelled. The teacher has defined an "acceptable level of mastery" as 16 correct (or 80%). These tests, sometimes called **content-referenced tests**, are concerned with the mastery of specific, defined skills; the student's performance on the test indicates whether he or she has mastered those skills. Examples of criterion-referenced questions would be

- Does John correctly read the word *happy*?
- Does Jane do eighth-grade math computation problems with 85 percent accuracy?
- Did Joe get 90 percent of the questions correct on the social studies exam?

As you can see, in criterion-referenced assessment, the emphasis is on correctly answering a certain percentage of a series of questions. The test giver is interested in what the student can and cannot do, rather than how his or her performance compares with those of other people (Salvia & Ysseldyke, 2007, p. 30).

An **informal reading inventory (IRI)** is an example of a criterion-referenced test. IRIs generally consist of two main sections: word recognition and passage reading. According to Bigge and Stump (1999),

> the interpretation of an IRI is based on criteria or levels of performance, and identifies three reading levels: independent, instructional, and frustration. The independent reading level is the level at which a student reads fluently and for pleasure (word recognition of 96% to 99% correct paired with correct comprehension of 75% to 90%). The instructional reading level is the level at which the student can experience success with assistance (word recognition of 92% to 95% correct paired with correct comprehension of 60% to 75%). The frustration level is the level at which the reading process breaks down for the student (word recognition of 90% to 92% or less paired with correct comprehension of 60% to 75% or less), as demonstrated by depressed comprehension and difficulties with word recognition (p. 197).

Standards-Referenced Tests

A recent variation of the criterion-referenced test is the **standards-referenced test**, or standards-based assessment. Many states and districts have adopted content standards (or "curriculum frameworks") that describe what students should know and be able to do in different subjects at various grade levels. They also have performance standards that define how much of the content standards students should know to reach the "basic," "proficient," or "advanced" level in the subject area. Tests are then based on the standards, and the results are reported in terms of these "levels," which, of course, represent human judgment. In some states, performance standards have been steadily increased, so that students continually have to know more to meet the same level.

Educators often disagree about the quality of a given set of standards. Standards are supposed to cover the important knowledge and skills students should learn—they define the "big picture." State standards should be well written and reasonable. Some state standards have been criticized for including too much, for being too vague, for being ridiculously difficult, for undermining higher-quality local curriculum and instruction, and for taking sides in educational and political controversies. If the standards are flawed or limited, tests based on them also will be. In any event, standards enforced by state tests will have—and are meant to have—a strong impact on local curriculum and instruction.

Ecological Assessment

Ecological assessment involves directly observing and assessing a child in the many environments in which he or she routinely operates. The purpose of conducting such an assessment is to probe how the different environments influence the student and his or her school performance. Critical questions to ask in an ecological assessment include:

- In which environments does the student manifest difficulties?
- Are there instances in which he or she appears to function appropriately?

- What is expected of the student academically and behaviorally in each type of environment?
- What differences exist in the environments in which the student manifests the greatest and the least difficulty?
- What implications do these differences have for instructional planning?

According to Overton (2009), an ecological assessment analyzes a "student's total learning environment" (p. 339). A thorough ecological assessment should include the following:

- Interaction between students, teachers, and others in the classroom and in other school environments
- Presentation of materials and ideas
- Selection and use of materials for instruction
- Physical arrangement and environment of the classroom or target setting
- Students' interactions in other environments

Ecological assessment can also draw on:

- The culture and beliefs of the child
- The teacher's teaching style
- The way time is used in the classroom
- Academic, behavioral, and social expectations within the learning environment

The components of an ecological assessment clearly reveal that it involves numerous aspects of the student's life to get a detailed picture of his or her situation.

Curriculum-Based Assessment

Direct assessment of academic skills is one alternative that has recently gained in popularity. Although a number of direct assessment models exist, they are similar in that they all suggest that assessment needs to be tied directly to instructional curriculum.

According to Cohen and Spenciner (2011), **curriculum-based assessment (CBA)** is an approach to linking instruction with assessment. CBA has three purposes: (1) to determine eligibility, (2) to develop the goals for instruction, and (3) to evaluate the student's progress in the curriculum. Based on the student's performance on a CBA instrument, teachers and other professionals can specify instructional goals. Because there is such a close link between assessment and instruction, it is possible to conduct CBA frequently in order to determine whether to make any changes in instruction or the curriculum. Data collection, interpretation, and intervention are all *integral* parts of CBA. Other terms for CBA are curriculum-referenced measurement, curriculum-embedded measurement, frequent measurement, continuous curriculum measurement, and therapeutic measurement.

CBA is useful because it:

- links curriculum and instruction.
- helps the teacher determine what to teach.
- can be administered frequently.
- is sensitive to short-term academic gains.
- assists in the evaluation of student progress and program evaluation.
- can be reliable and valid.

Whereas standardized commercial achievement tests measure broad curriculum areas and/ or skills, curriculum-based assessment (CBA) measures specific skills that are presently being taught in the classroom, usually basic skills. Several approaches to CBA have been developed (Hall & Mengel, 2002). Four common characteristics exist across these models:

- The measurement procedures assess students directly using the materials in which they are being instructed. This involves sampling items from the curriculum.
- Administration of each measure is generally brief in duration (typically 1–5 minutes).
- The design is structured such that frequent and repeated measurement is possible and measures are sensitive to change.
- Data are usually displayed graphically to allow monitoring of student performance.

"Tests" of performance in this case come directly from the curriculum. For example, a child may be asked to read from his or her reading book for one minute. Information about the accuracy and the speed of reading can then be obtained and compared with other students in the class, building, or district. CBA is quick and offers specific information about how a student may differ from his or her peers. Because the assessment is tied to curriculum content, it allows the teacher to match instruction to a student's current abilities and pinpoints areas in which curriculum adaptations or modifications are needed.

CBA also offers information about the accuracy and efficiency (speed) of performance. The latter is often overlooked when assessing a child's performance, but is an important piece of information when designing intervention strategies. CBA is also useful in evaluating short-term academic progress (Wright, 2007).

Curriculum-Based Measurement

Curriculum-based measurement (CBM) is an assessment method that involves timing tasks and then charting performance. CBM is most concerned with fluency. This means that we are looking at the rate at which a student is able to perform a given task. After assessing the speed at which the student performs the task, we then chart performance over time so that we can clearly see on a graph the student's progress (or decline) from the initial performance to the goal point. An example of curriculum-based measurement would be to examine the number of words correctly read from a book in 5 minutes and then continually chart the student's progress over the course of the school year with the goal being set at a predetermined number (e.g., 150 words).

How Does CBM Work?

According to McLane (2006), when CBM is used, each child is tested briefly each week. The tests generally last from 1 to 5 minutes. The teacher counts the number of correct and incorrect responses made in the time allotted to find the child's score. For example, in reading, the child may be asked to read aloud for one minute. Each child's scores are recorded on a graph and compared to the expected performance on the content for that year. The graph allows the teacher, and you, to see quickly how the child's performance compares to expectations. (Figure 2.1 is an example of what a CBM graph looks like.)

After the scores are entered on the graphs, the teacher decides whether to continue instruction in the same way, or to change it. A change is called for if the child's rate of learning progress is lower than is needed to meet the goal for the year.

The teacher can change instruction in any of several ways. For example, he or she might increase instructional time, change a teaching technique or way of presenting the material, or change a grouping arrangement (for example, individual instruction instead of small-group

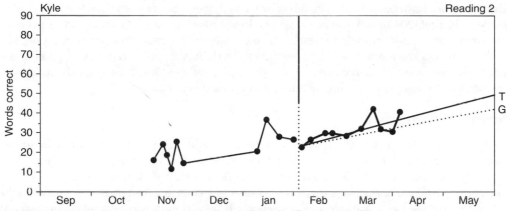

FIGURE 2.1 Example of Curriculum Based Measurement (CBM) graph for reading.

instruction). After the change, parents—and the teacher—can see from the weekly scores on the graph whether the change is helping their child. If it is not, then the teacher can try another change in instruction, and its success will be tracked through the weekly measurements.

Dynamic Assessment

Dynamic assessment refers to several different but similar approaches to evaluating student learning. One of the chief characteristics of dynamic assessment is the inclusion of a dialogue or interaction between the examiner and the student. The interaction allows the examiner to draw conclusions about the student's thinking processes (i.e., why he or she answers a question in a particular way) and his or her response to a learning situation (i.e., whether, with prompting, feedback, or modeling, the student can produce a correct response and what specific means of instruction produce and maintain positive change in the student's cognitive functioning).

Dynamic assessment may be framed as a constructivist approach to assessment. That is, the goal is to determine what students do, can do, and can do with help, and to devote less time and attention to comparing student performance to set standards or to norm-group performance in an attempt to identify deficiencies. In dynamic assessment,

> the assessment is focused on student learning and performance over time, and comparisons are made between a student's current and past performance. Additionally, dynamic assessment is concerned with learning what a student is able to do when provided supports in the form of prompts, cues, or physical supports, some of which naturally exist in the environment (Bigge & Stump, 1999, p. 182).

Typically, dynamic assessment involves a test–train–retest approach. The examiner begins by testing the student's ability to perform a task or solve a problem without help. Then, a similar task or problem is given to the student, and the examiner models how the task or problem is solved or gives the student cues to assist his or her performance. In Feuerstein's (1979) model of dynamic assessment, the examiner is encouraged to interact constantly with the student, an interaction that is called *mediation*, which is felt to maximize the probability that the student will solve the problem.

Dynamic assessment is a promising addition to current evaluation techniques. Because it incorporates a teaching component into the assessment process, this type of assessment may be particularly useful with students from minority backgrounds who may not have been exposed to the types of problems or tasks found on standardized tests. The interactional aspect of dynamic assessment also can contribute substantially to developing an understanding of the student's thinking process and problem-solving approaches and skills. Certainly, having detailed information about how a student approaches performing a task and how he or she responds to various instructional techniques can be highly relevant to instructional planning.

Portfolio Assessment

Perhaps the most important type of assessment for the classroom teacher is the **portfolio assessment**. According to Overton (2009), a **portfolio assessment** is "a collection of various types of products or assessments collected over time that demonstrate student progress" (p. 20). The collection must include student participation in selecting contents, the criteria for selection, the criteria for judging merit, and evidence of student self-reflection. A portfolio collection contains work samples, permanent products, and test results from a variety of instruments and measures. For example, a portfolio of reading might include a "student's test scores on teacher-made tests including curriculum-based assessments, work samples from daily work and homework assignments, error analyses on work and test samples, and the results of an informal reading inventory with miscues noted and analyzed" (p. 243).

Batzle (1992; cited in Bigge & Stump, 1999) identifies three general types of portfolios:

- *Working portfolio:* Teacher, student, and parents all contribute to the portfolio. Both works in progress and final product pieces are included.
- *Showcase portfolio:* The portfolio houses only the student's best work and generally does not include works in progress. The student manages the portfolio and decides what to place in it.
- *Teacher portfolio or record keeping:* The portfolio houses student test papers and work samples maintained by the teacher. It contains work not selected by the student for inclusion in the showcase portfolio.

When portfolios are used in the classroom, they allow teachers to assess student progress more closely over time, aid teachers and parents in communicating about students' performance, assist in program evaluation efforts, and provide a means through which students can actively participate with their teachers in the assessment process (Salvia & Ysseldyke, 2007).

There is some controversy about what should go into a portfolio, given that it could play a very important role in the educational future of a student. Teachers have been urged to create portfolios and structure them to help them make future decisions for their students. Yet the literature on portfolio assessment offers little practical guidance about (1) the types of decisions teachers should be making, (2) the characteristics of the content used for specific decisions, and (3) the criteria to guide decision making about grading, identification of academic weaknesses, instructional improvement, eligibility for entitlement programs, assessing educational outcomes, and educational reform (Salvia & Ysseldyke, 2007). Consequently, for portfolio assessment to be more useful in special education considerations, more research needs to be done and practical information and suggestions will need to be offered.

Authentic/Naturalistic/Performance-Based Assessment

Another technique that is becoming increasingly popular with classroom teachers to assess classroom performance is authentic assessment. This performance-based assessment technique involves the application of knowledge to real-life activities, real-world settings or a simulation of such a setting using real-life, real-world activities (Taylor, 2009). For example, when an individual is being assessed in the area of artistic ability, typically he or she presents artwork and is evaluated according to various criteria; it is not simply the person's knowledge of art, materials, artists, or history. Authentic assessment is sometimes referred to as naturalistic-based assessment or performance-based assessment. The terms can be used interchangeably. Each of the methods within **authentic/naturalistic/performance-based assessment** has common characteristics. These include the following (Herman et al., 1992, p. 6; cited in Bigge & Stump, 1999, p. 183):

- Ask students to perform, create, produce, or do something.
- Tap higher-level thinking and problem-solving skills.
- Use tasks that represent meaningful instructional activities.
- Invoke real-world applications.
- Let people, not machines, do the scoring, using human judgment.
- Require new instructional and assessment roles for teachers.

This new category of assessment is up and coming, and, as such, an agreement on the appropriate terminology to describe it is still to come.

Task Analysis

Task analysis is very detailed; it involves breaking down a particular task into the basic sequential steps, component parts, or skills necessary to accomplish the task. Task analysis is "a procedure for identifying the subskills that comprise a specific skill or behavior in order to assist a student in acquiring that skill or behavior. The behavior that will be acquired or eliminated is referred to as the target behavior" (Cohen & Spenciner, 2007, p. 316).

Taking this approach to assessment offers the teacher several advantages. For one, the process identifies what is necessary for accomplishing a particular task. It also tells the teacher whether the student can do the task, which part or skill causes the student to falter, and the order in which skills must be taught to help the student learn to perform the task.

Task analysis is an approach to assessment that goes far beyond the need to make an eligibility or program placement decision regarding a student. It can become an integral part of classroom planning and instructional decision making.

Outcome-Based Assessment

Outcome-based assessment has been developed, at least in part, to respond to concerns that education, to be meaningful, must be directly related to what educators and parents want the child to have gained in the end. Outcome-based assessment involves considering, teaching, and evaluating the skills that are important in real-life situations. Learning such skills will result in the student becoming an effective adult. Assessment, from this point of view, starts by identifying what outcomes are desired for the student (e.g., being able to use public transportation). In steps similar to what is used with task analysis, the team then determines what competencies are necessary for the outcomes to take place (e.g., the steps or subskills the student needs to have mastered in order to achieve the outcome desired) and identifies which subskills the student has mastered and which he or she still needs to learn. The instruction that is needed can then be pinpointed and undertaken (Pierangelo & Giuliani, 2009).

Learning Styles Assessment

Learning styles theory suggests that students may learn and problem solve in different ways, and that some ways are more natural for them than others. When they are taught or asked to perform in ways that deviate from their natural style, they are thought to learn or perform less well. Some of the common elements that may be included in **learning styles assessment** would be the way material is typically presented (visually, auditorily, tactilely) in the classroom, the environmental conditions of the classroom (hot, cold, noisy, light, dark), the child's personality characteristics, the expectations for success that the child and others hold, the response the child receives while engaging in the learning process (e.g., praise or criticism), and the type of thinking the child generally utilizes in solving problems (e.g., trial and error, analyzing). Identifying the factors that positively impact the child's learning may be very valuable in developing effective intervention strategies.

TESTING CONSIDERATIONS

There are many testing considerations that need to be understood when doing the assessment of a child for a suspected disability. This next section will address these testing considerations and explain the importance of each.

Selecting an Appropriate Instrument

Choosing an appropriate test for a given student requires investigation. It is extremely important that those responsible for test selection do not use only what is available to or what has "always been used" by the school district or school. The child's test results will certainly influence eligibility decisions, instructional decisions, and placement decisions, all of which have enormous consequences for the child. If the child is assessed with an instrument that is not appropriate for him or her, the data gathered are likely to be inaccurate and misleading, which in turn results in faulty decisions regarding that child's educational program. This is one of the reasons that many educators object vehemently to standardized testing as a means of making decisions about a student's strengths and weaknesses.

Therefore, selecting instruments with care is vital, as is the need to combine any information gathered through testing with information gathered through other approaches. Given the number of standardized tests available today, how do professionals in special education select an appropriate instrument for a given student? Here are some suggestions:

- Consider the student's skill areas to be assessed, and identify a range of tests that measure those skill areas. A variety of books can help evaluators identify what tests are available. One useful reference book is Pierangelo and Giuliani's (2007), *Special Educator's Comprehensive Guide to 301 Diagnostic Tests*. This book describes what each available test claims to measure, the age groups for which it is appropriate, whether it is group or individually administered (all testing of children with suspected disabilities must be individualized), how long it takes to administer the test, and much more.
- Investigate how suitable each test identified is for the student to be assessed, and select those that are most appropriate: A particularly valuable resource for evaluating tests is *The Fourteenth Mental Measurements Yearbook* (Plake & Impara, 2001), which describes tests in detail and includes expert reviews of many tests. This yearbook is typically available in professional libraries for teachers, university libraries, and in the reference section of many public libraries. Publishers of tests generally also make literature available to

help professionals determine whether a test is suitable for a specific student. This litera-ture typically includes sample test questions, information on how the test was developed, a description of what groups of individuals (e.g., ethnic groups, ages, grade levels) were included in the "norm" group and general guidelines for administration and interpretation.

- According to the publisher or expert reviewers, what, specifically, is the test supposed to measure? Is its focus directly relevant to the skill area(s) to be assessed? Will student results on the test address the educational questions being asked? (In other words, will the test provide the type of educational information that is needed?) If not, the test is not ap-propriate for that student and should not be used.

- Is the test valid and reliable? These are two critical issues in assessment (see Chapter 4). Validity refers to the degree to which the test measures what it claims to measure. For example, if a test claims to measure anxiety, a person's scores should be higher under a stressful situation than under a nonstressful situation. Reliability refers to the degree to which a child's results on the test are the same or similar over repeated testing. If a test is not reliable or if its reliability is uncertain—it does not yield similar results when the student takes the test again—then it should not be used. Test publishers make available specimen sets that will typically report the reliability and validity of the test.

- Is the content/skill area being assessed by the test appropriate for the student, given his or her age and grade? If not, there is no reason to use the test.

- If the test is norm-referenced, does the norm group resemble the student? This point was mentioned earlier and is important for interpreting results.

- Is the test intended to evaluate students, to diagnose the specific nature of a student's disability or academic difficulty, to inform instructional decisions, or to be used for research purposes? Many tests will indicate that a student has a disability or specific problem academically, but results will not be useful for instructional planning purposes. Additional testing may then be needed in order to understand fully what type of instruction is necessary for the student.

- Is the test administered in a group or individually? By law, group tests are not appropriate when assessing a child for the presence of a disability or to determine his or her eligibility for special education.

- Does the examiner need specialized training in order to administer the test, record student responses, score the test, or interpret results? In most, if not all, cases, the answer to this question is yes. If the school has no one trained to administer or interpret the specific test, then it should not be used unless the school arranges for the student to be assessed by a qualified evaluator outside of the school system.

- Will the student's suspected disability impact his or her taking the test? For example, many tests are timed tests, which means that students are given a certain amount of time to complete items. If a student has weak hand strength or dexterity, his or her performance on a timed test that requires holding a pencil or writing will be negatively affected by the disability. Using a timed test would be appropriate only for determining how speed affects performance. To determine the student's actual knowledge of a certain area, an untimed test would be more appropriate. It may also be possible to make accommodations for the student (e.g., removing time restrictions from a timed test). If an accommodation is made, however, results must be interpreted with caution. Standardized tests are designed to be administered in an unvarying manner; when accommodations are made, standardization is broken, and the norms reported for the test no longer apply.

- How similar to actual classroom tasks are the tasks the child is asked to complete on the test? For example, measuring spelling ability by asking a child to recognize a misspelled word may be very different from how spelling is usually measured in a class situation (reproducing words from memory). If test tasks differ significantly from classroom tasks, information gathered by the test may do little to predict classroom ability or provide information useful for instruction.

Selection of Test Content

Test content is an important factor when choosing between a norm-referenced test (NRT) and a criterion-referenced test (CRT). The content of an NRT test is selected according to how well it ranks students from high achievers to low. The content of a CRT test is determined by how well it matches the learning outcomes deemed most important. Although no test can measure everything of importance, the content selected for the CRT is selected on the basis of its significance in the curriculum, whereas that of the NRT is chosen by how well it discriminates among students.

Any national, state, or district test communicates to the public the skills that students should have acquired as well as the levels of student performance that are considered satisfactory. Therefore, education officials at any level should carefully consider content of the test which is selected or developed. Because of the importance placed on high scores, the content of a standardized test can be very influential in the development of a school's curriculum and standards of excellence.

Test Interpretation

As mentioned earlier, a student's performance on an NRT is interpreted in relation to the performance of a large group of similar students who took the test when it was first normed. For example, if a student receives a percentile rank score on the total test of 34, this means that he or she performed as well or better than 34 percent of the students in the norm group. This type of information can be useful for deciding whether or not a student needs remedial assistance or is a candidate for a gifted program. However, the score gives little information about what the student actually knows or can do. The validity of the score in these decision processes depends on whether or not the content of the NRT matches the knowledge and skills expected of the students in that particular school system.

Limitations of Testing

Even when all of these considerations have been observed, there are those who question the usefulness of traditional testing in making good educational decisions for children. Many educators concerned with the **limitations of testing** see traditional tests as offering little in the way of information useful for understanding the abilities and special needs of an individual child.

Another concern about the overuse of testing in assessment is its lack of usefulness in designing interventions. Historically, it has seemed as if tests have not been interpreted in ways that allow for many specific strategies to be developed. Although scores help to define the areas in which a student may be performing below his or her peers, they may offer little to determine particular instruction or curricular changes that may benefit the child.

Traditional tests often seem to overlap very little with the curriculum being taught. This suggests that scores may not reflect what the child really knows in terms of what is taught in the actual classroom. Other concerns include overfamiliarity with a test that is repeated regularly, inability to apply test findings in any practical way (i.e., generating specific recommendations based on test results), and difficulty in using such measures to monitor short-term achievement gains.

The sometimes circular journey from the referral to the outcome of the assessment process is frustrating. The teacher or parent requests help because the student is having problems, and the assessment results in information that more or less states, "The student is having problems."

It may be, however, that it is not that the tests themselves offer little relevant information but, rather, that the evaluators may fail to interpret them in useful ways. If we ask questions only related to eligibility (e.g., does this child meet the criteria as an individual with mental disabilities?) or about global ability (e.g., what is this child's intellectual potential?), then those are the questions that will be answered. Yet such information is not enough if the goal is to develop an effective and appropriate educational program for the student.

CONCLUSION

Various methods of assessment are available to use when evaluating a student for a possible disability. Both formal and informal measures of assessment are necessary to get the most complete picture of a student's abilities. Ultimately, it becomes necessary for you to understand all the different measures. Selecting instruments with care is vital, as is the need to combine any information gathered through testing with information gathered through other approaches. Given the number of standardized tests available today, it is your professional responsibility to be sure that you understand the various methods of assessments and the purpose of their use.

Vocabulary

Authentic assessment: This is a performance-based assessment technique that involves the application of knowledge to real-life activities, real-world settings, or a simulation of such a setting using real-life, real-world activities.

Basal: The level of mastery of a task below which the student would correctly answer all items on a test.

Ceiling: The point at which the student has made a predetermined number of errors, and therefore, all other items stop being administered because it is assumed that the student will continue to get the answers wrong.

Content-referenced tests: Tests that are concerned with the mastery of specific, defined skills; the student's performance on the test indicates whether he or she has mastered those skills.

Criterion: The standard by which criterion-referenced tests are scored. The criterion represents an acceptable level of mastery.

Criterion-referenced tests (CRTs):   Tests that are scored according to a standard, or criterion, that the teacher, school, or test publisher decides represents an acceptable level of mastery.

Curriculum-based assessment (CBA):   A type of direct evaluation. "Tests" of performance in this case come directly from the curriculum.

Curriculum-based measurement (CBM):   An assessment method that involves timing tasks and then charting performance.

Dynamic assessment: The goal of this type of assessment is to explore the nature of learning, with the objective of collecting information to bring about cognitive change and to enhance instruction.

Ecological assessment: Involves directly observing and assessing the child in the many environments in which he or she routinely operates.

Formal tests: Tests that assume a single set of expectations for all students and come with prescribed criteria for scoring and interpretation.

Informal reading inventories: Commercial and teacher-made instruments for diagnosing reading difficulties, assessing a student's progress, and planning interventions for a student.

Informal tests: Techniques that are not intended to provide a comparison to a broader group beyond the students in the local project.

Learning style assessment: An assessment that attempts to determine those elements that impact on a child's learning.

Limitations of testing: Traditional tests' lack of useful information about the needs and abilities of an individual.

Naturalistic-based assessment: A performance-based assessment technique that involves the application of knowledge to real-life activities, real-world settings, or a simulation of such a setting using real-life, real-world activities.

Norm group: A large number of children who are representative of all the children in that age group.

Norm-referenced tests (NRTs):   These tests are not interpreted according to an absolute standard or criterion (e.g., 8 out of 10 correct) but, rather, according to how the student's performance compares with that of a particular group of individuals.

Outcome-based assessment: Involves considering, teaching, and evaluating the skills that are important in real-life situations.

Performance-based assessment: See naturalistic-based assessment (terms used interchangeably).

Portfolio: A purposeful collection of student works that exhibits the student's efforts, progress, and achievement in one or more areas.

Portfolio assessment: The process of collecting a student's work to examine efforts, progress, and achievement in one or more areas.

Showcase portfolio: The portfolio houses only the student's best work and generally does not include works in progress. The student manages the portfolio and decides what to place in it.

Standardization: Refers to structuring test materials, administration procedures, scoring methods, and techniques for interpreting results.

Standardized tests: Tests with detailed procedures for administration, timing, scoring, and interpretation procedures that must be followed precisely to obtain valid and reliable results.

Standards-referenced tests: Tests that measure whether students meet standards of what they should know and be able to do in different subjects at various grade levels.

Task analysis: Involves breaking down a particular task into the basic sequential steps, component parts, or skills necessary to accomplish the task.

Teacher portfolio or record keeping: The portfolio houses student test papers and work samples maintained by the teacher. It contains work not selected by the student for inclusion in the showcase portfolio.

Working portfolio: Teacher, student, and parents all contribute to the portfolio. Both works in progress and final product pieces are included.

3 | BASIC STATISTICAL CONCEPTS

Key Terms

Bimodal distribution
Correlation
Correlation coefficient
Descriptive statistics
Frequency distribution
Interval scale of measurement
Mean
Measures of central tendency
Median

Mode
Multimodal distribution
Negative correlation
Negatively skewed distribution
Nominal scale of
    measurement
Normal curve
Normal distribution
Ordinal scale of measurement

Positive correlation
Positively skewed distribution
Range
Ratio scale of
    measurement
Skewed distribution
Standard deviation
Variance
Zero correlation

Chapter Objectives

Statistics! This one 10-letter word tends to instill more fear and anxiety in undergraduate and graduate students than any other word we know. We have learned from our experience as college professors that when we say we are going to cover statistics in our assessment courses, responses from students will be:

▪ Can we take this course pass/fail?

▪ What is the latest date to drop the course?

▪ I hate math—I always get confused!

▪ Do we really have to know this? If so, how come?

   The fact is, whether you are an avid fan of statistics or generally do not enjoy it, you absolutely have to know statistics when you are doing special education assessment. Statistics play a vital role in the understanding of disability awareness. Although there are numerous reasons to know statistics, of primary importance to special educators is that without a proper understanding of it, you cannot interpret test results.

   When large sets of data are being presented, it is important that they be organized in a fashion that makes some sense to the reader. In special education, this is done through methods known as **descriptive statistics.** Descriptive statistics summarize and describe data. In this chapter, we discuss basic descriptive statistics used every day in special education. After reading this chapter, you should be able to understand (and in some cases be able to calculate) the following:

▪ Scales of measurement

▪ Measures of central tendency (mean, median, and mode)

▪ Frequency distribution

▪ Range

▪ Variance

■ Standard deviation
■ Normal curve
■ Skewed distributions
■ Correlations

SCALES OF MEASUREMENT

The way data can be expressed in assessment often depends on the type of score one receives. In descriptive statistics, there are four scales of measurement that can be used to explain data: nominal, ordinal, interval, and ratio.

Nominal

In a **nominal scale of measurement,** nominal data are categorical data. They are created by assigning observations into various independent categories and then counting the frequency of occurrence within each of the categories (Lane, 2011). This is referred to as nose-counting data. It is a scale in which scores represent names that are weighted equally—for example, observing how many males versus females there are in a school.

With nominal data, the concept of quantity cannot be expressed for any individual unit of data. For example, the numbers on football jerseys are examples of nominal data. A person who wears number 20 is not two times better than the person who wears number 10. Examples of nominal data include telephone numbers, social security numbers, and species of birds.

Ordinal

Ordinal scales of measurement involve the rank order system. It is a scale in which scores indicate only relative amounts or rank order. When we discuss horse races and say first place, second place, and third place, we are using ordinal data. Although ordinal scales tell us rank, they do not tell us the distance between each subject. For example, even though we know which horse finished first, second, and third, we do not know by how much the first-place horse beat the second-place horse. In schools, class rank is a classic example of ordinal data.

Interval

An **interval scale of measurement** is one in which equal differences in scores represent equal differences in amount of the property measured, but with an arbitrary zero point. For example:

- Fahrenheit temperature: A temperature of 40 degrees is not twice as hot as 20 degrees. Also, zero degrees does not mean no temperature; it is an arbitrary zero point.
- IQ scores: A student with an IQ of 100 is not twice as smart as someone with an IQ of 50.

Ratio

A **ratio scale of measurement** has all the properties of an interval scale with the additional property of zero indicating a total absence of the quality being measured. A score of zero means zero. For example:

- Distance: The distance 15 feet is three times more than 5 feet.
- Duration: The duration 20 minutes is twice as long as 10 minutes.
- Weight: A 300-pound man is six times heavier than a 50-pound boy.
- On a math test in which a child gets four wrong and another gets eight wrong, the child who missed eight questions got twice as many wrong as the other child.

MEASURES OF CENTRAL TENDENCY

Most students have learned the **measures of central tendency** many times in their academic lives. So, for many of you, this may be a review. There are three ways to describe central tendency in a set of scores. These are mean, median, and mode.

The measures of central tendency can be very important to know because they organize and describe data to see how the data fall together or cluster. Central tendency shows how scores are distributed around a numerical representation of the average score (Overton, 2009).

Mean

The **mean** is the mathematical average of the distribution of scores. Statistically, the mean is represented by the symbol M. The way to calculate the mean score is simply to add up the scores in the distribution and divide by the number of units. For example, suppose the following scores were obtained in a distribution: 8, 10, 8, 14, and 40. Calculate the mean score.

CALCULATION OF THE MEAN

- Add up the scores (this is also referred to as summating or summation): $8 + 10 + 8 + 14 + 40 = 80$
- Count the number of units in the distribution. Here, there are five of them (8, 10, 8, 14, and 40 = 5 numbers in total).
- Take the total score in Step 1 and divide by the number of units calculated in Step 2: $80/5 = 16$

The mean is 16 (or you can write it as $M = 16$).

Important Point: *The mean is greatly affected by extreme scores.* For example, suppose four students take an exam and receive scores of 90, 95, 100, and 7 percent. The mean of the distribution is 73 percent. Notice though that three students did extremely well, but the one student who got a 7 percent took the mean from an A average to a C average.

Median

Another way to measure central tendency is to order the scores relative to where they fall in a distribution. The **median** is the middle score in a distribution. It is the point at which half the scores fall above and half the scores fall below. In the distribution 8, 10, 8, 14, and 40, what is the median?

CALCULATION OF THE MEDIAN

- Rank order the data from least to greatest. What you do is simply list the scores from the smallest number to the largest: 8, 8, 10, 14, 40.
- Now cross off the low score (8), then the high score (40). Repeat this step until there is only one number left. In our example you would next cross off the 8, then the 14. This leaves 10 as the middle number. The median is 10.

- Now, suppose the distribution of scores had an even number of units. For example: 8, 10, 12, 8, 14, and 40. Calculate the median. In this example, first rank order the data: 8, 8, 10, 12, 14, 40. After crossing out the high and low numbers, you are left with 10 and 12.
- To find the median, simply take the average of the two numbers left. This would make 11 the median score: $(10 + 12 = 22/2 = 11)$.

Important Point: *The median is less affected by extreme scores than is the mean.* For example, suppose four students take an exam and receive scores of 90, 95, 100, and 7 percent. Although the mean of the distribution is 73 percent, the median is 92.5 percent, a much better indication of how the four students did overall.

Mode

The **mode** is the most frequently occurring score in a distribution. For example: In the distribution 8, 10, 8, 14, and 40, what is the mode? The answer is 8. The number 8 occurs twice, whereas all other numbers occur only once.

What is the mode in the following distribution: 8, 10, 8, 10, 14, and 40? Here, the scores 8 and 10 occur twice; therefore, we have two modes: 8 and 10. When you have two modes in a distribution, it is referred to as a **bimodal distribution.** If you have three or more modes in your distribution, it is referred to as a **multimodal distribution.** For example, what is the mode of this distribution: 8, 10, 8, 10, 14, 14, and 40? Because 8, 10, and 14 are the most frequently occurring numbers (three of them), it is a multimodal distribution.

FREQUENCY DISTRIBUTION

To see data more clearly (and often the way to find the mode) in a distribution, it can be extremely helpful to set up a frequency distribution. A **frequency distribution** expresses how often a score occurs in a set of data. For example, suppose you had the following distribution of 11 students' scores on a spelling test:

Student Name	Spelling Test Score (%)
Ted	100
Carmen	85
Ralph	75
Juana	98
Celest	98
Mohammed	100
Joaquinne	95
Amy	80
Carol	85
Tony	85
Jesus	100

A frequency distribution sets up a much easier way to look at the data. To set up a frequency distribution, simply make three columns: Column 1—Test Score, Column 2—Tally,

Table 3.1 Frequency Distribution for Spelling Test Scores		
Test Score (%)	**Tally**	**Frequency**
75	I	1
80	I	1
85	III	3
95	I	1
98	II	2
100	III	3

Column 3—Frequency. Under each column fill in the appropriate information. Table 3.1 shows what the frequency distribution would look like for the above 11 students' spelling test scores.

Important Point: *When setting up a frequency distribution, always rank order the data from the smallest to the largest number or the largest to the smallest.* In Table 3.1, 75 is the smallest and 100 is the largest. Also, notice that when setting up a frequency distribution it is very easy to calculate the mode(s) simply by inspection. (The scores that most frequently occur are 85 and 100—seen by the 3s in the frequency column.)

RANGE

The **range** of a distribution is the difference between the high score and the low score in the distribution (range = high score − low score). For example, if we have a distribution of 8, 10, 8, 14, and 40, what is the range?

CALCULATION OF THE RANGE

1. Find the high score and the low score in the distribution: 40 and 8.
2. Subtract the low score from the high score: 40 − 8 = 32.
3. The range is 32.

Important Point: The range is very simple to determine, yet there is a serious problem with just giving the range of scores. Think about it: The range tells you nothing about the scores in between the high and low scores. And, if there is *one extreme score, it can greatly affect the range.* Suppose the distribution was 8, 9, 8, 9, 8, and 1,000. The range would be 992 (1,000 − 8 = 992). Yet, only one score is even close to 992, the 1,000.

Variance

When looking at scores within a distribution, it is often very helpful to know how the scores are spread out. In order to get a better idea of the spread of scores within a distribution, it is necessary to calculate the variance. The **variance** is a statistical concept that tells you the spread of scores within a distribution. The variance is an extremely important concept to understand because it is necessary in the calculation of the standard deviation and the analysis of data in the normal curve. (These two areas, discussed later in this chapter, are critical to understand as special educators.)

To explain the importance of variance, let's look at the following two distributions of scores on a 50-question spelling test (each score represents the number of words correctly spelled):

Scores for 5 students in Group A: 28, 29, 30, 31, 32

Scores for 5 students in Group B: 0, 20, 30, 40, 50

Calculate the mean for Groups A and B.

Mean of Group A = 30

Mean of Group B = 30

The mean of both groups is 30. Now, if you knew nothing about these two groups other than their mean scores, you might think they looked similar. However, the spread of scores in Group A (28 to 32) is much smaller than in Group B (10 to 50). Statistically, we say that the variance of Group B is greater than the variance in group A. According to Sattler (2001), the general rule is the greater the spread, the greater the variance. The fact that two different sets of scores have the same mean but different variances means that one has a larger range or spread of scores than the other.

STANDARD DEVIATION

In almost all cases, we determine the variance to calculate the standard deviation. *The standard deviation is the spread of scores around the mean.* It is an extremely important statistical concept to understand when doing assessment in special education (see normal curve explanation).

Important Point: *The standard deviation is calculated by taking the square root of the variance.* The steps sfor calculating standard deviation are the exact same steps for calculating the variance except that there is one extra step. After finding the variance, take the square root. This is the **standard deviation.**

NORMAL CURVE

According to Overton (2009), a **normal distribution** "hypothetically represents the way test scores would fall if a particular test is given to every single student of the same age or grade in the population for whom the test was designed. If educators could administer an instrument in this way and obtain a normal distribution, the scores would fall in the shape of a bell curve" (p. 108).

The **normal curve** (also referred to as the *bell curve*) tells us many important facts about test scores and the population. The beauty of the normal curve is that it never changes. As students, this is great for you because once you memorize it, it will never change on you (and, yes, you do have to memorize it at some point in your academic or professional career). Figure 3.1 shows how the normal curve is always represented.

Now, how does this help you? Well, let's take an example that you will come across numerous times in special education: IQ. The mean IQ score on many IQ tests is 100 and the standard deviation is 15. (The most popular IQ test is the Wechsler Scales of Intelligence; see Chapter 10.) Now, according to the normal curve, IQ on the Wechsler Scales is distributed as in Figure 3.2.

Given this information, there is so much we can say. First, notice that approximately 68 percent of the entire population has an IQ between 85 and 115 (–1 SD to +1 SD: 34% + 34% = 68%). Also, 13.5 percent of the population has an IQ between 115 and 130. Furthermore, about 95 percent of all the scores are found within 2 SD above and below the mean. (Look between the lines on the curve between –2 SD and + 2 SD. The percent of scores are 13.5% + 34% + 34% + 13.5%, which totals 95%.)

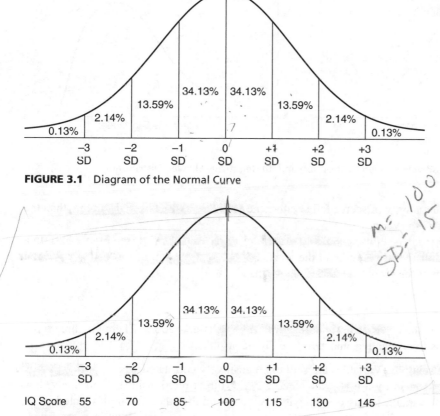

FIGURE 3.1 Diagram of the Normal Curve

FIGURE 3.2 Diagram of the Normal Curve for the WISC-IV with a Mean of 100 and a Standard Deviation of 15

Do you know what the requirements are for most gifted programs regarding minimum IQ scores (that have a mean of 100 and SD of 15)? By looking at the normal curve you may have figured it out—the minimum is normally an IQ of 130 for entrance. Why? Gifted programs will take only students who are 2 SD or more above the mean. In a sense, they want only those whose IQs are better than 97.5 percent of the population.

How about mental retardation? On the Wechsler Scales, the classification of mental retardation is determined if a child receives an IQ score below 70. Why 70? This score was not just randomly chosen. What we are saying is that in order to be mentally retarded, a student is usually 2 or more SD below the mean. In a sense, the child's IQ is only as high as 2.5 percent (or even lower) of the normal population (or, in other words, 97.5 percent or more of the population has a higher IQ than this child).

Skewed Distributions

As you may have noticed, the normal curve is *symmetrical*. This means that the left side of the bell is exactly the same shape as the right side. However, the normal curve may not always occur when you have only a small number of test scores in your distribution. When the population of a sample is not large, there may be a tendency for the scores to be *skewed*. A **skewed distribution**

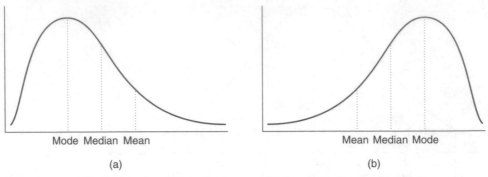

Mode Median Mean   Mean Median Mode

(a)   (b)

FIGURE 3.3   (a) Positively Skewed Distribution and (b) Negatively Skewed Distribution

is one in which the majority of scores fall at either the high end or the low end xsrather than the middle of a distribution (Venn, 1999).

A distribution can be either positively skewed or negatively skewed (see Figure 3.3). In a **positively skewed distribution,** more of the scores fall below the mean. In a **negatively skewed distribution,** more of the scores fall above the mean.

Correlations

Correlations tell us the relationship between two variables (Berk, 2007). There are three types of correlations: positive, negative, and zero (see Figure 3.4).

1. **Positive correlation:** Variables are said to be positively correlated when a high score on one is accompanied by a high score on the other (direct relationship). Conversely, low scores on one variable are associated with low scores on the other. Examples include:
   • IQ and academic achievement—as IQ increases, academic achievement increases.
   • Education and income—as education increases, income tends to increase.

2. **Negative correlation:** Variables are said to be negatively correlated when a high score on one is accompanied by a low score on the other (an inverse relationship). Conversely, low scores on one variable are associated with high scores on the other. Examples include:
   • Teacher stress and job satisfaction—as job stress increases, job satisfaction decreases.
   • Student anxiety and student performance—in general, as anxiety increases, student performance decreases.

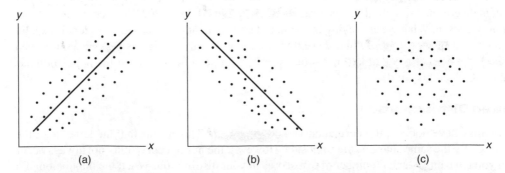

(a)   (b)   (c)

FIGURE 3.4   (a) Positive Correlation, (b) Negative Correlation, and (c) Zero Correlation

Table 3.2 Interpreting Correlation Coefficients

Correlation Coefficient	Statistical Interpretation
.00	*No relationship between the variables.* The two variables **never** occur together.
.01–.25	*Weak relationship.* The two variables **rarely** occur together.
.26–.50	*Moderate relationship.* The two variables occur together **sometimes.**
.51–.75	*Strong relationship.* The two variables occur together **often.**
.76–.99	*Very strong relationship.* The two variables occur together **very often.**
1.00	*Perfect relationship.* The two variables **always** occur together

3. **Zero correlation:** Here, there is *no relationship between the variables.* Examples include:

- Foot size and grades on exams—as foot size increases, nothing changes with respect to grades. They are not related whatsoever.
- Weight and intelligence test scores—as weight increases, nothing changes with respect to IQ. They are not related whatsoever.

When describing the relationship between any two variables, you determine the **correlation coefficient** (see Table 3.2). Statistically, this is represented by the letter r. Now, the general rules for correlations are as follows (Tabachnick & Fidell, 2007; Berk, 2007):

Correlations range from $+1.00$ to -1.00.

The closer you get to $+1.00$ or -1.00, the stronger the relationship

The closer you get to Zero, the weaker the relationship.

0.0 is the weakest correlation—no relationship between the variables.

For example, a correlation coefficient of $-.95$ tells you that there is a negative correlation ($-$ sign) and that there is a strong relationship (because .95 is close to 1.0). Finally, and perhaps the most important point with correlations, is this: *Correlations do not indicate cause and effect.* Just because two things are related to each other does not mean that one causes the other to occur. For example, there is a strong positive correlation between depression and anxiety (as depression goes up so does anxiety). But does the depression cause anxiety, or is the anxiety causing the depression? The fact is, you do not know. Therefore, when determining or reading about correlations, never lose sight of the fact that they indicate only relationships, never cause and effect.

CONCLUSION

Descriptive statistics play a very important role in the assessment process. The fact is, without statistics there would be no way to collect truly objective data to be interpreted. Statistics give us the opportunity to compare children to the norms in many different ways. Understanding statistics is a vital part of being an effective special educator.

Numerous results will be presented to you on a daily basis. Without the proper understanding or interpretation of data, you will not be able to critically evaluate and properly diagnose a child with a disability. Therefore, being able to look at data and make sense of it are fundamental professional responsibilities of special educators.

Vocabulary

Bimodal distribution: A distribution with two modes.

Correlation: The relationship between two variables.

Correlation coefficient: A numerical value that expresses the degree of relationship between two variables.

Descriptive statistics: Statistics that describe and summarize data in a meaningful fashion.

Frequency distribution: Expresses how often a score occurs in a set of data.

Interval scale of measurement: An interval scale is one in which equal differences in scores represent equal differences in amount of the property measured but with an arbitrary zero point.

Mean: The arithmetical average of the distribution of scores.

Measures of central tendency: The mean, median, and mode of a distribution of scores.

Median: The middle score in a distribution. It is the score that separates the top half of the test takers from the bottom half.

Mode: The score in the distribution that most frequently occurs.

Multimodal distribution: A distribution with three or more modes.

Negative correlation: An inverse relationship: Variables are said to be negatively correlated when a high score on one is accompanied by a low score on the other. Conversely, low scores on one variable are associated with high scores on the other.

Negatively skewed distribution: A distribution in which more of the scores fall above the mean.

Nominal scale of measurement: Nominal data are categorical data. Assigning observations into various independent categories and then counting the frequency of occurrence within each of the categories creates a nominal scale.

Normal curve (bell curve):   In this frequency polygon, most of the scores cluster around the mean. The farther above or below the mean a score appears, the less frequently it occurs.

Normal distribution: Represents the way test scores would fall if a particular test is given to every single student of the same age or grade in the population for whom the test was designed.

Ordinal scale of measurement: Ordinal scales involve the rank order system. It is a scale in which scores indicate only relative amounts or rank order.

Positive correlation: A direct relationship: Variables are said to be positively correlated when a high score on one is accompanied by a high score on the other. Conversely, low scores on one variable are associated with low scores on the other.

Positively skewed distribution: A distribution in which more of the scores fall below the mean.

Range: The difference between the high score and the low score in the distribution (Range = High Score − Low Score).

Ratio scale of measurement: A scale having interval properties except that a score of zero indicates a total absence of the quality being measured. A score of zero means zero.

Skewed distribution: A distribution in which the majority of scores falls at either the high end or the low end rather than the middle of a distribution.

Standard deviation: The spread of scores around the mean.

Variance: A statistical concept that tells the spread of scores within a distribution.

Zero correlation: No relationship between the variables, so that a change in one is not associated with a change in the other.

Practice Problems

3.1. Given the following set of IQ scores from students, calculate the mean:

Student Name	IQ Score
Billy	100
Juan	110
Carmela	75
Fred	120
Yvonne	95
Amy	80
Carmen	85

3.2. Given the following IQ scores, calculate the median:

Student Name	IQ Score
Ravi	100
Jesus	110
Carmela	75
Fred	120
Yvonne	95
Amy	80
Chenel	85

75, 80, 85, 95, 100, 110, 120

3.3. Given the following IQ scores, calculate the median:

Student Name	IQ Score
Ralph	100
Marguarita	110
Mike	75
Fred	120
Juanna	95
Amy	80
Carol	85
Ricky	85

85 + 95   180/2 (90)

75, 80, 85, 85, 95, 100, 110, 120

3.4. Given the following spelling test scores, calculate the mode:

Student Name	Score
Edwin	100
Marguarita	85
Tom	75
Fredrika	100
Juan	95
Amy	80
Caroline	85
Ravi	85

3.5. Given the following spelling test scores, calculate the mode:

Student Name	Score
Ed	100
Joe	85
Miguel	75
Jean	100
Joan	95
Jose	80
Carol	85
Tony	85
Cory	100

85, 100

3.6. For the following set of numbers, (a) create a frequency distribution and (b) calculate the mode: 20, 50, 45, 50, 25, 40, 20, 55, 20, 60, 33, 45, 33, 20.

3.7. For the following distribution, calculate the range: 20, 50, 45, 50, 25, 40, 20, 55, 20, 60, 33, 45, 33, 20.

3.8. For the following 10-point Reading Quiz scores, find the measures of central tendency, find the range, and draw a frequency distribution:

Student Name	Score
Caitlyn	10
Erin	8
Tom	7
Kate	6
Lynn	9
Miguel	9
Jen	5
Carol	6
Tony	9
Mohammed	10

3.9. For the following correlations, list them in order from strongest correlation to weakest correlation.

a.   −.67
b.   +.53
c.   −.91
d.   +.03
e.   −.47

Answers to Practice Problems

3.1. M = 95.   To solve this problem, first summate the IQ scores. This total is 665. Now count the number of IQ scores. There are 7 of them. Now take 665/7, and you get 95 as the mean IQ score.

3.2. 95.   Rank order the data from lowest score to highest score: 75, 80, 85, 95, 100, 110, 120. Now, cross off the low and high scores (75 and 120). Do it again (80 and 110). Do it again (85 and 100). You are left with 95 as the median.

3.3. 90.   Rank order the data from lowest score to highest score: 75, 80, 85, 85, 95, 100, 110, 120. Now, cross off the low and high scores (75 and 120). Do it again (80 and 110). Do it again (85 and 100). You are now left with 85 and 95. Take the average and you get 90 as the median.

3.4. 85.   The test score of 85 occurs three times, **the most in the distribution.**

3.5. 85 and 100.   The test scores of 85 and 100 each occur three times, the most in the distribution.

3.6. (a). Test

Score	Tally	Frequency
20	IIII	4
25	I	1
33	II	2
40	I	1
45	II	2
50	II	2
55	I	1
60	I	1

(b). The mode is 20.

3.7. The range is 40. The range is calculated by taking the high score (60) and subtracting the low score (20), which equals 40.

3.8. Reading

Quiz Score	Tally	Frequency
5	I	1
6	II	2
7	I	1
8	I	1
9	III	3
10	II	2

The mode is 9. The mean is 7.9. The median is 8.5. The range is 5.

3.9. strongest to weakest: c, a, b, e, d.

4 | VALIDITY AND RELIABILITY

Key Terms

Alternate forms reliability
Concurrent validity
Construct validity
Constructs
Content validity
Convergent validity
Criterion-related validity

Discriminant validity
Interrater reliability
Obtained score
Predictive validity
Reliability
Reliability coefficient
Reliable test scores

Split-half reliability
Standard error of measurement (SEM)
Target behavior
Test–retest reliability
Validity
Validity coefficient

Chapter Objectives

This chapter focuses on two very important concepts—*validity* and *reliability*. In order to use any instrument in the assessment process, federal law mandates that the tests be both validated and reliable. What does that mean? How does an evaluator determine which tests are the most valid and reliable? There are many types of validity and reliability that are important to know when doing an assessment in special education. After reading this chapter, you should be able to understand the following:

■ The purpose for needing valid and reliable measures

■ The most utilized and important types of validity seen in special education assessment

■ The most utilized and important types of reliability seen in special education assessment

VALIDITY

Validity denotes the extent to which an instrument is measuring what it is supposed to measure. Validity is the most essential quality needed in a measuring instrument. Obviously, if an instrument is not producing the information that it is supposed to, it is essentially worthless. The greater the validity of a test, the greater our confidence that it measures what it is designed to measure (Cohen & Spenciner, 2011). Questions about validity are of ultimate importance for special educators because they address whether an instrument fulfills the function for which it was created. Accordingly, effort must be put into determining the validity of any measuring instrument that is to be used in a study. This section covers the most important and often utilized types of validity seen in special education assessment.

Criterion-Related Validity

Criterion-related validity is a method for assessing the validity of an instrument by comparing its scores with another criterion (or *criteria*—the plural of *criterion*) known already to be a measure of the same trait or skill. Simply stated, the instrument in question is compared with another instrument that has already been established as being valid. The closer the two tests are to each other, the better the criterion-related validity.

Criterion-related validity is usually expressed as a correlation between the test in question and the criterion measure. This correlation coefficient is referred to as a **validity coefficient.** The closer the correlation coefficient is to +1.00, the stronger the criterion-related validity (see Chapter 3 for a review of correlations). Consequently, when students completing both instruments obtain similar scores, the instrument in question is said to have high criterion-related validity (Overton, 2009).

If you created a new achievement test, the readers would have to know how it compares with an already established and valid achievement test. To establish criterion-related validity for your test, administer your test and then administer an already established test to the same group of students. Whether you give the criterion test soon after or at a much later time will determine the type of criterion-related validity you have chosen.

With respect to criterion-related validity, it is important to understand that a test is only as valid as the criterion measure. If a new test developer reports a high validity coefficient between his or her new test and a criterion test that is not considered valid, this correlation does not make the new test valid. Therefore, when evaluating criterion-related validity, you must not only look at how strong the validity coefficient is (i.e., how close it is to +1.00), but also examine the criterion measure to which it was compared (Salvia & Ysseldyke, 2007).

There are two types of criterion-related validity: (1) concurrent validity and (2) predictive validity. The ultimate difference between concurrent and predictive validity is the time at which scores on the criterion measure are obtained.

Concurrent validity is the extent to which a procedure correlates with the current behavior of subjects. It refers to how precisely a person's present performance (e.g., a test score) estimates that person's performance on the criterion measure administered at approximately the same time (Cohen & Spenciner, 2011).

To do a concurrent validity study, both measures must be given in close proximity. Normally, the administration of each of the two measures should not exceed more than two weeks. The procedure consists of administering the first instrument (i.e., the instrument to be validated) and very shortly thereafter, administering the criterion measure. Correlating the data from the two instruments then determines the concurrent validity (Overton, 2009).

Predictive validity is the extent to which a procedure allows accurate predictions about a subject's future behavior. It is a measure of a specific instrument's ability to predict future performance on some other measure or criterion at a later date (Overton, 2009). For example, many colleges believe that the SAT has predictive validity with respect to how well a student will do in college. Similarly, the Graduate Record Exam is often required by admissions committees for graduate school because it is believed to have high predictive validity for future academic performance in graduate school.

Content Validity

Content validity refers to whether the individual items of a test represent what you actually want to assess. When we evaluate content validity, we are asking, "Does the content of our measure fairly and accurately reflect the content desired to be measured?" Thus, when we are measuring academic achievement with a new achievement test, we ask, "Is the score that we obtain truthfully measuring the actual academic achievement of the student?" Overall, content validity describes how well a test's items reflect the area of learning to be assessed (Venn, 2007).

According to the Standards for Educational and Psychological Tests (American Psychological Association, 1999),

> to demonstrate the content validity of a set of test scores, one must show that the behaviors demonstrated in testing constitute a representative sample of behaviors to be exhibited in a desired performance domain. An investigation of content validity requires that the test developer or test user specify his objectives and carefully define the performance domain in light of those objectives (p. 4).

For a test to have good content validity, it must contain the content in a representative fashion (Overton, 2009). For example, a 100-question social studies test on information about the United States that has 50 questions about the East Coast states and 50 questions about the Midwest states has not fairly represented the content of United States knowledge, because there are no questions pertaining to the Southern, Southwestern, or West Coast states. A good representation of content will always include several items for each domain, level, and skill being measured.

The questions college students might raise about an exam are often questions of content validity. A college exam is supposed to measure what students have learned. However, students sometimes feel an exam includes only questions about things they did not understand (Myers & Hansen, 2002).

Finally, when doing an assessment of the content validity of an instrument, you should seek the rationale for item selection as described in the test's technical manual. According to McLean, Wolery, and Bailey (2004),

> An initial test of content validity would be the extent to which the test developer convinces you that a thorough and systematic process has occurred in the selection of test content. Essentially, content validity is assessed through a logical analysis of the item development process of the actual items (p. 39).

Construct Validity

Construct validity is the extent to which a test measures a theoretical construct or attribute. **Constructs** are abstract concepts, such as intelligence, self-concept, motivation, aggression, and creativity, that can be observed by some type of instrument. They represent relatively abstract concepts that are difficult to define and therefore difficult to measure (Taylor, 2009).

A classic question of construct validity involves intelligence tests, which determine intelligence by measuring subjects in areas such as vocabulary or problem-solving ability. The question of whether intelligence is being measured by these particular variables is an assessment of the test's construct validity.

Because establishing construct validity entails a long and involved process, most tests provide little information about this type of validity. Construct validity is normally determined through extensive research studies using numerous and intensive statistical procedures. According to the Standards for Educational and Psychological Testing (APA, 1999), evidence of construct validity is not found in a single study; rather, judgments of construct validity are based on an accumulation of research results. Consequently, only the most well-established tests in special education present solid evidence of construct validity. A test's construct validity is often assessed by its convergent and discriminant validity. A test that has good **convergent validity** has high positive correlations with other tests measuring the same construct. In contrast, a test that has good **discriminant validity** has low correlations with tests that measure different constructs. For example, an academic achievement test should correlate highly with established academic achievement tests (convergent validity) and have lower correlations with social and cognitive measures (discriminant validity).

Factors Affecting Validity

Various factors can affect the validity of any test (Sattler, 2008). These include the following:

1. **Test-related factors:** These consist of, but are not limited to, such things as anxiety, motivation, speed, understanding test instructions, rapport, physical handicaps, language barriers, deficiencies in educational opportunities, and unfamiliarity with testing materials.
2. **The criterion to which you compare your instrument may not be well enough established:** If your comparison instrument is not valid, then the results you receive are to be questioned as to their validity.
3. **Intervening events:** These include life experiences such as the death of a parent, divorce, breakup with a boyfriend, and a move to a new school district that occur at the time of testing.
4. **Reliability:** If the reliability of a test is low, then the validity also will be low.

According to McLean, Wolery, and Bailey (2004),

> Validity is both separate and tied to reliability. Although conceptually they ask very different questions, it is a well accepted axiom in test development that test validity can be no higher than the test's reliability, and usually is considerably lower. This makes sense, for how could an unreliable or inconsistent measure have accuracy? However, the fact that a test is reliable does not mean that it has any validity for certain purposes. For example, a screening test may be perfectly reliable but be of no use in planning instructional programs (p. 42).

RELIABILITY

Reliability refers to the consistency of measurements. If a test lacks reliability, it is not stable, reproducible, predictable, dependable, meaningful, or accurate. In assessment, reliability relates to the confidence in an instrument to give the same score for a student if the test were given more than once. **Reliable test scores** are similar across various conditions and situations, including different evaluators and testing environments (Venn, 2007).

How do we account for an individual who does not get exactly the same test score every time he or she takes the test? Some possible reasons are the following (U.S. Department of Labor Employment and Training Administration (1999):

Test taker's temporary psychological or physical state: Test performance can be influenced by a person's psychological or physical state at the time of testing. For example, differing levels of anxiety, fatigue, or motivation may affect the applicant's test results.

Environmental factors: Differences in the testing environment, such as room temperature, lighting, noise, or even the test administrator, can influence an individual's test performance.

Test form: Many tests have more than one version or form. Items differ on each form, but each form is supposed to measure the same thing. Different forms of a test are known as parallel forms or alternate forms. These forms are designed to have similar measurement characteristics, but they contain different items. Because the forms are not exactly the same, a test taker might do better on one form than on another.

Multiple raters: In certain tests, scoring is determined by a rater's judgments of the test taker's performance or responses. Differences in training, experience, and frame of reference among raters can produce different test scores for the test taker.

These factors are sources of chance or random measurement error in the assessment process. If there were no random errors of measurement, the individual would get the same test score, the individual's "true" score, each time. The degree to which test scores are unaffected by measurement errors is an indication of the reliability of the test. Reliable assessment tools produce dependable, repeatable, and consistent information about students. To interpret test scores meaningfully and make useful assessment decisions, you need reliable instruments.

Reliability Coefficients

The statistic for expressing reliability is the **reliability coefficient,** which expresses the degree of consistency in the measurement of test scores. The symbol used to denote a reliability coefficient is the letter r with two identical subscripts (rxx). Reliability coefficients can range in value from 0.00 to 1.00. A reliability coefficient of $rxx = 0.00$ indicates absence of reliability, whereas a reliability coefficient of $rxx = 1.00$ demonstrates perfect reliability.

Acceptable reliability coefficients should never be below $rxx = .90$. A coefficient below $rxx = .90$ normally indicates inadequate reliability. A test should not be trusted if its reliability coefficient is low. High reliabilities are especially needed for tests used in individual assessment (Sattler, 2008). A reliability coefficient of $rxx = .95$ on a test means that 95 percent of a test score is accurate while only 5 percent consists of unexplained error. However, a test with a reliability coefficient of $rxx = .60$ does not have acceptable reliability because approximately 40 percent of the test score may be due to error (Venn, 2007).

Test–Retest Reliability

Test–retest reliability suggests that subjects tend to obtain the same score when tested at different times. For example, if an IQ test has strong test–retest reliability, a student who produces a low score now should also produce a low score later. Conversely, a student receiving a high score now should also produce a high score later. In other words, test–retest reliability is evident when there is a high positive correlation between the scores obtained from two testings (Heiman, 2002).

The reliability coefficient expresses the correlation between the scores obtained by the same students on two administrations of a test. According to Venn (2007), the critical factor with test–retest reliability is the length of time between testing. Too little time between testing and retesting inflates the reliability coefficient, whereas too much time deflates the reliability coefficient. In most cases, a two-week interval allows enough time to adjust from any learning that may take place from the first testing experience. Longer intervals may reduce the reliability estimate due to maturation of the students or the influence of other outside events (p. 77).

The usual procedure for obtaining a test–retest reliability coefficient is to administer the same test to the same group on two different occasions, usually within a short period of time. Generally, the shorter the retest interval, the higher the reliability coefficient, because within a shorter span of time there are fewer reasons for an individual's score to change (Sattler, 2008).

Split-Half Reliability or Internal Consistency

Split-half reliability (sometimes referred to as *internal consistency*) indicates that subjects' scores on some trials consistently match their scores on other trials. Typically, we make this determination by computing each subject's total odd score and correlating it with the even scores. For example, if the questions on an achievement test have split-half reliability, then subjects producing a low score on the odd questions should also obtain a low score on the even questions (Heiman, 2002).

Split-half reliability is a procedure for determining accuracy that involves correlating two halves of the same test. The steps in the process include giving a test once, splitting the test items in half, and comparing the results of the two halves to each other (Cohen & Spenciner, 2011). The reliability coefficient obtained is an estimate of the correlation between the items on each half of the test (Venn, 2007).

Interrater Reliability

Interrater reliability involves having two raters independently observe and record specified behaviors, such as hitting, crying, yelling, and getting out of the seat, during the same time period. For example, suppose two observers are to determine each time they see a certain child tap his pencil during a math lecture. Tapping the pencil during the math lecture is considered the **target behavior.** A target behavior is a specific behavior the observer is looking to record. After each observer determines the total number of times the target behavior occurs, the scores are compared, and an estimate of the percentage of agreement between the two observations is done (Venn, 2007). The reliability coefficient obtained in this case correlates the observations of two independent observers. According to Overton (2009), interrater reliability is normally done by administering the test and then having an objective scorer also score the test results. The results of the tests scored by the examiner are then correlated with the results obtained by the objective scorer to determine how much variability exists between the test scores. This information is especially important when tests with a great deal of subjectivity are used in making educational decisions.

The formula for interrater reliability is:

Number of agreements/Number of agreements + Disagreements × 100 = Percentage of agreements

For example, suppose you and another observer watch a child to see how many times she looks out the window during a science lesson. Then the two of you compare when you saw this behavior occurring. The results are listed below, indicating the interrater reliability for your observations.

Agree: 47 times

Disagree: 3 times

Therefore, 47/50 × 100 = 94% (.94). Because 90 percent or higher is our goal, there is adequate interrater reliability.

Practice Problem

4.1. In order to assess interrater reliability, you work with someone to examine how many times a child gets up from his chair over the course of the day. You agree with your partner 55 times but had different recordings on five separate occasions. What is the interrater reliability?

Answer to Practice Problem

4.1. 55/60 + 100 − 91.67% = **.917**
Important Point: Accuracy is the unit of measure that compares a child's performance against a standard (e.g., the dictionary). In the English language, *cat* is spelled *c-a-t*. One does not need interrater reliability when an accuracy standard is available.

Alternate Forms Reliability

With **alternate forms reliability,** also known as *equivalent forms reliability* or *parallel forms reliability,* two different forms of the same instrument are used. Alternate forms reliability is obtained by administering two equivalent tests to the same group of examinees (Cohen & Spencer, 2011). Determining alternate forms reliability requires a test developer to create two forms of the same test, give both forms to students, and compare the scores from the two forms. The reliability coefficient in this case describes the correlation between the scores obtained by the same students on the two forms of the test (Venn, 1999). If the two forms of the test are equivalent, they should have the same means and variances and a high reliability coefficient. If there is no error in measurement, an individual should earn the same score on both forms of the test (Sattler, 2008).

In alternate forms reliability, the items are matched for difficulty on each test (Overton, 2009). For example, if three items of long division are on one version of the test, then three long division problems need to be on the alternate form of the test at the same level of difficulty.

Several published achievement and diagnostic tests that are used in special education consist of two equivalent forms (Overton, 2009). The advantage of having alternate forms is that there are two tests of the same difficulty level that can be administered within a short time frame without the influence of practice effects. To determine alternate forms reliability, it is necessary that the time frame between giving the two forms of the instrument be as short as possible. This eliminates the chance that other factors might affect test performances (Taylor, 2009).

Standard Error of Measurement

When you administer a test you get a score. This score is known as the **obtained score.** In theory, the obtained score consists of two parts: the *true score* and the *error score.* The obtained score is the amount of the trait the child actually possesses (true score) plus the error of measurement (error score). According to Sattler (2008), the child's true score is a hypothetical construct; it cannot be observed. The theory assumes that the child possesses stable traits, that errors are random, and that the obtained score results from the addition of true and error scores.

Error exists when doing assessment. The fact is, we are human beings administering tests to human beings. Therefore, it is to be expected that neither the examiner nor the examinee will be "perfect." Errors should always be considered when giving tests. Special educators need to know that all tests contain errors, and that a single test score may not accurately reflect the student's true score (Overton, 2009).

Test manuals report a statistic called the **standard error of measurement (SEM)**. It gives the margin of error that you should expect in an individual test score because of imperfect reliability of the test. The SEM represents the degree of confidence that a person's "true" score lies within a particular range of scores. For example, an SEM of "2" indicates that a test taker's "true" score probably lies within 2 points in either direction of the score he or she receives on the test. This means that if an individual receives a 91 on the test, there is a good chance that the person's score lies somewhere between 89 and 93 (U.S. Department of Labor Employment and Training Administration (1999).

The SEM is a useful measure of the accuracy of individual test scores. The smaller the SEM, the more accurate the measurements. When evaluating the reliability coefficients of a test, it is important to review the explanations provided in the manual for the following:

Types of Reliability Used. The manual should indicate why a certain type of reliability coefficient was reported. The manual should also discuss sources of random measurement error that are relevant for the test.

How Reliability Studies Were Conducted. The manual should indicate the conditions under which the data were obtained, such as the length of time that passed between administrations of a given test in a test–retest reliability study. In general, reliabilities tend to drop as the time between test administrations increases.

The Characteristics of the Sample Group. The manual should indicate the important characteristics of the group used in gathering reliability information, such as education level, occupation, and so on. This will allow you to compare the characteristics of the people you want to test with the sample group. If they are sufficiently similar, then the reported reliability estimates will probably hold true for your population as well.

Factors Affecting Reliability

According to Sattler (2008), several factors can affect reliability:
1. **Test length:** The more items on a test and the more homogeneous they are, the greater the reliability.
2. **Test–retest interval:** The smaller the time interval between the administration of two tests, the smaller the chance of change and, hence, the higher the reliability is likely to be.
3. **Variability of scores:** The greater the variance of scores on a test, the higher the reliability estimate is likely to be. Small changes in performance have a greater impact on the reliability of a test when the range or spread of scores is narrow than when it is wide.
4. **Guessing:** The less guessing that occurs on a test, the higher the reliability is likely to be.
5. **Variation within the test situation:** The fewer variations there are in the test situation, the higher the reliability is likely to be. Factors include misleading or misunderstood directions, scoring errors, illness, and daydreaming.

CONCLUSION

In conclusion, an instrument or test should be both valid and reliable. Although both terms define two completely different concepts, they work together. A test needs to measure what it is supposed to measure and it must be consistent with its results. Therefore, as special educators, when you find out or hear about a new test and wonder if it is technically adequate, examine the various validity and reliability coefficients to determine whether the test will be useful. Remember, making determinations about classifications for children is very serious. Therefore, you always want to be able to defend your decisions by stating that when you did your assessment, you used the most valid and reliable instruments to make your conclusions and recommendations.

Vocabulary

Alternate forms reliability: Reliability obtained by administering two equivalent tests to the same group of examinees.

Concurrent validity: Refers to how precisely a person's present performance (e.g., a test score) estimates that person's performance on the criterion measure at approximately the same time.

Construct validity: The extent to which a test measures a theoretical construct or attribute.

Constructs: Theoretical concepts, such as self-esteem and intelligence, that can be observed by some type of instrument.

Content validity: Refers to whether the individual items of a test represent what you actually want to assess.

Convergent validity: A test that has good convergent validity has high positive correlations with other tests measuring the same construct.

Criterion-related validity: A method for assessing the validity of an instrument by comparing its scores with another criterion known already to be a measure of the same trait or skill.

Discriminant validity: A test that has good discriminant validity has low correlations with tests that measure different constructs.

Interrater reliability: Involves having two raters independently observe and record specified behaviors.

Obtained score: The score actually calculated in the assessment process.

Predictive validity: The extent to which a procedure allows accurate predictions about a subject's future behavior. It is a measure of a specific instrument's ability to predict future performance on some other measure or criterion at a later date.

Reliability: Refers to the consistency of measurements.

Reliability coefficient: Expresses the degree of consistency in the measurement of test scores.

Reliable test scores: A test score that produces similar scores across various conditions and situations, including different evaluators and testing environments.

Split-half reliability: Indicates that subjects' scores on some trials consistently match their scores on other trials.

Standard error of measurement (SEM): The amount of error that exists when using a specific instrument.

Target behavior: A specific behavior an observer is looking to record.

Test–retest reliability: Suggests that subjects tend to obtain the same score when tested at different times.

Validity: The extent to which a test measures what it is supposed to measure.

Validity coefficient: Criterion-related validity is usually expressed as a correlation between the test in question and the criterion measure. This correlation coefficient is referred to as a validity coefficient.

5 | SCORING TERMINOLOGY USED IN ASSESSMENT

Key Terms

Age equivalent
Chronological age
Data
Deciles
Grade equivalent

Percentile rank
  (percentile)
Protocol
Quartiles
Raw score

Scaled scores
Standard score
Stanine
T score
z score

Chapter Objectives

When you administer tests as special educators, you collect data. **Data** (*datum* is the singular) represent information gathered and collected during the assessment process. However, data need to be interpreted. You do not test a child and then come to the parent meeting with stacks upon stacks of data and test materials. On the contrary, you break the data down into statistical components that describe how the child performed on various parts of the assessment process. This chapter covers the various statistical ways in which data are reported to parents and school personnel when doing assessment. After reading this chapter, you should be able to understand the following:

- Calculation of age
- Raw scores
- Percentiles
- Standard scores
- *z* scores
- *T* scores
- Stanines
- Age equivalents
- Grade equivalents

CALCULATION OF AGE

Any time you test a child, perhaps the most important piece of information you must obtain is the child's age at the time of testing (known as **chronological age**). Miscalculating a child's chronological age will result in faulty interpretations and scores. Therefore, it is necessary to take your time and be sure of a child's chronological age when determining how old he or she is at the time of testing.

Now, you may be saying, why not just ask the child his or her age? The answer is threefold:

1. Many children do not know when they were born.
2. Children think they know their date of birth, but are incorrect.
3. Ages (when doing an evaluation) are broken down into years, months, and days, something that children would not normally know.

For example, you may calculate that a child has a chronological age of 7-9-13. This means that the child is 7 years, 9 months, and 13 days old. If you determine that a child is 11-5-17, this represents a child who is 11 years, 5 months, and 17 days old.

Now, on every test you give as a special educator, there normally will be a box on the **protocol** (the booklet in which you record the child's response) to calculate the child's chronological age. The box almost always looks like this:

	YEAR	MONTH	DAY
Date of Test	_____	_____	_____
Date of Birth	_____	_____	_____
Chronological Age	_____	_____	_____

To calculate age, the first step is simply to fill in the appropriate lines for Date of Test and Date of Birth. For example, a child who was tested on November 25, 2011, and who was born on July 9, 1997, would have these data in the following box:

	YEAR	MONTH	DAY
Date of Test	2011	11	25
Date of Birth	1997	7	9
Chronological Age	_____	_____	_____

Date of Test of November 25, 2011, is represented by 2011-11-25, whereas Date of Birth of July 9, 1997, is represented by 1997-7-9. Now all you have to do is subtract the Date of Birth from the Date of Test to find the child's Chronological Age.

Important Point: Always start the subtraction process from RIGHT to LEFT (i.e., subtract the days, then the months, and last, the years). You must always follow this procedure!

	YEAR	MONTH	DAY
Date of Test	2011	11	25
Date of Birth	1997	7	9
Chronological Age	14	4	16

This child is 14-4-16: 14 years, 4 months, and 16 days old. (On many tests, if the days are over 15, the age is rounded up to 14-5.) Now, suppose you have a child whose Date of Test

Days is less than his Date of Birth Days. All you need to do is subtract 1 from the Date of Test Months and add 30 to the Date of Test Days (you are simply replacing 1 month with 30 days). For example: Suppose you have a child who was tested on August 11, 2011. He was born on May 23, 2001. The box would look like this:

	YEAR	MONTH	DAY
Date of Test	2011	7 8	30×11 3 41
Date of Birth	2001	5	23
Chronological Age	10	2	18

You cannot subtract 23 from 11, so simply subtract 1 from the Date of Test Months ($8 - 1 = 7$) and add 30 to Date of Test Days ($11 + 30 = 41$). Now the box looks like this:

	YEAR	MONTH	DAY
Date of Test	2011	7	41
Date of Birth	2001	5	23
Chronological Age			

Now, simply subtract as you normally would:

	YEAR	MONTH	DAY
Date of Test	2011	7	41
Date of Birth	2001	5	23
Chronological Age	10	2	18

This child is 10-2-18. (For assessment purposes, the child's age probably would be recorded as 10-3.)

Now, suppose the Date of Test Months is less than the Date of Birth Months. Here, subtract 1 from the Date of Test Years and add 12 to the Date of Test Months (you are replacing 1 year with 12 months). For example: Suppose you tested a child born on November 4, 2004. She was tested on April 15, 2009. Calculate her age at the time of testing.

	YEAR	MONTH	DAY
Date of Test	2009-1	+12 4 16	15
Date of Birth	2004	11	4
Chronological Age	4	5	11

Subtract the Days as you normally would and you get 11 days. However, you cannot subtract 11 from 4 Months. Therefore, subtract 1 from the Date of Test Years (2009 − 1 = 2008) and add 12 to the Date of Test Months (4 + 12 = 16). Subtract as you normally would. Now, the box looks like this:

	YEAR	MONTH	DAY
Date of Test	2008	16	15
Date of Birth	2004	11	4
Chronological Age	4	5	11

This child was 4-5-11 when tested.

If you can do this problem, then you should be able to do any calculation of age. Try this one: A child is tested on March 14, 2011. He was born on December 29, 2004. What was his age at the time of testing? (In both situations, the Date of Test Days and Months are less than those of the Date of Birth.)

Answer: This child is 6-2-15.

Just for fun, suppose that you were tested today. Calculate how old you are today.

RAW SCORES

When you administer any test, the first step in scoring almost always will be to calculate the number of correct items the student obtained. For example, if a student took a 20-question spelling test in your class, the first thing you would do is determine how many words the student spelled correctly. This score is known as the raw score. The **raw score** normally indicates the number of items correctly answered on a given test. In almost all cases, it is the first score a teacher obtains when interpreting data. A raw score is a test score that has not been weighted, transformed, or statistically manipulated.

In general, raw scores by themselves mean very little. For example, suppose the student in your class got 18 out of 20 correct on the spelling test. The number 18 has no real meaning. What is important is what you do with the 18. For example, most teachers would say the student got 18 out of 20 and turn it into a percentage indicating that the student got 90 percent (18/20 is 90%) on this test.

PERCENTILE RANKS (PERCENTILES)

A **percentile rank** (often referred to as a **percentile**) is a score indicating the percentage of people or scores that occur at or below a given score. For example, if you have a percentile rank of 75 in a class, this means that you did as well as or better than 75 percent of the students in the class. A percentile rank of 16 means that you scored as well as or better than only 16 percent of the population. Percentile ranks range from the lowest (1st percentile) to the highest (99th percentile). A percentile rank of 83 means that a student has scored as well as or better than 83 percent of the students taking a test. Notice, however, it does not mean that the student got a test score of 83 percent. The percentage correct on a test is not the same as the percentage of people scoring below a given score, the percentile rank. The 50th percentile normally signifies the average ranking or average performance.

There are two other types of percentiles used in assessment: quartiles and deciles. **Quartiles divide scores into four units: 1–25, 26–50, 51–75, and 76–99.** The first quartile (1–25) marks the lower quarter (bottom 25%) or bottom fourth of all scores, whereas the fourth quartile represents the upper quarter (top 25%). **Deciles divide scores into tenths or ten equal units.** For example, the sixth decile is the point at which 60 percent of the scores fall below, whereas the ninth decile is the point at which 90 percent of the scores fall below.

In assessment, percentile ranks are very important because they indicate how well a child did when compared to the norms on a test. Knowing that a child had a percentile rank of 97 on a test would tell you that he is exceptional in this testing area; knowing that he got a percentile rank of 7 would tell you that this is an area of weakness.

Important Point: It should be noted that there is a serious drawback to percentiles. According to Venn (2007),

> The major drawback to percentiles involves the unequal length of percentile units, especially at the extremes. This characteristic results in a tendency to overemphasize differences near the middle and underemphasize difference near the ends. In other words, the difference between 50 and 55 may be less than the difference between 90 and 95. This inequality occurs because percentiles, which are calculated from ranked data, designate relative standing, not absolute differences (p. 104).

Calculation of Percentile

Suppose 20 students take an exam. The scores of these 20 students are: 70, 70, 70, 73, 76, 78, 79, 80, 82, 84, 84, 87, 88, 90, 94, 60, 62, 65, 67, 69.

Billy is the student who got an 80 on this exam. What is his percentile?
Calculation of percentile can be done in an easy 3-step process.

Step 1: Sort the test scores so they are in order from lowest to highest score.

Our Example: Here are the 20 test scores in order from lowest to highest: 60, 62, 65, 67, 69, 70, 70, 70, 73, 76, 78, 79, 80, 82, 84, 84, 87, 88, 90, 94

Step 2: To calculate the percentile of a given test score, the formula to use is (Adkins, 2010):

$$L/N(100) = P$$

L: is the total number of test scores <u>less than</u> the score obtained by the student

N: is the total number of test scores

P: is the percentile

Our Example:

Billy got a score of 80.

L is the number of tests with scores less than 80 (which is 12; test scores 60, 62, 65, 67, 69, 70, 70, 70, 73, 76, 78, and 79 are all less than 80).

N is the total number of test scores (which is 20; 60, 62, 65, 67, 69, 70, 70, 70, 73, 76, 78, 79, 80, 82, 84, 84, 87, 88, 90, 94).

P is the percentile we are calculating.

So, this gives us L = 12 and N − 20.

Step 3: Divide out L/N to get the decimal equivalent. Multiply this by 100. (Discard any digits to the right of the decimal point, leaving you with a whole number). This is your percentile (Adkins, 2010).

Our Example: 12/20 = .60.

Multiply by 100: .60 × 100 = 60.00

Remove the decimal points: 60

Billy's percentile is 60. Billy scored at the 60th percentile.

STANDARD SCORES

A **standard score** is a score that has been transformed to fit a normal curve, with a mean and standard deviation that remain the same across ages. Normally, standard scores have a mean of 100 and a standard deviation (SD) of 15. Perhaps the most well-known version of the standard score with a mean of 100 and an SD of 15 is the Wechsler Intelligence Scales (see Chapter 10 on assessment of intelligence). Using this scoring system, a child with a standard score of 115 would be 1 standard deviation above the mean, whereas a child with a standard score of 85 would be 1 standard deviation below the mean. Also, the percentage of scores between a standard score of 85 and 115 is 68 percent. (If this is unclear, refer to Chapter 4 for a review of the normal curve.) Often, when doing assessment, you will have to tell parents and administrators the standard scores the child received on the given test and the appropriate classification that they represent. For some tests with a mean of 100 and a standard deviation of 15, the general classification system may appear as follows:

STANDARD SCORE	CLASSIFICATION
Less than 70	Developmental Delay
70–79	Well Below Average or Borderline
80–89	Low Average
90–109	Average
110–119	High Average
120–129	Superior
130 and higher	Very Superior

Important Point: The classification system shown is only one form of representing standard scores. Different tests may use different ranges and terminology.

The standard score of 100 with a mean of 15 is the most often common representation of standard scores. However, other types of standard scores also represent test performance. The three other types of standard scores that you will come across in doing assessment are *z* scores, *T* scores, and stanines.

SCALED SCORES

Many tests used for assessment of children have subtests that comprise the entire test. For each subtest, a student receives a raw score. This raw score is often transformed into a scaled score. A **scaled score** is a conversion of a student's raw score on a test to a common scale that allows for a numerical comparison between students. Scaled scores are very specific subtest scores. In many cases, scaled scores range from 1 to 19 with a mean of 10 (Table 5.1). They follow the following classification format:

SCALED SCORE	CLASSIFICATION
1–3	Developmental Delay
4–5	Well Below Average
6–7	Low Average
8–12	Average
13–14	High Average
15–16	Superior
17–19	Very Superior

For example, if a student gets only a scaled score of 7 on a reading subtest but a 13 on a math subtest, this indicates a much greater strength with respect to math than with reading, compared to the norms of the age group.

Table 5.1 Relationship among Ranges of Scores, Scaled Scores, and Percentiles

RANGE	SCALED SCORE	PERCENTILE
Very Superior	19	99.9
Very Superior	18	99.6
Very Superior	17	99.6
Superior	16	98.6
Superior	15	95.6
High Average	14	91.6
High Average	13	84.6
Average	12	75.6
Average	11	63.6
Average	10	50.6
Average	9	37.6
Average	8	25.6
Low Average	7	16.6
Low Average	6	9.6
Well Below Average	5	5.6
Well Below Average	4	2.6
Developmental Delay	3	1.6
Developmental Delay	2	0.4
Developmental Delay	1	0.1

Z SCORES

A z **score** indicates how many standard deviations a score is above or below the mean. A z score is a standard score distribution with a mean of zero and a standard deviation of one. For example, if a student has a z score of +1.0, this means that he scored 1 standard deviation above the mean on the test. If a student has a z score of −1.7, this means that she scored 1.7 standard deviations below the mean. To calculate z scores, the formula is

$$z = (\text{Test Score} - \text{Mean Score})/\text{Standard Deviation}$$

For example, suppose a student had an IQ of 130 on an IQ test with a mean of 100 and a standard deviation of 15. Use the formula:

$$(130 - 100)/15 = +2.0$$

A student with a 130 IQ would be 2.0 standard deviations above the mean. (You already knew this from the normal curve.)

T SCORES

A **T score** is another way to express test performance. T scores have a mean of 50 with a standard deviation of 10. Therefore, if you have a T score of 40 you are 1 standard deviation below the mean, whereas a T score of 60 would be 1 standard deviation above the mean. To calculate T scores:

$$T = 50 + 10z$$

For example, a student who scored 1.5 standard deviations above the mean would have a T score of 65 because T = 50 + 10(1.5). Here the 1.5 represents 1.5 standard deviations above the mean, which is $z = 1.5$.

STANINES

A **stanine,** an abbreviation for *standard nines,* is a type of standard score that has a mean of 5 and an SD of 2. Stanine scores can range from 1 to 9. A stanine of 7 is 1 SD above the mean (5 + 2). A stanine of 9 is 2 SD above the mean (5 + 2 + 2). Conversely, a stanine of 3 is 1 SD below the mean (5 − 2) and a stanine of 1 is 2 SD below the mean (5 − 2 − 2).

COMPARING z SCORES, T SCORES, AND STANINES

The table that follows and Figure 5.1 can help you to remember how standard deviations, z scores, T scores, and stanines compare to each other.

STANDARD DEVIATION	z SCORE	T SCORE	STANINE
−2.0	−2.0	30	1.0
−1.0	−1.0	40	3.0
0.0 (mean score)	0.0	50	5.0
+1.0	+1.0	60	7.0
+2.0	+2.0	70	9.0

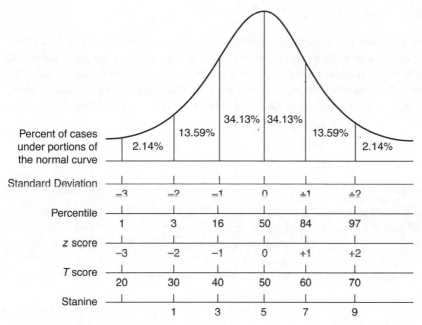

FIGURE 5.1 The Normal Curve.

AGE EQUIVALENT SCORES

An **age equivalent** is a very general score that is used to compare the performance of children at the same age with one another. It is the estimated age level that corresponds to a given score. Age equivalent scores are almost always given in years and months. For example, a child who gets an age equivalent score of 11-5 is performing as well as the average 11-year, 5-month-old child.

GRADE EQUIVALENT SCORES

A **grade equivalent** is a very general score that is used to compare the performance of children in the same grade with one another. It is the estimated grade level that corresponds to a given score. Grade equivalent scores are almost always given in years and months in school. For example, a child who gets a grade equivalent score of 3.5 is performing as well as the average student in the third grade, 5th month.

    Important Point: Age equivalent scores do not compare the performance of the child with children at the age given by the age equivalent score. What they do compare is the child's raw score—the score achieved on the assessment measure—with the average raw score of students in the norm group who took the same test. Likewise, a 6.5 grade equivalent score does not mean that a student is performing as well as the average student in grade 6 midway through the year. It does mean that the student's raw score on the assessment measure was equal to the average raw score of students at the 6.5 level in the norm group.

CONCLUSION

It is evident that there are numerous ways to express test scores in assessment. The fact is, no one way is superior to all others. However, the more information you can give parents and administrators, the more objective and solid the case you make for determination of a disability or in planning a program. Consequently, being able to determine, calculate, and express the various scores from testing in a clear and cogent manner is a very important responsibility of a special educator.

Vocabulary

Age equivalent: A very general score that is used to compare the performance of children at the same age with one another.

Chronological age: The child's actual age.

Data: Information gathered and collected during the assessment process.

Deciles: Division of scores into tenths or ten equal units. For example, the sixth decile is the point at which 60 percent of the scores fall below, whereas the ninth decile is the point at which 90 percent of the scores fall below.

Grade equivalent: A very general score that is used to compare the performance of children in the same grade with one another.

Percentile rank (Percentile):   A score indicating the percentage of people or scores that occur at or below a given score. If you have a percentile rank of 75, this means that you did as well as or better than 75 percent of the students in the class.

Protocol: The booklet where responses and scores are recorded.

Quartiles: Division of scores into four quarters: 1–25, 26–50, 51–75, and 76–99. The first quartile (1–25) marks the lower quarter (bottom 25%) or bottom fourth of all scores, whereas the fourth quartile represents the upper quarter (top 25%).

Raw score: The raw score indicates the number of items correctly answered on a given test. In almost all cases, it is the first score a teacher obtains when interpreting data.

Scaled scores: A conversion of a student's raw score on a test to a common scale that allows for a numerical comparison between students

Standard score: A score that has been transformed to fit a normal curve, with a mean and standard deviation that remain the same across ages.

Stanine: An abbreviation for *standard nines,* it is a type of standard score that has a mean of 5 and a standard deviation of 2. Stanine scores can range from 1 to 9.

***T* scores:**   Another way to express test performance. *T* scores have a mean of 50 with a standard deviation of 10.

***z* score:**   Indicates how many standard deviations a score is above or below the mean. A *z* score is a standard score distribution with a mean of zero and a standard deviation of one.

Practice Problems

5.1. Given the following numerical representation of a child's age, write, in words, his age: 14-3-24.

5.2. A student is 13 years, 7 months, and 12 days old. How would her age be expressed numerically?

5.3. A child was tested on June 12, 2004. He was born on January 20, 1994. Calculate his age at the time of testing.

5.4. A child was born on July 24, 1996. She was tested on May 28, 2005. Calculate her age at the time of testing.

5.5. A child was tested on February 13, 2007. He was born on August 21, 993. What was his age at the time of testing?

5.6. On a test, 1 point represents a correct answer while 0 points represents an incorrect answer. On this test, Sally got the following correct and incorrect answers: 0, 1, 0, 1, 1, 0, 1, 1, 1, 0.
What is Sally's raw score?

5.7. For the following standard scores, assuming a mean of 100 and an SD of 15, give the appropriate classification:

1. 97   **2.** 57
3. 103   **4.** 117
5. 84   **6.** 72
7. 125   **8.** 139

5.8. A student gets a 75 on a test with a mean of 90 and a standard deviation of 10. How many standard deviations above or below the mean did this student score?

5.9 Calculate the T score of a student who scored 1.5 standard deviations below the mean on a test.

Answers to Practice Problems

5.1. 14 years, 3 months, and 24 days old.
5.2. 13-7-12.
5.3. 10-4-22.
5.4. 8-10-4.
5.5. 13-5-22.
5.6. 6.
5.7. 1. Average, **2.** Developmental Delay, **3.** Average, **4.** High Average, **5.** Low Average, **6.** Well Below Average or Borderline, **7.** Superior, **8.** Very Superior.

5.8. $z = (75 - 90)/10 = -15/10 = -1.5$. The student scored 1.5 standard deviations below the mean.
5.9. 35.
$T = 50 + 10(-1.5)$
$T = 50 - 15$
$T = 35$

THE SPECIAL EDUCATION PROCESS

The process of identifying a student with a suspected disability is referred to as the *special education process*. This process involves a variety of steps that must follow federal, state, and district guidelines. These guidelines have been created to protect the rights of students, parents, and school districts. Working together within these guidelines allows for a thorough and comprehensive assessment of a student and the proper special education services and modifications, if required. When a student is having difficulty in school, the professional staff make many attempts to resolve the problem. When these interventions do not work, a more extensive look at the student is required.

The remaining chapters in this text outline in detail the step-by-step process that is normally followed in special education. A brief explanation of this assessment continuum follows. Each step is covered in depth in the chapters noted.

Step 1. Prereferral: When concerns are realized by the classroom teacher, he or she attempts simple classroom interventions such as meeting with the child, extra help, simplified assignments, parent conferences, and peer tutoring. At this point, Tier I RTI strategies are also introduced by the classroom teacher. These are high-quality instructional and behavioral supports that are provided for all students in general education. Chapter 6 focuses on the most talked about new area of intervention, *response to intervention* (RTI). RTI plays a critical role in the referral or nonreferral of children for evaluations for suspected disabilities. In this chapter, frequently asked questions about RTI and its importance are addressed.

- If unsuccessful, then:

Step 2. Child study team and prereferral strategies: When teachers realize that Tier I RTI strategies are not working, they will move to Tier II RTI strategies. These students whose performance and rate of progress lag behind those of peers in their classroom, school, or district may receive more specialized prevention or remediation within general education.

At this point the teacher may also choose to find out more in-depth information on the child that may shed light on other factors which may be contributing to the lack of performance. This would normally result in a referral to the school's Child Study Team. Referral to a school-based *child study team* (sometimes called the *prereferral team* or *pupil personnel team*) for a more comprehensive look at the child, and a prereferral intervention plan is usually made by the classroom teacher (although anyone can make a request for a meeting). More involved prereferral strategies are considered, such as direct classroom intervention strategies that include the following: classroom management, classroom modifications, observation by professional staff, observation and analysis of teaching methods, in-school counseling, assessment of environment, extra help, classroom modifications, change of program, consolidation of program, disciplinary actions, further parent conferences, medical referral, and so forth (discussed in Chapter 7).

- If strategies prove unsuccessful, then:

Step 3. Screening: The child is screened for a suspected disability by members of the school staff, such as the school psychologist, educational evaluator, and speech and language clinician. If screening reveals a possible suspected disability, then a referral for a more comprehensive assessment (discussed in Chapter 7) is made to:

Step 4. Multidisciplinary team (MDT): This team is made up of parents, school staff, and other professionals. When required, they decide which evaluations and professionals will be involved in this specific assessment. The team then provides a thorough and comprehensive assessment for possible special education services. Assessments may include such measures as standardized tests, portfolio assessments, curriculum-based assessment, criterion-referenced assessments, and the like (discussed in Chapter 2 and Chapters 8 through 15). If the findings of this team indicate the existence of a disability, then:

Step 5. Putting it all together: Once the MDT team completes the assessment, members of the team determine the strengths and weaknesses of the student; a possible diagnostic category; level of severity of the problem; recommendations to the school, teachers, and parents; and other information that later will be used to determine any appropriate special education recommendations (discussed in Chapter 16).

Step 6. Writing a professional report: Once the members of the team establish their findings, they should write up a professional report (discussed in Chapter 17) clearly outlining their findings. This report will be part of the materials that go to the *eligibility committee*.

Step 7. Preparation for presentation to the eligibility committee: The MDT puts together the information packet for the presentation to the eligibility committee. This packet contains all the necessary forms, reports, and results of assessment that will be used to determine possible classification and special education services (discussed in Chapter 18).

Step 8. Eligibility committee meetings: Once the packet is complete, an eligibility committee meeting (*committee on special education, IEP committee, eligibility committee*) is scheduled. This committee determines whether the student meets the criteria for a disability, a special education program, and services (discussed in Chapter 18). If the student is classified, then:

Step 9. IEP development and alternate planning: Final IEP development occurs and placement is instituted (discussed in Chapter 19). If eligibility is not accepted, alternate planning is formulated and suggested by the eligibility committee to the local school (also discussed in Chapter 19).

6

RESPONSE TO INTERVENTION

Key Terms

At risk
Core academic subjects
Early intervening services
Fidelity
Intervention
National Research Center on
  Learning Disabilities (NRCLD)

Office of Special Education
  Programs (OSEP)
Progress monitoring
Research-based
Research-based interventions
Response to intervention (RTI)
Schoolwide screening

Specific learning disability (SLD)
Tiered or multitiered service
  delivery model
Universal screening

Chapter Objectives

The focus of this chapter will be to present a basic overview of response to intervention.
After reading this chapter, you should have a basic understanding of the following:

- Overview of response to intervention (RTI)

- Purpose of RTI

- Importance of RTI

- History of RTI

- Core principles of RTI

- Events that led to changes in learning disability identification in IDEA 2004

- Rationale for replacing the discrepancy model with RTI

- Major issues related to using the concept of ability–achievement discrepancy

- The role RTI should play in identifying children with specific learning disabilities

- Can RTI be used as the sole determinant for SLD classification?

- In the big picture, how does RTI fit into the LD determination process?

- Multitiered service delivery model

- Continuum of intervention support for at-risk students

- Focus of Tier I

- Focus of Tier II

- Focus of Tier III

- Importance of parent involvement for successful RTI programs

- Fidelity

- The RTI process for teachers

- What teachers need in terms of professional development and RTI

OVERVIEW OF RESPONSE TO INTERVENTION

The response to intervention (RTI) process is a multitiered approach to providing services and interventions to struggling learners at increasing levels of intensity. RTI can be used for making decisions about general, compensatory, and special education, creating a well-integrated and seamless system of instruction and intervention guided by child outcome data. RTI is an initiative that takes place in the general education environment. RTI calls for early identification of learning and behavioral needs, close collaboration among teachers and special education personnel and parents, and a systemic commitment to locating and employing the necessary resources to ensure that students make progress in the general education curriculum.

The **National Research Center on Learning Disabilities** (NRCLD, 2007) defines RTI as

> an assessment and intervention process for systematically monitoring student progress and making decisions about the need for instructional modifications or increasingly intensified services using progress monitoring data.

RTI is an integrated approach to service delivery that encompasses general, remedial, and special education through a multitiered service delivery model. It utilizes a problem-solving framework to identify and address academic and behavioral difficulties for all students using scientific, research-based instruction. Essentially, RTI is the practice of (a) providing high-quality instruction/intervention matched to all students' needs and (b) using learning rate over time and level of performance to (c) make important educational decisions to guide instruction (National Association of State Directors of Special Education, 2005). RTI practices are proactive, incorporating both prevention and intervention, and are effective at all levels from early childhood through high school.

PURPOSE OF RTI

RTI is intended to reduce the incidence of "instructional casualties" by ensuring that students are provided high-quality instruction with fidelity. By using RTI, districts can provide **interventions** to students as soon as a need arises. This is very different, for example, from the methods associated with the aptitude achievement discrepancy models traditionally used for **specific learning disability (SLD, also referred to as LD)** identification, which have been criticized as a "wait to fail" approach.

IDEA 2004 allows the use of a student's "response to scientific, research-based intervention" (20 U.S.C. 1414 (B)(6)(A)) as part of an evaluation. **Response to intervention** (RTI) functions as an alternative for learning disability (LD) evaluations within the general evaluation requirements of IDEA 2004. The statute continues to include requirements that apply to all disability categories, such as the use of validated, nonbiased methods, and evaluation in all suspected areas of difficulty. IDEA 2004 adds a new eligibility concept that prohibits children from being found eligible for special education if they have not received instruction in reading that includes the five essential components of reading instruction identified by the Reading First Program. These requirements are those recognized by the National Reading Panel: phonemic awareness, phonics, reading fluency (including oral reading skills), vocabulary development, and reading comprehension strategies. RTI is included under this general umbrella. By using RTI, it is possible to identify students early, reduce referral bias, and test various theories for why a child is failing. It was included in the law specifically to offer an alternative to discrepancy models.

A key element of an RTI approach is the provision of **early intervening services** when students first experience academic difficulties, with the goal of improving the achievement of all students, including those who may have LD. In addition to the preventive and remedial services this approach may provide to at-risk students, it shows promise for contributing data useful for identifying LD. Thus, a student exhibiting (1) significantly low achievement and (2) insufficient RTI may be regarded as being at risk for LD and, in turn, as possibly in need of special education and related services. The assumption behind this paradigm, which has been referred to as a dual discrepancy (Fuchs, Fuchs, & Speece, 2002), is that when provided with quality instruction and remedial services, a student without disabilities will make satisfactory progress. The concept behind RTI has always been the focus of the teaching/learning process and a basic component of accountability in general education. In other words, does instruction (i.e., strategies, methods, interventions, or curriculum) lead to increased learning and appropriate progress? In the past few years, RTI has taken on a more specific connotation, especially in the Individuals with Disabilities Education Improvement Act of 2004 (IDEA, 2004), as an approach to remedial intervention that also generates data to inform instruction and identify students who may require special education and related services. Today, many educators, researchers, and other professionals are exploring the usefulness of an RTI approach as an alternative that can provide (1) data for more effective and earlier identification of students with LD and (2) a systematic way to ensure that students experiencing educational difficulties receive more timely and effective support (Gresham, 2002; Learning Disabilities Roundtable, 2002, 2005; National Research Council, 2002; President's Commission on Excellence in Special Education, 2002).

IMPORTANCE OF RTI

According to current early reading research, all except a very few children can become competent readers by the end of the third grade. RTI is a process that provides immediate intervention to struggling students at the first indication of failure to learn. Through systematic screening of all students in the early grades, classroom teachers identify those who are not mastering critical reading skills and provide differentiated intervention to small groups of students. Continuous progress monitoring of students' responses to those interventions allows teachers to identify students in need of additional intervention and to adjust instruction accordingly.

Response to intervention is about building better readers in the early grades and consists of multitiered reading instruction in the general education classroom. In an RTI model, *all* students receive high-quality reading instruction and struggling readers receive additional and increasingly more intense intervention. Early intervention and prevention of reading difficulties are fundamental to the process. However, if a student's learning history and classroom performance warrant, a multidisciplinary team may determine that the student has a disability and needs special education services to ensure continued and appropriate academic progress.

Three major developments concerning the education of students with learning problems have coalesced to establish RTI as a promising approach. First, longstanding concerns about the inadequacies of the ability–achievement discrepancy criterion—which was a component of the Individuals with Disabilities Education Act of 1997 for identifying LD—have accentuated the need to develop alternative mechanisms for the identification of LD. At the LD Summit of August 2001, sponsored by the Office of Special Education Programs, RTI was the alternative proposed by several researchers (e.g., Gresham, 2002; Marston, 2001).

Second, special education has been used to serve struggling learners who do not have LD or other disabilities. An RTI approach has been suggested as a way to reduce referrals to special education by providing well-designed instruction and intensified interventions in general education, thereby distinguishing between students who perform poorly in school due to factors such as inadequate prior instruction from students with LD who need more intensive and specialized instruction.

A third major reason for the increased interest in an RTI approach has been the abundance of recent research on reading difficulties, in particular, the national network of research studies coordinated by the National Institute of Child Health and Human Development (NICHD). A number of NICHD research studies have demonstrated that well-designed instructional programs or approaches result in significant improvements for the majority of students with early reading.

History of RTI

RTI is not a new approach. It is recognizable under other names such as *dynamic assessment, diagnostic teaching*, and *precision teaching*. Those terms, however, have been applied to approaches used to maximize student progress through sensitive measurement of the effects of instruction. RTI applies similar methods to draw conclusions and make LD classification decisions about students. The underlying assumption is that using RTI will identify children whose intrinsic difficulties make them the most difficult to teach. Engaging a student in a dynamic process like RTI provides an opportunity to assess various hypotheses about the causes of a child's difficulties, such as motivation or constitutional factors like attention.

CORE PRINCIPLES OF RTI   In general, RTI is comprised of seven core principles that represent recommended RTI practices (Mellard, 2003). These principles represent systems that must be in place to ensure effective implementation of RTI systems and establish a framework to guide and define the practice.

1. **Use all available resources to teach all students.** RTI practices are built on the belief that all students can learn. RTI requires that educators shift their focus from the student to the intervention. The initial evaluation no longer focuses on "what is wrong with the student"; instead, there is a shift to an examination of the curricular, instructional, and environmental variables that affect inadequate learning progress. Once the correct set of intervention variables has been identified, schools must then provide the means and systems for delivering resources so that effective teaching and learning can occur. In doing so, schools must provide resources in a manner that is directly proportional to students' needs. This will require districts and schools to reconsider current resource allocation systems so that financial and other support structures for RTI practices can be established and sustained.

2. **Use scientific, research-based interventions/instruction.** The critical element of RTI systems is the delivery of scientific **research-based interventions** with fidelity in general, remedial, and special education. This means that the curriculum and instructional approaches must have a high probability of success for the majority of students. By using research-based practices, schools efficiently use time and resources and protect students from ineffective instructional and evaluative practices. Because instructional practices vary in efficacy, ensuring that the practices and curriculum have demonstrated validity is an important consideration in the selection of interventions. In the absence of definitive research, schools should implement promising practices, monitor their effectiveness, and modify implementation based on the results.

3. **Monitor classroom performance.** General education teachers play a vital role in designing and providing high-quality instruction. Furthermore, they are in the best position to assess students' performance and progress against grade-level standards in the general education curriculum. This principle emphasizes the importance of general education teachers in monitoring student progress rather than waiting to determine how students are learning in relation to their same-aged peers based on results of statewide or districtwide assessments.

4. **Conduct universal screening/benchmarking.** By conducting **universal screening** and giving **benchmark tests** in all **core academic subjects** and behavior, school staff gain data on all students that indicate individual performance and progress compared to the peer group's performance and progress. These data form the basis for an initial examination of individual and group patterns on specific academic skills (e.g., identifying letters of the alphabet or reading a list of high-frequency words) as well as behavior skills (e.g., attendance, cooperation, tardiness, truancy, suspensions, and/or disciplinary actions). Universal screening is the least intensive level of assessment completed within an RTI system and helps educators and parents identify students early who might be **at risk.** Since screening data may not be as reliable as other assessments, it is important to use multiple sources of evidence in reaching inferences regarding students at risk.

5. **Use a multitier model of service delivery.** A RTI approach incorporates a **tiered** or **multitiered service delivery model** in which each tier represents an increasingly intense level of services associated with increasing levels of learner needs. The system described in this chapter reflects a three-tiered design. All multitiered systems, regardless of the number of levels chosen, should yield the same practical effects and outcomes.

   Tier I represents the largest group of students, approximately 80 to 90 percent, who are performing adequately within the core curriculum. Tier II comprises a smaller group of students, typically 5 to 10 percent of the student population. These students will need strategic interventions to raise their achievement to proficiency or above based on a lack of response to interventions at Tier I. Tier III contains the fewest students, usually 1 to 5 percent. These students will need intensive interventions if their learning is to be appropriately supported (Tilly, 2003).

   In an RTI system, all students receive instruction in the core curriculum supported by strategic and intensive interventions when needed. Therefore, all students, including those with disabilities, are found in Tiers I, II, or III. Important features, such as universal screening, progress monitoring, fidelity of implementation, and problem solving, occur within each tier. The basic tiered model reflects our knowledge that students in school have varying instructional needs. Thus, the nature of the academic or behavioral intervention changes at each tier, becoming more rigorous as the student moves through the tiers.

6. **Make data-based decisions.** Decisions within an RTI system are made by teams using problem solving and/or standard treatment protocol techniques. The purpose of these teams is to find the best instructional approach for a student with an academic or behavioral problem. Problem solving and standard treatment protocol decision making provide a structure for using data to monitor student learning so that good decisions can be made at each tier with a high probability of success. When using the problem-solving method teams answer four interrelated questions: (1) Is there a problem and what is it? (2) Why is it happening? (3) What are we going to do about it? (4) Did our interventions work (NASDSE, 2005)? Problem-solving and standard treatment protocol techniques ensure that decisions about a student's needs are driven by the student's response to high-quality interventions.

7. **Monitor progress frequently.** To determine if the intervention is working for a student, the decision-making team must establish and implement progress monitoring. **Progress monitoring** is the use of assessments that can be collected frequently and are sensitive to small changes in student behavior. Data collected through progress monitoring will inform the decision-making team whether changes in the instruction or goals are needed. Informed decisions about students' needs require frequent data collection to provide reliable measures of progress. Various curriculum-based measurements (CBM) are useful tools for monitoring students' progress.

RTI AND THE ASSESSMENT PROCESS

The role of RTI in the assessment process is one that needs to be determined so that special educators can determine how RTI effects making referrals for special education services. The Virginia Department of Education's Office of Student Services (2009) answered questions concerning the role of RTI in the eligibility process for special education.

How is RTI used in the eligibility process?

RTI can be useful in the eligibility process in the following ways:

- By helping the eligibility group decide if more evaluation data is needed
- By documenting that the student was provided appropriate high-quality research-based instruction in general education settings, and that the instruction was delivered by qualified personnel
- By providing data to the eligibility group as one part of the evaluation process used to determine if the student has a disability that requires special education and related services.

RTI practices that help identify unexpected lower learning *levels* and lower learning *rates* practices implemented with fidelity will help school teams monitor student progress to decide when there is a need for additional information about a child that can only be gathered through comprehensive individual assessment obtained through the special education evaluation process.

WHEN USING RTI AS A COMPONENT OF ELIGIBILITY DETERMINATION, DOES A PATTERN OF STRENGTHS AND WEAKNESSES HAVE TO BE ESTABLISHED?   Yes. Whether RTI is used, or any other permissible method of identifying a specific learning disability or other disability, a pattern of strengths and weaknesses in performance, achievement, or both, must be established relative to age, grade level standards or intellectual development. This evidence/documentation must be considered as part of the evaluation as described in 34 CFR § 300.309.

Can eligibility for special education be determined solely by RTI?

No. RTI practices can assist eligibility groups in determining special education eligibility by providing useful information to the evaluation and eligibility process, as well as determining the educational needs of the child. The information obtained through RTI progress monitoring will provide the eligibility group with documentation that the student's lack of academic progress is not the result of inappropriate instruction in reading or mathematics, or the result of limited English proficiency (34 CFR §§ 300.301 through 300.311).

Can a child be found eligible for special education services without using RTI?

Yes, as long as the eligibility team's decision is compliant with state regulations that outline the individual disability identification requirements and procedures. However, as noted in the RTI guidance document, when a student is suspected of having a specific learning disability, the data collected during the course of RTI is an assessment that is part of the evaluation leading to the eligibility determination process.

Events That Led to Changes in LD Identification in IDEA 2004

Through decades of educational practice, it has become generally accepted that a "severe discrepancy" is *in fact* a learning disability and/or a proxy for a learning disability and its underlying processing disorders. It is now widely acknowledged that there is not a scientific basis for the use of a measured IQ achievement discrepancy as either a defining characteristic of or a marker for LD. Though numerous authorities (Fletcher et al., 2005; Lyon et al., 2001; Stanovich, 2005) have identified problems with discrepancy models, it has persisted as the most widely used diagnostic concept. In the 1997 IDEA reauthorization process, the concern with discrepancy approaches reached a head and the U.S. **Office of Special Education Programs (OSEP)** committed to a vigorous program of examining and summarizing evidence around LD identification. That effort resulted in the Learning Disabilities Summit, as well as subsequent roundtable meetings involving representatives of major professional organizations. While preparing for the 2004 IDEA reauthorization, OSEP conducted the 2002 Learning Disabilities Roundtable to generate a series of consensus statements about the field of learning disabilities. With respect to the use of discrepancy formulas, the members stated:

> Roundtable participants agree there is no evidence that ability–achievement discrepancy formulas can be applied in a consistent and educationally meaningful (i.e., reliable and valid) manner. They believe SLD eligibility should not be operationalized using ability–achievement discrepancy formulas.

Rationale for Replacing the Discrepancy Model with RTI

Response to intervention offers the promise of "building better readers" through the provision of differentiated instruction based on data from ongoing assessments for all students in the early grades. That is, all students receive scientifically research-based reading instruction and, most importantly, struggling readers receive additional instructional time and research-based reading interventions within the structure and context of the general education classroom. In essence, RTI replaces the practice of "waiting to fail" with deliberate early intervention and prevention.

Major Issues Related to Using the Concept of Ability–Achievement Discrepancy

Issue 1: Discrepancy models fail to differentiate between children who have LD and those who have academic achievement problems related to poor instruction, lack of experience, or other problems. It is generally agreed that the ability–achievement discrepancy model was influenced by research conducted by Rutter and Yule (1975; Reschly et al., 2003). This research found two groups of low-achieving readers, one with discrepancies and one without. This finding formed the basis for the idea that a discrepancy was meaningful for both classification and treatment purposes. Later analyses of this research, and attempts to replicate it, have failed to produce support for the "two group" model for either purpose. In fact, it is now accepted that reading occurs in a normal distribution and that students with dyslexia or severe reading problems represent the lower end of that distribution (Fletcher et al., 2002).

Issue 2: Discrepancy models discriminate against students outside of "mainstream" culture and students who are in the upper and lower ranges of IQ. Due to psychometric problems, discrepancy approaches tend to under-identify children at the lower end of the IQ range and over-identify children at the upper end. This problem has been addressed by various formulas that correct for the regression to the mean that occurs when two correlated measures are used. However, using regression formulas does not address issues such as language and cultural bias in IQ tests, nor does it improve the classification function of a discrepancy model (Steubing et al., 2002).

Issue 3: Discrepancy models do not effectively predict which students will benefit from or respond differentially to instruction. The research around this issue has examined both progress and absolute outcomes for children with and without discrepancy, and has not supported the notion the two groups will respond differentially to instruction (Stanovich, 2005). Poor readers with discrepancies and poor readers without discrepancies perform similarly on skills considered to be important to the development of reading skills (Gresham, 2002).

Issue 4: The use of discrepancy models requires children to fail for a substantial period of time—usually years—before they are far enough behind to exhibit a discrepancy. To show a discrepancy, two tests need to be administered—an IQ test, such as the Wechsler Intelligence Scale for Children, and an achievement test, such as the Woodcock-Johnson Tests of Achievement. Because of limitations of achievement and IQ testing, discrepancies often do not "appear" until late second, third, or even fourth grade. Educators and parents have experienced the frustration of knowing a child's skills are not adequate and not typical of the child's overall functioning and being told to "wait a year" to rerefer the child. While waiting for a discrepancy to appear, other persistent problems associated with school failure develop such as poor self-concept, compromised motivation, vocabulary deficits, and deficits associated with limited access to written content.

The Consideration of RTI in the Process of Determining Specific Learning Disabilities (SLD)

RTI is being strongly considered as part of the SLD identification process because it has the potential to address areas of the SLD definition and construct that are not adequately assessed with current approaches. If the features of RTI are implemented correctly

- There is some assurance that students are being exposed to high-quality instruction in the general education classroom by stipulating that schools use evidence-based instructional practices and routinely monitor the progress of all students.
- There is an emphasis on underachievement through its focus on discrepancy models that examine whether a student is failing to respond to instruction through both low overall achievement and inability to make adequate progress.
- They encourage access to early intervention because, with the regular monitoring of progress, at-risk students are identified early, and an infrastructure for the appropriate delivery of services already is established.

- They are designed to address many students with achievement problems, so the label of learning disability is applied only for those students who fail to respond to multiple levels of intervention efforts.
- They are meant to be applied as multiple measures of child performance rather than to limit determination to a single point in time.

THE ROLE RTI SHOULD PLAY IN IDENTIFYING CHILDREN WITH SPECIFIC LEARNING DISABILITIES

When considering adopting an RTI approach for identifying students with specific learning disabilities (SLD), school districts should keep in mind a number of provisions of IDEA 2004. Under IDEA 2004 schools districts may but are no longer required to consider whether a student has a severe discrepancy between achievement and intellectual ability. At the same time, IDEA 2004 gives school districts the flexibility to determine that a student has an SLD using RTI data. Proponents point out that identifying SLD through RTI shifts the emphasis of the evaluation process from documenting the student's disability to the student's instructional needs. RTI emphasizes this shift of focus through documentation of a student's persistent failure to progress even after receiving intense and sound scientifically research-based interventions in the general education curriculum.

IDEA 2004 is silent about the exact criteria school districts may use in establishing SLDs. It is expected that when final federal regulations are published, specific criteria will be established and states will be provided clarifying guidance regarding these procedures. Until that time, districts implementing RTI are strongly encouraged to use established approaches for using RTI data to identify SLDs. The following procedure is recommended:

After appropriate CBM probes have been applied, and after attempts have been made to implement at least two Tier III interventions with fidelity, a student should be considered nonresponsive when the student's level of academic achievement has (a) been determined to be significantly lower than that of his or her peers, and (b) the gap between the student's achievement and that of his or her peers increases (or does not significantly decrease). Absent other information to explain the lack of achievement, students who are nonresponsive at Tier III should be suspected of having a disability.

Once a referral for special education is initiated the school district must determine whether an initial comprehensive evaluation is required to determine the presence of a disability. Unless mitigating information exists to explain why the student was nonresponsive at Tier III, an initial evaluation, for which the school district must obtain written consent from a parent or guardian, will be completed. A comprehensive evaluation may or may not require additional testing but should include a formal observation of the student by a team member unless a recent observation was completed by a team member prior to the evaluation. If the student's evaluation team determines that the existing data developed through the RTI process is sufficient to complete the evaluation report in all suspected areas of disability, additional information does not need to be obtained. If the existing data do not establish the need for special education services, further assessment may be needed to rule out the possibility of a qualifying disability, including a disability in a category other than SLD.

The Use of RTI in the SLD Classification

Although RTI addresses some significant shortcomings in current approaches to SLD identification and other concerns about early identification of students at risk for reading problems, RTI should be considered as merely one important element within the larger context of the SLD determination process. Implementing RTI allows schools to have more confidence that they are providing appropriate learning experiences to all students while identifying and targeting early those students who may be at risk for reading or math problems but who do not necessarily have a learning disability. Although IDEA 2004 provides flexibility to local education agencies (LEAs) in determining SLD identification procedures, the following recommendations by the National Joint Committee on Learning Disabilities (2005) should help guide the development of these procedures:

> Decisions regarding eligibility for special education services must draw from information collected from a comprehensive individual evaluation using multiple methods including clinical judgment and other sources of relevant information. Students must be evaluated on an individual basis and assessed for intra-individual differences in the seven domains that comprise the definition of SLD in the law—listening, thinking, speaking, reading, writing, spelling, and mathematical calculation. Eligibility decisions must be made through an interdisciplinary team, must be student-centered and informed by appropriate data, and must be based on student needs and strengths.

As schools begin to execute a process of decision making more clinical than statistical in nature, ensuring through regulations that this team of qualified professionals represents all competencies necessary for accurate review of comprehensive assessment data will be critical.

One of the advantages of RTI is the timely identification of children who struggle with learning. RTI is not intended as a stand-alone approach to determining specific learning disabilities, but it can be a key component of a comprehensive approach to disability determination. In an RTI model, if a student does not respond to robust high-quality instruction and intervention that is progress monitored over time, he or she may indeed be determined to have a learning disability. The benefit of RTI for these at-risk students is the wealth of meaningful instructional data provided for use in creating well-targeted individualized instructional programs and evidence-based instructional interventions. In addition RTI sets in place a student progress monitoring process that facilitates communication and promotes ongoing meaningful dialogue between home and school.

Although RTI addresses some significant shortcomings in current approaches to SLD identification and other concerns about early identification of students at risk for reading problems, RTI should be considered to be one important element within the larger context of the SLD determination process. RTI as one component of SLD determination is an insufficient sole criterion for accurately determining SLD. As part of a larger process, RTI provides the following information about a student:

1. Indication of the student's skill level relative to peers or a criterion benchmark
2. Success or lack of success of particular interventions
3. Sense of the intensity of instructional supports that will be necessary for the student to achieve

Incorporating this information into SLD determination procedures has the potential to make important contributions to identifying students with SLDs in schools. In addition to an RTI process that helps ensure appropriate learning experiences and early intervention, identification of SLD should include a student-centered, comprehensive evaluation that ensures students who have a learning disability are accurately identified.

Although IDEA 2004 provides flexibility to LEAs in determining SLD identification procedures, the following recommendations by the NJCLD should help guide the development of these procedures (2005):

- Decisions regarding eligibility for special education services must draw on information collected from a comprehensive individual evaluation using multiple methods, including clinical judgment and other sources of relevant information.
- Students must be evaluated on an individual basis and assessed for intra-individual differences in the seven domains that comprise the definition of SLD in the law: listening, thinking, speaking, reading, writing, spelling, and mathematical calculation.
- Eligibility decisions must be made through an interdisciplinary team, must be student-centered and informed by appropriate data, and must be based on student needs and strengths.
- As schools begin to execute a process of decision making that is more clinical than statistical in nature, ensuring through regulations that this team of review of comprehensive assessment data will be critical.

Processes for SLD identification have changed and will continue to do so. Within that context, remembering that RTI is but one resource for use in the SLD determination process is important. More broadly speaking, RTI procedures have the distinction that when implemented with fidelity, they can identify and intervene for students early in the educational process, thereby reducing academic failure among students.

MULTITIERED SERVICE DELIVERY MODEL

An RTI approach incorporates a multitiered model of educational service delivery in which each tier represents increasingly intense services that are associated with increasing levels of learner needs. The various tier interventions are designed to provide a set of curricular/instructional processes aimed at improving student response to instruction and student outcomes.

Much discussion continues surrounding the issues of how many tiers constitute an adequate intervention (O'Connor, Tilly, Vaughn, & Marston, 2003). Most frequently, RTI is viewed as a three-tiered model, similar to those used for other service delivery practices, such as positive behavioral support. Figure 17.1 depicts a three-tiered model as conceived in an RTI framework.

Like other models, RTI is meant to be applied on a schoolwide basis, in which the majority of students receive instruction in Tier I (the general classroom), students who are at risk for reading and other learning disabilities are identified (such as through **schoolwide screening**) for more intense support in Tier II, and students who fail to respond to the interventions provided in Tier II may then be considered for specialized instruction in Tier III.

The application of RTI is typically understood within the context of a multi-tiered model or framework that delineates a continuum of programs and services for students with academic difficulties. Although no universally accepted model or approach currently exists, the many possible variations can be conceptualized as elaborations on or modifications of the following three-tiered model:

Tier I: High-quality instructional and behavioral supports are provided for all students in general education.

- School personnel conduct universal screening of literacy skills, academics, and behavior.
- Teachers implement a variety of research-supported teaching strategies and approaches.
- Ongoing curriculum-based assessment and continuous progress monitoring are used to guide high-quality instruction.

- Students receive differentiated instruction based on data from ongoing assessments.

Tier II: Students whose performance and rate of progress lag behind those of peers in their classroom, school, or district receive more specialized prevention or remediation within general education.

- Curriculum-based measures are used to identify which students continue to need assistance and with what specific kinds of skills.
- Collaborative problem solving is used to design and implement instructional support for students that may consist of a standard protocol or more individualized strategies and interventions.
- Identified students receive more intensive scientific, research-based instruction targeted to their individual needs.
- Student progress is monitored frequently to determine intervention effectiveness and needed modifications.
- Systematic assessment is conducted to determine the fidelity or integrity with which instruction and interventions are implemented.
- Parents are informed and included in the planning and monitoring of their child's progress in Tier II specialized interventions.
- General education teachers receive support (e.g., training, consultation, direct services for students), as needed, from other qualified educators in implementing interventions and monitoring student progress.

Tier III: Comprehensive evaluation is conducted by a multidisciplinary team to determine eligibility for special education and related services.

- Parents are informed of their due process rights and consent is obtained for the comprehensive evaluation needed to determine whether the student has a disability and is eligible for special education and related services.
- Evaluation uses multiple sources of assessment data, which may include data from standardized and norm-referenced measures; observations made by parents, students, and teachers; and data collected in Tiers I and II.
- Intensive, systematic, specialized instruction is provided and additional RTI data are collected, as needed, in accordance with special education time lines and other mandates.
- Procedural safeguards concerning evaluations and eligibility determinations apply, as required by IDEA 2004 mandates.

Standard protocol as used in describing Tier II refers to an approach in which students with similar difficulties (e.g., problems with reading fluency) are given a research-based intervention that has been standardized and shown to be effective for students with similar difficulties and uses a standard protocol to ensure implementation integrity (Fuchs et al., 2003).

Variations on this basic framework may be illustrated by options often found within Tier II. For example, Tier II might consist of two hierarchical steps, or subtiers (e.g., a teacher first collaborates with a single colleague and then, if needed, problem solves with a multidisciplinary team, creating in effect a four-tiered model). Alternatively, more than one type of intervention might be provided within Tier II (e.g., both a standard protocol and individualized planning, based on the student's apparent needs).

RTI is a critical component of a multitiered service delivery system. The goal of such a system is to ensure that quality instruction, good teaching practices, differentiated instruction, and remedial opportunities are available in general education, and that special education is provided for students with disabilities who require more specialized services than can be provided in general education. The continuous monitoring of the adequacy of student response to instruction is particularly relevant to an RTI approach as a means of determining whether a student should move from one tier to the next by documenting that existing instruction and support are not sufficient. For example, in moving from Tier II to Tier III, insufficient responsiveness to high-quality, scientific, research-based intervention may be cause to suspect that a student has a disability and should be referred for a special education evaluation. In addition, however, the right of a parent, state education agency, or a local education agency to initiate a request for an evaluation at any time is maintained in IDEA 2004.

Focus of Tier I

Tier I is designed to meet the needs of a majority of the school population and has three critical elements:

a. A **research-based** core curriculum
b. Short cycle assessments for all students at least three times a year to determine their instructional needs
c. Sustained professional development to equip teachers with tools necessary for teaching content area effectively

In Tier I, the goal is to prevent failure and optimize learning by offering the most effective instruction possible to the greatest number of students. Instruction takes place in a regular education setting and is, for the most part, whole class (scientifically based) instruction that produces good results for most students. Based on data, classroom teachers monitor student progress and differentiate instruction for students who do not meet grade-level expectations.

Focus of Tier II

Tier II is for students who are falling behind same-age peers and need additional targeted interventions to meet grade-level expectations. In Tier II, the goal is to accelerate learning for students who need more intensive support. The interventions typically take place in a regular setting and may include instruction to small groups of students, targeted interventions, and frequent progress monitoring.

Focus of Tier III

Tier III is designed for students who still have considerable difficulty in mastering necessary academic and/or behavioral skills, even after Tier I and Tier II instruction and interventions. Tier III addresses students' needs through intensive individualized services. In Tier III, students receive intensive and highly focused intentional research-based instruction, possibly over a long period of time. Tier III involves students who did not respond to Tier II intervention. These students undergo a more formal diagnostic evaluation.

Importance of Parent Involvement for Successful RTI Programs

Involving parents at all phases is a key aspect of a successful RTI program. As members of the decision-making team, parents can provide a critical perspective on students, thus increasing the likelihood that RTI interventions will be effective. For this reason, schools must make a concerted effort to involve parents as early as possible, beginning with instruction in the core curriculum. This can be done through traditional methods such as parent–teacher conferences, regularly scheduled meetings, or by other methods. This must be done by notifying parents of student progress within the RTI system on a regular basis.

Districts and schools should provide parents with written information about its RTI program and be prepared to answer questions about RTI processes. The written information should explain how the system is different from a traditional education system and about the vital and collaborative role that parents play within the RTI system. The more parents are involved as players, the greater the opportunity for successful RTI outcomes.

Because RTI is a method of delivering the general education curriculum for all students, written consent is not required before administering universal screenings, CBMs, and targeted assessments within a multitiered RTI system when these tools are used to determine instructional needs. However, when a student fails to respond to interventions and the decision is made to evaluate a student for special education eligibility, written consent must be obtained in accordance with special education procedures. When developing screening measures, districts should also consider the parallel measures that may be used for evaluation.

Failure to communicate and reach out to parents will lead to confusion, especially among parents who believe their children have a learning disability. Schools may also want to provide other means for keeping parents engaged and informed:

- Involving them in state and local planning for RTI adoption
- Providing them written information on their right to refer their child at any time for special education evaluation as stipulated in IDEA 2004
- Providing written material that outlines the criteria for determining eligibility under IDEA 2004 and the role of RTI data in making LD determinations

Taking measures to build strong, productive relationships with parents can only increase the likelihood that students will benefit greatly from the RTI model.

FIDELITY

Fidelity refers to the degree to which RTI components are implemented as designed, intended, and planned. Fidelity is achieved through sufficient time allocation, adequate intervention intensity, qualified and trained staff, and sufficient materials and resources. Fidelity is vital in universal screening, instructional delivery, and progress monitoring.

THE RTI PROCESS FOR TEACHERS

An RTI outcome vital to the effectiveness of a school system is that *all teachers*, both general and special educators, will feel an increased accountability for student learning as well as strengthened confidence in their own skills and knowledge related to teaching reading. The goal of all students learning to read will be a unifying force that includes all staff and all students. All teachers will see themselves as part of a system that delivers high-quality instruction that continually assesses student progress and that provides extra help and extra time to meet the needs of students.

If we are to close the achievement gap in schools, roles of school personnel will change. Collaboration among teachers will increase in order to determine student needs, designate resources, and maximize student learning. Genuine access to and participation in the general curriculum for students with disabilities may require a shift in the way we think about and ultimately provide special education and related services. Building better readers must become the collective responsibility of all teachers so that all students achieve.

Although RTI presents a promising way of addressing many issues associated with SLD identification, unanswered implementation questions remain. We must ask how many issues relevant to SLD determination are due to the specific assessment components as well as the limited fidelity with which those components were implemented (e.g., appropriate learning experiences, prereferral intervention, application of exclusion clause, and ability–achievement discrepancy). Further, we must consider how well states, districts, or schools could implement an assessment process that incorporates significant changes in staff roles and responsibilities (i.e., most dramatically for general education staff) while lengthening the duration of disability determination assessment and possibly lengthening service time.

Another significant consideration is that current research literature provides scant scientific evidence on how RTI applies in curricular areas other than reading and beyond primary or elementary school-age children. In conjunction with the standards that have been developed (NCSESA, 1996; NCTM, 2000), science-based research needs to be conducted using the RTI construct in the areas of science and mathematics. Utilizing an RTI framework across educational disciplines, as well as grade levels, is synergistic with the No Child Left Behind Act of 2001 and promotes the idea that schools have an obligation to ensure that all students participate in strong instructional programs that support multifaceted learning.

What Teachers Need in Terms of Professional Development and RTI

Teachers of students with learning disabilities will need to acquire specialized knowledge to individualize instruction, to build skills, and recommend modifications and accommodations needed for students with learning disabilities to be successful in the general curriculum.

Within the RTI framework, professional development will be needed to prepare these teachers in the following skills and knowledge (Division for Learning Disabilities of the Council for Exceptional Children, 2006):

- Understanding and ability to apply pedagogy related to cognition, learning theory, language development, behavior management, and applied behavioral analysis
- Possession of a substantial base of knowledge about criteria for identifying scientific, research-based methodology and instructional programs useful for students with learning disabilities and individualization of instruction
- Proficiency in providing direct skill instruction in reading, writing, spelling, math, and listening and learning strategies
- Ability to adjust instruction and learning supports based on student progress, observation, and clinical judgment
- Ability to conduct comprehensive evaluations that include standardized assessment measures, informal assessment, and behavioral observations
- Ability to translate evaluations into meaningful educational recommendations
- Guidance in explaining test results to help parents and teachers understand the student's needs and the recommendations generated during the assessment process
- Strengthening of communication skills to function as collaborative partners and members of problem-solving teams
- Knowledgeability about the legal requirements of IDEA 2004, federal and state regulations, and the history of learning disabilities

Vocabulary

At risk: A term used for children who may, in the future, have problems with their development that may affect learning or development.

Core academic subjects: English; language arts; reading; mathematics; science; the arts, including music and visual arts; social studies, which includes civics, government, economics, history, and geography; and modern and classical languages.

Early intervening services: Refers to a broad application of scientifically based prevention and support services for students who are not identified as needing special education programs or service but who need additional academic and behavioral support to succeed in the general education classroom.

Fidelity: Refers to the intensity and accuracy with which instruction and intervention are implemented.

Intervention: Instructional strategies and curricular components used to enhance student learning.

National Research Center on Learning Disabilities (NRCLD): A joint project of researchers at Vanderbilt University and the University of Kansas with funding provided by the U.S. Department of Education, Office of Special Education Programs. NRCLD is part of a federal effort to find improved research-based ways of identifying students with learning disabilities.

Office of Special Education Programs (OSEP): The Office of Special Education Programs is a federal program of the U.S. Department of Education dedicated to improving results for infants, toddlers, children, and youth with disabilities ages birth through 21 by providing leadership and financial support to assist states and local districts.

Progress monitoring: A set of assessment procedures for determining the extent to which students are benefiting from classroom instruction.

Research-based (Activities, Practices, Instruction, Intervention, or Treatment): Interventions or treatment approaches that have been scientifically demonstrated to be effective, regardless of the discipline that developed them.

Research-based interventions: Instructional strategies and curricular components used to enhance student learning. The effectiveness of these interventions is backed by experimental design studies that have been applied to a large study sample, show a direct correlation between the intervention and student progress, and have been reported in peer-reviewed journals.

Response to intervention: A system used at schools to screen, assess, identify, plan for, and provide interventions to *any* student at risk of school failure due to academic or behavior needs. It is an assessment and intervention process for systematically monitoring student progress and making decisions about the need for instructional modifications or increasingly intensified services using progress monitoring data.

Schoolwide screening (also known as *universal screening*): An assessment characterized as a quick, low-cost, repeatable test of age-appropriate critical skills (e.g., identifying letters of the alphabet or reading a list of high-frequency words) or behaviors (e.g., tardiness or discipline reports). Measures are not too complicated and can be administered by someone with a minimal amount of training.

Specific learning disability (SLD): A categorical condition considered important for providing legal protections and entitlements. Under IDEA 2004, SLD is defined as "a disorder of one or more of the basic psychological processes involved in understanding or using language, spoken or written, which disorder may manifest itself in [the] imperfect ability to listen, think, speak, read, write, spell, or do mathematical calculations. Such term includes such conditions as perceptual disabilities, brain injury, minimal brain dysfunction, dyslexia, and developmental aphasia. Such term does not include a learning problem that is primarily the result of visual, hearing, or motor disabilities, of mental retardation, of emotional disturbance, or of environmental, cultural, or economic disadvantage."

Tiered or multitiered service delivery model: Provides tiers of increasingly intense interventions directed at more specific deficits and at smaller segments of the population.

7 THE CHILD STUDY TEAM AND PREREFERRAL STRATEGIES

Key Terms

Change of program
Classroom management
    techniques
Consolidation of program
Disciplinary action
Hearing test

Help classes
In-school counseling
Medical exam
Parent interview
Prereferral strategies
Progress report

Referral to Child Protective
    Services
Remedial reading or math services
Screening
Team meeting with teachers
Vision test

Chapter Objectives

This chapter focuses on the child study team and the various prereferral procedures that school systems use. After reading this chapter, you should be able to do the following:

■ Understand the purpose of the child study team
■ Understand the role of RTI in the assessment process
■ Understand the purpose of prereferral strategies
■ Identify the prereferral strategies used most often in school systems

THE CHILD STUDY TEAM

Initially, teachers will provide the majority of students instruction in Tier I RTI strategies. These high-quality instructional and behavioral supports are provided for all students in general education. Examples include:

- School personnel conduct universal screening of literacy skills, academics, and behavior.
- Teachers implement a variety of research-supported teaching strategies and approaches.
- Ongoing curriculum-based assessment and continuous progress monitoring are used to guide high-quality instruction.
- Students receive differentiated instruction based on data from ongoing assessments.

When progress monitoring and teacher observation show that Tier I RTI strategies are not working, they will move to Tier II RTI. These students whose performance and rate of progress lag behind those of peers in their classroom, school, or district may receive more specialized prevention or remediation within general education. This includes:

- Curriculum-based measures are used to identify which students continue to need assistance and with what specific kinds of skills.
- Collaborative problem solving is used to design and implement instructional support for students that may consist of a standard protocol or more individualized strategies and interventions.
- Identified students receive more intensive scientific, research-based instruction targeted to their individual needs.
- Student progress is monitored frequently to determine intervention effectiveness and needed modifications.
- Systematic assessment is conducted to determine the fidelity or integrity with which instruction and interventions are implemented.
- Parents are informed and included in the planning and monitoring of their child's progress in Tier II specialized interventions.
- General education teachers receive support (e.g., training, consultation, direct services for students), as needed, from other qualified educators in implementing interventions and monitoring student progress.

At this point the teacher may also choose to find out more in-depth information on the child that may shed light on other factors that may be contributing to the student's lack of performance. This would normally result in a referral to the school's Child Study Team. The Child Study Team is a school-based team, often known as the child study team (CST), school building-level committee (SBLC), pupil personnel team (PPT), or prereferral team (PRT), depending on the state in which the student resides. Depending on the type of referral, this team may be drawn from the following staff members:

- Child's classroom teacher
- Principal
- School psychologist
- Special education teacher
- School nurse
- Social worker
- Speech/language clinician
- Guidance counselor (secondary level)

Many school districts recommend or require that, before a formal assessment of a student for possible placement in special education occurs, his or her teacher meet with this prereferral team to discuss the nature of the problem and what possible modifications to instruction or the classroom might be made. These procedures are known as prereferral strategies. **Prereferral strategies** have arisen out of a number of research studies documenting faulty referral practices, such as the over-referral of students who come from backgrounds that are culturally or linguistically different from the majority culture, those who are hard to teach, or those who are felt to have behavioral problems.

This process recognizes that many variables affect learning; rather than first assuming that the difficulty lies within the student, the prereferral team and the teacher look specifically at what variables (e.g., classroom, teacher, student, or an interaction of these) might be affecting this particular student. Examining student records and work samples and conducting interviews and observations are part of the team's efforts. These approaches to gathering data are intended to specify the problem more precisely and to document its severity. Modifications to the teacher's approach, to the classroom, or to student activities may then be suggested, attempted, and documented. It is important for teachers to keep track of the specific modifications they attempt with a student who is having trouble learning or behaving, because these can provide valuable information to the school-based team if the student is referred for a comprehensive assessment.

Prior to doing an evaluation for possible classification and placement in special education, it is important to make sure that the school has made every effort to remediate the learning and/ or behavioral problems through other means. The assessment process is a very significant and important piece in addressing such concerns but should never be the first step. Before full batteries of tests are administered, various preventive measures should be tried in efforts to remediate further difficulties. The rest of this chapter is devoted to discussing the prereferral procedures used most often in school systems.

The members of the CST (the prereferral team) usually meet on a regular basis, once or twice a week depending on the caseload. Normally, there is a chairperson on the CST to whom the entire faculty and staff can make referrals during the week prior to each meeting. For example, if the CST meets on Friday, a teacher can go to the chairperson on Tuesday and say: "I have been trying to work with Mary Bell by making some changes in my class. However, she does not seem to be responding, and I am becoming increasingly concerned about her deterioration. I think I need help and would like to discuss her at the next team meeting."

Such a statement would allow the teacher to come to the team meeting and help develop more formal and comprehensive prereferral strategies that can then be attempted in the classroom. The next statement typifies a different need: "We have been working with Luther Santos for a while on prereferral strategies but they do not seem to be working. Therefore, I would like to meet with the CST again to discuss Luther because he is still doing very poorly in my class and nothing we developed is working." This type of statement would probably require the team to consider screening Luther for a suspected disability because prereferral strategies have been attempted over a period of time and under a variety of conditions and have made no impact.

The chairperson then puts Mary Bell and Luther Santos on the list of students to discuss at the next CST meeting. He or she informs the members of the CST in writing that both are on the CST agenda. It is each team member's responsibility to bring any important and relevant documentation on Mary Bell and Luther Santos to the next CST meeting.

When the CST meets, team members discuss whatever agenda is put forth for that particular day. On some days, there may be very little to discuss whereas on other days, the CST meeting may run for a few hours based on the number of students that need to be discussed.

Examples of Referral Forms to the CST

Many schools utilize a referral form procedure that teachers submit to indicate the possibility of a high-risk student. This is usually the first step in the referral process. The form then goes to the child study team for discussion and future direction. The initial section of these forms is usually the same, containing basic identifying information. The differences are usually in the body of the form. Figures 7.1 and 7.2 are two examples of how this form might be used for referral to the CST.

As shown in Figure 7.1, the classroom teacher has made several attempts to resolve Mary's issues prior to a referral to the CST. When she realized that her attempts were not working, she decided to take her concerns to the CST for a more formal analysis of Mary's situation. At this point, the team, along with the classroom teacher, will develop prereferral strategies for Mary in an attempt to resolve her issues in hopes that a formal referral for a comprehensive assessment is not required.

The referral in Figure 7.2 was made after meetings with the CST established a prereferral intervention strategy plan. This plan had been in operation for several weeks by the time the teacher made the referral.

REFERRAL FORM TO THE CHILD STUDY TEAM

Student Name: Mary Bell

Grade Level: 5

Teacher Name: Mrs. Brown

Parents' Names: Julie/Robert

Date of Referral: November 21, 2011

Date of Birth: 9/21/01

Chronological Age: 10-2

Phone: (516) 555-9876

Please answer the following questions:

What symptoms is the child exhibiting that are of concern at this time?

Mary is having a great deal of problems learning in my class. She rarely hands in work, fails tests, procrastinates, makes excuses, and avoids handing in homework assignments.

What have you tried that has worked?

The only thing that seems to work is contacting her parents, but that is short-lived. Any noticeable changes last for only a day or two and Mary is right back to her patterns.

What have you tried that does not seem to work toward alleviating these symptoms?

I have attempted peer tutoring, limiting assignments, change of seat, parent conferences, small group interventions, and shorter but more frequent assignments to see if she could accomplish anything, but nothing has worked.

What are the child's present academic levels of functioning?

From informal testing, I consider Mary to be functioning at a low average level in all academic skills and ability.

Any observable behavioral or physical limitations?

Mary tends to squint a great deal, but does not seem to have any physical limitations.

What is the child's social behavior like?

Mary seems to avoid any social contact with the other children. She spends a great deal of her time alone on the playground and rarely talks to others. She seems to have no friends.

Current performance estimates (below, on, or above grade level)

Reading: ___below___   **Math:** ___below___   **Spelling:** ___below___

Have the parents been contacted? yes x   no ____.   If not, why not? _____

Further comments?

Parents are very cooperative and concerned. Not sure what to do next.

FIGURE 7.1   Example of Referral Form to Child Study Team

REFERRAL FORM TO THE CHILD STUDY TEAM

Student Name: Luther Santos   **Date of Referral:** February 11, 2011

Grade Level: 3   **Date of Birth:** 2/1/02

Teacher Name: Mrs. Davis   **Chronological Age:** 9-0

Parents' Names: Dalia/Lorenzo   **Phone:** (516) 555-7843

Please answer the following questions:

What symptoms is the child exhibiting that are of concern at this time?

Despite numerous intervention strategies, Luther continues not to follow class or school rules, bothers other children when they are working, gets up out of his seat constantly, throws things at other children, does not finish his class work, and defies authority.

What have you tried that has worked?

Small group instruction in which I can closely monitor Luther by having him close to me. But even that is difficult.

What have you tried that does not seem to work toward alleviating these symptoms?

I have worked with the school psychologist in consultation, tried behavioral plans, behavior modification techniques, parent conferences, small group work, changing his seat, modifying the class environment, and giving him more work in the morning when he seems to have the most attention. He is also receiving in-school counseling and has been observed several times. We have reviewed his work samples and tests and have instituted changes as a result of the weaknesses we have found. We have been trying this intervention plan for several weeks but nothing seems to be working.

What are the child's present academic levels of functioning?

From informal testing I consider Luther to be a very capable boy if he were able to focus. His skills all seem to be at least average, and his ability seems above average based on some of the comments he makes and vocabulary he uses.

Any observable behavioral or physical limitations?

Luther cannot sit still for more than two to three minutes, cannot focus on work for more than a few minutes, and asks questions constantly and at inappropriate times. He does not seem to have any physical limitations and is very good in sports although he has little patience for following rules.

What is the child's social behavior like?

Luther is liked by some children in the class because he is good at sports. However, many of the boys are losing patience because he will walk off during a game when he doesn't feel like playing.

Current performance estimates (below, on, or above grade level)

Reading: _____   **Math:** _____   **Spelling:** _____

Have the parents been contacted?   yes _____ no _____ .   If not, why not? _____

Further comments?

Parents do not feel that he is that bad. Father indicated that he was the same way in school and grew out of it.

FIGURE 7.2   Example of Referral Form to Child Study Team

In the case of Luther, the teacher and the CST have already attempted numerous prereferral strategies in an attempt to improve Luther's class behavior and performance. However, according to the teacher, nothing seems to be working. At this point, the CST might consider screening Luther for a suspected disability. If team members find evidence of a suspected disability, they will make a formal referral for a comprehensive assessment with the parents' permission.

The Child Study Team Meeting

Once a referral is made to the CST, personnel involved on the team will gather as much available information as possible prior to the meeting in order to better understand the child and his or her educational patterns. This information may come from a variety of sources, and the presentation of this information at the meeting is crucial in the determination of the most appropriate direction to proceed. Schools usually have a wealth of information about all of the students, distributed among a number of people and a number of records. Gathering and reviewing this information after a referral, and prior to screening, could reduce the need for more formal testing and provide a very thorough picture of the child's abilities and patterns.

Sources of Student Information

SCHOOL RECORDS.   School records can be a rich source of information about the student and his or her background. For instance, the number of times the student has changed schools may be of interest. Frequent school changes can be disruptive emotionally, as well as academically, and may be a factor in the problems that have resulted in the student's being referred to the CST.

PRIOR ACADEMIC ACHIEVEMENT.   The student's past history of grades is usually of interest to the CST. Is the student's current performance in a particular subject typical of the student or is the problem being observed something new? Are patterns noticeable in the student's grades? For example, many students begin the year with poor grades and then show gradual improvement as they get back into the swing of school. For others, the reverse may be true: During the early part of the year, when prior school material is being reviewed, they may do well, with declines in their grades coming as new material is introduced. Also, transition points such as beginning the fourth grade or middle school may cause some students problems; the nature and purpose of reading, for example, tends to change when students enter the fourth grade, because reading to learn content becomes more central. Similarly, middle school requires students to assume more responsibility for long-term projects (Hoy and Gregg, 1994). These shifts may bring about a noticeable decline in grades.

PRIOR TEST SCORES.   Test scores are also important to review. Comparing these scores to a student's current classroom performance can indicate that the student's difficulties are new ones, perhaps resulting from some environmental change that needs to be more fully investigated. Further, the comparison may show that the student has always found a particular skill area to be problematic. "In this situation, the current problems the student is experiencing indicate that the classroom demands have reached a point that the student requires more support to be successful" (Hoy & Gregg, 1994, p. 37).

GROUP STANDARDIZED ACHIEVEMENT TEST RESULTS.   A great deal of information can be obtained from group achievement test results. Whereas individual tests should be administered when evaluating a child's suspected disability, group achievement results may reflect certain very important patterns. Most schools administer group achievement tests annually or every few years. If these results are available on a student, you may want to explore the various existing patterns. It is helpful to have several years of results to analyze. Over time this type of pattern can be more reliable for interpretation.

ATTENDANCE RECORDS.   Attendance records can provide the CST with a great deal of important information, especially if team members know what they are looking for. Many patterns are symptomatic of more serious concerns, and being able to recognize these patterns early can only facilitate the recognition of a potential high-risk student. When we look at a student's attendance profile over the years, several things may stand out. For instance, a child's pattern of absences might include consistent absences during a specific part of the year, as is the case with some students who have respiratory problems or allergies. In other cases, there may be a noticeable pattern of declining attendance that may be linked to a decline in motivation, an undiagnosed health problem or a change within the family. Specific points to keep in mind when reviewing attendance records include the following:

1. **The number of days absent in the student's profile:** Ordinarily, more than 10 days a year may need to be investigated for patterns. If a child is out more than 15 to 20 days, this could be indicative of a serious issue if a medical or some other logical reason did not substantiate the absences.
2. **The patterns of days absent:** Single days may indicate the presence of possible school avoidance, phobia, or dysfunctional or chaotic home environment.

PRIOR TEACHER REPORTS.   Comments written on report cards or in permanent record folders can provide the CST with a different perspective on the child under a different style of teaching. Successful years and positive comments may be clues to the child's learning style and the conditions under which he or she responds best. Also, write-ups about conferences between previous teachers and parents can provide information important to understanding the child's patterns and history.

GROUP IQ TEST INFORMATION.   This information is usually found in the permanent record folder. Many schools administer a group IQ type of test (e.g., Otis Lennon—7) in grades 3, 6, and 9. It is important to be aware that the term *school abilities index* has replaced the term *IQ* or *intelligence quotient* on many group IQ tests.

PRIOR TEACHER REFERRALS.   The CST should investigate school records for prior referrals from teachers. There could have been a time when a teacher referred a student but no action was taken due to time of year, parent resistance, delay in procedures, and so on. These referrals may still be on file and may reveal useful information.

MEDICAL HISTORY IN THE SCHOOL NURSE'S OFFICE.   The CST should also investigate school medical records for indications of visual or hearing difficulties, prescribed medication that may have an effect on the child's behavior (e.g., antihistamines), or medical conditions in need of attention or that could be contributing to the child's present difficulties.

STUDENT WORK.   Often, an initial part of the assessment process includes examining a student's work, either by selecting work samples that can be analyzed to identify academic skills and deficits or by conducting a portfolio assessment, whereby folders of the student's work are examined (see Chapter 3). When collecting work samples, the teacher selects work from the areas in which the student is experiencing difficulty and systematically examines them. The teacher might identify such elements as how the student was directed to do the activity (e.g., orally, in writing), how long it took the student to complete the activity, the pattern of errors (e.g., reversals when writing), and the pattern of correct answers. Analyzing the student's work in this way can yield valuable insight into the nature of his or her difficulties and suggest possible solutions.

RECOMMENDATIONS BY THE CHILD STUDY TEAM—PREREFERRAL STRATEGIES

After analyzing all of the information presented at the meeting, the CST has to make a decision: What does it recommend at this point? If this is the first time a student is being reviewed by the team, then the CST is very likely to recommend prereferral strategies to the teacher. As previously mentioned, these are techniques and suggestions to attempt to resolve the child's issues without the need for a more comprehensive assessment. What are the benefits of prereferral intervention?

- Alternatives are reviewed and referrals made to other programs. Instructional assistance can be provided if needed.
- Collaboration with the teacher on Tier II RTI strategies takes place.
- Students who do not have a disability, but who need instructional support, will receive it in the regular program.
- Problem solving happens as a team facilitates professional growth in needed areas; staff development is formative and directly in response to teacher needs.
- Teachers in the regular program develop a network of peer support.
- Referrals to special education are more valid; that is, students are more likely to truly have a disability.

Prereferral Intervention Strategies

TEAM MEETING WITH TEACHERS.   A **team meeting with teachers** is a prereferral procedure whereby teachers who have previously worked with or have ideas about this student come together to determine what strategies can be implemented for remediation. In this prereferral procedure, teachers share information about a student to identify patterns of behavior reflective of some particular condition or disability. Sometimes, a group meeting with all of the child's teachers can preclude the need for further involvement. One or several teachers may be using techniques that could benefit others also working with the child. By sharing information or observations, it is possible to identify patterns of behavior reflective of some particular condition or disability. Once this pattern is identified, the student may be handled in a variety of ways without the need for more serious intervention.

PARENT INTERVIEWS.   A **parent interview** as a prereferral procedure involves meeting with the parent(s) to discuss what motivates this child along with finding out any family information that may be contributing to the child's behavior in the classroom (e.g., recent separation, death of a loved one). Meeting the parent(s) is always recommended for a child having difficulty in school. This initial meeting can be informal, with the purpose of clarifying certain issues and gathering pertinent information that may help the child as well as the teacher in the classroom. If testing or serious intervention is required, then a more formal and in-depth parent meeting will take place.

MEDICAL EXAM. The CST should try to rule out any possibility of a medical condition causing or contributing to the existing problems. If the teacher or any other professional who works with the child feels that there is any possibility of such a condition, and the need for a complete medical workup is evident, then a recommendation for a **medical exam** should be made. Available records should be reviewed, and if they are inadequate in light of the presenting problems and symptoms, outside recommendations to the parents such as a neurological examination or ophthalmological examination should be considered.

HEARING TEST. A **hearing test** should be one of the first prereferral procedures recommended if one has not been administered to the student within the past 6 months to 1 year. Be aware of inconsistencies in test patterns from year to year that might indicate a chronic pattern. Some symptoms that might indicate the need for an updated audiological examination are when the child

- Turns head when listening
- Asks you to repeat frequently
- Consistently misinterprets what he or she hears
- Does not respond to auditory stimuli
- Slurs speech, speaks in a monotone voice, or articulates poorly

VISION TEST. As with the hearing exam, this evaluation should be one of the first prereferral procedures recommended. Again, if a **vision test** has not been done within 6 months to a year, then request this immediately. Possible symptoms that may necessitate such an evaluation are when the child

- Turns head when looking at board or objects
- Squints excessively
- Rubs eyes frequently
- Holds books and materials close to the face or at unusual angles
- Suffers frequent headaches
- Avoids close work of any type
- Covers an eye when reading
- Consistently loses place when reading

CLASSROOM MANAGEMENT TECHNIQUES. There are times when the real issue may not be the child but rather the teaching style of the classroom teacher—that is, having unrealistic expectations, being critical, or being overly demanding. In such instances, help for the teacher can come in the form of classroom management techniques. **Classroom management techniques** are strategies developed to help handle various problems and conflicts within a classroom. An administrator, psychologist, or any realistic and diplomatic team member who feels comfortable with this type of situation may offer these practical suggestions to the teacher. There are many classroom techniques and modifications that should be tried before taking more serious steps. These include the following:

- Display daily class schedule with times so that the student has a structured idea of the day ahead
- Change seating

- Seat the student with good role models
- Use peer tutors when appropriate
- Limit number of directions
- Simplify complex directions
- Give verbal as well as written directions
- Provide extra work time
- Shorten assignments
- Modify curriculum but change content only as a last resort
- Identify and address preferred learning styles
- Provide manipulative materials
- Provide examples of what is expected
- Use color coding of materials to foster organizational skills
- Develop a homework plan with parental support
- Develop a behavior modification plan if necessary
- Uses lots of positive reinforcement
- Use technology as an aid

HELP CLASSES.   Certain children may require only a temporary support system to get them through a difficult academic period. Some schools provide extra (nonspecial) education services, such as **help classes** that may be held during lunch or before or after school. These classes can clarify academic confusion that could lead to more serious problems if not addressed.

REMEDIAL READING OR MATH SERVICES.   **Remedial reading or math services** are academic programs within a school designed to help the student with reading or math by going slower in the curriculum or placing him or her with a smaller number of students in the classroom for extra attention. These services can be recommended when reading or math is the specific area of concern. Remedial reading and math classes are not special education services and can be instituted as a means of alleviating a child's academic problems.

IN-SCHOOL COUNSELING.   **In-school counseling** is normally done by the school psychologist, social worker, or guidance counselor, and is designed to help the child deal with the issues that are currently problematic for him or her. Sometimes, a child may experience a situational or adjustment disorder (a temporary emotional pattern that may occur at any time in a person's life without a prior history of problems) resulting from separation, divorce, health issues, newness to school district, and so on. When this pattern occurs, it may temporarily interfere with the child's ability to concentrate, remember, or attend to tasks. Consequently, a drop in academic performance can occur. If such patterns occur, the school psychologist may want to institute in-school counseling with the parent's involvement and permission. This recommendation should be instituted only to address issues that can be resolved in a relatively short period of time. More serious issues may have to be referred to outside agencies or professionals for longer treatment.

PROGRESS REPORTS.   A **progress report** is a synopsis of the child's work and behavior in the classroom sent home to the parents in order to keep them updated on the child's strengths and weaknesses over a period of time (e.g., every day, each week, biweekly, or once a month). Sometimes, a child who has fallen behind academically will "hide" from the real issues by avoiding reality. Daily progress reports for a week or two at first and then weekly reports may provide the child with the kinds of immediate gratification and positive feedback necessary to get back on track. They offer the child a greater sense of hope and control in getting back to a more normal academic pattern.

DISCIPLINARY ACTION.   This recommendation is usually made when the child in question needs a structured boundary set involving inappropriate behavior. If a child demonstrates a pattern of inappropriate behavior, **disciplinary action** is usually used in conjunction with other recommendations because such patterned behavior may be symptomatic of a more serious problem. The appropriate disciplinary actions necessary should be discussed with the school psychologist, and how it should be implemented must be carefully considered before it begins.

CHANGE OF PROGRAM.   A **change of program** involves examining the child's program and making adjustments to his or her schedule based on the presenting problem. This recommendation usually occurs when a student has been placed in a course that is not suited to his or her ability or needs. If a student is failing in an advanced class, then the student's program should be changed to include more modified classes.

CONSOLIDATION OF PROGRAM.   There are times when reducing a student's course load is necessary. **Consolidation of a program** involves taking the student's program and modifying it so that the workload is decreased. If a child is "drowning in school," then that child's available energy level may be extremely limited. In such cases, you may find that he or she is failing many courses. Temporarily consolidating or condensing the program allows for the possibility of salvaging some courses, because the student's available energy will not have to be spread so thin.

REFERRAL TO CHILD PROTECTIVE SERVICES.   Child Protective Services is a state agency designed to investigate cases of possible neglect and abuse of children. A **referral to Child Protective Services** (CPS) is mandated for all educators if there is a suspicion of abuse or neglect. The school official or staff does not have a choice as to referral if such a suspicion is present. Referrals to this service may result from physical, sexual, or emotional abuse and/or educational, environmental, or medical neglect.

INFORMAL ASSESSMENT TECHNIQUES.   As discussed in Chapter 3, other prereferral intervention strategies may be used in the form of various methods of informal assessment.

SCREENING.   If the CST feels the prereferral strategies are not working after a realistic period of time, team members may recommend a **screening** for a suspected disability. The source of this suspicion may emanate from the team, a staff member, or the parent. Keep in mind that the team does not have to diagnose a specific disability, but only suspect one in order to begin the referral for a more comprehensive assessment to a multidisciplinary team. This team (see Chapter 8) will administer a comprehensive evaluation conducted by several professionals to decrease the possibility of subjective and discriminatory assessment.

Informal Screening Tools.   Informal screening tools may include a variety of tests and procedures that can be sensitive enough to allow team members to determine the presence of a suspected disability. Other than the very obvious cases involving attempted suicide, neglect, abuse, and so on, which must be dealt with immediately, a child with a suspected disability is defined as a child who exhibits one or more of the following symptoms for more than 6 months:

- Serious inconsistencies in intellectual, emotional, academic, or social performance
- Inconsistency between ability and achievement and/or ability and classroom performance
- Impairment in one or more life functions, that is, socialization, academic performance, or adaptive behavior

To accomplish this screening, team members utilize

- Abbreviated intelligence tests
- Selected subtests or screening versions of individual achievement tests
- Informal reading inventories
- Checklists
- Observation scales
- Rating scales
- Prereferral data already discussed

If the screening determines the possibility of a suspected disability, then the CST must make a more formal referral to the district's multidisciplinary team for a comprehensive assessment. This process is discussed in Chapter 8.

CONCLUSION

Although all of these suggestions need not be tried before an evaluation is attempted, parents may be more willing to sign a release for evaluation if they see that other channels have been used and proven unsuccessful. The goal of prereferral procedures is to make sure that all avenues have been explored before the time is invested in doing a comprehensive assessment on a child. If a few modifications can be made to a child's school day that can alleviate the problem at hand, this will benefit all involved.

Vocabulary

Change of program: Examining the child's program and making schedule adjustments based on the presenting problem.

Classroom management techniques: Strategies created to help handle various problems and conflicts within a classroom.

Consolidation of a program: Taking the student's program and modifying it so that the workload is decreased.

Disciplinary action: A prereferral procedure whereby a child is placed in a structured boundary set because of inappropriate behavior.

Hearing test: A prereferral procedure used to determine whether an auditory problem is causing or contributing to a student's problems.

Help classes: Classes that provide a student with extra help in a given subject outside of the normal school day.

In-school counseling: Counseling, normally by the psychologist or social worker, designed to help the child deal with the issues that are currently problematic for him or her.

Medical exam: A prereferral procedure used to determine whether a medical condition is causing or contributing to a student's problems.

Parent interview: Meeting with the parent to discuss what motivates this child along with finding out any family information that may be contributing to the child's behavior in the classroom (e.g., recent separation, death of a loved one).

Prereferral strategies: Many school systems recommend or require that, before an individualized evaluation of a student is conducted for possible placement in special education, the teacher meet with an assistance team to discuss the nature of the problem and what possible modifications to instruction or the classroom might be made. These procedures are known as prereferral strategies.

Progress report: A synopsis of the child's work and behavior in the classroom sent home to the parents to keep them updated on the child's strengths and weaknesses over a period of time.

Referral to Child Protective Services: A state agency designed to investigate cases of possible neglect and abuse of children.

Remedial reading or math services: Academic programs within a school designed to help students with math or reading by going slower in the curriculum or placing them with a smaller number of students in the classroom for extra attention.

Screening: A prereferral strategy to determine whether a comprehensive assessment for special education is warranted.

Team meeting with teachers: A prereferral procedure whereby teachers who have worked with or who have ideas about the student come together to determine what helpful strategies can be implemented.

Vision test: A prereferral procedure used to determine whether a visual problem is causing or contributing to a student's problems.

THE MULTIDISCIPLINARY TEAM AND PARENTAL PARTICIPATION IN THE ASSESSMENT PROCESS

Key Terms

Academic history
Audiologist
Behavioral consultant
Classroom teacher
Developmental history
Educational diagnostician
Family history

Formal referral
Guidance counselor
Identifying data and family
  information
Occupational therapist
Parent intake
Parents (on the MDT)

Physical therapist
School nurse
School psychologist
School social worker
Social history
Special education teacher
Speech/language clinician

Chapter Objectives

This chapter focuses on the multidisciplinary team (MDT) and parental participation in the assessment process. After reading this chapter, you should be able to understand the following:

- Multidisciplinary team (MDT)
- Purpose of the MDT
- Membership of the MDT
- Formal referral for a suspected disability
- Contents of a referral to the MDT
- Initial referral to the MDT from the school staff
- Initial referral to the MDT from a parent/guardian
- Assessment plans, consent for evaluation
- Assessment options of the MDT
- Parental participation in the assessment process
- How to conduct parent intakes and interviews
- Parent intakes
- Confidentiality

PURPOSE OF THE MULTIDISCIPLINARY TEAM

As a result of the IDEA 2004 regulations, schools are moving toward a more global approach for the identification of students with suspected disabilities through the development of a district-based team. This team may be referred to as the multidisciplinary team (MDT), multifactor team (MFT), or school-based support team (SBST), depending on the state in which the student resides. Throughout this text, we refer to this team as the multidisciplinary team. This team usually comes into operation when the local school-based team (child study team) has conducted a screening and suspects a disability. Once that is determined, then the MDT takes over. This team is mandated by IDEA 2004 so that the child and parents are guaranteed that any comprehensive evaluation be conducted by different professionals to decrease the possibility of subjective and discriminatory assessment.

The role of the MDT is to work as a single unit in determining the possible cause, contributing behavioral factors, educational status, prognosis (outcome), and recommendations for a student with a suspected disability. The MDT's major objective is to bring together many disciplines and professional perspectives to help work on a case so that a single person is not required to determine and assimilate all of the factors that affect a particular child. The MDT is responsible for gathering all the necessary information on a child in order to determine the most effective and practical direction for his or her education. In many states, the MDT's findings are then reviewed by another committee (sometimes referred to as the *eligibility committee, IEP committee*, or *committee on special education*). Its role is to determine whether the findings of the MDT fall within the guidelines for classification of the student as having an exceptionality and requiring special education services (more on the process of eligibility in Chapter 18). In accomplishing this task, the team members employ several types of assessments and collect data from many sources.

To further comply with IDEA 2004, each local agency must ensure that

  a. Assessment materials and other evaluation materials are selected and administered so as not to be discriminatory on a racial or cultural basis.
  b. Assessment materials are provided and administered in the language and form most likely to yield accurate information on what the child knows and can do academically, developmentally, and functionally, unless it is not feasible to so provide or administer.
  c. Tests and other assessment materials have been validated for the specific purpose for which they are used.
  d. Tests and other assessment materials are administered by trained personnel in conformance with the instructions provided by the producer of the tests and other assessment materials, except that individually administered tests of intellectual or emotional functioning shall be administered by a credentialed school psychologist.
  e. Tests and other assessment materials are selected and administered to best ensure that a test administered to a pupil with impaired sensory, manual, or speaking skills produces test results that accurately reflect the pupil's aptitude, achievement level, or any other factors the test purports to measure and not the pupil's impaired sensory, manual, or speaking skills, unless those skills are the factors the test purports to measure.
  f. No single procedure is used as the sole criterion for determining an appropriate educational program for an individual with exceptional needs.
  g. The pupil is assessed in all areas related to the suspected disability including, where appropriate, health and development, vision, including low vision, hearing, motor abilities,

language function, general ability, academic performance, self-help, orientation and mobility skills, career and vocational abilities and interests, and social and emotional status. A developmental history is obtained, when appropriate. For pupils with residual vision, a low vision assessment shall be provided.

h. Persons knowledgeable of that disability shall conduct the assessment of a pupil, including the assessment of a pupil with a suspected low incidence disability. For instance, if the screening reveals a suspected learning disability then a learning disabilities specialist becomes part of the team. If the child is suspected of having a hearing impairment then an audiologist becomes a member of the team. Special attention shall be given to the unique educational needs, including, but not limited to, skills and the need for specialized services, materials, and equipment (IDEA 2004, sec. 614 et seq.).

MEMBERSHIP OF THE MULTIDISCIPLINARY TEAM

Although specific state regulations may differ on the membership of the MDT, the members are usually drawn from individuals and professionals within the school and community. Depending on the school in which you work, your role may be different from that of another professional with the same title in a different school (i.e., your roles and responsibilities as an educational evaluator in one school may be different from those of an evaluator in another school). Listed here are the general roles and responsibilities of members of a multidisciplinary team:

School psychologist: The role of the school psychologist on the MDT usually involves the administration of individual intelligence tests, projective tests, personality inventories, and the observation of the student in a variety of settings.

School nurse: The role of the school nurse is to review all medical records, screen for vision and hearing, consult with outside physicians, and make referrals to outside physicians, if necessary.

Classroom teacher: The classroom teacher's role is to work with the local school-based child study team to implement prereferral strategies, and plan and implement, along with the special education team, classroom strategies that create an appropriate working environment for the student.

School social worker: The social worker's role on the MDT is to gather and provide information concerning the family system. This may be accomplished through interviews, observations, conferences, and so forth.

Special education teacher: The roles of the special education teacher include consulting with parents and classroom teachers about prereferral recommendations, administering educational and perceptual tests, observing the student in a variety of settings, screening students with suspected disabilities, writing IEPs, including goals and objectives with the team (based on assessed needs), and recommending intervention strategies to teachers and parents.

Educational diagnostician: This professional administers a series of evaluations including norm-referenced and criterion-referenced tests, observes the student in a variety of settings, and makes educational recommendations that get applied to the IEP as goals and objectives.

Physical therapist: The physical therapist is called on to evaluate a child who may be experiencing problems in gross motor functioning, living and self-help skills, and vocational skills necessary for the student to be able to function in certain settings. This professional may be used to screen, evaluate, provide direct services, or consult with the teacher, parent, or school.

Behavioral consultant: A behavioral consultant works closely with the team in providing direct services or consultation on issues involving behavioral and classroom management techniques and programs.

Speech/language clinician: This professional is involved in screening for speech and language developmental problems, provides a full evaluation on a suspected language disability, provides direct services, and consults with staff and parents.

Audiologist: This professional is called on to evaluate a student's hearing for possible impairments and, as a result of the findings, may refer the student for medical consultation or treatment. The audiologist may also assist in helping students and parents obtain equipment (i.e., hearing aids) that may affect the child's ability to function in school.

Occupational therapist: The occupational therapist is called on to evaluate a child who may be experiencing problems in fine motor skills and living and self-help skills. This professional may be used to screen; evaluate; provide direct services; consult with the teacher, parent, or school; and assist in obtaining the appropriate assistive technology or equipment for the student.

Guidance counselor: This individual may be involved in providing aptitude test information, providing counseling services, working with the team on consolidating, changing, or developing a student's class schedule, and assisting the child study team in developing prereferral strategies.

Parents: The parent plays an extremely important role on the MDT in providing input for the IEP, working closely with members of the team, and carrying out, assisting, or initiating academic or management programs within the child's home (parents' roles will be discussed in more detail later in this chapter).

FORMAL REFERRAL FOR A SUSPECTED DISABILITY

Once the CST determines that a suspected disability may exist, a **formal referral** is made to the multidisciplinary team. A formal referral is nothing more than a form starting the special education process. A referral for evaluation and possible special education services is initiated by a written request. However, you should understand that people other than the CST have the right under due process to initiate a formal referral for a child with a suspected disability. Depending on state regulations, these could include

- The child's parent, advocate, person in parental relationship, or legal guardian
- A classroom teacher
- Any professional staff member of the public or private school district
- A judicial officer—a representative of the court
- A student on his or her own behalf if he or she is 18 years of age or older or an *emancipated minor* (a person under the age of 18 who has been given certain adult rights by the court)

- The chief school officer of the state or his or her designee responsible for the welfare, education, or health of children

The Contents of a Referral to the MDT

This signed formal referral is usually sent to the MDT so that the team can begin the process of formal assessment. At the same time, the referral is sent to the chairperson of the eligibility committee (discussed in Chapter 19) indicating that a child with a suspected disability will be reviewed by the committee in the near future. This referral should be in written form and dated. This makes it official and gives a start date because time lines are involved. A referral from the CST should include a great deal of information to assist the MDT in its assessment. Further documentation as to why a possible disability exists, descriptions of attempts to remediate the child's behaviors (prereferral strategies), or performance prior to the referral should all be included. All of these are important, especially the attempts that have been made prior to the referral. Remember, the district should try to keep the child in the mainstream, and the documentation it provides at this step in the process should ensure that it has done everything possible before beginning the referral process (prereferral options previously discussed in Chapter 7).

Referrals from the CST for a formal assessment are forwarded to the MDT. If the referral is not from the parents, the district must inform the parents in writing immediately that their child has been referred for assessment of a suspected disability. The referral states that the child may have a disability that adversely affects educational performance. An important point to remember is that a referral to the MDT does not necessarily mean that the child has a disability. It signals that the child is having learning and/or behavioral difficulties, and that there is a concern that the problem may be due to a disability.

Initial Referral to the MDT from the School Staff

As previously stated, once the CST has determined that a disability may exist, the team must alert the chairperson of the MDT that a child with a suspected disability is being referred for review. This, in all actuality, begins the special education process. At this time, the team may fill out a form like the one in Figure 8.1.

Initial Referral to the MDT from a Parent/Guardian

An initial referral to the MDT from the school staff alerts the chairperson of the MDT that the local school has made every attempt to resolve the student's difficulties prior to the formal referral. The form also informs the chairperson that the parental rights have been followed. In other cases, a student's parent or guardian may initiate a referral to the MDT for suspicion of a disability under special education laws or Section 504 of the Rehabilitation Act. A fully completed referral form and any relevant information is sent to the appropriate special education administrator. Usually, on the receipt of the parent's referral, the chairperson of the MDT will send to the parent/guardian an assessment plan (discussed next) and the parent's due process rights statement. The building principal is also notified of the referral. When the possibility of a suspected disability of a child is brought to the school's attention *by the parent,* then the form presented in Figure 8.2 is filled out and forwarded.

INITIAL REFERRAL TO THE MDT FROM THE SCHOOL STAFF

To: Chairperson of the MDT

From: Bill Wethers   **School:** Harrison   **Date:** 5/15/11

Name/Title: Chairperson of the Child Study Team

The following student is being referred to the MDT for suspicion of a disability:

Student Name: Rosa Carlarzo   **Sex:** F   **Grade:** 5

Ethnicity: Hispanic

Parent/Guardian Name: Livia/Carlos

Address: 12 High Court

City: Birchwood Glen   **State:** NY   **Zip:** 15789

Telephone: (914) 555-9867   **Date of Birth:** 3/2/01

Current Program Placement: Regular mainstream

Teacher (Elem): Mrs. Buglia

Reasons for Referral: Describe the specific reason and/or needs that indicate the suspicion of a disability. Specify reason why referral is considered appropriate and necessary.

Rosa is being referred for a formal assessment as the result of a suspected learning disability. The school has attempted a variety of prereferral strategies but has been unable to change Rosa's level of impaired performance. Rosa exhibits severe problems in processing information, retaining information, and expressing her ideas on paper. Although she is a bright girl, and articulates appropriately, her written expression is well below average. Rosa also needs a great deal of attention, encouragement, and monitoring in the classroom. She is not a self-starter and tends to avoid academic tasks.

Describe recent attempts to remediate the pupil's performance prior to referral, including regular education interventions such as remedial reading and math, teaching modifications, behavior modifications, speech improvement, parent conferences, and the like and the results of those interventions.

The referral is considered necessary at this time because Rosa continues to do poorly in school despite classroom modifications, parent training and conferences, portfolio assessment, observation, remedial reading and math intervention, and changes in teaching strategies and management. The results of these intervention strategies have been unsuccessful and have even added to Rosa's sense of frustration and lack of confidence.

Do you have a signed Parent Assessment Plan? yes _X_ **no** _____ **(If yes, send copy attached.)**

Is there an attendance problem? yes _X_ **no** _____

Language spoken at home? English

Did student repeat a grade? yes _____ **no** _X_ **If yes, when?** _____

Is an interpreter needed? yes _____ **no** _X_ **Deaf:** _____

Is a bilingual assessment needed? yes _____ **no** _X_ **If yes, what language?** _____

Is student eligible to receive ESL (English as a Second Language) services?

yes _____ **no** _X_

If yes, how many years receiving ESL services? _NA_ If yes, determine how student's educational, cultural, and experiential background were considered to determine if these factors are contributing to the student's learning or behavior problems.

TEST SCORES WITHIN LAST YEAR

(e.g., Standardized Achievement, Regents Competency, etc.)

TEST NAME	AREA MEASURED	PERCENTILE
1. Wechsler Ind. Achievement Test Screening	Basic Reading	22
2. Wechsler Ind. Achievement Test Screening	Reading Comp.	18
3. Wechsler Ind. Achievement Test Screening	Numerical Operations	12
4. Wechsler Ind. Achievement Test Screening	Oral Expression	67
5. Wechsler Ind. Achievement Test Screening	Written Expression	11

Has school staff informed parent/guardian of referral to MDT?

yes _X_ no _____ By whom? School psychologist

What was the reaction of the parent/guardian to the referral? Positive

To Be Completed by School Nurse—Medical Report Summary

Any medication? yes _____ no _X_ If yes, specify: _____

Health Problems? yes _____ no _X_ If yes, specify: _____

Scoliosis screening: Positive _____ Negative _X_

Date of Last Physical: 8/10 Vision results: Normal

Hearing results: Normal

Relevant medical information: None

Nurse/teacher signature: _____

Principal's signature: _____

To Be Completed by the Appropriate Administrator

Date received: _____ Signature: _____

Chairperson: _____

Date notice and consent sent to parent/guardian: _____

Parent consent for initial evaluation received: _____

Date agreement to withdraw referral received: _____

Projected eligibility meeting date: _____

If eligible, projected date of implementation of services: _____

Projected eligibility board of education meeting date: _____

FIGURE 8.1 Initial Referral to the MDT from the School Staff

INITIAL REFERRAL TO THE MDT FROM A PARENT/GUARDIAN

To: Chairperson of the MDT

Re: Brian Leader   **Date of Birth:** 7/12/98

I am writing to refer my child Brian, age 13, for consideration of an educational disability under special education laws and/or under Section 504 of the Vocational Rehabilitation Act (mental or physical impairment that substantially limits one of life's functions). I am concerned about my child's educational difficulties in the following areas: severe and historic reading and writing difficulties.

Parent Name/Signature: _____

Address: 20 Carbondale Rd
            Beverly Hills, CA 90210

Telephone No: (314) 555-0507

Date of Referral: 11/9/11

School: Wilson Middle School   **Grade:** 8

Please attach any relevant evaluations or documents or information that support the referral.

Date received by MDT chairperson: _____

FIGURE 8.2   Initial Referral to the MDT from a Parent/Guardian

Important Point: If a release for testing (assessment plan) is not secured at a separate meeting, the chairperson of the MDT will mail one to the parent along with the letter indicating that a referral has been made. However, no formal evaluations may begin until the district has received signed permission from the parent or guardian.

ASSESSMENT PLANS—CONSENT FOR EVALUATION

Prior to any assessment, the MDT must secure an agreement by the parent to allow the members of the team to evaluate the child. This release is part of the assessment plan and should have the following characteristics:

- Use language easily understood by the general public.
- Be provided in the primary language of the parent or other mode of communication used by the parent, unless to do so is clearly not feasible.
- Explain the types of assessments to be conducted.
- State that no individualized education program (IEP) will result from the assessment without the consent of the parent.
- State that no assessment shall be conducted unless the written consent of the parent is obtained prior to the assessment. The parent shall have at least 15 days (may vary from state to state) from the receipt of the proposed assessment plan to arrive at a decision. Assessment may begin immediately upon receipt of the consent.

- Note in the copy of the notice of parent rights the right to record electronically the proceedings of the eligibility committee meetings.
- Provide that the assessment shall be conducted by persons competent to perform the assessment, as determined by the school district, county office, or special education local plan area.
- Provide that any psychological assessment of pupils must be conducted by a qualified school psychologist.
- Provide that any health assessment of pupils shall be conducted only by a credentialed school nurse or physician who is trained and prepared to assess cultural and ethnic factors appropriate to the pupil being assessed.

ASSESSMENT OPTIONS OF THE MULTIDISCIPLINARY TEAM

Only when the parents have been informed of their rights, a release has been obtained, and the assessment plan has been signed can assessment begin. The MDT has several evaluation options from which to choose. The MDT most often assesses a child with a suspected disability using the evaluations discussed in the following sections.

Academic Achievement Evaluation

An academic achievement evaluation (see Chapter 9) is frequently recommended when a child's academic skill levels (reading, writing, math, and spelling) are unknown or inconsistent. The evaluation will determine strengths and weaknesses in the child's academic performance.

THE PRIMARY OBJECTIVES OF AN ACADEMIC ACHIEVEMENT EVALUATION

- Help determine the child's stronger and weaker academic skill areas. The evaluation may give useful information when making practical recommendations to teachers about academic expectations, areas in need of remediation, and how to best present information to assist the child's ability to learn.
- Help the teacher gear the materials to the learning capacity of the individual child. A child reading 2 years below grade level may require modified textbooks or greater explanations prior to a lesson.
- Develop a learning profile that can help the classroom teacher understand the best way to present information to the child and therefore increase the child's chances of success.
- Help determine whether the child's academic skills are suitable for a regular class or so severe that a more restrictive educational setting is required—that is, an educational setting or situation best suited to the present needs of the student other than a full-time regular class placement (resource room, self-contained class, special school, etc.).
- Use an achievement battery that covers enough skill areas to make an adequate diagnosis of academic strengths and weaknesses.

SOME SYMPTOMS THAT MIGHT SUGGEST THE RECOMMENDATION
FOR SUCH AN EVALUATION

- Consistently low test scores on group achievement tests
- Indications of delayed processing when faced with academic skills
- Labored handwriting after grade 3
- Poor word recall

- Poor decoding (word attack) skills
- Discrepancy between achievement and ability
- Consistently low achievement despite remediation

In most cases of a suspected disability, the academic achievement evaluation is always a part of the formal evaluation.

Intellectual and Psychological Evaluation

Intellectual and psychological evaluations are appropriate when the child's intellectual ability is unknown or when there is a question about his or her inability to learn (see Chapter 9 and Chapter 10). It is useful when the CST suspects a potential learning, emotional, or intellectual problem. The psychological evaluation can rule out or rule in emotionality as a primary cause of a child's problem. Ruling this factor out is necessary before a diagnosis of learning disabled (LD) can be made.

OBJECTIVES OF A PSYCHOLOGICAL EVALUATION

- Determine the child's present overall levels of intellectual ability
- Determine the child's present verbal intellectual ability
- Determine the child's non-language intellectual ability
- Explore indications of greater potential
- Find possible patterns involving learning style—that is, verbal comprehension, concentration, and the like
- Ascertain possible influences of tension and anxiety on testing results
- Determine the child's intellectual ability to deal with present grade-level academic demands
- Explore the influence of intellectual ability as a contributing factor to a child's past and present school difficulties—that is, limited intellectual ability found in retardation

SOME SYMPTOMS THAT MIGHT SIGNAL THE NEED FOR SUCH AN EVALUATION

- High levels of tension and anxiety exhibited in behavior
- Aggressive behavior
- Lack of motivation or indications of low energy levels
- Patterns of denial
- Oppositional behavior
- Despondency
- Inconsistent academic performance, ranging from very low to very high
- History of inappropriate judgment
- Lack of impulse control
- Extreme and consistent attention-seeking behavior
- Pattern of provocative behavior

As with the academic assessment, the psychological evaluation is a normal part of a referral for a suspected disability.

Perceptual Evaluation

A perceptual evaluation (see Chapter 12) is suggested when the team suspects discrepancies in the child's ability to receive and process information. This assessment may focus on a number of perceptual areas including:

- **Auditory modality:** The delivery of information through sound
- **Visual modality:** The delivery of information through sight
- **Tactile modality:** The delivery of information through touch
- **Kinesthetic modality:** The delivery of information through movement
- **Reception:** The initial receiving of information
- **Perception:** The initial organization of information
- **Association or organization:** Relating new information to other information and giving meaning to the information received
- **Memory:** The storage or retrieval process that facilitates the associational process to give meaning to information or help in relating new concepts to other information that might have already been learned
- **Expression:** The output of information through vocal, motor, or written responses

THE PRIMARY OBJECTIVES OF THE PERCEPTUAL ASSESSMENT

- Help determine the child's stronger and weaker modality for learning. Some children are visual learners, some are auditory, and some learn well through any form of input. However, if a child is a strong visual learner in a class in which the teacher relies on auditory lectures, then it is possible that his or her ability to process information may be hampered. The evaluation may give useful information for making practical recommendations to teachers about how to best present information to assist the child's ability to learn.
- Help determine a child's stronger and weaker process areas. A child having problems in memory and expression will very quickly fall behind the rest of his or her class. The longer these processing difficulties continue, the greater the chance for development of secondary emotional problems (emotional problems resulting from continued frustration with the ability to learn).
- Develop a learning profile that can help the classroom teacher understand the best way to present information to the child, thereby increasing the child's chances of success.
- Help determine whether the child's learning process deficits are suitable for a regular class or so severe that a more restrictive educational setting is required—that is, an educational setting or situation best suited to the present needs of the student other than a full-time regular class placement (resource room, self-contained class, special school).

Oral Language Evaluation

This recommendation (see Chapter 13) usually occurs when the child is experiencing significant delays in speech or language development, problems in articulation, or problems in receptive or expressive language.

SOME SYMPTOMS THAT MIGHT WARRANT SUCH AN EVALUATION

- Difficulty pronouncing words through grade 3
- Immature or delayed speech patterns
- Difficulty labeling thoughts or objects
- Difficulty putting thoughts into words

Occupational Therapy Evaluation

This evaluation (see Chapter 15) may be considered by the team when the child is exhibiting problems involving fine motor upper-body functions. Examples of these would include abnormal movement patterns, sensory problems (sensitive to sound, visual changes, etc.), hardship with daily living activities, organizational problems, attention span difficulties, equipment analysis, and interpersonal problems.

Physical Therapy Evaluation

When the child is exhibiting problems with lower body and gross motor areas, physical therapy evaluation (see Chapter 15) may be considered. Examples of these might be range of motion difficulties; architectural barrier problems; problems in posture, gait, and endurance; and joint abnormalities.

PARENTAL PARTICIPATION IN THE ASSESSMENT PROCESS

Once the CST has made a formal referral for assessment to the MDT for a child with a suspected disability, the parents need to be called in to provide pertinent background information that will assist in the assessment process. The participation of the parents is crucial to this process.

Although designing, conducting, interpreting, and paying for the assessment are the school system's responsibilities, parents have an important part to play before, during, and after the evaluation. There is a range of ways that parents may involve themselves in the assessment of their child. The extent of their involvement, however, is a personal decision and will vary from family to family.

Waterman (1994) lists parental options, responsibilities, and expectations prior to an assessment for a suspected disability:

- Parents may initiate the assessment process by requesting that the school system evaluate their child for the presence of a disability and the need for special education.
- Parents must be notified by the school, and give their consent, before any initial evaluation of the child may be conducted.
- Parents may wish to talk with the professional responsible for conducting the evaluation to find out what the evaluation will involve.
- Parents may find it very useful to become informed about assessment issues in general and any specific issues relevant to their child (e.g., assessment of minority children, use of specific tests or assessment techniques with a specific disability).
- Parents should advocate for a comprehensive evaluation of their child—one that investigates all skill areas apparently affected by the suspected disability and that uses multiple means of collecting information (e.g., observations, interviews, alternative approaches).
- Parents may suggest specific questions to the MDT they would like to see addressed through the assessment.
- Parents should inform the MDT of any accommodations the child will need (e.g., removing time limits from tests, conducting interviews/testing in the child's native language, adapting testing environment to child's specific physical and other needs).
- Parents should inform the MDT if they themselves need an interpreter or other accommodations during any of their discussions with the school.
- Parents may prepare their child for the assessment process, explaining what will happen and, where necessary, reducing the child's anxiety. It may help the child to know that he or she will not be receiving a "grade" on the tests.

- Parents need to share with the MDT their insights into the child's background (developmental, medical, and academic) and past and present school performance.
- Parents may wish to share with the MDT any prior school records, reports, tests, or evaluation information available on their child.
- Parents may need to share information about cultural differences that can illuminate the MDT's understanding of the student.
- Parents need to make every effort to attend interviews the MDT may set up with them and provide information about their child.

How to Conduct Parent Intakes and Interviews

There may be times when a member of the MDT is called on to do a **parent intake**, a gathering of pertinent information from a parent. A thorough parent intake is a crucial part of the assessment process. The parents can offer information on a child that is not seen by teachers or other staff members and may have profound effects on the outcome of the assessment. This may involve interviewing the parent to obtain a complete **Family history**. In some cases, this part of the assessment process may be difficult to obtain because of a number of variables—parents' work restrictions, inability to obtain child care for younger siblings, resistance, or apathy.

In many schools, the psychologist or social worker will normally meet with the parents to collect this information. However, it is important that all members of the MDT understand the process in case anyone is asked to do the interview. When the interview is arranged, there are several things to recognize and consider before a parent meeting.

WHEN CONDUCTING A PARENT INTAKE, YOU SHOULD TRY TO DO THE FOLLOWING:

- Help the parent(s) feel comfortable and at ease by setting up a receptive environment.
- If possible, hold meetings in a pleasant setting, around a table rather than behind a desk. An effort to ease tension should be made, such as offering simple refreshments or encouraging parents to take brief notes so they feel more in control of your information.
- Never view parents as adversaries even if they are angry or hostile. Any anger or hostility that the parents may exhibit could be a defense because they may not be aware of what the evaluator will be asking or because they may have experienced negative school meetings over the years. Because this may be an opportunity for parents to "vent," evaluators should listen and strive to understand their concerns without being defensive.
- Inform parents every step of the way as to the purpose of meetings and the steps involved in the assessment process. Parents need to be reassured that no recommendation will be made or implemented without their input and permission.
- Inform parents of the types, names, and purposes of the evaluation instruments chosen by the MDT. Parents need to be reassured that the evaluation is looking for a way to help the child.

Reassure parents about the confidentiality of information gathered about their child. They should know which individuals on the team will be seeing the information and the purpose for their review of the facts. Evaluators should also make every effort to make parents feel free to call with any questions or concerns they may have.

Goals of a Parent Intake

A parent intake should be done with sensitivity and diplomacy. Keep in mind that although some questions may not be of concern to most parents, they may be perceived as intrusive by others.

The questions should be specific enough to help in the diagnosis of the problem, but not so specific as to place the parent in a vulnerable and defensive position. There are four main areas usually covered in a parent intake:

1. **Identifying data and family information:** Confirmation of names, addresses, phone numbers, and dates of birth; siblings' names, ages, and dates of birth; parents' occupations; other adults residing within the home; marital status of parents; and so on.
2. **Developmental history:** Length of delivery; type of delivery; complications if any; approximate ages of critical stages, that is, walking and talking; hospital stays; illnesses other than normal ones; sleeping habits; eating habits; high fevers; last eye exam; last hearing exam; falls or injuries; traumatic experiences; medications; and any prior developmental testing.
3. **Academic history:** Number of schools attended, types of schools attended, adjustment to kindergarten, best school year, worst school year, best subject, worst subject, prior teacher reports, prior teacher comments, and homework behavior.
4. **Social history:** The child's groups or organizations; social behavior in a group situation; hobbies, areas of interest, circle of friends, sports activities. Shown in Figure 8.3 is an example of a parent intake completed by the school social worker. Here, the intake was done with the mother of the child, Mrs. Bali Shah.

PARENT INTAKE FORM
Identifying Data

Name of Student: Ravi Muhas   **Date of Intake:** 4-10-11

Address: 12 Conner Street, South Hills, NY 11223

Phone: (631) 555-7863   **Date of Birth:** 3/4/02   **Age:** 9-1

Siblings: Brothers: (names and ages) Mohammed age 15

Sisters: (names and ages) Sari age 4

Mother's name: Bali   **Father's name:** Moshi

Mother's occupation: Medical technician

Father's occupation: Accountant

Referred by: Teacher   **Grade:** 4   **School:** Holland Avenue

Developmental History

Length of pregnancy: Full term   **Type of delivery:** Forceps

Complications: Apgar score 7, jaundice at birth

Long hospital stays: None

Falls or injuries: None

Allergies: Early food allergies, none recently

Medication: None at present

Early milestones (i.e., walking, talking, toilet training):
According to parent, Ravi was late in walking and talking in comparison to brother. He was toilet trained at three years of age. Parent added that he seemed to be slower than usual in learning basic concepts.

Traumatic experiences: None

Previous psychological evaluations or treatment (please explain reasons and dates):
None. However, parent indicated that it was suggested by first-grade teacher but the teacher never followed through.

Previous psychiatric hospitalizations: None

Sleep disturbances: Trouble falling asleep; somnambulism (sleepwalking) at age five but lasted only a few weeks; talks a great deal in his sleep lately

Eating disturbances: Picky eater, likes sweets

Last vision and hearing exams and results: Last eye test in school indicated 20/30 vision. Last hearing test in school was inconclusive. Parent has not followed through on nurse's request for an outside evaluation.

Exooooively high fovoro: No

Childhood illnesses: Normal ones

Academic History

Nursery school experience: Ravi had difficulty adjusting to nursery school. The teacher considered him very immature and his skills were well below those of his peers. He struggled through the year.

Kindergarten experience (adjustment, comments, etc.):   Ravi's difficulties increased. According to the parent, he had problems with reading and social difficulties. His gross- and fine-motor skills were immature.

First grade through sixth grade (teacher's comments, traumatic experiences, strength areas, comments, etc.):   According to past teachers, Ravi struggled through the early elementary school years. He was nice and polite and at times tried hard. But in the later grades (2 and 3), his behavior and academics began to falter. Teachers always considered referral but felt he might grow out of it.

Subjects that presented the most difficulty: Reading, math, spelling

Subjects that were the least difficult: Science

Most recent report card grades (if applicable):   Ravi has received mostly NEEDS TO IMPROVE on his report card.

Social History

Groups or organizations: Tried Boy Scouts but dropped out. Started Little League but became frustrated.

Social involvement as perceived by parent: Inconsistent. He does not seem to reach out to kids, and lately he spends a great deal of time alone.

Hobbies or interests: Baseball cards, science

FIGURE 8.3   Example of a Parent Intake Form

CONFIDENTIALITY

Information about the child collected through assessment automatically becomes a part of a child's school records. The school district should establish policies regarding confidentiality of information contained in the school record, such as informing the parent and the child (above age 18) of their right to privacy, who has access to the information, and their right to challenge those records should they be inaccurate, misleading, or otherwise inappropriate. To communicate this information to the parent, handouts describing the district's policy on confidentiality of school records are usually given out on the day of the parent intake.

Because professionals conducting the evaluation are involved in collecting confidential information about a child's health status and educational development, it is very important that verbal as well as written accounts of the child's performance be held in the strictest confidence. Personnel involved in the evaluation should treat their own impressions and concerns about the children they see in a confidential manner and should refrain from talking about children and their performance with people not directly involved with conducting the evaluation. If parents ask how their child is doing during the evaluation, explain that the screening results are meaningful only after all the testing has been completed and their child's performance in all areas is recorded. You should also inform them at this time that they are entitled to receive a complete typed report from the evaluation personnel. The person in charge of evaluation may choose to designate certain persons responsible for answering specific questions about the evaluation instruments, children's responses, and reports.

Conclusion

The MDT plays a critical role in the assessment of a child with a suspected disability. An effective MDT works as an interdisciplinary team to make many of the most important decisions for a child and his or her possible future in special education. By working as a professional team, the members of the MDT have the opportunity to help numerous children. An efficient MDT gathers much data and takes significant time to analyze each child's potential problems. In the end, its recommendations may be the most important ones for children who are in need of services.

It is very important to remember that referring a child for a suspected disability could have tremendous impact on his or her life. Because this is a formal referral for special education, it has legal implications, and therefore, it is extremely important that the MDT follow all procedures, complete all necessary forms, and make sure that it complies with the specific time limits required by the state in which the child resides.

Parents have many rights during the assessment process. Regardless of race, creed, color, socioeconomic status, and so on, all parents are afforded the same legal rights and protections under federal law. The differences arise in the parents' exercising of their rights. Some parents will be heavily involved in their child's assessment for a suspected disability, whereas others will show little, if any, interest—only signing the release form and never participating or attending any optional sessions for them. Parents need to be aware of their rights. As a special educator, there are many ways to make parents comfortable when you meet with them. Remember, most parents are scared and confused about the entire process. Normally, all they want is for their child to be evaluated so that success, both in and out of school, becomes a future possibility.

Once written consent of the parent or legal guardian is given for assessment, the MDT moves to the evaluation phase of the assessment process. The next several chapters address the various evaluation instruments available to the MDT in the formal evaluation of a child with a suspected disability.

Vocabulary

Academic history: A section of the parent intake form that asks about number of schools attended, types of schools attended, adjustment to kindergarten, best school years, worst school year, best subject, worst subject, prior teacher reports, prior teacher comments, and homework behavior.

Audiologist: This professional will be called on to evaluate a student's hearing for possible impairments, and as a result of the findings, may refer the student for medical consultation or treatment. The audiologist may also assist in helping students and parents obtain equipment—that is, hearing aids that may improve the child's ability to function in school.

Behavioral consultant: A behavioral consultant works closely with the team in providing direct services or consultation on issues involving behavioral and classroom management techniques and programs.

Classroom teacher: The member of the MDT who works with the CST to implement prereferral strategies and plans and implements any classroom techniques to help the student.

Developmental history: A section of the parent intake form that asks about length of delivery, type of delivery, complications if any, approximate ages of critical stages (i.e., walking, talking), hospital stays, illnesses other than normal last eye exam, last hearing exam, falls or injuries, traumatic experiences, medications, and any prior testing.

Educational diagnostician: Administers a series of evaluations including norm-referenced and criterion-referenced tests, observes the student in a variety of settings, and makes educational recommendations that get applied to the IEP as goals and objectives.

Family history: A description of the family life situation over time.

Formal referral: Once the CST determines that a suspected disability may exist, a formal referral is made. It is nothing more than a form starting the special education process.

Guidance counselor: This individual may be involved in providing aptitude test information; providing counseling services; working with the team on consolidating, changing, or developing a student's class schedule; and assisting the child study team in developing prereferral strategies.

Identifying data and family information: A section of the parent intake form that asks about confirmation of names, addresses, phone numbers, dates of birth; siblings' names, ages, and dates of birth; parents' occupations; other adults residing within the home; marital status of parents.

Occupational therapist: The occupational therapist is called on to evaluate a child who may be experiencing problems in fine motor skills and living and self-help skills. This professional may be used to screen; evaluate; provide direct services; consult with the teacher, parent, or school; and assist in obtaining the appropriate assistive technology or equipment for the student.

Parent intake: A gathering of pertinent information from a parent.

Parents (on the MDT):   The parent plays an extremely important role on the MDT in providing input for the IEP, working closely with other members of the team, and carrying out, assisting, or initiating academic or management programs within the child's home.

Physical therapist: The physical therapist is called on to evaluate a child who may be experiencing problems in gross motor functioning, living and self-help skills, and vocational skills necessary for the student to be able to function in certain settings. This professional may be used to screen, evaluate, provide direct services, or consult with the teacher, parent, or school.

School nurse: The member of the MDT who reviews all medical records, screens for vision and hearing, and handles other medical concerns.

9 ASSESSMENT OF ACADEMIC ACHIEVEMENT

Key Terms

Achievement tests
Affective comprehension
Applications
Arithmetic
Composition
Content
Critical comprehension
Disregard of punctuation
Handwriting
Hesitation
Incorrect algorithm

Incorrect number fact
Incorrect operation
Inferential comprehension
Insertion
Inversion
Lexical comprehension
Listening comprehension
Literal comprehension
Manuscript
Mathematics
Miscue

Omissions
Operations
Qualitative miscues
Quantitative miscues
Random error
Spelling
Substitution
Word attack skills
Word recognition tests

Chapter Objectives

This chapter examines all of the various issues surrounding assessment of academic achievement in special education. It focuses on what to expect on tests of reading, spelling, writing, mathematics, and on comprehensive achievement tests available to special educators today. After reading this chapter, you should be able to do the following:

▪ Understand the purpose of achievement tests

▪ Understand why individually administered achievement tests are preferable to group achievement tests

▪ Discuss oral reading and miscues associated with it

▪ Understand the different types of reading comprehension

▪ Understand word recognition and word attack skills

▪ Thoroughly evaluate the various reading assessment measures

▪ Understand written composition and the tests associated with it

▪ Differentiate between mathematics and arithmetic

▪ Identify and thoroughly evaluate the various arithmetic tests

▪ Identify and thoroughly evaluate tests that measure spelling ability

▪ Identify and thoroughly evaluate the various comprehensive achievement tests

ACHIEVEMENT TESTS

One of the most important parts of assessment in the special education process is to assess academic achievement. **Achievement tests** are tests designed to assess the academic progress of a student. A student's academic achievement skills are reviewed to determine how well he or she is performing in core skill areas such as reading, writing, mathematics, and spelling. The information obtained from the academic battery of tests is important for both the planning and the evaluation of instruction. It is important to remember that individual achievement tests (rather than group-administered tests) are preferred for assessment of school performance in special education. When doing an evaluation for identification and/or placement in special education, achievement tests always will be individually administered. Individually administered achievement tests are used because they

- Are designed to assess children at all ages and grade levels
- Can assess the most basic skills of spelling, math, and reading
- Allow the examiner to observe a child's test-taking strategies
- Can focus on a specific area of concern
- Can be given in oral, written, or gestural format
- Allow the examiner to observe the child's behavior in a variety of situations

READING

Reading provides a fundamental way for individuals to exchange information. It is also a means by which much of the information presented in school is learned. As a result, reading is the academic area most often associated with academic failure. Reading is a complex process that requires numerous skills for its mastery. Consequently, identifying the skills that lead to success in reading is extremely important (Pierangelo & Giuliani, 2009).

Numerous reading tests are available for assessing a student's ability to read. Choosing which test to use depends on what area needs to be assessed. Different reading tests measure different reading subskills: oral reading, reading comprehension, word attack skills, and word recognition.

Oral Reading

A number of tests or parts of tests are designed to assess the accuracy and fluency of a student's ability to read aloud. According to Salvia and Ysseldyke (2007), different oral reading tests record different behaviors as errors or miscues in oral reading. Common errors seen on oral reading tests include, but are not limited to, the following:

- **Omissions:** The student skips individual words or groups of words.
- **Insertion:** The student inserts one or more words into the sentence being orally read.
- **Substitution:** The student replaces one or more words in the passage by one or more meaningful words.
- **Gross mispronunciation of a word:** The student's pronunciation of a word bears little resemblance to the proper pronunciation.
- **Hesitation:** The student hesitates for two or more seconds before pronouncing a word.
- **Inversion:** The student changes the order of words appearing in a sentence.
- **Disregard of punctuation:** The student fails to observe punctuation; for example, may not pause for a comma, stop for a period, or indicate a vocal inflection, a question mark, or an exclamation point.

ANALYZING ORAL READING MISCUES. An oral reading error is often referred to as a **miscue.** A miscue is the difference between what a reader states is on a page and what is actually on the page. According to Vacca, Vacca, and Grove (1986), differences between what the reader says and what is printed on the page are not the result of random errors. Instead, these differences are "cued" by the thought and language of the reader, who is attempting to construct what the author is saying. Analysis of miscues can be of two types:

1. **Quantitative miscues:** With this type of miscue analysis, the evaluator counts the number of reading errors made by the student.
2. **Qualitative miscues:** With this type of miscue analysis, the focus is on the quality of the error rather than the number of different mistakes. It is not based on the problems related to word identification, but rather on the differences between the miscues and the words on the pages. Consequently, some miscues are more significant than others.

According to John (1985), a miscue is *significant* if it affects meaning. Miscues are generally significant when

1. The meaning of the sentence or passages is significantly changed or altered, and the student does not correct the miscue.
2. A nonword is used in place of the word in the passage.
3. Only a partial word is substituted for the word or phrase in the passage.
4. A word is pronounced for the student.

Miscues are generally *not significant* when

5. The meaning of the sentence or passage undergoes no change or only minimal change.
6. They are self-corrected by the student.
7. They are acceptable in the student's dialect.
8. They are later read correctly in the same passage.

Through miscue analysis, teachers can determine the extent to which the reader uses and coordinates graphic, sound, syntactic, and semantic information from the text. According to Goodman and Burke (1972), to analyze miscues you should ask at least four crucial questions:

- **Does the miscue change meaning?** If it does not, then it is semantically acceptable within the context of the sentence or passage.
- **Does the miscue sound like language?** If it does, then it is grammatically acceptable within the context. Miscues are grammatically acceptable if they sound like language and serve as the same parts of speech as the text words.
- **Do the miscue and the text word look and sound alike?** Substitution and mispronunciation miscues should be analyzed to determine how similar they are in approximating the graphic and pronunciation features of the text words.
- **Was an attempt made to self-correct the miscue?** Self-corrections are revealing because they demonstrate that the reader is attending to meaning and is aware that the initial miscuing did not make sense.

Reading Comprehension

Reading comprehension assesses a student's ability to understand what he or she is reading. Many children can read, yet do not understand what they have read. Therefore, when doing a reading assessment, it is always necessary to assess not only decoding but also the ability to understand what is being decoded. Diagnostic reading tests often assess six kinds of reading comprehension skills. According to Salvia and Ysseldyke (2007), these are:

1. **Literal comprehension:** The student reads the paragraph or story and is then asked .questions based on it.
2. **Inferential comprehension:** The student reads a paragraph or story and must interpret what has been read.
3. **Listening comprehension:** The student is read a paragraph or story by the examiner and is then asked questions about what the examiner has read.
4. **Critical comprehension:** The student reads a paragraph or story and then analyzes, evaluates, or makes judgments about what he or she has read.
5. **Affective comprehension:** The student reads a paragraph or story, and the examiner evaluates his or her emotional responses to the text.
6. **Lexical comprehension:** The student reads a paragraph or story, and the examiner assesses his or her knowledge of vocabulary words.

When evaluating the reading behavior of a child on reading comprehension subtests, it is important for the evaluator to ask the following questions:

- Does the student *guess* at answers to the questions presented?
- Does the student *show unwillingness to read* or make attempts at reading?
- Does the student *skip* unknown words?
- Does the student *disregard* punctuation?
- Does the student exhibit *inattention* to the story line?
- Does the student *drop the tone of his or her voice* at the end of sentences?
- Does the student *display problems with sounding out* word parts and blends?
- Does the student *exhibit a negative attitude* toward reading?
- Does the student *express difficulty attacking* unknown words?

Word Recognition Skills

The purpose of **word recognition tests** are to explore the student's ability with respect to sight vocabulary. According to Salvia and Ysseldyke (2007),

> A student learns the correct pronunciation of letters and words through a variety of experiences. The more exposure a student has to specific words and the more familiar those words become, the more readily he or she recognizes those words and is able to pronounce them correctly (p. 419).

Word recognition subtests form a major part of most diagnostic reading tests. Students who recognize many words are said to have good sight vocabularies or good word recognition skills.

Word Attack Skills

When assessing the reading abilities of the student, evaluators will often examine the word attack–word analysis skills of the child. **Word attack skills** are those used to derive meaning and/or pronunciation of a word through context clues, structural analysis, or phonics. In order to assess the word attack skills of the student, the examiner normally reads a word to the student who must then identify the consonant, vowel, consonant cluster, or digraph that has the same sound as the beginning, middle, or ending letters of the word.

Summary of Reading Assessment

Although most reading tests do cover many of these areas of assessment, each has its own unique style, method of scoring and interpretative value. However, when looking at a student's reading behavior, regardless of the test administered, one must address certain questions:

- Does the student have excessive body movements while reading?
- Does the student prefer to read alone or in a group?
- How does the student react to being tested?
- Does the student avoid reading?
- When the student reads, what types of materials will he or she read?
- Does the student read at home?
- Does the student understand more after reading silently than after listening to someone read the material orally?
- Does the student value reading?
- Is the student's failure mechanical or is he or she deficient in comprehension?

READING ASSESSMENT MEASURES

Many different reading assessment measures are used for determining reading strengths and weaknesses. The various reading tests used in school systems to assess reading abilities follow.

Dynamic Indicators of Basic Early Literacy Skills-6th Edition (DIBELS)

Authors: Roland H. Good III, PhD and Ruth Kaminski, PhD

Description of Test: The DIBELS helps to quickly and accurately predict reading success in young students by measuring underlying skills such as comprehension, sound recognition, and word use. Results can predict performance on year end achievement testing and standardized educational assessments, and facilitate early intervention to improve scores. Because it is sensitive to even small improvements in reading skills, the DIBELS can evaluate instruction effectiveness after short intervals. It includes empirically validated instructional goals for each grade and skill level, which can serve as achievable targets.

Administration Time: DIBELS is comprised of a series of 1-minute tests that indicate students' progress toward competence and chances for success in all areas of basic early literacy skills in kindergarten through grade six. Using these measures, teachers can discover students' long-term reading and literacy progress. Through seven 1-minute tests, DIBELS can predict student literacy schoolwide, enabling teachers and administrators to better address gaps and deficits as necessary. These assessments are designed to take approximately 10 minutes per student.

Age/Grade Levels: Kindergarten to Grade 6

Subtest Information: The DIBELS contains seven subtests that measure distinct reading-related skills. The number and type of subtests that are administered to a child depend on his or her grade level. To administer a subtest, the teacher leads the student through a simple task such as naming letters, reading nonsense words, or constructing a sentence.

Each DIBELS subtest contains a Benchmark Assessment and a Progress Monitoring form. Benchmark Assessments are given to students at the beginning, middle, and end of the school year. They use different tasks for each evaluation to prevent practice effects. When a child's scores indicate the need for development in a particular area, the teacher can use the Progress Monitoring forms as frequently as necessary to evaluate the effectiveness of interventions. Progress Monitoring evaluations contain up to 20 different tasks that are equivalent in difficulty, so students do not repeat the same tasks.

The 7 subtests of the DIBELS are:

1. *Initial Sound of Fluency:* Identification and production of beginning word sounds
2. *Phoneme Segmentation Fluency:* Segmentation of words into phonemes
3. *Nonsense Word Fluency:* Naming upper- and lowercase letters
4. *Letter Naming Fluency:* Letter-sound matching and letter blending
5. *Oral Reading:* Reading text aloud
6. *Retell Fluency:* Reading comprehension
7. *Word Use Fluency:* Use of specific words in sentences

Gates-MacGinitie Silent Reading Tests–4th Edition (GMRT- 4)

Authors: Walter MacGinitie, Ruth MacGinitie, Katherine Maria, and Lois G. Dreyer

Description of Test: The GMRT- 4 comprises a series of multiple-choice pencil-and-paper subtests designed to measure silent reading skills.

Administration Time: About 1 hour

Age/Grade Levels: Grades 1 through 12

Subtest Information: The test provides a comprehensive assessment of reading skills in two domains:

• *Comprehension*—This subtest domain assesses the ability to read and understand whole sentences and paragraphs.
• *Vocabulary*—This subtest domain assesses reading vocabulary. The difficulty of the task varies with the grade level.

Gray Diagnostic Reading Tests–2nd Edition (GDRT-2)

Authors: Brian R. Bryant, J. Lee Wiederholt, and Diane P. Bryant

Description of Test: *The Gray Diagnostic Reading Tests–2nd Edition* (GDRT-2) has been revised and updated to reflect current research in reading. The GDRT-2 assesses students who have difficulty reading continuous print and who require an evaluation of specific abilities and weaknesses. Two parallel forms are provided to allow you to study a student's reading progress over time. Teachers and reading specialists will find this test useful and efficient in gauging reading skills progress.

Administration Time: 45 to 60 minutes

Age/Grade Levels: Ages 6 through 13

Subtest Information: The GDRT-2 has four core subtests, each of which measures an important reading skill. The four subtests are: (1) Letter/Word Identification, (2) Phonetic Analysis, (3) Reading Vocabulary, and (4) Meaningful Reading. The three supplemental subtests, Listening Vocabulary, Rapid Naming, and Phonological Awareness, measure skills that many researchers and clinicians think have important roles in the diagnosis or teaching of developmental readers or children with dyslexia.

Gray Oral Reading Tests–4th Edition (GORT-4)

Authors: J. Lee Wiederholt and Brian R. Bryant

Description of Test: The widely used and popular *Gray Oral Reading Tests–3rd Edition* (GORT-3) has been revised and all new normative data provided. The GORT-4 provides an efficient and objective measure of growth in oral reading and an aid in the diagnosis of oral reading difficulties.

Administration Time: The time required to administer each form of the GORT-4 will vary from 15 to 30 minutes. Although the test is best administered in one session, examiners may use two sessions if the reader becomes fatigued or uncooperative.

Age/Grade Levels: Ages 6 through 18

Subtest Information: The test consists of two parallel forms, each containing 14 developmentally sequenced reading passages with five comprehension questions and can be given to students ages 6-0 through 18-11. The GORT-4 provides examiners with a Fluency Score that is derived by combining the reader's performance in Rate (time in seconds taken to read each passage) and Accuracy (number of deviations from print made in each passage). The number of correct responses made to the comprehension questions provides examiners with an Oral Reading Comprehension Score. All four scores are reported in terms of standard scores, percentile ranks, grade equivalents, and age equivalents. The Fluency Score and the Oral Reading Comprehension Score are combined to obtain an Oral Reading Quotient.

Gray Silent Reading Tests (GSRT)

Authors: J. Lee Wiederholt and Ginger Blalock

Description of Test: The *Gray Silent Reading Tests* quickly and efficiently measure an individual's silent reading comprehension ability.

Administration Time: 15–30 minutes

Age/Grade Levels: Ages 7 through 24

Subtest Information: There are no subtests on the GSRT. This test consists of two parallel forms each containing 13 developmentally sequenced reading passages with five multiple-choice questions. It can be given individually or to groups. Each form of the test yields raw scores, grade equivalents, age equivalents, percentiles, and a Silent Reading Quotient.

Durrell Analysis of Reading Difficulty–3rd Edition (DARD-3)

Authors: Donald O. Durrell and Jane H. Catterson.

Description of Test: The DARD-3 has long served a population of experienced teachers whose primary purpose was to discover and describe weaknesses and faulty habits in children's reading. The kit includes an examiner's manual, student record booklets, tachistoscope, and a subtest presentation booklet containing reading passages.

Administration Time: 30 to 90 minutes

Age/Grade Levels: Grades 1 through 6

Subtest Information: The Durrell Analysis consists of 19 subtests designed to assess a student's reading and listening performance. They are included in the following sections:

- *Identifying Sounds in Words*—The examiner reads lists of words at increasing difficulty levels, and the student's score is based on the total number of identifying sounds in words that the student can recall correctly.
- *Listening Comprehension*—The examiner is directed to read one or two paragraphs aloud to determine the student's ability to comprehend information presented orally.
- *Listening Vocabulary*—This test requires the child to listen to a series of words and indicate the category to which it belongs.
- *Oral Reading*—The student reads orally and answers questions that require the recall of explicit information.
- *Phonic Spelling of Words*—The examiner reads lists of words at increasing difficulty levels, and the student's score is based on the total number of words he or she spells phonetically correctly.
- *Prereading Phonics Abilities Inventory*—This optional subtest includes syntax matching, naming letters in spoken words, naming phonemes in spoken words, naming lowercase letters, and writing letters from dictation.
- *Silent Reading*—The student reads silently and answers questions that require the recall of explicit information.
- *Sounds in Isolation*—This test assesses the student's mastery of sound/ symbol relationships—including letters, blends, digraphs, phonograms, and affixes.
- *Spelling of Words*—The examiner reads lists of words at increasing difficulty levels, and the student's score is based on the total number of words spelled correctly.
- *Visual Memory of Words*—The examiner reads visually presented lists of words at increasing difficulty levels, and the student's score is based on the total number of words the student can recall correctly when the word list is presented again.
- *Word Analysis*—The examiner reads lists of words at increasing difficulty levels, and the score is based on the total number of words that the child analyzes correctly.
- *Word Recognition*—The examiner reads lists of words at increasing difficulty levels, and the score is based on the total number of words that the child recognizes correctly.

Gates-McKillop-Horowitz Reading Diagnostic Tests

Authors: Arthur I. Gates, Anne S. McKillop, and Elizabeth Horowitz

Description of Test: This is an 11-part verbal and paper-and-pencil test. Not all parts need to be given to all students. Subtests are selected based on the student's reading levels and reading difficulties.

Administration Time: 40 to 60 minutes

Age/Grade Levels: Grades 1 through 6

Subtest Information: The subtests are listed and described below.

- *Auditory Blending*—The student is required to blend sounds to form a whole word.
- *Auditory Discrimination*—The student is required to listen to a pair of words and to determine whether the words are the same or different.
- *Informal Writing*—The student is required to write an original paragraph on a topic of his or her choice.
- *Letter Sounds*—The student is required to give the sound of a printed letter.
- *Naming Capital Letters*—The student is required to name uppercase letters.

- *Naming Lowercase Letters*—The student is required to name lowercase letters.
- *Oral Reading*—The student is required to read seven paragraphs orally. No comprehension is required.
- *Reading Sentences*—The student is required to read four sentences with phonetically regular words.
- *Reading Words*—The student is required to read 15 one-syllable nonsense words.
- *Recognizing and Blending Common Word Parts*—The student is required to read a list of nonsense words made up of common word parts.
- *Spelling*—The student is required to take an oral spelling test.
- *Syllabication*—The student is required to read a list of nonsense words.
- *Vowels*—The student is required to determine the vowel associated with a nonsense word presented by the examiner.
- *Words/Flash Presentation*—The student is required to identify words presented by a tachistoscope in half-second intervals.
- *Words/Untimed*—The student is required to read the same word list as resented in Words/Flash Presentation. However the student is given the opportunity to use word attack skills in an untimed setting.

Gilmore Oral Reading Test

Authors: John V. Gilmore and Eunice C. Gilmore

Description of Test: This test measures three aspects of oral reading competency: pronunciation, comprehension, and reading rate. It is used for diagnosing the reading needs of students identified as having reading problems.

Administration Time: 15 to 20 minutes

Age/Grade Levels: Grades 1 through 8

Subtest Information: The test is made up of 10 paragraphs in increasing order of difficulty that form a continuous story about episodes in a family group. There are five comprehension questions on each paragraph and a picture that portrays the characters in the story.

Nelson-Denny Reading Test

Authors: James I. Brown, Vivian Vick Fishco, and Gerald S. Hanna

Description of Test: *The Nelson-Denny Reading Test, Forms G and H,* is a reading survey test for high school and college students and adults. It assesses student achievement and progress in vocabulary, comprehension, and reading rate. The primary uses of the Nelson-Denny are as a screening test for reading problems, as a predictor of academic success, and as a measure of progress resulting from educational interventions.

Administration Time: 35 minutes; Extended-time administration: 56 minutes

Age/Grade Levels: High school and college students and adults

Subtest Information: A two-part test, the Nelson-Denny measures vocabulary development, comprehension, and reading rate. Part I (Vocabulary) is a 15-minute timed test; Part II (Comprehension and Rate) is a 20-minute test.

1. *Vocabulary:* Consists of 80 multiple-choice items, each with five response options. The words were drawn from high school and college textbooks and vary in difficulty.
2. *Comprehension:* Requires examinees to read five short passages (also drawn from high school and college textbooks) and to respond to 38 multiple-choice questions about the contents of these passages.

Slosson Oral Reading Test-Revised 3 (SORT-R3)

Authors: Richard L. Slosson; revised by Charles L. Nicholson

Description of Test: The new Slosson Oral Reading Test-Revised 3 (SORT-R3) is a multidimensional reading assessment tool which can be used for regular education testing populations and also for most special testing populations. The SORT-R3 gives a brief measure of reading ability and is most useful in identifying individuals with reading disabilities.

The SORT-R3 contains 200 words in ascending order of difficulty in groups of 20 words. These word groups approximate grade reading levels. Thus List 1 is equivalent to approximately the first grade level, List 2 is equivalent to approximately the second grade level, and so on. The same pattern continues throughout the word lists. The last group is listed as grades 9–12. This list contains the most difficult words, with words frequently encountered at the adult level.

The SORT-R3 is a quick and reliable screening test of reading word recognition can be readily used for all general student and adult testing populations as well as including additional adapted specialized scoring instructions for Adult Literacy Programs, the visually impaired, and others who have functional educational disabilities.

Administration Time: Untimed (3 to 5 minutes)

Age/Grade Levels: Preschool to Adult

Subtest Information: The test has no subtests.

Spache Diagnostic Reading Scales (DRS)

Author: George D. Spache

Description of Test: *The Diagnostic Reading Scales* consists of a battery of individually administered tests that are used to estimate the instructional, independent, and potential reading levels of a student.

Administration Time: 60 minutes

Age/Grade Levels: Grades 1 through 7 and poor readers in grades 8 through 12

Subtest Information: The subtests are listed and described below:

- *Auditory Comprehension*—The student is required to respond to questions orally about paragraphs read aloud by the examiner.
- *Oral Reading*—The student is required to read paragraphs aloud and answer questions orally.
- *Silent Reading*—The student is required to read a passage silently and to respond orally to questions asked by the examiner.

- *Supplementary Phonics Test*—This subtest measures the student's word attack skills and phonics knowledge.
- *Word Recognition List*—This test contains graded word lists that are used to determine a student's reading ability.

The Woodcock Reading Mastery Tests–Revised (WRMT-R)

Author: Richard W. Woodcock

Description of Test: *The Woodcock Reading Mastery Tests* (WMRT-R) is composed of six individually administered tests. There are two forms of the test, G and H. Form G includes all six tests, whereas Form H includes only four reading achievement tests.

Administration Time: 40 to 45 minutes

Age/Grade Levels: Grades K through 12

Subtest Information: Form G includes the following six subtests:

- *Letter Identification*—This test measures a student's skill in naming or pronouncing letters of the alphabet. Uppercase and lowercase letters are used.
- *Passage Comprehension*—In this subtest, the student must read silently a passage that has a word missing and then tell the examiner a word that could appropriately fill in the blank space. The passages are drawn from actual newspaper articles and textbooks.
- *Visual Auditory Learning*—The student is required to associate unfamiliar visual stimuli (rebuses) with familiar oral words and to translate sequences of rebuses into sentences.
- *Word Attack*—This test assesses skill in using phonic and structural analysis to read nonsense words.
- *Word Comprehension*—There are three parts to this section: Antonyms, Synonyms, and Analogies. In the Antonyms section, the student must read a word and then provide a word that means the opposite. In the Synonyms section, the student must provide a word with similar meanings to the stimulus words provided. In the Analogies section, the student must read a pair of words, ascertain the relationship between the two words, read a third word, and then supply a word that has the same relationship to the third word as exists between the initial pair of words read.
- *Word Identification*—This tests measures skill in pronouncing words in isolation.

Test of Reading Comprehension–4th Edition (TORC-4)

Authors: Virginia L. Brown, Donald D. Hammill, and J. Lee Wiederholt

Description of Test: Now available in a fully updated Fourth Edition, this multidimensional measure of silent reading comprehension is appropriate for grades 2 through 12 (ages 7-0 through 17-11). The TORC-4 is an excellent way to identify students who need to improve reading proficiency. It is also useful in documenting the effectiveness of remedial efforts.

Administration Time: 45 minutes or less

Age/Grade Levels: ages 7-0 through 17-11

Subtest Information: The TORC-4 is composed of five subtests assessing word identification and contextual meaning:

1. *Relational Vocabulary:* Items require the student to silently read a set of three related words, then consider another four words, choosing two that are associated with the original set of three.
2. *Sentence Completion:* Each item presents a sentence that is missing two words. The student silently reads each sentence, then selects from a list the pair of words that best completes it.
3. *Paragraph Construction:* After silently reading a series of sentences that are not in logical order, the student rearranges the sentences to form a coherent paragraph.
4. *Text Comprehension:* The student silently reads short passages and then answers five multiple-choice questions about each passage.
5. *Contextual Fluency:* Progressively more difficult passages (drawn from the Text Comprehension Subtest) are printed in uppercase letters without punctuation or spacing between words. As students read the passages, they attempt to recognize individual words, drawing a line between all those they can discern within a 3-minute time limit.

Stanford Diagnostic Reading Test–4th Edition (SDRT-4)

Authors: Bjorn Karlsen and Eric F. Gardner

Description of Test: The *Stanford Diagnostic Reading Test,* 4th Edition (SDRT-4), provides group-administered diagnostic assessment of the essential components of reading in order to determine students' strengths and needs. SDRT-4 includes detailed coverage of reading skills, including many easy questions, so teachers can better assess students struggling with reading and plan instruction appropriately.

Administration Time: 85 to 105 minutes

Age/Grade Levels: Grades K through 12

Subtest Information: Depending on age level, SDRT-4 consists of three subtests:

1. *Reading Vocabulary:* measures the range of words a child knows, based on grade-level expectations.
2. *Reading Comprehension:* measures how well a child understands and analyzes various types of reading material.
3. *Scanning Skills:* measures a child's ability to skim through reading material to find information.

Written Expression

Written language skills are critical for successful school performance (McLoughlin & Lewis, 2008). Writing is a highly complex method of expression involving the integration of eye–hand, linguistic, and conceptual abilities. As a result, it is usually the last skill children master. Whereas reading is usually considered the receptive form of a graphic symbol system, writing is considered the expressive form of that system. Assessment of written language can inform instruction by providing information on students' skills and abilities (Cohen & Spenciner, 2011). The primary concern in the assessment of composition skills is the content of the student's writing, not its form. The term *writing* refers to a variety of interrelated graphic skills, including:

Composition: The ability to generate ideas and to express them in an acceptable grammar, while adhering to certain stylistic conventions

Spelling: The ability to use letters to construct words in accordance with accepted usage

Handwriting: The ability to execute physically the graphic marks necessary to produce legible compositions or messages

Handwriting

Handwriting refers to the actual motor activity that is involved in writing. Most students are taught **manuscript** (printing) initially and then move to cursive writing (script) in later grades. There are those who advocate that only manuscript or only cursive should be taught. In truth, problems may appear among students in either system.

According to Taylor (2009), handwriting is the visible product of written expression; if handwriting is not readable, then the goal of written expression, namely communication, is affected (p. 325).

Handwriting skills are usually measured through the use of informal assessment measures—that is, CBA, CBM, portfolio assessments, rating scales, observation measures, or error analysis—rather than norm-referenced measures. Given the fact that most measures are informal, handwriting may or may not be part of a full psychoeducational battery. However, handwriting should always be evaluated, and examples need to be gathered and informally assessed if it appears to warrant concern.

Spelling

Spelling is one of the academic skills often included in the evaluator battery of individual achievement tests used in special education assessment. **Spelling** is the ability to use letters to construct words in accordance with accepted usage. Spelling ability is viewed by some teachers and school administrators equally with other academic skills. Being a poor speller does not necessarily mean that a child has a learning disorder. However, when poor spelling occurs with poor reading and/or arithmetic, then there is reason for concern. It appears that many of the learning skills required for good spelling are the same ones that enable students to become good readers (Pierangelo & Giuliani, 2009).

Spelling, like all written language skills, is well suited to work sample analysis because a permanent product is produced. Learning to spell is a developmental process, and young children go through a number of stages as they begin to acquire written language skills. Writing begins in the preschool years as young children observe and begin to imitate the act of writing.

Analysis of Spelling Skills

Several questions should be addressed before one begins to analyze the results of the spelling subtest (Pierangelo & Giuliani, 2009):

Does the child have sufficient mental ability to learn to spell?

This information can be obtained from the school psychologist if an intellectual evaluation was administered. However, if no such test was administered, then a group school abilities index may be present in the child's permanent folder.

Are the child's hearing, speech, and vision adequate?

This information can be obtained through the permanent record folder, information in the nurse's office, or informal screening procedures.

What is the child's general level of spelling ability according to teacher comments, past evaluations, or standardized tests?

Teacher comments and observations about the child's spelling history are very important to show patterns of disability. Also, look at standardized tests to see if patterns exist through the years on such tests.

Other information should be obtained from the classroom teacher as well. The teacher can offer you some foundational information on the child's patterns. You may want to ask the teacher for the following information:

- The child's attitude toward spelling in the classroom
- The extent to which the child relies on a dictionary in the classroom
- The extent of spelling errors in classroom written work
- Any patterns of procrastination or avoidance of written work
- The student's study habits and methods of work in the classroom
- The history of scores on classroom spelling tests
- Any observable handwriting difficulties
- Any evidence of fatigue as a factor in the child's spelling performance

Spelling Errors Primarily Due to Auditory or Visual Channel Deficits

Certain spelling errors may be evident in students with certain auditory channel deficits:

- **Auditory discrimination problems or cultural problems:** The child substitutes *t* for *d* or *sh* for *ch*.
- **Auditory discrimination problems:** The child confuses vowels, for example, spells *bit* as *bet*.
- **Auditory acuity or discrimination problems:** The child does not hear subtle differences in or discriminate between sounds and often leaves vowels out of two-syllable words.
- **Auditory–visual association:** The child uses a synonym such as *house* for *home* in spelling.
- **Auditory–visual associative memory:** The child takes wild guesses with little or no relationship between the letters or words used and the spelling words dictated, such as spelling *dog* for *home* or writing *phe* for *home*.

Certain spelling errors may be evident in students with certain visual channel deficits:

- **Visual memory problems:** The child visualizes the beginning or the ending of words but omits the middle of the words, for example, spells *hppy* for *happy*.
- **Visual memory sequence:** The child gives the correct letters but in the wrong sequence, for example, writes the word *the* as *teh* or *hte*.
- **Visual discrimination problems:** The child inverts letters, writing *u* for *n*, *m* for *w*.
- **Visual memory:** The child spells words phonetically that are nonphonetic in configuration, for example, *tuff* for *tough*.

TESTS OF WRITTEN LANGUAGE

Many different assessment measures are used for determining written language. Listed next are the various tests of written expression tests.

Test of Early Written Language–2nd Edition (TEWL-2)

Author: Wayne P. Hresko

Description of Test: The TEWL-2 was developed to assess early writing abilities and covers the five areas of writing transcription, conventions of print, communication, creative expression, and record keeping. The TEWL-2 has a total of 42 items. The starting items vary by age level. An item is graded as 1 if correct and 0 if incorrect. Each item counts equally, although some require more responses or information than others. It is individually administered.

Administration Time: 10 to 30 minutes

Age/Grade Levels: Ages 3 through 7

Subtest Information: The test consists of two subtests: The selection of items and the development of the subtests are grounded in the available research literature and other evidence of developing literacy ability. Item types were selected only if recognized experts in the field have related them to developing literacy abilities. The TEWL-2 is a companion to the TOWL-4 for extending the assessment range to younger children.

- *Basic Writing Quotient*—Basic Writing is a subtest (i.e., component) area that results in a standard score quotient. This quotient is a measure of a child's ability in such areas as spelling, capitalization, punctuation, sentence construction, and metacognitive knowledge. The Basic Writing Subtest may be given independent of the Contextual Writing Subtest.
- *Contextual Writing Quotient*—Contextual Writing is a subtest (i.e., component) area that results in a standard score quotient. This quotient is a measure of a child's ability to construct a story when provided with a picture prompt. This subtest measures such areas as story format, cohesion, thematic maturity, ideation, and story structure. Both Form A and Form B consist of 14 items. A detailed, expanded scoring guide is provided to assist in scoring the Contextual Writing Subtest. The Contextual Writing subtest may be given independently of the Basic Writing subtest.
- *Global Writing Quotient*—This composite quotient is formed by combining the standard scores for the Basic Writing Quotient and the Contextual Writing Quotient.

Test of Written Language–4th Edition (TOWL-4)

Authors: Donald D. Hammill and Stephen C. Larsen

Description of Test: The fourth edition of *Test of Written Language* (TOWL-4) is a norm-referenced, comprehensive diagnostic test of written expression. It is used to (a) identify students who write poorly and, therefore, need special help, (b) determine students' particular strengths and weaknesses in various writing abilities, (c) document students' progress in special writing programs, and (d) measure writing in research.

Administration Time: 60–90 minutes

Age/Grade Levels: Ages 9-0 through 17-11

Subtest Information: The TOWL-4 has two forms (i.e., Form A and Form B), each of which contains seven subtests. The subtests represent the conventional, linguistic, and conceptual aspects of writing. Subtests 1–5 use contrived formats; subtests 6–7 use a spontaneously written story to assess important aspects of language. The subtests are:

1. *Vocabulary*—The student writes a sentence that incorporates a stimulus word. *e.g.:* For *"ran,"* a student writes, *"I ran up the hill."*
2. *Spelling*—The student writes sentences from dictation, making proper use of spelling rules.
3. *Punctuation*—The student writes sentences from dictation, making proper use of punctuation and capitalization rules.
4. *Logical Sentences*—The student edits an illogical sentence so that it makes better sense (*e.g.:* *"John blinked his nose"* is changed to *"John blinked his eye"*).
5. *Sentence Combining*—The student integrates the meaning of several short sentences into one grammatically correct written sentence (*e.g.:* *"John drives fast"* is combined with *"John has a red car,"* making *"John drives his red car fast"*).
6. *Contextual Conventions*—The student writes a story in response to a stimulus picture. Points are earned for satisfying specific arbitrary requirements relative to orthographic (*e.g.:* punctuation, spelling) and grammatic conventions (*e.g.:* sentence construction, noun–verb agreement).
7. *Story Composition*—The student's story is evaluated relative to the quality of its composition (*e.g.:* vocabulary, plot, prose, development of characters, and interest to the reader).

Test of Written Expression (TOWE)

Authors: Ron McGee, Brian Bryant, Stephen Larsen, and Diane Rivera

Description of Test: The *Test of Written Expression* (TOWE) provides a comprehensive yet efficient norm-referenced assessment of writing achievement. The TOWE, which can be administered conveniently to individuals or groups of students, uses two assessment methods to evaluate a student's writing skills. The first method involves administering a series of 76 items that tap different skills associated with writing. The second method requires students to read or hear a prepared story starter and use it as a stimulus for writing an essay (i.e., the beginning of the story is provided, and the writer continues the story to its conclusion).

Administration Time: 60 minutes

Age/Grade Levels: Ages 6 through 14

Subtest Information: The TOWE provides two separate assessment methods for measuring a comprehensive set of writing skills including:

- Ideation
- Vocabulary
- Grammar
- Capitalization
- Punctuation
- Spelling

Writing Process Test (WPT)

Authors: M. Robin Warden and Thomas Hutchinson

Description of Test: The norm-referenced *Writing Process Test* (WPT) is a direct measure of writing that requires the student to plan, write, and revise an original composition.

The WPT assesses both written product and writing process. The test can be administered individually or in groups.

Administration Time: 45 minutes

Age/Grade Levels: Ages 8 through 19

Subtest Information: The test rates the writer's effort on two scales, Development and Fluency. The six Development Scales assess Purpose and Focus, Audience, Vocabulary, Style and Tone, Support and Development, and Organization and Coherence. The six Fluency Scales assess Sentence Structure and Variety, Grammar and Usage, Capitalization and Punctuation, and Spelling.

Test of Written Spelling–4th Edition (TWS-4)

Authors: Stephen C. Larsen and Donald D. Hammill

Description of Test: The revised TWS-4 is a norm-referenced test of spelling administered using a dictated word format. The TWS-4 now has two alternate or equivalent forms (A and B) that make it more useful in test–retest situations. The TWS-4 is appropriate for students in grades 1 through 12 as well as for those in remedial programs. The TWS was developed after a review of 2,000 spelling rules. The words to be spelled are drawn from 10 basal spelling programs and popular graded word lists. The results of the TWS-4 may be used for four specific purposes: to identify students whose scores are significantly below those of their peers and who might need interventions designed to improve spelling proficiency, to determine areas of relative strength and weakness in spelling, to document overall progress in spelling as a consequence of intervention programs, and to serve as a measure for research efforts designed to investigate spelling.

Administration Time: 20 minutes

Age/Grade Levels: Ages 6 through 18 (Grades 1–12)

Subtest Information:

- Predictable words
- Unpredictable words

MATH

Mathematical thinking is a process that begins early in most children. Even before formal education begins, children are exposed to various situations that involve the application of mathematical concepts. As they enter formal schooling, they take the knowledge of what they had previously learned and begin to apply it in a more formal manner.

It is necessary to understand that mathematics and arithmetic are actually two different terms. Although most people use them interchangeably, they each have distinct meanings. **Mathematics** refers to the study of numbers and their relationships to time, space, volume, and geometry. **Arithmetic** refers to the operations or computations performed. Mathematics involves many different abilities. These include:

- Solving problems
- Recognizing how to interpret results

- Applying mathematics in practical situations
- Using mathematics for prediction
- Estimating
- Using computational skills
- Understanding measurement
- Creating and reading graphs and charts

All schools, whether regular or special education, use some form of mathematical assessment. Schools begin the process of teaching math skills in kindergarten and proceed throughout the child's formal education. Even at the college level, mathematics is often a core requirement in many liberal arts schools. In general, next to reading, mathematics is probably the area most frequently assessed in school systems.

Mathematics can be assessed at the individual or group level. Consequently, it is a skill that is stressed and measured by various tests in schools. Mathematics tests often cover a great many areas. However, according to Salvia and Ysseldyke (2007), three types of classifications are involved in diagnostic math tests. Each classification measures certain mathematical abilities:

- **Content:** This consists of numeration, fractions, geometry, and algebra.
- **Operations:** This consists of counting, computation, and reasoning.
- **Applications:** This consists of measurement, reading graphs and tables, money and budgeting time, and problem solving.

Furthermore, according to the National Council of Supervisors of Mathematics (1978), basic mathematical skills include:

- Arithmetic computation
- Problem solving
- Applying mathematics in everyday situations
- Alertness to the reasonableness of results
- Estimation and approximation
- Geometry
- Measurement
- Reading charts and graphs
- Using mathematics to predict
- Computer literacy

Although less attention is given to the assessment of mathematics than reading (Taylor, 2009), it is an essential component that should be included when doing a comprehensive assessment of a child for a suspected disability. There are fewer diagnostic math tests than diagnostic reading tests. However, math assessment is more clear-cut. Most diagnostic math tests generally sample similar behaviors.

Analysis and Interpretation of Math Skills

According to McLoughlin and Lewis (2008), mathematics is one of the school subjects best suited for error analysis because students respond in writing on most tasks, thereby producing a permanent record of their work. Also, there is usually only one correct answer to mathematics questions and problems, and scoring is unambiguous. Today, the most common use of error analysis in mathematics is assessment of computation skills.

McLoughlin and Lewis (2008) identified four error types in computational analysis:

- **Incorrect operation:** The student selects the incorrect operation. For example, the problem requires subtraction, and the student adds.
- **Incorrect number fact:** The number fact recalled by the student is inaccurate. For example, the student recalls the product of 9×6 as 52.
- **Incorrect algorithm:** The procedures used by the student to solve the problem are inappropriate. The student may skip a step, apply the correct steps in the wrong sequence, or use an inaccurate method.
- **Random error:** The student's response is incorrect and apparently random. For example, the student writes 100 as the answer to 42×6 (p. 386).

Different types of errors can occur in the mathematics process other than these four mentioned. For example, a student may make a mistake or error in applying the appropriate arithmetical operations. Such an example would be $50 - 12 = 62$. Here, the student used the operation of addition rather than subtraction. The student may understand how to do both operations, but consistently gets these types of questions wrong on the tests he or she takes due to the improper use of the sign involved.

Another problem that the student may encounter is a *slip*. When a slip occurs, it is more likely due to a simple mistake rather than a pattern of problems. For example, if a child correctly subtracts $20 - 5$ in eight problems but for some reason not in the ninth problem, the error is probably due to a simple slip rather than a serious operational or processing problem. One error on one problem is not an error pattern. Error patterns can be assessed by analyzing all correct and incorrect answers. When designing a program plan for a particular child in mathematics, it is critical to establish not only the nature of the problems but also the patterns of problems that occur in the child's responses.

Also, handwriting can play an important role in mathematics. Scoring a math test often involves reading numbers written down on an answer sheet by the student. If a student's handwriting is difficult to interpret or impossible to read, this can create serious problems for the evaluator with respect to obtaining valid scores. When a student's handwriting is not clear on a math test, it is important that the evaluator ask the student to help him or her read the answers. By doing so, the evaluator is analyzing the math skills that need to be assessed rather than spending his or her time trying to decode the student's responses.

ASSESSMENT OF MATHEMATICAL ABILITIES

Many different arithmetic assessment measures are used for determining strengths and areas of need. Commonly used mathematics tests that school systems use to assess students' abilities follow.

Key Math Diagnostic Arithmetic Tests–Revised/Normative Update (Key Math-R/NU)

Authors: Austin J. Connolly, William Nachtman, and E. Milo Pritchett

Description of Test: The Key Math-R/NU is a point-to and paper-and-pencil test measuring math skills in 14 areas. Two forms of the Key Math-R are available to use: Forms A and B. Each form contains 258 items. The materials include a test manual, two easel kits for presentation of test items, and individual record forms for recording responses.

Administration Time: Approximately 30 to 45 minutes

Age/Grade Levels: Ages 5 to 22

Subtest Information: The test is broken down into three major areas consisting of 13 subtests:

- *Basic Concepts*—This part has three subtests that investigate basic mathematical concepts and knowledge: Numeration, Rational Numbers, and Geometry.
- *Operations*—This part consists of basic computation processes: Addition, Subtraction, Multiplication, Division, and Mental Computation.
- *Applications*—This part focuses on the functional applications use of mathematics necessary to daily life: Measurement, Time and Money, Interpretation of Data, Problem Solving, and Estimation.

Test of Mathematical Abilities–2nd Edition (TOMA-2)

Authors: Virginia L. Brown, Mary E. Cronin, and Elizabeth McEntire

Description of Test: The TOMA-2 comprises five paper-and-pencil subtests that assess various areas of mathematical ability.

Administration Time: 60 to 90 minutes

Age/Grade Levels: Ages 8 through 18

Subtest Information: The test consists of four core subtests and one supplemental subtest:

- *Attitude Toward Math (supplemental subtest)*—The child is presented with various statements about math attitudes and must respond with *agree, disagree,* or *don't know.*
- *Computation*—In this subtest, students are presented with computational problems consisting of basic operations and involving manipulation of fractions, decimals, money, percentages, and so on.
- *General Information*—In this subtest, the examiner reads the student questions involving basic general knowledge, and the student must reply orally. This subtest is usually administered individually.
- *Story Problems*—In this subtest, the student reads brief story problems that contain extraneous information and must extract the pertinent information required to solve the problems. Work space is provided for calculation.
- *Vocabulary*—In this subtest, students are presented with mathematical terms that they are asked to define briefly as they are used in a mathematical sense.

Stanford Diagnostic Mathematics Test–4th Edition (SDMT-4)

Authors: Harcourt Brace Educational Measurement

Description of Test: The *Stanford Diagnostic Mathematics Test,* 4th Edition (SDMT-4), measures competence in the basic concepts and skills that are prerequisite to success in mathematics, while emphasizing problem solving and problem-solving strategies. SDMT-4 identifies specific areas of difficulty for each student so that teachers can plan appropriate intervention. Designed to be group administered, SDMT-4 provides both multiple-choice and optional free response assessment formats. Students select and apply problem-solving strategies and use their reasoning and communication skills.

Administration Time: Varies with age according to mathematical ability

Age/Grade Levels: Grades 1 through 12

Subtest Information: There are six levels of testing on the SDMT-4 that assess concepts, applications, and computation:

- Red Level: Grades 1.5–2.5
- Orange Level: Grades 2.5–3.5
- Green Level: Grades 3.5–4.5
- Purple Level: Grades 4.5–6.5
- Brown Level: Grades 6.5–8.9
- Blue Level: Grades 9.0–12.9

Comprehensive Mathematical Abilities Test (CMAT)

Authors: Wayne P. Hresko, Paul L. Schlieve, Shelley R. Herron, Colleen Swain, and Rita J. Sherbenou

Description of Test: Based on actual materials used to teach math in schools and on state and local curriculum guides, the CMAT represents a major advance in the accurate assessment of the mathematics taught in today's schools. All items reflect real-world problems using up-to-date, current information and scenarios. Use as few as two subtests or as many as 12, depending on your purpose for testing.

Administration Time: 30 minutes to 2 hours

Age/Grade Levels: Ages 7 through 18

Subtests: The CMAT has six core subtests:

- *Addition*
- *Subtraction*
- *Multiplication*
- *Division*
- *Problem Solving*
- *Charts, Tables, and Graphs*

There are also six supplemental subtests:

- *Algebra*
- *Geometry*
- *Rational Numbers*
- *Time*
- *Money*
- *Measurement*

For most testing purposes, you will only want to give the core subtests, which can be administered in about 40 minutes. The supplemental subtests are used in those relatively few instances of need for information about higher-level mathematics ability.

Test of Early Mathematics Ability–3rd Edition (TEMA-3)

Authors: Herbert P. Ginsburg and Arthur J. Baroody

Description of Test: The TEMA-3 measures the mathematics performance of children between ages 3-0 to 8-11 and is also useful with older children who have learning problems in mathematics. It can be used as a norm-referenced measure or as a diagnostic instrument to determine specific strengths and weaknesses. Thus, the test can be used to measure progress, evaluate programs, screen for readiness, discover the bases for poor school performance in mathematics, identify gifted students, and guide instruction and remediation.

Administration Time: 40 minutes

Age/Grade Levels: Ages 3 through 8

Subtests: The test measures informal and formal (school-taught) concepts and skills in the following domains: numbering skills, number-comparison facility, numeral literacy, mastery of number facts, calculation skills, and understanding of concepts. It has two parallel forms, each containing 72 items.

COMPREHENSIVE TESTS OF ACADEMIC ACHIEVEMENT

The following tests are comprehensive in their assessment of academic areas. These tests normally offer a thorough approach to the assessment of a child's strengths and weaknesses in reading, writing, math, and spelling.

Brigance Comprehensive Inventory of Basic Skills–Revised (CIBS-R)

Author: Albert Brigance

Description of Test: As with its criterion-referenced application, the CIBS–R is designed to be administered in classroom settings, by teachers. Accordingly, the standardization and validation of the CIBS–R was conducted largely by teachers who administered the test to their own students in classroom settings. This means that the CIBS–R produces a complete range of data on students' skill levels as demonstrated under real-life, everyday conditions. The standardized portions of the CIBS–R are designed to meet state and federal assessment requirements. This means that the CIBS–R can be used as the educational portion of the battery that identifies children with learning disabilities, giftedness, or other exceptionalities. Specifically, the CIBS–R produces grade equivalents, age equivalents, percentiles, and quotients in six of the seven areas of achievement designated under the Individuals with Disabilities Education Act, for the detection of learning disabilities (basic reading skills, reading comprehension, math calculation, math reasoning, written language, and listening comprehension). The CIBS–R also provides data on students' information-processing skills in order to detect students with learning disabilities caused by processing deficits. Ultimately, the CIBS–R shows how students are progressing and identifies their strengths and weaknesses across skill areas (Glascoe, 2011).

Administration Time: Specific time limits are listed on many tests; others are untimed.

Age/Grade Levels: Grades pre-K through 9

Subtest Information: There are four subtest areas including 154 pencil-and-paper or oral-response tests:

- *Readiness*—The skills assessed include color naming; visual discrimination of shapes, letters, and short words; copying designs; drawing shapes from memory; drawing a person; gross motor coordination; recognition of body parts; following directional and verbal instructions; fine motor self-help skills; verbal fluency; sound articulation; personal knowledge; memory for sentences; counting; alphabet recitation; number naming and comprehension; letter naming; and writing name, numbers, and letters.
- *Reading*—This area evaluates word recognition, oral reading, comprehension, oral reading rate, word analysis (auditorily and while reading), meaning of prefixes, syllabication, and vocabulary.
- *Language Arts*—This area assesses cursive handwriting, grammar and mechanics, spelling, and reference skills.
- *Mathematics*—This area assesses rote counting, writing numerals in sequence, reading number words, ordinal concepts, numeral recognition, writing to dictation, counting in sets, Roman numerals, fractions, decimals, measurement (money, time, calendar, linear/liquid/ weight measurement, temperature), and two- and three-dimensional geometric concepts.

Kaufman Tests of Educational Achievement–2nd Edition (KTEA-II)

Authors: Alan S. Kaufman and Nadren L. Kaufman

Description of Test: The KTEA II is an individually administered battery that gives a flexible, thorough assessment of the key academic skills in reading, math, written language, and oral language.

Administration Time: Comprehensive Form: (pre K–K) 25 minutes; (grades 1−2) 50 minutes; (grades 3+) 70 minutes. Brief Form: (ages 4½ to Adult) 20−30 minutes

Age/Grade Levels: Ages 4½ through 25 (Comprehensive Form), 4½ through Adult (Brief Form)

Subtest Information: The test contains 14 subtests making up five composite scores:

- **Reading Composite**
  Letter & Word Recognition
  Reading Comprehension
  Phonological Awareness
  Nonsense Word Decoding
  Word Recognition Fluency
  Decoding Fluency
  Associated Fluency
  Naming Facility

- **Math Composite**
  Math Concepts & Applications
  Math Computation

- **Written Language Composite**
  Written Expression
  Math Computation

- **Oral Language Composite**
  Listening Comprehension
  Oral Expression

- **Comprehensive Achievement Composite**

Peabody Individual Achievement Test–Revised/Normative Update (PIAT-R/NU)

Author: Frederick C. Markwardt, Jr.

Description of Test: The PIAT-R is used in special education for identifying academic deficiencies. It is made up of six subtests. The most typical response format on the PIAT-R is multiple-choice. The student is shown a test plate with four possible answers and asked to select the correct response.

Administration Time: 50 to 70 minutes

Age/Grade Levels: Ages 5 through 22; Level 1 (grades K through 1) and Level 2 (grades 2 through 12)

Subtest Information: The test's six subtests include:

- *General Information*—This subtest has 100 open-ended questions that are presented orally. They measure the student's factual knowledge related to science, social studies, humanities, fine art, and recreation.
- *Reading Recognition*—There are 100 items. Items 1 through 16 are multiple choice and measure prereading skills. Items 17 through 100 measure decoding skills and require the student to read aloud individually presented words.
- *Reading Comprehension*—This subtest consists of 82 items and measures the student's ability to draw meaning from printed sentences.
- *Spelling*—Items 1 through 15 are multiple-choice tasks that assess reading skills. Items 16 through 100 require the student to select from four possible choices the correct spelling of a word read orally by the examiner.
- *Written Expression*—This subtest has two levels. Level 1 consists of 19 copying and dictation items that are arranged in order of ascending difficulty. In Level 2, the child is presented with one or two picture plates and given 20 minutes to write a story about the picture.
- *Mathematics*—In this subtest, the student is asked the question orally and must select the correct response from four choices. Questions cover topics ranging from numerical recognition to trigonometry.

Wechsler Individual Achievement Test–3rd Edition (WIAT-III)

Author: David Wechsler

Description of Test: The WIAT-III is a comprehensive academic achievement test that measures listening, speaking, reading, writing, and mathematics skills. The WIAT-III is suitable for use in a variety of clinical, educational, and research settings, including schools, clinics, private practices, and residential treatment facilities. WIAT III results can be used to: identify the academic strengths and weaknesses of a student; inform decisions regarding eligibility for educational services, educational placement, or diagnosis of a specific learning disability; and design instructional objectives and plan interventions.

Administration Time: Varies by grade level and number of subtests administered

Age/Grade Levels: Ages 4-0–50-11

Subtest Information: The WIAT-III consists of the following subtests:

Listening Comprehension: The student listens to vocabulary words and points to a picture that illustrates each word, and then listens to passages and answers questions about each one.

Oral Expression: The student is shown pictures and is asked to name the concept shown in each picture. Then the student says words from a given category and repeats sentences.

Reading Comprehension: The student reads passages aloud or silently under un-timed conditions, and then answers open-ended questions about each one.

Word Reading: The student reads aloud a list of increasingly difficult words.

Pseudoword Decoding: The student reads aloud a list of increasingly difficult nonsense words.

Oral Reading Fluency: The student reads passages aloud, and then orally responds to comprehension questions.

Sentence Composition: The student combines the information from two or three sentences into single sentences that mean the same thing, and then the student writes meaningful sentences that use specific words.

Essay Composition: The student writes an essay within a 10-minute time limit.

Spelling: The student writes single words that are dictated within the context of a sentence.

Math Problem Solving: Depending upon the grade and ability level of the student, the student solves untimed math problems related to basic skills (counting, identifying shapes, etc.), everyday applications (time, money, word problems, etc.), geometry, and algebra.

Numerical Operations: Depending upon the grade and ability level of the student, the student solves un-timed written math problems in the following domains: basic skills, basic operations with integers, geometry, algebra, and calculus.

Math Fluency—Addition: The student solves written addition problems within a 60 second time limit.

Math Fluency—Subtraction: The student solves written subtraction problems within a 60-second time limit.

Math Fluency—Multiplication: The student solves written multiplication problems within a 60-second time limit.

Wide Range Achievement Test–4th Edition (WRAT4)

Authors: Gary S. Wilkinson and Gary J. Robertson

Description of Test: The WRAT4 is a norm-referenced test that measures the basic academic skills of word reading, sentence comprehension, spelling, and math computation. It was standardized on a representative national sample of over 3,000 individuals ranging in age from 5 to 94 years. The normative sample was selected according to a stratified national sampling procedure with proportionate allocation controlled for age, gender, ethnicity, geographic region, and parental/obtained education as an index of socioeconomic status. Alternate forms, designated the Blue Form and the Green Form, were developed and equated during standardization by use of a commonperson research design. Derived scores were developed for both age- and grade-referenced groups. Standard scores, percentile ranks, stanines, normal curve equivalents, grade equivalents, and Rasch ability scaled scores are provided.

The Blue Form and the Green Form can be used interchangeably with comparable results, thus permitting retesting within short periods of time without the potential practice effects that may occur from repeating the same items. The alternate forms also can be administered together (i.e., Combined Form) in a single examination. For those interested in a more qualitative assessment of academic skills, the Combined Form provides an additional opportunity for performance observance.

Administration Time: Approximately 15 to 25 minutes for individuals ages 5 to 7 years; approximately 35 to 45 minutes for individuals ages 8 years and older

Age/Grade Levels: Ages 5 through Adult

Subtest Information:

- *Word Reading*—Measures letter and word decoding through letter identification and word recognition.
- *Sentence Comprehension*—Measures an individual's ability to gain meaning from words and to comprehend ideas and information contained in sentences through the use of a modified cloze technique.
- *Spelling*—Measures an individual's ability to encode sounds into written form through the use of a dictated spelling format containing both letters and words.
- *Math Computation*—Measures an individual's ability to perform basic mathematics computations through counting, identifying numbers, solving simple oral problems, and calculating written mathematics problems.

In addition to providing derived scores and interpretive information for the subtests, the WRAT4 yields a Reading Composite score, obtained by combining the Word Reading and Sentence Comprehension standard scores.

Woodcock Johnson III Tests of Achievement/Normative Update (WJ-III/NU)

Authors: Richard W. Woodcock, Kevin S. McGrew, and Nancy Mather

Description of Test: The WJ III NU Tests of Achievement has two parallel forms (A and B) that are divided into two batteries—Standard and Extended. The Standard Battery includes tests 1 through 12 that provide a broad set of scores. The 10 tests in the Extended Battery provide more in-depth diagnostic information on specific academic strengths and weaknesses. Examiners can administer the Standard Battery either alone or with the Extended Battery.

Practitioners use the WJ III NU Tests of Achievement to help assess students for learning disabilities and to determine if they need special services. IDEA 2004 requires the use of a variety of assessment tools and strategies to gather relevant, functional, developmental, and academic information about the student. The WJ III NU Tests of Achievement include tests and clusters that directly parallel those outlined by IDEA and provide sound procedures for determining learning variances between abilities and achievement.

Administration Time: Varies, about 5 minutes per test (approximately 60 to 70 minutes)

Age/Grade Levels: Ages 2 to 90+; Grades K–12, college

Subtest Information: The subtests in the Achievement Battery measure six curriculum areas: Reading, Oral Language, Written Language, Mathematics, Academic Knowledge, and Supplemental (Taylor, 2009; Cohen & Spenciner, 2011; McLoughlin & Lewis, 2008).

Reading

- *Letter*-Word Identification—Measures the ability to identify letters and words in isolation
- *Reading Fluency*—Requires the student to read printed statements and indicate whether they are true or false
- *Passage Comprehension*—Measures the ability to read a short passage and to identify the missing word
- *Word Attack* (Extended Battery)—Assesses a student's ability to apply phonics and instructional analysis skills using nonsense words
- *Reading Vocabulary* (Extended Battery)—Assesses the ability to supply one-word synonyms and antonyms after reading words

Oral Language

- *Story Recall*—The student is required to listen to short stories on audiotape and then must retell each story.
- *Understanding Directions*—The student must listen to commands on audiotape and then point to objects shown in pictures as directed.
- *Picture Vocabulary* (Extended Battery) Measures the ability to identify objects.
- *Oral Comprehension* (Extended Battery)—The student must listen to sentences that are incomplete on audiotape and then must state the word that is missing.

Mathematics

- *Calculation*—Assesses the ability to solve mathematical calculations using a booklet in which the student can respond in writing.
- *Math Fluency*—Number fact problems are given to the student, who must solve them in 3 minutes.
- *Applied Problems*—The student solves word problems.
- *Quantitative Concepts* (Extended Battery)—Assesses the ability to identify mathematics terms, formulas, and number patterns.

Written Language

- *Spelling*—The student is required to spell words that are dictated to him or her.
- *Writing Fluency*—The student must create and write simple sentences.
- *Writing Samples*—The student is required to write sentences based on prompts from the examiner.
- *Editing* (Extended Battery)—Measures the ability to correct errors in written passages.

Academic Knowledge

- *Academic Knowledge* (Extended Battery)—This subtest consists of three parts: Science, Social Studies and Humanities. The examiner reads questions to the student and the student answers them orally.

Supplemental

- *Story Recall-Delayed*—Anywhere from 30 minutes to 8 days after administering the *Story Recall* subtest, this subtest is administered and asks the student to tell the rest of the story.
- *Spelling of Sounds* (Extended Battery)—Assesses knowledge of letter combinations that form regular patterns in written English.
- *Sound Awareness* (Extended Battery)—Assesses a student's ability to rhyme words and to remove, substitute, and reverse parts of words in order to make new words.
- *Punctuation & Capitalization* (Extended Battery)—Assesses the ability to correctly use punctuation and capitalization.

Test of Academic Achievement Skills–Revised (TAAS-R)

Author: Morrison F. Gardner

Description of Test: The TAAS-R measures a child's reading, arithmetic, and spelling skills. It is an excellent tool for diagnosing learning disabilities when used in conjunction with other standardized tests.

Administration Time: 15 to 25 minutes

Age/Grade Levels: Ages 5 through 15

Subtest Information: The revision of the Test of Academic Achievement Skills has strengthened all of the original subtests and includes a new subtest—*Oral Reading Stories and Comprehension*. In addition to the new subtest, the revision includes the following subtests:

- *Spelling*—Students write letters and words from dictation.
- *Letter Reading and Word Reading*— Students decipher and pronounce letters and words.
- *Listening Comprehension*—Students listen to stories, understand, and remember in order to answer questions about the stories.
- *Oral Reading Stories and Comprehension*
- *Arithmetic*—This subtest consists of word problems and computation.

Hammill Multiability Achievement Test (HAMAT)

Authors: Donald D. Hammill, Wayne P. Hresko, Jerome J. Ammer, Mary E. Cronin, and Sally S. Quinby

Description of Test: The HAMAT is designed for use by psychologists, educational diagnosticians, counselors, and other professionals concerned with the assessment of academic achievement.

Administration Time: 30 to 60 minutes

Age/Grade Levels: Ages 7 through 17

Subtest Information: The HAMAT consists of the following subtests:

- *Reading*—This subtest consists of a series of paragraphs based on the cloze procedure.
- *Writing*—Students write sentences from dictation, stressing correctness.

- *Mathematics*—This subtest measures students' mastery of number facts and ability to complete mathematical calculations.
- *Facts*—Students answer questions based on the content of social studies, science, history, and literature.

Diagnostic Achievement Battery-3rd edition (DAB-3)

Authors: Phyllis Newcomer

Description of Test: The DAB-3 is designed to assess children's abilities in listening, speaking, reading, writing, and mathematics. It is a revision of one of the most popular and useful individual tests of school achievement. The DAB-3 uses 14 short subtests to identify a child's strengths and weaknesses across several areas of achievement.

Administration Time: 90 to 120 minutes

Age/Grade Levels: Ages 6-0 through 14-11

Subtest Information: The DAB-3 uses 14 short subtests to identify a child's strengths and weaknesses across several areas of achievement:

1. *Story Comprehension*
2. *haracteristics*
3. *Synonyms*
4. *Grammatical Completion*
5. *Alphabet/Word Knowledge*
6. *Reading Comprehension*
7. *Capitalization*
8. *Punctuation*
9. *Spelling*
10. *Contextual Language*
11. *Story Construction*
12. *Math Reasoning*
13. *Math Calculation*
14. *Phonemic Analysis*

Scores from these subtests can be combined to form eight composites:

1. *Total Achievement*
2. *Listening*
3. *Speaking*
4. *Reading*
5. *Writing*
6. *Mathematics*
7. *Spoken Language*
8. *Written Language*

Conclusion

Assessing academic achievement is a vital component of the assessment process. Understanding where a child has strengths and weaknesses in academic areas is necessary if you are going to diagnose a possible disability. There are numerous areas professionals can assess when giving an achievement test. Regardless of the number of areas, reading, writing, math, and spelling are part of every initial assessment battery for possible classification and/or placement in special education. We always need to know how a child compares academically, relative to the norms of the population. Therefore, all special educators should be able to read scores from achievement tests and, at a minimum, have a general understanding of what the assessment measures test and the purpose of the testing. For those who must administer achievement batteries, it is essential that a complete, thorough, valid, and reliable battery be given.

Vocabulary

Achievement tests: Tests designed to assess the academic progress of a student. A student's academic achievement skills are reviewed to determine how well he or she is performing in core skill areas such as reading, spelling, mathematics, and writing.

Affective comprehension: The student reads a paragraph or story, and the examiner evaluates the student's emotional responses to the text.

Applications: In math, this consists of measurement, reading graphs and tables, money and budgeting, time, and problem solving.

Arithmetic: The operations or computations performed in math.

Composition: The ability to generate ideas and to express them in an acceptable grammar, while adhering to certain stylistic conventions.

Content: In math, this consists of numeration, fractions, geometry, and algebra.

Critical comprehension: The student reads a paragraph or story and then analyzes, evaluates, or makes judgments on what he or she has read.

Disregard of punctuation: The student fails to observe punctuation—for example, may not pause for a comma, stop for a period, or indicate a vocal inflection, a question mark, or an exclamation point.

Gross mispronunciation: The student's pronunciation of a word bears little resemblance to the proper pronunciation.

Handwriting: The actual motor activity that is involved in writing.

Hesitation: The student hesitates for two or more seconds before pronouncing a word.

Incorrect algorithm: The procedures used by the student to solve the problem are inappropriate.

The student may skip a step, apply the correct steps in the wrong sequence, or use an inaccurate method.

Incorrect number fact: The number fact recalled by the student is inaccurate. For example, the student recalls the product of 9 and 6 as 52.

Incorrect operation: The student selects the incorrect operation. For example, the problem requires subtraction and the student adds.

Inferential comprehension: The student reads a paragraph or story and must interpret what has been read.

Insertion: The student inserts one or more words into the sentence being orally read.

Inversion: The student changes the order of words appearing in a sentence.

Lexical comprehension: The student reads a paragraph or story, and the examiner assesses his or her knowledge of vocabulary words.

Listening comprehension: The student listens to a paragraph or story read by the examiner and is then asked questions about what was read.

Literal comprehension: The student reads the paragraph or story and is then asked factual questions based on it.

Manuscript: Printing in writing.

Mathematics: The study of numbers and their relationships to time, space, volume, and geometry.

Miscue: The difference between what a reader states is on a page and what is actually on the page.

Omissions: The student skips individual words or groups of words when reading aloud.

Operations: In math, this consists of counting, computation, and reasoning.

Qualitative miscues: With this type of miscue analysis, the focus is on the quality of the error rather than the number of different mistakes.

Quantitative miscues: With this type of miscue analysis, the evaluator counts the number of reading errors made by the student.

Random error: The student's response is incorrect and apparently random. For example, the student writes 100 as the answer to $42 + 6$.

Spelling: The ability to use letters to construct words in accordance with accepted usage.

Substitution: The student replaces one or more words in the passage by one or more meaningful words.

Word attack skills: Those skills used to derive meaning and/or pronunciation of a word through context clues, structural analysis, or phonics.

Word recognition tests: Tests that explore the student's ability with respect to sight vocabulary.

School psychologist: The member of the MDT who normally administers intelligence tests, projective tests, personality inventories, and does observations of a student in a variety of settings.

School social worker: The member of the MDT who gathers and provides information concerning the family system.

Social history: A section of the parent intake form that asks about groups or organizations, social behavior in a group situation, hobbies, areas of interest, circle of friends, sports activities.

Special education teacher: The member of the MDT who consults with parents and teachers about prereferral recommendations, administers educa tional tests, and observes the student in a variety of settings.

Speech/language clinician: This professional will be involved in screening for speech and language developmental problems, be asked to provide a full evaluation on a suspected language disability, provide direct services, and consult with staff and parents.

10 | ASSESSMENT OF INTELLIGENCE

Key Terms

Adaptive behavior
Average
Borderline
Developmental delay
Full Scale IQ
High average

Intellectually deficient
Intelligence
IQ
Low average
Mental retardation
Performance subtests

Scaled scores
Superior
Verbal subtests
Very superior

Chapter Objectives

This chapter discusses the importance of intelligence testing in the special education process. After reading this chapter, you should be able to understand the following:

- The complexity of intelligence
- The purpose of intelligence testing
- What IQ scores represent
- Classification of IQ scores
- The Wechsler Scales of Intelligence
- Other measures of intellectual ability

INTELLIGENCE

It is very important to assess a child's intellectual functioning in an evaluation for special education; however, intelligence testing is an area of great controversy. Defining intelligence is not an easy task, and many different theorists have conflicting views on the nature of intelligence. Ask yourself what this means: "Sally is intelligent." What do you think you know about Sally? Is she smart? Bright? Exceptional? A great test taker? Has good common sense? Maybe—maybe not. The fact is, two people may be very intelligent yet have very different capabilities, strengths, and weaknesses. Although the term *intelligence* is not easily defined, we use the following definition. **Intelligence** is a general term referring to the ability to learn and to behave adaptively (Morris, 2001). In essence, intelligence is one's ability to learn new tasks and also be able to adapt to the situations one faces (referred to as **adaptive behavior**—see Chapter 11).

In special education, intelligence testing is usually completed by a psychologist. However, all professionals in special education need to understand intelligence tests and their purpose, because by learning how to interpret the results of intellectual measures, you can substantiate a diagnosis, help determine learning styles, assist in making recommendations, and arrive at accurate levels of intellectual expectation.

The Purpose of Intelligence Testing

Intelligence tests are psychological tests that are designed to measure a variety of mental functions, such as reasoning, comprehension, and judgment (Encyclopedia of Mental Disorders, 2011). Intelligence tests are most helpful (and probably most appropriate) when they are used to determine specific skills, abilities, and knowledge that a child either has or does not have. When such information is combined with other evaluation data, it can be directly applied to school programming. Intelligence tests attempt to measure a number of skills, including the following:

- Social judgment
- Level of thinking
- Language skills
- Perceptual organization
- Processing speed
- Spatial abilities
- Common sense
- Long- and short-term memory
- Abstract thinking
- Motor speed
- Word knowledge

Many of these skills depend on the experience, culture, training, and intact verbal abilities of the child being tested. However, responses to items concerning perceptual organization, processing speed, and spatial abilities depend less on experience and verbal skill than on hand-eye coordination and reasoning abilities.

Intelligence tests can yield valuable information about a student's ability to process information. In order to learn, every person must take in, make sense of, store, and retrieve information from memory in an efficient and accurate way. Each of us can process certain kinds of information more easily than others. In school, children need certain skills to function effectively, such as listening attentively so that other movements, sounds, or sights do not distract them. They must be able to understand the words spoken to them. This often requires children to hold multiple pieces of information in memory (e.g., page number, questions to answer) in order to act upon them. For example, they must be able to find the words they need to express themselves and, ultimately, commit these words to paper. This involves another whole series of processing skills such as holding a writing implement, coordinating visual and motor actions, holding information in memory until it can be transferred to paper, transforming sounds into written symbols, and understanding syntax, punctuation, and capitalization rules. They also must be able to interpret the nonverbal messages of others, such as a frown, a smile, a shake of the head. Moreover, they must do all of these things quickly and accurately and often in a setting with many distractions.

A thorough interpretation of an intelligence test can yield information about how effectively a child processes and retrieves information. Most individually administered intelligence tests can determine, at least to some degree, a child's ability to attend, process information quickly, distinguish relevant from less relevant details, put events in sequence, and retrieve words from memory. Ultimately, the goal of intelligence tests is to obtain an idea of the person's intellectual potential (Encyclopedia of Mental Disorders, 2011).

IQ Scores

When children take intelligence tests they normally receive an overall IQ score. **IQ** is an abbreviation for *intelligence quotient.* The IQ score often represents a measure of the child's overall potential relative to the norms of his or her age group. On almost all intelligence tests, the mean IQ score is 100 with a standard deviation of 15.0 (a popular exception is the Stanford-Binet–4, which has a standard deviation of 16).

When a child receives an IQ score, a classification often accompanies it. The following is a list of the various IQ scores one can obtain on most intelligence tests, the classifications that directly apply, and the percentages of children who are included (assuming a mean of 100 and an SD of 15):

IQ RANGE	CLASSIFICATION	PERCENT INCLUDED
130 and over	Very Superior	2.2
120–129	Superior	6.7
110–119	High Average	16.1
90–109	Average	50.0
80–89	Low Average	16.1
70–79	Borderline	6.7
	Well Below Average	
69 and below	Mental Retardation Developmentally Delayed Intellectually Deficient	2.2

Once an IQ score is calculated, the psychologist can make several determinations and report back to parents, teachers, and all members of the assessment team the following information:

- The child's present overall levels of intellectual functioning
- The child's present verbal intellectual functioning
- The child's nonlanguage intellectual functioning
- Indications of greater intellectual potential
- Possible patterns involving learning style, for example, verbal comprehension and concentration
- Possible influence of tension and anxiety on testing results
- Intellectual capability to deal with present grade-level academic demands
- The influence of intellectual functioning as a contributing factor to a child's past and present school difficulties—for example, test results showing limited intellectual level of development found in mental retardation

Advantages and Disadvantages of IQ Testing and IQ Scores

Research suggests that there are both advantages and disadvantages to IQ testing (Bank, 2011; Zisko, 2010; Encyclopedia of Mental Disorders, 2011; Ireland, 2010)

Advantages

- IQ testing assesses a wide variety of human behaviors better than any other measure that has been developed.
- IQ tests may be helpful in identifying academically gifted children. Even though an IQ test is not an indisputable measure of intelligence, it can single out children who show exceptional promise at a young age.
- IQ tests can help identify learning disabilities. IQ tests are designed to uncover learning potential. Therefore, an IQ test can help clarify whether a student who is struggling in school is being hampered by a learning disability or may be running up against a limitation in learning potential.
- Since the IQ tests can identify the potential for academic achievement, schools can begin to develop students in a way that takes advantage of their natural talents.
- IQ testing allows professionals to have a uniform way of comparing a person's performance with that of other people who are similar in age.
- IQ testing provides information on cultural and biological differences among people.
- IQ tests are very strong predictors of academic achievement and provide an outline of a person's mental strengths and weaknesses. Many times the scores have revealed talents in many people, which have led to an improvement in their educational opportunities. Teachers, parents, and psychologists are able to devise individual curricula that matches a person's level of development and expectations.
- IQ testing can identify students and individuals that may benefit from extra assistance, leading them to a better quality of life.
- Behavioral observations during IQ testing can provide a lot of information about personality characteristics of the examinee and their adjustment to stress and anxiety.

Disadvantages

- A central criticism of intelligence tests is that psychologists and educators use these tests to distribute the limited resources of our society. These test results are used to provide rewards such as special classes for gifted students, admission to college, and employment. Those who do not qualify for these resources based on intelligence test scores may feel angry and as if the tests are denying them opportunities for success.
- IQ tests also do not account for the effect on performance of such factors as malnutrition or other adverse affects of poverty.
- Many intelligence tests produce a single intelligence score. This single score is often inadequate in explaining the multidimensional.
- Intelligence tests only measure a sample of behaviors or situations in which intelligent behavior is revealed. For instance, some intelligence tests do not measure a person's everyday functioning, social knowledge, mechanical skills, and/or creativity (Encyclopedia of Mental Disorders, 2011).
- IQ testing can be used to classify children into stereotyped categories, which limit their freedom to choose fields of study.
- IQ test results can be misinterpreted as well as abused. IQ test results tend to vary among racial groups, which has given rise to theories perpetuated by such books as

The Bell Curve, which claim that some racial groups are inherently more intelligent than others. However, other books, such as *The Mismeasure of Man,* point out that cultural biases have been demonstrated in the development of many standardized tests, including IQ tests.

- IQ scores are not a measure of innate fixed ability or representative of all problem-solving situations. The tests tend to look at test results as absolute facts reflecting permanent characteristics in an individual.
- IQ scores are not concerned with the underlying processes involved in problem solving. They focus on the final product or outcome rather than on the steps involved in reaching the outcome. The practitioner may apply labels quickly and easily, without attempting to examine the specific strengths and weaknesses that might make precise therapeutic interventions or knowledgeable recommendations possible.
- IQ scores have limited usefulness in assessing minority groups with divergent cultural backgrounds. Research suggests that minorities tend to be at a disadvantage because of deficiencies in motivation, lack of practice, lack of familiarity with culturally loaded items, and difficulties in establishing rapport.

MEASURES OF INTELLECTUAL ABILITY

The Wechsler Scales of Intelligence

Many intelligence tests are used in special education and schools choose different tests based on personal preference and the strengths and weaknesses that each test exhibits. This section briefly summarizes some of the intelligence tests most often used by school systems.

The Wechsler Scales are one of the most widely used individual evaluation measures of intelligence used in today's schools. Although usually administered by psychologists, much useful information can be obtained by all special educators from the Wechsler Scales. Because of likely contact with this test, it is critical that special education teachers understand the nature of the scores and the implications of the results. A child's learning style, indications of greater potential, strengths and weaknesses, organizational skills, processing abilities, reasoning abilities, and adjustment to timed tasks are examples of useful information that can be obtained from this test.

The Wechsler Scales used for preschool children (*Wechsler Preschool Primary Scales of Intelligence:* WPPSI-III) and the Wechsler Scale used for individuals age 17 and older (*Wechsler Adult Intelligence Scale–3rd edition:* WAIS-IV) consist of two separate parts—the Verbal and Performance tests. The Verbal test is a group of **verbal subtests** that assess a student's verbal abilities. The Performance Test consists of a group of **performance subtests** that measure areas of intellectual functioning not involving verbal abilities.

On the Wechsler Scale for Children, *Wechsler Intelligence Scale for Children–4th edition* (WISC-IV), there are four parts called Composite Indexes.

- Verbal Composite Index (VCI)
- Perceptual Reasoning Index (PRI)
- Working Memory Index (WMI)
- Processing Speed Index (PSI)

All Wechsler Scales of Intelligence produce a Full Scale IQ Score (on the WISC-IV it is referred to as the Full Scale Index-FSIQ), representing the child's overall IQ score.

Author: David Wechsler

Description of Test: Three tests for different age levels each comprise two areas of assessment: Verbal and Performance. The verbal section assesses auditory/vocal tasks (auditory input and vocal output), whereas the performance areas examine visual/vocal and visual/motor tasks (visual input and vocal or motor output).

- *Wechsler Preschool and Primary Scale of Intelligence–Revised* (WPPSI-III)
- *Wechsler Intelligence Scale for Children–IV* (WISC-IV)
- *Wechsler Adult Intelligence Scale–III* (WAIS-IV)

Administration Time: 60 to 75 minutes

Age/Grade Levels: The three tests are designed for children from ages 2-6 to Adult. The age ranges for the three Wechsler tests are

- WPPSI-III: ages 2-6 to 7-3 years
- WISC-IV: ages 6-0 to 16-11 years
- WAIS-III: ages 17-0 years and older

Subtest Information: The three Wechsler Scales consist of a total of 21 possible subtests. Unless otherwise noted, all subtests are contained in each scale.

WECHSLER SUBTESTS (IN ALPHABETICAL ORDER)

- *Animal House*—Measures ability to associate meaning with symbol, visual–motor dexterity, flexibility, and speed in learning tasks (WPPSI-R only).
- *Arithmetic*—Measures mental alertness, concentration, attention, arithmetic reasoning, reaction to time pressure, and practical knowledge of computational facts. This is the only subtest directly related to the school curriculum and is greatly affected by anxiety.
- *Block Design*—Measures ability to perceive, analyze, synthesize, and reproduce abstract forms; visual–motor coordination; spatial relationships; general ability to plan and organize.
- *Cancellation*—Measures processing speed using random and structured animal target forms, which are common nonanimal objects (WISC-IV and WAIS IV only).
- *Coding*—Measures ability to associate meaning with symbol, visual–motor dexterity (pencil manipulation), flexibility, and speed in learning tasks (WPPSI-III and WISC-IV only).
- *Comprehension*—Measures social judgment, commonsense reasoning based on past experience, and practical intelligence.
- *Digit Span*—Measures attention, concentration, immediate auditory memory, auditory attention, and behavior in a learning situation. This subtest correlates poorly with general intelligence.
- *Digit Symbol*—Measures ability to associate meaning with symbol, visual–motor dexterity (pencil manipulation), flexibility, and speed in learning tasks (WAIS-IV only).
- *Fluid Weights*-Measures fluid reasoning (WAIS-IV only)
- *Geometric Design*—Measures a child's pencil control and visual–motor coordination, speed and accuracy, and planning capability (WPPSI-R only).
- *Information*—Measures general information acquired from experience and education, remote verbal memory, understanding, and associative thinking. The socioeconomic background and reading ability of the student may influence the subtest score.
- *Letter–Number Sequencing*—Measures working memory (adapted from WAIS-IV); child is presented a mixed series of numbers and letters and repeats them, putting numbers first in numerical order and then letters in alphabetical order (WISC-IV only).

- *Matrix Reasoning*—Measures fluid reasoning (highly reliable subtest on WAIS-IV and WPPSI-III); child is presented with a partially filled grid and asked to select the item that properly completes the matrix.
- *Mazes*—Measures ability to formulate and execute a visual–motor plan, pencil control and visual–motor coordination, speed and accuracy, and planning capability (WPPSI-R and WISC-IV only).
- *Object Assembly*—Measures immediate perception of a total configuration, part–whole relationships, and visual–motor/spatial coordination (WPPSI-III).
- *Picture Arrangement*—Measures visual perception, logical sequencing of events, attention to detail, and ability to see cause–effect relationships (WISC-IV and WAIS-IV only).
- *Picture Completion*—Measures visual alertness to surroundings, remote visual memory, attention to detail, and ability to isolate essential from nonessential detail.
- *Picture Concepts*—Measures fluid reasoning, perceptual organization, and categorization (requires categorical reasoning without a verbal response); from each of two or three rows of objects, child selects objects that go together based on an underlying concept (WPPSI-III and WISC-IV only).
- *Picture Naming*—Measures spoken vocabulary, expressive language ability, and word retrieval from long-term memory (WPPSI-III only).
- *Receptive Vocabulary*—Measures ability to recognize the meaning of a word (WPPSI-III only).
- *Sentences*—Measures attention, concentration, immediate auditory memory, auditory attention, and behavior in a learning situation (WPPSI-III only).
- *Similarities*—Measures abstract and concrete reasoning, logical thought processes, associative thinking, and remote memory.
- *Symbol Search*—Measures visual discrimination (WPPSI-III and WISC-IV only).
- *Visual Puzzles*—Measures fluid reasoning (WAIS-IV only)
- *Vocabulary*—Measures a child's understanding of spoken words, learning ability, general range of ideas, verbal information acquired from experience and education, and kind and quality of expressive language. This subtest is relatively unaffected by emotional disturbance, but is highly susceptible to cultural background and level of education. It is also the best single measure of intelligence in the entire battery.
- *Word Reasoning*—Measures reasoning with verbal material; child identifies underlying concept given successive clues (WPPSI-III and WISC-IV only).

COMPOSITE SCORES FOR THE WISC-IV. To make interpretation more clinically meaningful, the dual IQ and Index structure from WISC-III has been replaced with a single system of four composite scores (consistent with the four Index scores in WISC-III) and the Full Scale IQ. This new system helps you better understand a child's needs in relation to contemporary theory and research in cognitive information processing.

Note: *indicates that the subtest is not included in the Index total score.

VERBAL COMPREHENSION INDEX (VCI):

Similarities

Vocabulary

Comprehension

**Information*

**Word Reasoning*

PERCEPTUAL REASONING INDEX (PRI):

Block Design

Picture Concepts

Matrix Reasoning
*Picture Completion

WORKING MEMORY INDEX (WMI):

Digit Span

Letter–Number Sequencing
*Arithmetic

PROCESSING SPEED INDEX (PSI):

Coding

Symbol Search

*Cancellation

SCALED SCORES ON THE WECHSLER TESTS.   For each subtest on the Wechsler Tests, a student receives a raw score. This raw score is then transformed into a scaled score (see Chapter 6 for a review). **Scaled scores** are very specific subtest scores ranging from 1 to 19, with a mean of 10. They follow the following classification format:

SCALED SCORE	CLASSIFICATION
1–3	Developmental Delay
4–5	Borderline
6–7	Low Average
8–12	Average
13–14	High Average
15–16	Superior
17–19	Very Superior

For example, a scaled score of 7 on the Vocabulary subtest with a 13 on the Comprehension subtest indicates a student with much greater strength in comprehension than vocabulary, compared to age group norms. Moreover, when detecting learning disabilities in psychoeducational assessment for a given child, such a great variance in the distribution of scaled scores is often present with a learning disability.

The protocol reveals many things about the test, and its cover contains a great deal of useful information. The first thing to look at is the pattern of scaled scores that appears next to the raw scores (the number of correct responses on a given test) on the front of the protocol. Scale scores can range from 1 to 19, with 10 considered the midpoint. Ranges of scaled scores as noted in the previous chart can be related to percentiles as shown by the following chart. To get a better idea of the value of a scaled score, simply multiply it by 10, and that will give you a rough idea of the correlated IQ value. It is from these scaled scores that our investigation of greater potential begins.

Table 10.1	Relationship among IQ Ranges, Scaled Scores, and Percentiles	
RANGE	**SCALED SCORE**	**PERCENTILE**
Very Superior	19	99.9
Very Superior	18	99.6
Very Superior	17	99
Superior	16	98
Superior	15	95
Above Average	14	91
Above Average	13	84
Average	12	75
Average	11	63
Average	10	50
Average	9	37
Average	8	25
Low Average	7	16
Low Average	6	9
Borderline	5	5
Borderline	4	2
Mental Retardation	3	1
Mental Retardation	2	0.4
Mental Retardation	1	0.1

Note: This chart is used only for a general relationship between IQs, scaled scores, and percentiles, and is not statistically exact. The conversion tables used by the psychologist in deriving the actual IQ from test results are different and are located within the manual.

The scaled scores are calculated to get three separate IQ scores: *Verbal IQ, Performance IQ,* and a **Full Scale IQ** (the student's overall IQ score). When there is a discrepancy between the Verbal and Performance sections on the Wechsler tests, this is one indication of a possible learning disability.

The IQ results from the Wechsler Scales may not always indicate an individual's true intellectual potential. Although the Wechsler Scales are valid tests, the resulting scores can be influenced by many factors—tension, poor self-esteem, language difficulties, culture—and may not be valid, therefore necessitating further analysis. To determine if the resulting scores are valid, four indicators of an individual's true ability are applied to the results of the test. Any one indicator by itself should bring into question the validity of the results and initiate an analysis of the factors that may contribute to such variability.

OTHER MEASURES OF INTELLIGENCE

There are many other measures of intelligence used for assessment in special education. Some of the most popular ones are discussed in this section.

- *The Stanford-Binet Intelligence Scales, 5th edition* (SBIS-5)
- *Kaufman Assessment Battery for Children* (KABC)

- *Kaufman Brief Intelligence Test* (KBIT)
- *Slosson Intelligence Test–Revised 3rd edition* (SIT-R3)
- *Comprehensive Test of Nonverbal Intelligence-2nd edition* (CTONI-2)
- *Test of Nonverbal Intelligence, 4th edition* (TONI-4)
- *Otis-Lennon School Ability Test, 8th Edition* (OLSAT-8)
- *Woodcock-Johnson III, Normative Updates Tests of Cognitive Ability* (WJ III COG)

The Stanford-Binet Intelligence Scale, 5th Edition (SB-5)

Authors: Gaile Roid

Description of Test: The SB5 is an individually administered assessment of intelligence and cognitive abilities.

Administration Time: The SB5 includes many untimed tasks with an average testing time of 45 to 60 minutes.

Age/Grade Levels: Ages 2 to Adult

Subtest Information: The SB5 consists of five Factors covering 10 Domains (subtests):

Fluid Reasoning (FR)

Nonverbal Fluid Reasoning*

Verbal Fluid Reasoning

Knowledge (KN)

Nonverbal Knowledge

Verbal Knowledge*

Quantitative Reasoning (QR)

Nonverbal Quantitative Reasoning

Verbal Quantitative Reasoning

Visual–Spatial Processing (VS)

Nonverbal Visual–Spatial Processing

Verbal Visual–Spatial Processing

Working Memory (WM)

Nonverbal Working Memory

Verbal Working Memory

After completing both Routing Tests (starred subtests), administer all nonverbal subtests, followed by all verbal subtests.

Kaufman Assessment Battery for Children–2nd Edition (KABC-II)

Authors: Alan S. Kaufman and Nadeen L. Kaufman

Description of Test: This individually administered intelligence test was developed to minimize the influence of language and acquired facts and skills on the measurement of a child's intellectual ability.

Administration Time: 25 to 55 minutes (core battery, Luria model), 35 to 70 minutes (core battery, CHC model)

Age/Grade Levels: Ages 3 to 18

Subtest Information:

- *Face Recognition*—This test requires the child to choose from a group photo one or two faces that are exposed briefly.
- *Gestalt Closure*—This test requires the child to name an object or scene from a partially constructed inkblot.
- *Hand Movements*—The child is required to perform a series of hand movements presented by the examiner.
- *Magic Windows*—This test requires the child to identify a picture that the examiner exposes slowly through a window—only a small part is shown.
- *Matrix Analogies*—This test requires the child to choose a meaningful picture or abstract design that best completes a visual analogy.
- *Number Recall*—The child is required to repeat a series of digits in the same sequence as presented by the examiner.
- *Photo Series*—This test requires the child to place photographs of an event in the proper order.
- *Spatial Memory*—This test requires the child to recall the placement of a picture on a page that was briefly exposed.
- *Triangles*—This test requires the child to assemble several identical triangles into an abstract pattern.
- *Word Order*—The child is required to touch a series of silhouettes of objects in the same order as presented verbally by the examiner.

Kaufman Brief Intelligence Test–2nd Edition (KBIT-2)

Authors: Alan S. Kaufman and Nadeen L. Kaufman

Description of Test: The KBIT-2 is an assessment device for developing and evaluating remedial programs for those with mental disabilities. It may also be used for normal children from birth to age 10. It is a brief, individually administered screener of verbal and nonverbal ability.

Administration Time: Approximately 20 minutes

Age/Grade Levels: Ages 4 to Adult

Subtest Information: KBIT-2 measures two distinct cognitive abilities through two scales—Crystallized and Fluid.

- Crystallized (Verbal) Scale contains two item types: Verbal Knowledge and Riddles
- Fluid (Nonverbal) Scale is a Matrices subtest

Slosson Intelligence Test–Revised 3rd edition (SIT-R3)

Authors: Richard L. Slosson; Revised by Charles L. Nicholson and Terry L. Hibpshman

Description of Test: The *Slosson Intelligence Test–Revised 3rd edition* (SIT-3) is a quick, reliable, user-friendly instrument for evaluating crystallized verbal intelligence in children and adults. In addition to being one of the few measures assessing the infant, toddler, and preschool years (two and above), it can also be used with individuals with Severely/Profoundly disabilities because its IQ scales range from 36 to 164.

Administration Time: 10 to 20 minutes

Age/Grade Levels: Preschool to Adult

Subtest Information: The SIT-R3 test items are derived from the following cognitive domains: Information, Comprehension, Arithmetic, Similarities and Differences, Vocabulary, and Auditory Memory. Cognitive areas of measurements include:

- *Vocabulary:* 33 items
- *General Information:* 29 items
- *Similarities and Differences:* 30 items
- *Comprehension:* 33 items
- *Quantitative:* 34 items
- *Auditory Memory:* 28 items

Comprehensive Test of Nonverbal Intelligence–2nd edition (CTONI-2)

Authors: Donald D. Hammill, Nils A. Pearson, and Lee Wiederholt

Description of Test: The *CTONI-2* is a norm-referenced test that uses nonverbal formats to measure general intelligence of children and adults whose performance on traditional tests might be adversely affected by subtle or overt impairments involving language or motor abilities. The *CTONI-2* measures analogical reasoning, categorical classification, and sequential reasoning

Administration Time: 60 minutes

Age/Grade Levels: Ages 6-0 to 89-11

Subtest Information: The *CTONI-2* measures analogical reasoning, categorical classification, and sequential reasoning, using six subtests in two different contexts: Pictures of familiar objects (e.g., people, toys, animals) and geometric designs (unfamiliar sketches and drawings). The six subtests are:

1. Pictorial Analogies
2. Geometric Analogies
3. Pictorial Categories
4. Geometric Categories
5. Pictorial Sequences
6. Geometric Sequences

Test of Nonverbal Intelligence–4th Edition (TONI-4)

Authors: Linda Brown, Rita J. Sherbenou, and Susan Johnsen

Description of Test: The *Test of Nonverbal Intelligenc–Fourth Edition* is a practical, easy-to-use, norm-referenced instrument that measures an individual's intelligence. The administration and response format are pragmatic with simple oral instructions, requiring test takers to answer only with simple but meaningful gestures such as pointing, nodding, or blinking. This test can be used for those who have language, hearing, or motor impairments, or are not familiar with mainstream American culture.

Administration Time: 15 to 20 minutes

Age/Grade Levels: Ages 6-0 to 89-11

Subtest Information: There are no subtests on the TONI-4. However, the TONI-4 has two equivalent forms: Form A and Form B. Each form consists of 60 items, all of which are abstract/figural (i.e., void of pictures or cultural symbols), thus educational, cultural, or experiential backgrounds will not adversely affect test results. All items are arranged in easy-to-difficult order. Each item contains one or more of the eight salient characteristics: shape, position, direction, rotation, contiguity, shading, size, and movement.

Otis-Lennon School Ability Test–8th Edition (OLSAT-8)

Authors: Arthur S. Otis and Roger T. Lennon

Description of Test: OLSAT-8 measures the cognitive abilities that relate to a student's ability to learn in school. By assessing a student's abstract thinking and reasoning abilities, OLSAT-8 supplies educators with information they can use to enhance the insight that traditional achievement tests provide.

Administration Time: A–C (Grades K through 2), 75 minutes over two sessions; Levels D–G (Grades 3 through 12), 60 minutes

Age/Grade Levels: Grades K through 12

Subtest Information: The test is broken down into five clusters:

- *Verbal Comprehension*—This cluster includes following directions, antonyms, sentence completion, and sentence arrangement.
- *Verbal Reasoning*—This cluster includes logical selection, verbal analogies, verbal classification, and inference.
- *Pictorial Reasoning*—This cluster includes picture classification, picture analogies, and picture series.
- *Figural Reasoning*—This cluster includes figural classification, figural analogies, and figural series.
- *Quantitative Reasoning* (given in Levels E–G)—This cluster includes number series, numeric inference, and number matrix.

Woodcock-Johnson III, Normative Updates Tests of Cognitive Ability (WJ III COG)

Authors: Richard W. Woodcock, Kevin S. McGrew, and Nancy Mather

Description of Test: The WJ III COG provides a comprehensive system for measuring general intellectual ability, specific cognitive abilities, scholastic aptitude, oral language, and academic achievement.

Administration Time: Varies, about 5 minutes per test; 7 tests (35–40 minutes)

Age/Grade Levels: Ages 2.0 to 90+ years; Grades K.0 to graduate school

Subtest Information: There are 10 tests in the Standard Battery, and an additional 10 in the Extended Battery, allowing for a considerably detailed analysis of cognitive abilities. The Cattell-Horn-Carroll theory factors that this test examines are: Comprehension-Knowledge, Long-Term Retrieval, Visual-Spatial Thinking, Auditory Processing, Fluid Reasoning, Processing Speed, Short-Term Memory and Quantitative Knowledge and Reading-Writing Ability. A General Intellectual Ability (GIA) or Brief Intellectual Ability (BIA) may be obtained.

Standard Battery Subtests
1. Verbal Comprehension
2. Visual-Auditory Learning
3. Spatial Relations
4. Sound Blending
5. Concept Formation
6. Visual Matching
7. Numbers Reversed
8. Incomplete Words
9. Auditory Working Mem.
10. Vis-Aud. Learn.–Delayed

Extended Battery Subtests
1. General Information
2. Retrieval Fluency
3. Picture Recognition
4. Auditory Attention
5. Analysis-Synthesis
6. Decision Speed
7. Memory for Words
8. Rapid Picture Naming
9. Planning
10. Pair Cancellation

CONCLUSION

Intelligence tests are very important in the determination of various disabilities. As you will see later in this book, a determination of whether a child has a learning disability, emotional disturbance, or mental retardation cannot be done without an IQ score. When all is said and done, IQ scores give the special educator a solid indicator of a child's overall potential. Furthermore, when properly evaluated, intelligence tests can uniquely describe in detail numerous strengths and weaknesses of a child as no other tests can do. Utilizing these data appropriately is critical for future placement, recommendations, expectations, and appropriate services for a child.

Vocabulary

Adaptive behavior: The effectiveness or degree with which individuals meet the standards of personal independence and social responsibility expected for age and cultural groups.

Average: A classification that refers to an IQ score of 90 to 109, with a mean of 100 and standard deviation of 15.

Borderline: A classification that refers to an IQ score of 70 to 79, with a mean of 100 and standard deviation of 15.

Developmentally delayed: A classification that refers to an IQ score of 69 or below, with a mean of 100 and standard deviation of 15 (see also *intellectually deficient* and *mental retardation*).

Full Scale IQ: On the Wechsler Scales, the student's overall IQ score.

High average: A classification that refers to an IQ score of 110 to 119, with a mean of 100 and standard deviation of 15.

Intellectually deficient: A classification that refers to an IQ score of 69 and below, with a mean of 100 and standard deviation of 15.

Intelligence: A general term referring to the ability to learn and to behave adaptively.

IQ: An abbreviation for intelligence quotient. It is the score one receives on the IQ test.

Low average: A classification that refers to an IQ score of 80 to 89, with a mean of 100 and standard deviation of 15.

Mental retardation: A classification on the Wechsler Tests that refers to an IQ score of 69 and below, with a mean of 100 and standard deviation of 15.

Performance subtests: Sections on IQ tests that measure a child's nonverbal abilities.

Scaled score: Scores on the Wechsler scales ranging from 1 to 19 (with a mean of 10 and a standard deviation of 3) that are calculated to provide three separate IQ scores: Verbal IQ, Performance IQ, and a Full Scale IQ.

Superior: A classification that refers to an IQ score of 120 to 129, with a mean of 100 and standard deviation of 15.

Verbal subtests: Sections on IQ tests that measure a child's verbal abilities.

Very superior: A classification that refers to an IQ score of 130 and over, with a mean of 100 and standard deviation of 15.

11 | ASSESSMENT OF BEHAVIOR

Key Terms

Adaptive behavior

Anecdotal recording

Apperception tests

Behavioral intervention plan

Duration recording

Event recording

Functional behavioral assessment

Interview

Latency recording

Projective drawing tests

Rating scales

Sentence completion tests

Structured interview

Target behaviors

Unstructured interview

Chapter Objectives

This chapter focuses on the assessment of behavior. After reading this chapter, you should be able to understand the following:

▪ The purpose of a behavioral assessment

▪ Observational techniques

▪ Recording behaviors

▪ Interviews

▪ A student's behavior during testing

▪ Psychological tests

▪ Projective drawing tests

▪ Apperception tests

▪ Sentence completion tests

▪ Adaptive behavior

▪ Functional behavioral assessment

▪ Behavioral intervention plans

ASSESSING PROBLEM BEHAVIOR

When a referral is made for a child who is suspected of having a disability, a behavioral and emotional assessment is a normal part of the evaluation. Behavioral and emotional measures are usually administered and reported on by the school psychologist. The behavior of a given child can have a serious impact on his or her learning processes. For example, a child with problems staying on task or focusing may have the intelligence to do math or social studies but consistently gets low grades because he or she cannot sit still in order to complete the assignments given by the teacher (Pierangelo & Giuliani, 2009).

Behaviors that are not appropriate in school can occur for many different reasons, including

- Attention deficit problems
- Problems with teachers of certain classes
- Emotional disturbance
- Depression
- Environmental factors at home
- Anxiety

When behaviors are believed to contribute to a child's problems in school, a variety of methods can be used for assessment. Because there are so many different possible scenarios involving a child acting inappropriately in school, it is critical to do a thorough behavioral assessment. If future placement in special education programs notes behavior issues, the reasons and the nature of the appropriate services will be more easily clarified.

Observation

Observation as part of the assessment process is often done when parents, teachers, or any other individuals working with a child feel there are possible concerns involving emotional, social, or behavioral issues. The purpose of observation is to gain an awareness of what factors, if any, are influencing the behavior that the child is exhibiting. To do a complete and thorough observation, it is critical to include the following situations:

- **Observation of a specific situation:** Here, an observation of the child is done during a specified time, such as during lunchtime, recess, or show and tell.
- **Observation in various settings:** Here, an observation of the child is done across different settings, such as in the classroom, on the playground, and during band.
- **Observation at different times during the day:** Here, an observation of the child is done in the morning, in the afternoon, and by parents in the evening.

There are many different ways to record a child's behavior for assessment purposes. Regardless of method, the first goal of observation is to determine the target behaviors. **Target behaviors** are those that the observer seeks to record when doing the observation. For example, an observer could be looking for how many times a child taps his or her pencil during a 30-minute period. Here, the target behavior would be tapping the pencil. Once the target behavior is established, recording of behaviors can begin. In assessment, various types of recordings are often used when doing an observation. Four of the most common are:

- **Anecdotal recording:** Here, the observer records behaviors and interactions within a given time frame (e.g., recording a child's behavior from 9:00 A.M. to 9:30 A.M.).
- **Event recording:** Here, the observer is looking specifically for one or more target behaviors and records the frequency with which they occur. Event recording is also referred to as *frequency counting* because the observer is simply counting the number of times a behavior occurs (e.g., recording the number of times a child gets out of his chair in a given period of time).
- **Latency recording:** Here, the observer determines the amount of time between a given stimulus for the child and the response (e.g., the time it takes a student to get out her pencil after the teacher says, "Take out your pencil").

- **Duration recording:** Here, the observer notes the amount of time a target behavior occurs (e.g., watching a child for 1 hour who is supposed to be reading—the child reads only 12 minutes of that time).

By doing such observations, information about the child becomes much more comprehensive. Collectively, observations should provide the following:

- The nature of the most frequently seen behaviors
- Information that can be related to the types of services the child may need
- Information to help with intervention plans and instructional goals for the child
- An understanding of how the child is currently functioning in certain areas

Later, this can be compared to the child's behavior after intervention begins. Therefore, progress can be measured from the first observation (baseline) to after a plan or program has been implemented for the child to determine if it is actually working and signs of progress are being noticed.

Interviews

Besides observations, interviews become a very important part of the behavioral assessment. An **interview** is a method of gathering information that is conducted face to face between two people (the interviewer and the interviewee), whereby recorded responses to questions are obtained. Interviews can be very effective because they are personal, emotional, and flexible. Interviews can be of two types:

- **Structured interview:** An interview in which the individual is asked a specific set of predetermined questions in a controlled manner.
- **Unstructured interview:** An interview in which the questions are not predetermined, thereby allowing for substantial discussion and interaction between the interviewer and interviewee.

Parents, teachers, and the child should be interviewed in order to gain insight into the nature and history of the child's difficulties. It is important to interview the child because the evaluator needs to know whether the child has any awareness that there is a concern about his or her behaviors and the degree to which he or she may be willing to change.

UNDERSTANDING A STUDENT'S BEHAVIOR DURING ASSESSMENT

There are many behaviors that should be watched when doing an assessment for a child with a suspected disability. It is important that evaluators consider carefully any peculiarities exhibited by a student during evaluation. Almost any peculiarity can be seen as either a symptom or a problem. For example, a student who hesitates for long periods before answering may be doing so as a symptom of difficulty processing information or as a symptom of low self-esteem. However, this hesitation itself becomes a problem during evaluation because it slows the student down considerably and therefore limits strong performance. Evaluations must consider what peculiarities reveal as well as the impact they have. Accordingly, the following behaviors should be recorded in the final report: adjustment to the situation, reaction time, nature of responses, verbalizations, organizational approach used during testing, adaptability, and attitude.

Adjustment to the Situation

Children's adjustment to a new situation (e.g., initial meeting with evaluator, IQ testing, fine motor testing, etc.) can vary greatly. The significance of any adjustment period is not necessarily the student's initial reactions but the duration of the period of maladjustment. Some children may be initially nervous and uptight but relax as time goes on with the reassurance of the examiner. However, children who maintain a high level of discomfort throughout the sessions may be harboring more serious problems.

Elements of the testing environment itself should be considered as possible distracters for the student being tested. Noise, poor lighting, the presence of antagonistic peers, even an intimidating examiner can adversely impact a student during testing. It is the evaluator's responsibility to limit such variables and to consider the special needs of each student. Examiners should be aware of any overt signs of tension (observable behaviors indicative of underlying tension) exhibited by a child that may affect the outcome of the test results: constant leg motion, little or no eye contact with the examiner, consistent finger or pencil tapping. Any oppositional behaviors (behaviors that test the limits and guidelines of the examiner) should also be noted: singing or making noises while being tested, keeping a jacket on or covering most of his or her face with a hat, and so forth. If this type of tension is extreme, the examiner may want to note in the report the effects of such factors on performance and alert the reader to the possibility that the results may be minimal indicators of ability.

Reaction Time

The speed with which a child answers questions can indicate several things. The child who impulsively answers incorrectly without thinking may have high levels of anxiety that interfere with the ability to concentrate before responding. On the other hand, the child who blocks or delays may be afraid of reaction or criticism and may be using these techniques to ward off what he or she perceives will be an ego-deflating situation.

Nature of Responses

The types of responses a child gives during an evaluation may indicate certain difficulties. For example, a child who constantly asks to have questions repeated may have hearing difficulties. (Hearing and vision acuity should be determined prior to a testing situation.) Or the child who asks to have questions repeated may be having problems processing information and may need more time to understand what is being asked. If a child is overtly negative or self-defeating in responding—for example, "I'm so stupid" or "I'll never get any right"—the child is probably exhibiting a very low level of self-esteem or hiding a learning problem.

Verbalizations

A student's verbal interaction with the examiner during an evaluation can be very telling. Some children with high levels of anxiety may try to vent their tension through constant verbalizations. Of course, the tension can interfere with their ability to think clearly and to focus on task, and the verbalizing can also disrupt hearing and thought processes. Examiners should also be aware that verbal hesitations may indicate other problems: immature speech patterns, expressive language problems, poor self-esteem, or lack of understanding of the question due to limited intellectual capacity.

Organizational Approach Used During Testing

A child who sizes up a situation and systematically approaches a task using trial and error may have excellent internal organization, the ability to concentrate, and low levels of tension and anxiety. However, some children with emotional problems may also perform well on short-term tasks because they see it as a challenge and can organize themselves to perform well over a relatively short period of time. Their particular problems in organization and consistency may come when they are asked to perform this way over an extended period of time. On the other hand, some children become less organized under the stress of a time constraint. A child's organizational and performance styles when dealing with a task under time restrictions are factors considered in the investigation of his or her overall learning style.

Children with chaotic internal organization may appear to know what they are doing, but the overall outcome of the task indicates a great deal of energy input with very low production. They essentially "spin their wheels," and the energy output is a cover for not knowing what to do. Children with attention deficit/hyperactivity disorder also may exhibit a confused sense of organization. However, there are other factors besides attention span that go into the diagnosis of this disorder, discussed later in this chapter.

Adaptability

The ability of a student to adapt or shift from one task to another without difficulty is a very important factor in determining learning style and may be one predictor for the successful completion of a task. A student's ability to shift without expending a great deal of energy results in more available resources for the next task. A student who is rigid and does not adapt well uses much available energy to switch tasks, thereby reducing the chances of success on a new task.

The ability to sustain interest may also be a direct result of available energy. A child who loses interest quickly may be immature, overwhelmed, or preoccupied. Some of these reactions may be normal for the early ages. However, as the child gets older, such reactions may be symptomatic of other factors (e.g., learning problems, emotional issues, or limited intellectual capacity).

Attitude

The attitude that a child demonstrates toward a testing situation may be reflective of his or her attitude within the classroom. A child who is oppositional or uncooperative may be one who needs to feel in control of the situation. The more controlling a child is, the more out of control he or she feels. A child needs control to secure predictability in dealing with situations despite energy levels lowered by conflict and tension. Children under tension do not adapt well and are easily thrown by new situations or people. By controlling a situation or a person, they know what to expect. On the other hand, a child who tries hard to succeed may do so for several reasons, such as parental approval or personal satisfaction. He or she may enjoy success and find the tasks normally challenging. Generally, this type of child is not thrown by a mistake and can easily move to the next task without difficulty.

All behavior is essentially a message, and the way a child reacts to being tested can be a clue to learning style or problem areas. The evaluator who can attend to a child's behavior by being aware of significant signs may come to a better understanding of the child's needs and may learn even more about the child than the test results will indicate.

ASSESSING EMOTIONAL AND SOCIAL DEVELOPMENT

Assessment of emotional and social development is not an easy task. Throughout the course of a given day, children are involved in many situations with different people. It is not like assessing math or reading whereby we can normally compare numbers of a given child to national norms and make conclusions based on the quantifiable data. A child may act completely different with one person than another. Assessment of a child's behaviors involves knowledge about the following:

- The degree to which the child believes that personal behaviors make a difference in his or her life
- The child's tolerance for frustration
- General activity level
- The child's self-view
- How the child responds emotionally
- How much conflict the child is experiencing

Psychological Tests

There are numerous psychological tests used in the assessment of behavior in children. Psychological tests are almost always administered exclusively by the school psychologist. One of the most common types of psychological tests is called a *projective test,* which tries to elicit feelings from the student about life through projection of emotions onto the test stimuli. The three most common types of projective test used in school systems for assessment are projective drawing tests, apperception tests, and sentence completion tests.

A **projective drawing test** requires an individual to respond to indistinct stimuli. The individual's interpretation of the stimuli is meant to reveal personality traits. The tests are used to get the child to "project" his feelings about himself onto paper. The examiner looks for certain patterns in the drawings and the way the child handles what is being asked (e.g., a child who draws away from everyone else may have low self-esteem, or a child who takes the pencil and writes very hard on the paper may be exhibiting anger).

Goodenough-Harris Drawing Test (GHDT)

Authors: Florence L. Goodenough and Dale B. Harris

Description of Test: Developed in 1926 and revised in the late 1940s, the GHDT's purpose is to assess mental maturity nonverbally. The test is a formal system of administering and scoring human figure drawings to screen children for intellectual maturity as well as emotional problems. Practitioners can detect children who are at risk of having an emotional disturbance by comparing the scores obtained on their figure drawings with the scores from a normative sample.

Administration Time: 15 to 20 minutes

Age/Grade Levels: Ages 3 to 15-11, but the preferred ages are 3 to 10

Subtest Information: The Goodenough-Harris Drawing Test is composed of two scales: Man and Woman. Performance may be scored by a short, holistic method with Quality Scale Cards or by a more detailed method. Each drawing may also be scored for the presence of up to 73 characteristics.

Draw-A-Person: Screening Procedure for Emotional Disturbance (DAP:SPED)

Authors: Jack A. Naglieri, Timothy J. McNeish, and Achilles N. Bardos (1991)

Description of Test: The purpose of the DAP:SPED is to identify emotional or behavioral disorders. The test comprises a formal system of administering and scoring human figure drawings to screen children for emotional problems. Practitioners can detect children who are at risk of having an emotional disturbance by comparing the scores obtained on their figure drawings with the scores from the normative sample.

Administration Time: 15 minutes

Age/Grade Levels: Ages 6 to 17

Subtest Information: There are no subtests. The DAP:SPED scoring system is composed of two types of criteria, or items. With the first type, eight dimensions of each drawing are scored; a separate template for each age group is provided. With the second type of criteria, each drawing is rated according to 47 specific items. Cutoff scores are divided into three categories: additional assessment is not indicated; additional assessment is indicated; and additional assessment is strongly indicated.

Apperception Tests

Apperception tests require a child to view various picture cards and "tell a story" about what is shown. The child would normally tell a story of what happened before, during, and after the scene shown. Apperception tests try to elicit central themes from the child. For example, a child may consistently tell stories of loneliness, sadness, or perhaps anger. The examiner normally writes down every word the child says in narrative form and then tries to decipher general patterns of self-thoughts that the child may be projecting.

Children's Apperception Test (CAT)

Authors: Leopold Bellack and Sonya Sorel Bellak

Description of Test: This projective technique presents situations of special concern to children. It consists of 10 animal pictures in a social context that involve the child in conflict, identities, roles, family structures, and interpersonal interaction. This test uses a storytelling technique for personality evaluation. It employs pictures of animal figures in a variety of situations because it is assumed that children will be more comfortable expressing their feelings with pictures of animals than of humans.

Administration Time: Untimed

Age/Grade Levels: Ages 5 to 10

Subtest Information: There are no subtests.

Thematic Apperception Test (TAT)

Author: Henry A. Murray

Description of Test: Created in 1943, the TAT is still a widely used projective test that helps assess an individual's perception of interpersonal relationships. The 31 picture cards included in the TAT are used to stimulate stories or descriptions about relationships or social situations and can help identify dominant drives, emotions, sentiments, conflicts, and complexes.

Administration Time: Variable (31 picture cards/2 series of 10 cards for boys, girls, men, and women)

Age/Grade Levels: Age 10 and older

Subtest Information: No subtests. Individuals react (orally or in writing) to a series of picture cards.

Sentence Completion Tests

Sentence completion tests provide the beginning of a sentence that the student needs to finish. The "fill-ins" are believed to give indications of the emotions and feelings that the student is experiencing. Sentence completion tests can be extremely useful because one response can elicit many questions to ask the child in future interviews. For example, if a child responds to "I could do better if _____" with the response "I tried harder," you can later ask the child many questions about why his effort is poor or not up to a certain level.

Examples From a Sentence Completion Test

1. I wish _____
2. When I grow up _____
3. My mother _____
4. My best subject is _____
5. I wish my teacher would _____
6. On the school bus _____
7. I could do better if _____

Rating Scales

Rating scales are often given not only to the student but also to the parents and teachers. A rating scale gives a statement about a behavior of a child whereupon the individual (*the rater*) has to rate the frequency, intensity, and/or duration. By rating various situations, the examiner gets an idea of the child's strengths and weaknesses. Raters are normally asked to evaluate whether a given behavior is present or absent. The tremendous value of a rating scale is that it allows the examiner to get a differing viewpoint from other people who interact with the child. A teacher may have a different perception of a child's behavior than a parent does. By getting various viewpoints, a more comprehensive evaluation of the child's daily functioning can be established.

Conners 3rd Edition™ (Conners 3)

Author: C. Keith Conners

Description of Test: Conners 3rd Edition™ (Conners 3™) is the result of four years of extensive product research and development (Multi-Health Systems, 2011). School psychologists, clinicians, psychiatrists, pediatricians, child protection agencies, and mental health workers can count on the Conners 3 to be a reliable and dependable tool capable of supporting them in the diagnostic and identification process.

Based on the solid findings and key elements of its predecessor, the Conners' Rating Scales–Revised (CRS–R™), the Connors 3 offers a thorough assessment of ADHD. The Conners 3 now addresses comorbid disorders such as Oppositional Defiant Disorder and Conduct Disorder. Each parent, teacher, and self-report form is available in full-length and short versions.

The Conners 3–Parent (Conners 3–P)

The Conners 3–P assesses behaviors and other concerns in children from the age of 6–18. Both full-length and short [Conners 3–P (S)] versions are available. The full-length version provides more comprehensive results, and is recommended for both initial evaluations and comprehensive reevaluations. The short version provides evaluation of the key areas of inattention, hyperactivity/impulsivity, learning problems, executive functioning, aggression, and peer relations, making it an ideal measurement when time is limited or for follow-up testing/treatment monitoring. When used in conjunction with teacher ratings, differences between home and school are highlighted.

The Conners 3–Teacher (Conners 3–T)

The Conners 3 T assesses behaviors and other concerns in children from the age of 6–18 years old. Both full-length and short versions are available. The full-length version provides more comprehensive results, and is recommended for both initial evaluations and reevaluations. The short version provides evaluation of the key areas of inattention, hyperactivity/impulsivity, learning problems/executive functioning, aggression, and peer relations, making it an ideal measurement when time is limited or for follow-up testing. When used with the parent form, differences between home and school are highlighted.

The Conners 3–Self-Report (Conners 3–SR)

The Conners 3–SR measures behaviors and other concerns in children 8–18 years old. Both full-length and short versions are available. The full-length version provides more comprehensive results, and is recommended for initial evaluations and comprehensive reevaluations. The short version provides evaluation of the key areas of inattention, hyperactivity/impulsivity, learning problems, aggression, and family relations, making it an ideal measure when time is limited or for follow-up testing.

Conners 3 Global Index (Conners 3GI™)

The Conners 3GI is a fast and effective measure of general psychopathology and a helpful tool in monitoring treatment and intervention. The Conners 3GI is included in the full-length Conners 3 (for parent and teacher forms) or can be purchased separately.

Conners 3 ADHD Index (Conners 3AI™)

The Conners 3 offers a 10-item ADHD index (Conners 3AI). The brief index works well when screening a large group of children and adolescents to see if further assessment of ADHD is warranted. Additionally, this form can be used to monitor the effectiveness of treatment plans and measure the child's response to intervention. This form is available in parent, teacher, and self-report versions. The Conners 3AI is included in the full-length Conners 3rd Edition™ (Multi-Health Systems, 2011).

Administration Time: Approximately 20 minutes

Age/Grade Levels: Ages 6-0 to 17-11

Subtest Information: The Conners 3 is composed of the following scales:

Empirical Scales

- *Hyperactivity/Impulsivity*
- *Executive Functioning*
- *Learning Problems*
- *Aggression*
- *Peer Relations*
- *Family Relations*

DSM-IV-TR Symptom Scales

- *ADHD Hyperactive/Impulsive*
- *ADHD Inattentive*
- *ADHD Combined*
- *Oppositional Defiant Disorder*
- *Conduct Disorder New*

Validity Scales

- *Positive Impression*
- *Negative Impression*
- *Inconsistency Index*

Rational Scale

- *Inattention*

Attention Deficit Disorders Evaluation Scale–3rd Edition (ADDES-3)

Author: Stephen B. McCarney, Ed.D.

Description of Test: The Attention Deficit Disorders Evaluation Scale–3rd Edition (ADDES-3) enables educators, school and private psychologists, pediatricians, and other medical personnel to evaluate and diagnose ADHD in children and youth from input provided by primary observers of the student's behavior. The scale is available in two versions: *School Version,* a reporting form for educators, and *Home Version,* a reporting form for parents.

Administration Time: The Home Version can be completed by a parent or guardian in approximately 12 minutes and includes 46 items representing behaviors exhibited in and around the home environment. The School Version can be completed in approximately 15 minutes and includes 60 items easily observed and documented by educational personnel.

Age/Grade Levels: Ages 4 through 18

Subtest Information: The subscales, *Inattentive* and *Hyperactive–Impulsive,* are based on the current subtypes of ADHD. The ADDES-3 was developed from research in behavior disorders, learning disabilities, and ADHD; current literature in psychology, neurology, and education; and current practices in identification and diagnosis. The results provided by the scale are commensurate with criteria used by educational, psychiatric, and pediatric professionals to identify ADHD in children and youth.

Attention Deficit Disorders Evaluation Scale: Secondary-Age Student (ADDES-S)

Author: Stephen B. McCarney

Description of Test: There are two versions of this test: (1) Home Version, completed by parents, has 46 items that assess certain behaviors in the home, and (2) School Version has 60 items that teachers must rate. The ADDES-S is based on the APA definition of attention deficit/hyperactivity disorder (DSM-IV) and the criteria most widely accepted by educators and mental health providers.

Administration Time: The School Version can be completed in approximately 15 minutes and includes 60 items easily observed and documented by educational personnel.

Age/Grade Levels: Ages 11 to 18

Subtest Information: The subscales, *Inattentive* and *Hyperactive,* are based on the most currently recognized subtypes of ADHD.

ASSESSMENT OF ADAPTIVE BEHAVIOR

The assessment of adaptive behavior is a very important part of the overall assessment process. **Adaptive behavior** refers to the effectiveness or degree with which individuals meet the standards of personal independence and social responsibility expected for age and cultural groups. When doing an evaluation of adaptive behavior, the examiner should focus on a number of areas. These areas include:

Communication Skills	Self-Care
Community Use	Home Living
Self-Direction	Social Skills
Health and Safety	Leisure
Functional Academics	Work Skills

Understanding adaptive behavior is very important when working with or assessing the population with mental retardation. Adaptive behavior is a required area of assessment when a classification of mental retardation is being considered for a student. IDEA 2004 specifies "deficits in adaptive behavior" as one of the two characteristics necessary for a student to be so classified (the other being "significantly subaverage general intellectual functioning").

There are many different ways an evaluator can measure adaptive behavior. Because these measures are often used to assess persons with lower levels of intellectual functioning, the student being evaluated may not have to directly take part in the evaluation. The way many of these diagnostic assessment instruments work is that the examiner records information collected from a third person who is familiar with the student (e.g., parent, teacher, direct service provider). Perhaps the greatest problem with doing an assessment on adaptive behavior is the fact that many of the scales and tests do not have high validity and reliability. Also, there are serious concerns about the cultural bias of the tests. Consequently, great care must be taken when selecting the most appropriate measure for an individual student. It is imperative with minority students to develop an understanding of the types of behaviors considered adaptive (and thus appropriate) in the minority culture before making diagnostic judgments about the particular functioning of a student.

AAMR Adaptive Behavior Scale, Residential and Community–2nd Edition (ABS-RC:2)

Authors: Kazuo Nihira, Henry Leland, and Nadine Lambert

Description of Test: The test is intended for persons with disabilities in residential and community settings. It measures various domain areas and is available as a kit or as software for administration and scoring.

Administration Time: 15 to 30 minutes

Age/Grade Levels: Ages 18 to Adult

Subtest Information: The test has no subtests.

AAMR Adaptive Behavior Scale–School (ABS-S:2)

Authors: Nadine Lambert, Kazuo Nihira, and Henry Leland

Description of Test: There are 16 subscores measured from this test. The test includes an examiner's manual, examiner booklets, computer scoring systems, and profile summary forms.

Administration Time: 15 to 30 minutes

Age/Grade Levels: Ages 3 through 18

Subtest Information: The scale is divided into two parts. Part I focuses on personal independence and is designed to evaluate coping skills considered important to independence and responsibility in daily living. The skills within Part I are grouped into nine behavior domains:

Independent Functioning	Numbers and Time
Physical Development	Prevocational/Vocational Activity
Economic Activity	Self-Direction
Language Development	Responsibility
Socialization	

Part II of the scale contains content related to social adaptation. The behaviors in Part II are assigned to seven domains:

Social Behavior	Social Engagement
Conformity	Disturbing Interpersonal Behavior
Trustworthiness	Stereotyped and Hyperactive Behavior
Self-Abusive Behavior	

The Adaptive Behavior Evaluation Scale–Revised (ABES-R)

Author: Stephen B. McCarney

Description of Test: The ABES-R consists of 105 items assessing adaptive behaviors that are not measured by academic skill testing, but are necessary for success in an educational setting.

Administration Time: 20 to 25 minutes

Age/Grade Levels: Norms are for students from grades K through 12

Subtest Information: The test comprises 10 adaptive skill areas:

Communication Skills Self-Direction
Self-Care Health and Safety
Home Living Functional Academics
Social Skills Leisure
Community Use Work Skills

Vineland Adaptive Behavior Scales–2nd Edition (VABS-2)

Authors: Sara S. Sparrow, Domenic V. Cicchetti, and David A. Balla

Description of Test: Vineland Adaptive Behavior Scales are used to identify individuals who have mental retardation, developmental delays, brain injuries, and other impairments.

Administration Time: Survey Interview and Parent/Caregiver Rating Forms 20 to 60 minutes

Age/Grade Levels: Survey Interview Form, Parent/Caregiver Rating Form, Expanded Interview Form—Birth to Adult; Teacher Rating Form—Ages 3 through 21

Subtest Information: All Vineland-II forms aid in diagnosing and classifying mental retardation and other disorders, such as autism, Asperger syndrome, and developmental delays. As with the current Vineland, the content and scales of Vineland-II were organized within a three domain structure: Communication, Daily Living, and Socialization. This structure corresponds to the three broad domains of adaptive functioning recognized by the American Association of Mental Retardation: Conceptual, Practical, and Social. In addition, Vineland-II offers a Motor Skills Domain and an optional Maladaptive Behavior Index to provide more in-depth information about children.

Developmental Assessment for the Severely Handicapped–2nd Edition (DASH-2)

Authors: Mary Kay Dykes and Jane Erin

Description of Test: The assessment system is a developmentally sequenced, fine-grained, behaviorally defined criterion-referenced measure of current and developing skills in different domains. The instrument may be useful in identifying and measuring very discrete changes in behavior in very low-functioning individuals in order to pinpoint skills and facilitate training.

Administration Time: 120 to 180 minutes

Age/Grade Levels: Individuals functioning within the developmental range of birth to 8 years

Subtest Information: The DASH-2 consists of five pinpoint scales that assess performance in the following areas:

- Dressing
- Feeding
- Toileting
- Home Routines
- Travel and Safety

Adaptive Behavior Inventory (ABI)

Authors: Linda Brown and James E. Leigh

Description of Test: The ABI evaluates the functional daily living skills of school-age children. The ABI can be used to quickly screen students suspected of meeting the criteria for mental retardation or emotionally disturbance, or to reevaluate those already enrolled in special education programs.

Administration Time: Administration time is approximately 5 minutes per scale, less than half an hour for the entire instrument.

Age/Grade Levels: Ages 5 through 18 years of age.

Subtest Information: The ABI is composed of 150 brief items covering five scales: Self-Care Skills, Communication Skills, Social Skills, Academic Skills, and Occupational Skills. It is completed by a classroom teacher or another professional who has regular contact with the child being evaluated. He or she rates the child on each item, using a four-point scale ranging from "does not perform the skill in question" to "has mastered the skill."

FUNCTIONAL BEHAVIORAL ASSESSMENT AND BEHAVIORAL INTERVENTION PLANS

A **functional behavioral assessment** (FBA) is a problem-solving strategy utilized by educators, parents, and agency personnel to design an effective plan for helping children learn and choose more appropriate behaviors. These interventions assist the child by specifically identifying these behaviors, as well as the overall context within which they occur. The outcome of an FBA is a behavioral intervention plan that defines the team's strategy for addressing the behaviors, including timelines, role responsibilities, and consequence methods. The FBA should be seen as part of a continuum of evaluation and reevaluation procedures, not as an isolated practice reserved only for disciplinary proceedings.

According to the Center for Collaboration and Effective Practice (2011):

Functional behavioral assessment is generally considered to be a problem-solving process for addressing student problem behavior. It relies on a variety of techniques and strategies to identify the purposes of specific behavior and to help IEP teams select interventions to directly address the problem behavior. Functional behavioral assessment should be integrated, as appropriate, throughout the process of developing, reviewing, and, if necessary, revising a student's IEP.

A functional behavioral assessment looks beyond the behavior itself. The focus when conducting a functional behavioral assessment is on identifying significant, pupil-specific social, affective, cognitive, and/or environmental factors associated with the occurrence (and non-occurrence) of specific behaviors. This broader perspective offers a better understanding of the function or purpose behind student behavior. Behavioral intervention plans based on an understanding of "why" a student misbehaves are extremely useful in addressing a wide range of problem behaviors.

In fact, during any educational evaluation of a child or review of a child's IEP, an FBA must be conducted if problem behaviors need to be addressed. The results are then considered during the development of the IEP. Documentation regarding intervention strategies that have already been tried, as well as the positive or negative results they achieved, is very important for ensuring a quality FBA and BIP.

The 1997 Amendments to IDEA were explicit in what they required of an IEP team addressing behavioral problems of children with disabilities:

> The team should explore the need for strategies and support systems to address any behavior that may impede the learning of the child with the disability or the learning of his or her peers (614(d)(3)(B)(i));
>
> In response to disciplinary actions by school personnel, the IEP team should, within 10 days, meet to formulate a functional behavioral assessment plan to collect data for developing a behavior intervention plan, or if a behavior intervention plan already exists, the team must review and revise it (as necessary), to ensure that it addresses the behavior upon which disciplinary action is predicated (615(k)(i)(B)); and
>
> States shall address the needs of in-service and pre-service personnel (including professionals and paraprofessionals who provide special education, general education, related services, or early intervention services) as they relate to developing and implementing positive intervention strategies (653(c)(3)(D)(vi).

The discipline amendments of the 1997 Individuals with Disabilities Education Act (IDEA) reauthorization required local education agencies to conduct a functional behavior assessment to address behavior of a child with a disability who is removed for over 10 days during a given school year, if such an assessment was not done prior to the behavior subject to disciplinary action.

A functional behavior assessment is also the basis of a positive behavior intervention plan, which is a required component of individualized education programs (IEPs) for students with disabilities with behavioral needs. If a child's behavior impedes his or her learning or that of others, the IEP must consider positive behavioral interventions, strategies, and supports to address that behavior. Statutory requirements also specify that the regular education teacher participate in the development of the child's IEP, assisting the team in the determination of appropriate positive behavioral interventions and strategies.

Functional behavioral assessments are used to address the behavioral support needs of people who have a full range of problem behaviors. Examples could include self-injury, hitting and biting, violent and aggressive attacks, property destruction, disruptive behaviors, or verbal abuse. Those who exhibit problem behaviors might have developmental disability, mental retardation, mental illness, emotional or behavioral disorders, traumatic brain injury or a birth injury, communication disorders, an autism spectrum disorder, a chromosomal syndrome, or no diagnostic label at all. These persons might vary greatly in their needs for behavioral support and in their ability to communicate their needs. Some behaviors may serve an important function for a person who has no other way to communicate. Some individuals may have only nonverbal or unacceptable behavior as a means of expressing medical needs, physical discomfort, or reactions to medications.

Effective behavioral support is used to reduce problem behaviors and encourage new skills for interaction in our communities. At one time the emphasis was on designing consequences for behavior, but recent trends emphasize comprehensive interventions that include teaching new skills and rearranging conditions that "trigger" the problem behavior.

Functional behavior assessment is a process of examining a relationship between behavior and the environment. It is not just a "review" of a person with problem behaviors. All behavior is believed to have a function—a way for a person to meet certain needs and desires—even when others disapprove and the behavior is considered inappropriate. Functional behavior assessments are conducted to understand the structure and function of behavior. If the purpose of the behavior from the student's perspective is known, a behavioral intervention plan can be designed that teaches an alternative adaptive behavior.

A functional behavior assessment is accepted practice and a professional standard that should precede behavioral interventions. Information about when, where, and why behaviors occur is invaluable in building effective behavioral support. Some interventions done without a plan can make behaviors worse.

A functional behavior assessment is the primary tool for planning behavioral support. It is not a checklist, a formal test, or a medical diagnosis that matches a predesigned treatment plan or intervention. The purpose of the functional assessment is to gather information and use it to redesign an environment that "works" for people with communication, developmental, or behavioral disabilities. The assessment process requires collaborative participation of the person with the disability, those who know the person best, and the support of a person trained in behavioral analysis.

A functional behavior assessment contains the following five items:

1. A clear description of the problem behaviors, including behaviors that occur together.
2. Identification of the events, times, and situations that predict when the problem behaviors will occur or will not occur, across the range of settings and times in the child's day.
3. Identification of the consequences that maintain the problem behaviors—the "payoff" (what the student gains by the behavior, such as attention, avoidance of a task, or a preferred toy).
4. Development of hypotheses that describe the behaviors, specific situations in which they occur, and what reinforces or maintains them.
5. Collection of direct observation data to test and support at least one hypothesis.

Intervention planning may determine needed environmental changes before addressing direct strategies of managing the student's behavior. This is very important if the natural environment must provide ongoing proper conditions for the positive behaviors to occur routinely and be maintained over time. Making a change in the setting and keeping that constant might be easier and more effective than maintaining a more artificial, complex system of reinforcements for a behavior management plan, especially over a long period of time.

A functional behavior assessment should include systematic data collection and a willingness to explore various elements of the instructional process. Assessment of the learning environment assumes that student success involves an interaction of the student, the teacher, and the setting. A functional behavioral assessment directs professionals to identify undesirable or unacceptable behaviors, to identify multiple points for potential intervention of the settings in which the behavior occurs, and to provide a basis for teaching positive, acceptable behaviors.

The purpose of a functional assessment is to gather information in order to understand a student's problem behavior. However, an FBA goes beyond the "symptom" (the problem behavior) to the student's underlying motivation to "escape," "avoid," or get something. OSEP and other government-sponsored research as well as educators' and psychologists' experience has demonstrated that behavior intervention plans stemming from the knowledge of why a student misbehaves (i.e., based on a functional behavioral assessment) are extremely useful in addressing a wide range of problems.

Often, the functions of a behavior are not inappropriate; rather, it is the behavior itself that is judged appropriate or inappropriate. If the IEP team determines through an FBA that a student is seeking attention by acting out, they can develop a plan to teach the student more appropriate ways to gain attention, thereby filling the student's need for attention with an alternative or replacement behavior that serves the same function as the inappropriate behavior. At the same time, strategies may be developed to decrease or even eliminate opportunities for the student to engage in inappropriate behavior.

Identifying the reasons for behavior will take many forms, and while the IDEA advises an FBA approach to determine specific contributors to behavior, it does not require or suggest specific techniques or strategies to use when assessing that behavior. However, several key steps are common to most FBAs:

1. *Verify the seriousness of the problem.* Many classroom problems can be eliminated by the consistent application of standard and universal discipline strategies of proven effectiveness. Only when these strategies have not resulted in significant improvement on the part of the student should school personnel go forward with an FBA.

2. *Define the problem behavior in concrete terms.* School personnel need to pinpoint the behavior causing learning or discipline problems and to define that behavior in terms that are simple to measure and record. For example, a problem behavior might be "Trish is aggressive." A concrete description is "Trish hits other students during recess when she does not get her way."

3. *Collect data on possible causes of problem behavior.* The use of a variety of techniques will lead the IEP team to a better understanding of the student behavior. Key questions include the following: Is the problem behavior linked to a skill deficit? Is there evidence to suggest that the student does not know how to perform the skill? Does the student have the skill but for some reason not perform it consistently? Also, a probing discussion with the student may yield an enhanced understanding of what, in each context, causes problem behavior.

4. *Analyze the data.* A data triangulation chart is useful in identifying possible stimulus-response patterns, predictors, maintaining consequences, and likely function(s) of the problem behavior. A problem behavior pathway chart can be used to sequentially arrange information on setting antecedents, the behavior itself, and consequences of the behavior that might lead to its maintenance.

5. *Formulate and test a hypothesis.* After analyzing the data, school personnel can establish a plausible explanation (hypothesis) regarding the function of the behaviors in question. This hypothesis predicts the general conditions under which the behavior is most and least

likely to occur as well as the consequences that maintain it. The team can then experimentally manipulate some of the relevant conditions affecting the behavior. If the behavior remains unchanged following this environmental manipulation, the team can reexamine the hypothesis with a view to altering it.

The practice of conducting functional behavioral assessments of behavior that interferes with positive student outcomes allows IEP teams to develop more effective and efficient behavior intervention plans. Emphasis should be on enlarging student capacity to profit from instruction, which can be accomplished by designing pupil-specific interventions that not only discourage inappropriate behaviors, but teach alternative behaviors, and provide the student with the opportunity and motivation to engage in that behavior. If done correctly, the net result of behavioral assessments is that school personnel are better able to provide an educational environment that addresses the learning needs of all students (Center for Effective Collaboration and Practice, 2011).

Behavior Intervention Plans

If the IEP team determines that a child's behavior(s) is interfering with his or her learning, or that of other students, a **behavioral intervention plan** (BIP) must be developed. This plan consists of the positive intervention strategies and supports selected by the team to address the child's inappropriate behaviors. As with an FBA, however, a BIP is not only used to react to disciplinary situations, but may be created for any child demonstrating challenging behaviors. This is a tool that is often very effective in reducing the need for more extreme disciplinary measures, such as suspension or expulsion.

The student's BIP should include positive strategies, programs or curricular modifications, and supplementary aids and supports required to address the behaviors of concern. It is helpful to use the data collected during the FBA to develop the plan and to determine the discrepancy between the child's actual and expected behavior.

Intervention plans that emphasize skills needed by the student to behave in a more appropriate manner and that provide proper motivation will be more effective than plans that simply control behavior. Interventions based on control often only suppress the behavior, resulting in a child manifesting unaddressed needs in alternative, inappropriate ways. Positive plans for behavioral intervention, on the other hand, will address both the source of the problem and the problem itself and foster the expression of needs in appropriate ways.

It is good practice for IEP teams to include two evaluation procedures in an intervention plan: one procedure designed to monitor the consistency with which the management plan is implemented, the other designed to measure changes in behavior.

In addition, IEP teams must determine a time line for implementation and reassessment and specify how much behavior change is required to meet the goal of the intervention. Assessment completion should be within the time lines prescribed by the IDEA. If a student already has a BIP, the IEP team may elect to review and modify it or they may determine that more information is necessary and conduct an FBA. IDEA states that a behavior intervention plan based on an FBA should be considered when developing the IEP if a student's behavior interferes with his or her learning or the learning of classmates. To be meaningful, plans need to be reviewed at least annually and revised as often as needed. However, the plan may be reviewed and reevaluated whenever any member of the child's IEP team feels it is necessary.

A BIP, guided by information gained from an FBA, is the overall strategy the team has designed to increase or reduce a definable set or pattern of behaviors demonstrated by a child. This strategy may include the following:

- Teaching preventive and deescalation techniques to staff, parents, and peers
- Teaching crisis-response techniques
- Teaching the child appropriate replacement behaviors
- Providing positive and negative consequences to the child

Although each BIP will differ according to the needs demonstrated by different children, some common aspects include the following:

- Defining the target behavior in measurable terms
- Changing some of the "who, what, when, and where" information derived from the FBA
- Teaching the child new ways to meet his or her needs (i.e., identifying another behavior or skill that will be taught so the child can accomplish his or her purpose in a more acceptable way)
- Teaching others, including staff members and peers, how to react to the child's behavior in a way that will reinforce appropriate behavior
- Teaching how to manage a crisis situation, if appropriate
- Creating an appropriate data collection system that measures progress toward the desired goals and objectives of the plan
- Scheduling a review date to reconsider the plan

Prior to implementing a behavior intervention plan, all staff dealing with the child must be trained to execute the plan consistently. A time line for collecting necessary materials, making environmental arrangements, training staff, and starting the plan also needs to be established. Specific tasks should be clearly assigned to all the individuals involved. Once this is accomplished, the plan is ready to implement.

After the BIP has been implemented for at least 2 weeks, the team should meet and review the impact the plan is having. Part of this review should consider how successfully the BIP has been implemented and followed by staff members, as well as how successful the BIP has been in preventing or changing the target problem behavior. If the procedures and steps that have been taken are determined ineffective, alternative interventions may be selected. If interventions are repeatedly found to be ineffective, the IEP team may wish to consider further evaluation or a different placement.

No reasonable or valid procedure is excluded from being used in a BIP. However, discipline management procedures must be selected and supervised with the utmost care. These procedures may include time-outs, physical restraints, or "room clears," among others. If any extraordinary procedures are required, they shall be considered by the IEP team (including the parent), who must:

- Document the validity of the procedure
- Document the need for the procedure with objective data
- Document the training of the staff who will use the procedure

In conducting a functional behavioral assessment and developing a behavioral intervention plan, education personnel should draw upon a range of communication and interpersonal skills. Like knowledge of assessment itself, IEP team members may need special training in the skills of successful collaboration, such as time management, group problem-solving (including "brainstorming" strategies), active listening, and conflict resolution processes, to mention a few.

If team members are to conduct the assessment, they may also need training in the skills and knowledge required to conduct a functional behavioral assessment and use of behavior intervention techniques. As with other collaborative efforts, building-level administrative and collegial support is essential to a successful outcome. The value and appropriateness of student and parent involvement in the process also should be carefully considered. Too often they are excluded from activities when they have much to offer (Center for Effective Collaboration and Practice, 2011).

CONCLUSION

Assessment of behavior is essential for a comprehensive evaluation of a child for special education. Understanding the psychological makeup of a child can help tremendously with recommendations for future educational programs. Psychological tests play a very important role in the understanding of a student's behavior. Using many different psychological tests helps to identify general themes and patterns in the child's emotional well-being. When properly conducted, an assessment of a child's social and emotional development greatly enhances the assessment process because it enables us to try and understand the child's emotional state at the time of testing.

Vocabulary

Adaptive behavior: The effectiveness or degree with which individuals meet the standards of personal independence and social responsibility expected for age and cultural groups.

Anecdotal recording: An observer records all behaviors and interactions within a given time frame (e.g., recording a child's behavior from 9:00 to 9:30 A.M.).

Apperception tests: Tests that require the child to view various picture cards and "tell a story" about what is shown. Apperception tests try to elicit central themes from the child.

Behavioral intervention plan: A plan consisting of the positive intervention strategies and supports selected by the team to address the child's inappropriate behaviors.

Duration recording: An observer notes the amount of time a target behavior occurs (e.g., watching a child for one hour who is supposed to be reading—the child reads only 12 minutes of that time).

Event recording: An observer is looking specifically for one or more target behaviors and records the frequency with which they occur. Event recording is also referred to as frequency counting because the observer is simply counting the number of times a behavior occurs (e.g., the number of times a child gets out of his chair in a given period of time).

Functional behavioral assessment (FBA):   The process of determining why a student engages in challenging behavior and how the student's behavior relates to the environment.

Interview: A research method conducted face to face between two people (the interviewer and the interviewee) whereby recorded responses to questions are obtained.

Latency recording: An observer determines the amount of time between a given stimulus for the child and the response (e.g., the time it takes a student to get out her pencil after the teacher says, "Take out your pencil").

Projective drawing tests: Tests that simply ask the child to draw a picture. The tests are used to get the child to "project" personal feelings about him- or herself onto paper.

Rating scales: Scales that are often given not only to the student but also to parents and teachers. A rating scale gives a statement about a behavior of a child whereupon the individual has to rate the frequency, intensity, and/or duration.

Sentence completion tests: Tests that provide the student with a beginning of a sentence that the student needs to finish. The "fill-ins" are supposed to give indications of the emotions and feelings that the student is experiencing.

Structured interview: An interview in which individuals are asked a specific set of predetermined questions in a controlled manner.

Target behaviors: Specific behaviors an observer seeks to record when doing the observation.

Unstructured interview: An interview in which the questions are not predetermined, thereby allowing for substantial discussion and interaction between the interviewer and interviewee.

12 ASSESSMENT OF PERCEPTUAL ABILITIES

Key Terms

Association or organization
Auditory association
Auditory discrimination
Auditory long-term memory
Auditory modality
Auditory motoric expression
Auditory sequential memory
Auditory short-term memory
Auditory vocal expression
Expression

Gustatory modality
Kinesthetic modality
Memory
Multisensory approaches
Olfactory modality
Perception
Reception
Tactile modality
Visual association
Visual coordination

Visual discrimination
Visual figure–ground discrimination
Visual form perception
Visual long-term memory
Visual modality
Visual motoric expression
Visual sequential memory
Visual short-term memory
Visual spatial relationships
Visual vocal expression

Chapter Objectives

This chapter discusses the importance of assessment of perceptual abilities in the special education process. After reading this chapter, you should understand the following:

■ The purpose of perceptual evaluations
■ Visual perception
■ Assessment of visual perception
■ Auditory perception
■ Assessment of auditory perception
■ Comprehensive measures of perceptual abilities

THE LEARNING PROCESS

The perceptual evaluation is theoretically based on the concept of the learning process. When we evaluate a child's perceptual abilities, we are looking to see if there is a deficit in some area of the learning process that may be slowing down the processing of information, thereby interfering in the child's ability to receive, organize, memorize, or express information. Severe deficits in the learning process can have adverse effects on a child's ability to function in the classroom.

To understand how learning takes place, we must first understand the process by which information is received and the manner in which it is processed and expressed. In very simple terms, the learning process can be described in the following way:

- Step 1: Input of Information
- Step 2: Organization of Information
- Step 3: Expression of Information

Information is received in some manner and is filtered through a series of internal psychological processes. As information progresses along this "assembly line," it is given meaning, organized in some fashion, and then expressed through a variety of responses. To understand how learning takes place, we must first understand the specific parts that make up the learning process. There are six modalities or channels (avenues through which information is received):

- **Auditory modality:** The delivery of information through sound
- **Visual modality:** The delivery of information through sight
- **Tactile modality:** The delivery of information through touching
- **Kinesthetic modality:** The delivery of information through movement
- **Gustatory modality:** The delivery of information through taste
- **Olfactory modality:** The delivery of information through smell

Skills are usually taught using all six modalities in the primary grades—nursery school through grade 1. By grade 2, most teachers teach through approximately four of the modalities with a greater emphasis on visual and auditory input. By the upper elementary grades, this can shift to skill development through the use of only two modalities, visual and auditory. Generally, this remains the source of informational input in most classrooms until possibly college, at which level information in many cases is presented through only one modality, auditory (lectures).

Children should be taught using **multisensory approaches** (the input of information through a variety of receptive mechanisms—i.e., seeing, hearing, touching, etc.) whenever possible because increased sensory input enhances retention of information. Information is delivered to the senses through one or several of the previously mentioned modalities. Once received, the information goes through a series of processes that attempts to give meaning to the material received. Several processes comprise the learning process:

- **Reception:** The initial receiving of information.
- **Perception:** The initial organization of information.
- **Association or organization:** Relating new information to other information and giving meaning to the information received.
- **Memory:** The storage or retrieval process that facilitates the associational process to give meaning to information or help in relating new concepts to other information that might have already been learned. This process involves short-term, long-term, and sequential memory.
- **Expression:** The output of information through vocal, motoric, or written responses.

THE PURPOSE OF PERCEPTUAL EVALUATIONS

Now that you have some understanding of how the learning process functions, we can explore the objectives of the perceptual evaluation:

- **To help determine the child's stronger and weaker modality for learning:** Some children are visual learners, some are auditory, and some learn best through any form of input. However, if a child is a strong visual learner in a class in which the teacher relies on auditory lectures, it is possible the child's ability to process information may be hampered. The evaluation may give us this information, which is very useful when making practical recommendations to teachers about how best to present information to assist the child's ability to learn.

- **To help determine a child's stronger and weaker process areas:** A child having problems in memory and expression will quickly fall behind the rest of the class. The longer these processing difficulties continue, the greater the chance for secondary emotional problems to develop (emotional problems resulting from continued frustration with the ability to learn).

- **To develop a learning profile:** This can help the classroom teacher understand the best way to present information to the child, and therefore, increase his or her chances of success.

- **To help determine if the child's learning process deficits are suitable for a regular class:** Along with other information and test results, the child may require a more restrictive educational setting (an educational setting or situation best suited to the present needs of the student other than a full-time regular class placement—e.g., resource room, self-contained class, special school, etc.).

VISUAL PERCEPTION

Visual perception is considered to be one of the more important specific ability areas in early assessment because of the assumed relationship between visual perception deficits and reading performance. The following assessment area skills are most often associated with visual perception:

- **Visual coordination:** The ability to follow and track objects with coordinated eye movements
- **Visual discrimination:** The ability to differentiate visually the forms and symbols in one's environment
- **Visual association:** The ability to organize and associate visually presented material in a meaningful way
- **Visual long-term memory:** The ability to retain and recall general and specific long-term visual information
- **Visual short-term memory:** The ability to retain and recall general and specific short-term visual information
- **Visual sequential memory:** The ability to recall in correct sequence and detail prior visual information
- **Visual vocal expression:** The ability to reproduce vocally prior visually presented material or experiences
- **Visual motoric expression** (visual motor integration): The ability to reproduce motorically prior visually presented material or experiences
- **Visual figure–ground discrimination:** The ability to differentiate relevant stimuli (the figure) from irrelevant stimuli (the background)
- **Visual spatial relationships:** The ability to perceive the relative positions of objects in space
- **Visual form perception** (visual constancy): The ability to discern the size, shape, and position of visual stimuli

Diagnostic Symptoms for Visual Perceptual Disabilities

There are many symptoms that may indicate problems in a certain perceptual area. Some of these are observable, whereas others are discovered through intakes and testing. What follows is a list of symptoms that may reflect perceptual disabilities in a variety of visual areas.

General Visual Perceptual Problems

The student

- Exhibits poor motor coordination
- Is awkward motorically—frequent tripping, stumbling, bumping into things, having trouble skipping and jumping
- Demonstrates restlessness, short attention span, perseveration
- Exhibits poor handwriting, artwork, drawing
- Exhibits reversals of *b, d, p, q, u, n* when writing (beyond a chronological age of 7 or 8)
- Inverts numbers (17 for 71); reverses as well
- Gives correct answers when teacher reads test, but cannot put answers down on paper
- Exhibits poor performance on group achievement tests
- Appears brighter than test scores indicate
- Has poor perception of time and space

Visual Receptive Process Disability

The student

- Does not enjoy books, pictures
- Fails to understand what is read
- Is unable to give a simple explanation of contents of a picture
- Is unable to categorize pictures

Visual Association Disability

The student

- Is unable to tell a story from pictures; can only label objects in the pictures
- Is unable to understand what he or she reads
- Fails to handle primary workbook tasks
- Needs auditory cues and clues

Manual Expressive Disability

The student

- Has poor handwriting and drawing
- Communicates infrequently with gestures
- Is poor at "acting out" ideas, feelings
- Is clumsy, uncoordinated
- Plays games poorly; can't imitate other children in games

Visual Memory Disability

The student

- Exhibits frequent misspellings, even after undue practice
- Misspells own name frequently
- Cannot write alphabet, numbers, computation facts
- Identifies words one day and fails to the next

Assessment of Visual Perception

There are many assessment measures used in school systems to assess visual–motor integration and perceptual abilities. This section examines the most commonly used visual–motor perceptual measures and identifies the strengths and weaknesses of each.

BEERY™ VMI: Beery-Buktenica Developmental Test of Visual-Motor Integration–Sixth Edition (VMI-6)

Author: Keith E. Beery

Description of Test: *Beery-VMI,* now in its sixth edition, offers a convenient and economical way to screen for visual–motor deficits that can lead to learning, neuropsychological, and behavior problems. The VMI-6 helps assess the extent to which individuals can integrate their visual and motor abilities. The Short Format and Full Format tests present drawings of geometric forms arranged in order of increasing difficulty that the individual is asked to copy.

Administration Time: 15 minutes

Age/Grade Levels: Ages 2 to 100

Subtest Information: There are no subtests.

Test of Gross Motor Development–2nd Edition (TGMD-2)

Author: Dale Ulrich

Description of Test: The TGMD-2 assesses common motor skills. The primary uses of this test are to

- Identify children who are significantly behind their peers in gross motor skill development
- Assist in the planning of an instructional program in gross motor skill development
- Evaluate the gross motor program

The test is a multiple-item task performance test consisting of two subtests. The examiner records observations in a student record book. The TGMD-2 allows examiners to administer one test in a relatively brief time and gather data for making important educational decisions.

Administration Time: 15 minutes

Age/Grade Levels: Ages 3 to 10

Subtest Information:

- *Locomotion*—This subtest measures the run, gallop, hop, leap, horizontal jump, and slide skills that move a child's center of gravity from one point to another.

- *Object Control*—This subtest measures the ability to strike a stationary ball, as well as stationary dribble, catch, kick, underhand roll, and overhand throw skills that include projecting and receiving objects.

Bender Visual–Motor Gestalt Test (BVMGT)

Author: Lauretta Bender

Description of Test: Originally published in 1938 by Lauretta Bender, MD, the *Bender Visual–Motor Gestalt Test* has been one of the most widely used psychological tests. The *Bender Visual–Motor Gestalt Test, 2nd Edition* (Bender-Gestalt II) updates this classic assessment and continues its tradition as a brief test of visual–motor integration that may provide interpretive information about an individual's development and psychological functioning.

Administration Time: 5 to 10 minutes (14 stimulus cards), 5 minutes (visual, motor tests)

Age/Grade Levels: Ages 3 and older

Subtest Information: There are no subtests; patient reproduces Gestalt figures presented on stimulus cards.

Developmental Test of Visual Perception–2nd Edition (DTVP-2)

Authors: Donald Hammill, Nils Pearson, and Judith Voress

Description of Test: The test is designed to measure specific visual perceptual abilities and to screen for visual perceptual difficulties at early ages. The DTVP-2 is a revision of the *Developmental Test of Visual Perception* (Frostig et al., 1966). The DTVP-2 is a comprehensive diagnostic instrument for assessing the visual-processing skills of children.

Administration Time: Varies based on individual ability levels

Age/Grade Levels: Ages 4 to 10

Subtest Information: The tasks are arranged in increasing order of difficulty in eight areas:

- *Eye Motor Coordination*—This task requires the child to draw lines between increasingly narrow boundaries. These may include straight, curved, or angled lines.
- *Figure–Ground*—This task requires the child to distinguish and then outline embedded figures between intersecting shapes.
- *Form Constancy*—This task requires the child to discriminate common geometric shapes presented in different shapes, sizes, positions, and textures from other similar shapes.
- *Position in Space*—This test requires the child to distinguish between figures in an identical position and those in a reversed rotated position.
- *Spatial Relations*—This task requires the child to copy simple forms and patterns by joining dots.
- *Copying*—The child is asked to copy increasingly complex figures from model drawings.
- *Visual Closure*—The child is required to view a geometric figure and then select the matching figure from a series of figures that all have missing parts.
- *Visual–Motor Speed*—On this test, the child is required to draw special marks in selected geometric designs on a page filled with various designs.

Motor-Free Visual Perceptual Test–3rd Edition (MVPT-3)

Authors: Ronald Colarusso and Donald D. Hammill

Description of Test: Designed to assess visual perception without reliance on an individual's motor skills, the MVPT-3 is particularly useful with those who may have learning, cognitive, motor, or physical disabilities.

Administration Time: 20 minutes

Age/Grade Levels: Ages 4 to Adult

Subtest Information: The MVPT-3 measures skills without copying tasks. It contains many new, more difficult items at the upper end for older children and adults. Tasks include matching, figure–ground, closure, visual memory, and form discrimination. Stimuli are line drawings. Answers are presented in multiple-choice format. Responses may be given verbally or by pointing.

AUDITORY PERCEPTION

Auditory perception has long been a concern for special educators because of its relationship to speech and language development. The areas that comprise auditory perception are:

- **Auditory discrimination:** The ability to differentiate auditorily the sounds in one's environment
- **Auditory association:** The ability to organize and associate auditorily presented material in a meaningful way
- **Auditory long-term memory:** The ability to retain and recall general and specific long-term auditory information
- **Auditory short-term memory:** The ability to retain and recall general and specific short-term auditory information
- **Auditory sequential memory:** The ability to recall in correct sequence and detail prior auditory information
- **Auditory vocal expression:** The ability to reproduce vocally prior auditorily presented material or experiences
- **Auditory motoric expression:** The ability to reproduce motorically prior auditorily presented material or experiences

Diagnostic Symptoms for Auditory Perceptual Disabilities

As previously indicated, a major objective of a perceptual evaluation is to identify those areas that may have a direct impact on a child's ability to process information adequately and that may interfere in his or her academic achievement. What follows is a list of symptoms that may reflect perceptual disabilities in a variety of auditory areas.

General Auditory Perceptual Indicators

The student

- Appears less intelligent than IQ tests indicate
- Does many more things than one would expect: puts puzzles together, fixes broken objects, and so on

- Appears to have a speech problem
- May emphasize wrong syllables in words
- May sequence sounds oddly
- May use "small words" incorrectly
- Appears not to listen or comprehend
- Watches teacher's or adult's faces intently, trying to grasp words

Auditory Receptive Process Disability

The student

- Fails to comprehend what he or she hears
- Exhibits poor receptive vocabulary
- Fails to identify sounds correctly
- Fails to carry out directions

Auditory Association Disability

The student

- Fails to enjoy being read to by someone else
- Has difficulty comprehending questions
- Raises hand to answer question but gives foolish response
- Is slow to respond; takes a long time to answer
- Has difficulty with abstract concepts presented auditorily

Verbal Expressive Disability

The student

- Mispronounces common words
- Uses incorrect word endings and plurals
- Omits correct verbal endings
- Makes grammatical or syntactical errors that do not reflect those of his or her parents
- Has difficulty blending sounds

Auditory Memory Disability

The student

- Does not know address or phone number
- Fails to remember instructions
- Has difficulty memorizing nursery rhymes or poems
- Has difficulty knowing the alphabet

Assessment of Auditory Perception

There are many tests used in school systems to assess auditory perceptual skills. This section examines the most commonly used auditory perceptual measures and identifies the strengths and weaknesses of each test.

Goldman-Fristoe-Woodcock Test of Auditory Discrimination (G-F-W TAD)

Authors: Ronald Goldman, Macalyne Fristoe, and Richard W. Woodcock

Description of Test: The *Goldman-Fristoe-Woodcock Test of Auditory Discrimination* is specifically designed to assess young children. Geared to children's vocabulary levels and limited attention spans, the test moves rapidly as responses are made by pointing to appealing pictures of familiar objects. Writing and speaking are not required. In this two-part test the examiner presents a test plate containing four drawings to the subject. The subject responds to a stimulus word (presented via audiocassette to ensure standardized presentation) by pointing to one of the drawings on the plate.

Administration Time: 20 to 30 minutes

Age/Grade Levels: Ages 4 to Adult

Subtest Information: The test has three parts:

- *Training Procedure*—During this time, the examinee is familiarized with the pictures and the names that are used on the two subtests.
- *Quiet Subtest*—In this subtest, the examinee is presented with individual words in the absence of any noise. This subtest provides a measure of auditory discrimination under ideal conditions.
- *Noise Subtest*—In this subtest, the examinee is presented with individual words in the presence of distracting background noise on the tape. This subtest provides a measure of auditory discrimination under conditions similar to those encountered in everyday life.

Lindamood Auditory Conceptualization Test–3rd Edition (LAC-3)

Authors: Charles Lindamood and Patricia Lindamood

Description of Test: The LAC-3 is an individually administered, norm-referenced assessment that measures an individual's ability to perceive and conceptualize speech sounds using a visual medium. Because of the importance of these auditory skills to reading, the results are helpful for speech-language pathologists, special educators, and reading specialists. The LAC-3 also measures the cognitive ability to distinguish and manipulate sounds, which success in reading and spelling requires.

Administration Time: 20 to 30 minutes

Age/Grade Levels: Ages 5 through 18

Subtest Information: There are no formal subtests but the test is divided into four parts:

- *Precheck*—This five-item subtest is designed to examine a child's knowledge of various concepts—for example, same/different, first/last.
- *Category I, Part A*—This subtest consists of 10 items in which the student is asked to identify certain isolated sounds and determine whether they are the same or different.
- *Category I, Part B*—This subtest requires the student to identify isolated sounds, sameness or difference, and also their order.
- *Category II*—This subtest consists of a list of 12 items in which the student must change sound patterns when sounds are added, omitted, substituted, shifted, or repeated.

Test of Auditory Processing Skills–3rd Edition (TAPS-3)

Author: Morrison F. Gardner

Description of Test: The TAPS-3 is a reshaping of the *Test of Auditory Perceptual Skills* (authored by M. Gardner). The most obvious change is that there are no longer two "levels" of the test—the TAPS-3 offers seamless coverage for ages 4 through 18 years. The TAPS-3 measures what a person does with what is heard, and is intended to be used along with other tests as part of a battery. It is designed to be used by speech-language pathologists, audiologists, school psychologists, and other testing professionals.

Administration Time: Approximately 10 to 15 minutes

Age/Grade Levels: Ages 4–0 to 18–11

Subtest Information: The test is divided into nine subtests:

• Word Discrimination
• Phonological Segmentation
• Phonological Blending
• Numbers Forward
• Numbers Reversed
• Word Memory
• Sentence Memory
• Auditory Comprehension
• Auditory Reasoning

Wepman Test of Auditory Discrimination–2nd Edition (ADT-2)

Authors: Joseph M. Wepman and William M. Reynolds

Description of Test: The ADT-2 is a quick way to individually screen children for auditory discrimination—and to identify those who may have difficulty learning the phonics necessary for reading. Using a very simple procedure, the ADT assesses a child's ability to recognize the fine differences between phonemes used in English speech. The examiner reads aloud 40 pairs of words, and the child indicates, verbally or gesturally, whether the words in each pair are the same or different.

Administration Time: 10 minutes

Age/Grade Levels: Ages 4 to 8

Subtest Information: There are no subtests on this instrument. The mode of presentation is the same for all editions of the test. The test consists of 40 word pairs of similar sounding words or contrasts of similar words. The child has to say if the word pairs read aloud are the same or different.

COMPREHENSIVE MEASURES OF PERCEPTUAL ABILITIES

Besides the assessment measures already discussed under visual and auditory perception, there are many comprehensive measures of perceptual ability. These tests are sometimes referred to as *multiprocess tests* (tests that contain a variety of subtests used to measure many perceptual areas). The following is a review of some available comprehensive perceptual tests.

Bruininks-Oseretsky Test of Motor Proficiency–2nd Edition (BOT-2)

Author: Robert Bruininks

Description of Test: The *Bruininks-Oseretsky Test of Motor Proficiency-2* is an individually administered measure of gross and fine motor skills. It is a physical performance and paper-and-pencil assessment measure containing eight subtests. The examiner observes and records the student's performance on certain tasks, and the student is given a booklet in which he completes cutting and paper-and-pencil tasks. BOT-2 assesses the motor proficiency of all students, ranging from those who are normally developing to those with moderate motor-skill deficits. It can also be used for developing and evaluating motor training programs.

Administration Time: The complete battery takes 45 to 60 minutes; the short form takes 15 to 20 minutes.

Age/Grade Levels: Ages 4–6 to 14–5

Subtest Information: The test consists of eight subtests:

- *Fine Motor Precision:* seven items (e.g., cutting out a circle, connecting dots)
- *Fine Motor Integration:* eight items (e.g., copying a star, copying a square)
- *Manual Dexterity:* five items (e.g., transferring pennies, sorting cards, stringing blocks)
- *Bilateral Coordination:* seven items (e.g., tapping foot and finger, jumping jacks)
- *Balance:* nine items (e.g., walking forward on a line, standing on one leg on a balance beam)
- *Running Speed and Agility:* five items (e.g., shuttle run, one-legged side hop)
- *Upper-Limb Coordination:* seven items (e.g., throwing a ball at a target, catching a tossed ball)
- *Strength:* five items (e.g., standing long jump, sit-ups)

Detroit Tests of Learning Aptitudes–4th Edition (DTLA-4)

Author: Donald D. Hammill

Description of Test: The DTLA-4 is a multiple-item, oral-response, and paper-and-pencil battery of 11 subtests. The test provides the examiner with a profile of the student's perceptual abilities and deficiencies.

Administration Time: 50 to 120 minutes

Age/Grade Levels: Ages 6 through 17

Subtest Information: The DTLA-4 contains 11 subtests that are grouped into three domains. Within each domain there are two subareas called *composites*. Listed below are the subtests included in each domain:

Linguistic Domain

1. *Verbal Composite*—This composite tests the student's knowledge of words and their use using the following subtests:

Basic Information	*Story Construction*
Picture Fragments	*Word Opposites*
Reversed Letters	*Word Sequences*
Sentence Imitation	

    2. *Nonverbal Composite*—This composite does not involve reading, writing, or speech and uses the following subtests:

Design Reproduction	*Story Sequences*
Design Sequences	*Symbolic Relations*

Attentional Domain

1. *Attention-Enhanced Composite*—This composite emphasizes concentration, attending, and short-term memory, using the following subtests:

Design Reproduction	*Sentence Imitation*
Design Sequences	*Story Sequences*
Reversed Letters	*Word Sequences*

2. *Attention-Reduced Composite*—This composite emphasizes long-term memory, using the following subtests:

Basic Information	*Symbolic Relations*
Picture Fragments	*Word Opposites*
Story Construction	

Motoric Domain

1. *Motor-Enhanced Composite*—This subtest emphasizes complex manual dexterity, using the following subtests:

Design Reproduction	*Reversed Letters*
Design Sequences	*Story Sequences*

2. *Motor-Reduced Composite*—This subtest requires very little motor involvement and uses the following subtests:

Basic Information	*Story Construction*
Picture Fragments	*Word Opposites*
Sentence Imitation	*Word Sequences*

Illinois Test of Psycholinguistic Abilities–3rd Edition (ITPA-3)

Authors: Donald A. Hammill, Nancy Mather, and Rhia Roberts

Description of Test: The ITPA-3 is an effective measure of children's spoken and written language. All of the subtests measure some aspect of language, including oral language, writing, reading, and spelling.

Administration Time: 45 to 60 minutes

Age/Grade Levels: Ages 5 through 12

Subtest Information:

Spoken Language

- *Spoken Analogies*—The examiner says a four-part analogy, of which the last part is missing. The child then tells the examiner the missing part. For example, in response to "Birds fly, fish _____ ," the child might say "swim."

- *Spoken Vocabulary*—The examiner says a word that is actually an attribute of some noun. For example, the examiner may say, "I am thinking of something with a roof," to which the child might respond "house."
- *Morphological Closure*—The examiner says an oral prompt with the last part missing. For example, the examiner says, "big, bigger, _____," and the child completes the phrase by saying "biggest."
- *Syntactic Sentences*—The examiner says a sentence that is syntactically correct but semantically nonsensical (e.g., "Red flowers are smart"). The child repeats the sentence.
- *Sound Deletion*—The examiner asks the child to delete words, syllables, and their phonemes from spoken words. For example, the examiner might ask the student to say "weekend" without the "end."
- *Rhyming Sequences*—The examiner says strings of rhyming words that increase in length, and the child repeats them (e.g., "noon," "soon," "moon").

Written Language

- *Sentence Sequencing*—The child reads a series of sentences silently and then orders them into a sequence to form a plausible paragraph. For example, if the following three sentences were rearranged in B, C, A order they would make sense: A. I go to school. B. I get up. C. I get dressed.
- *Written Vocabulary*—After reading an adjective (e.g., "A broken ____"), the child responds by writing a noun that is closely associated with the stimulus word (e.g., "vase" or "mirror").
- *Sight Decoding*—The child pronounces a list of printed words that contain irregular parts (e.g., "would," "laugh," "height," "recipe").
- *Sound Decoding*—The child reads aloud phonically regular names of make-believe animal creatures (e.g., Flant, Yang).
- *Sight Spelling*—The examiner reads aloud irregular words one by one in a list. The child is given a printed list of these words, in which the irregular part of the words and one or more phonemes are missing. The child writes in the omitted part of the words. For example, the examiner says, "said"; the child sees s___d and writes in the missing letters, *ai*.
- *Sound Spelling*—The examiner reads aloud phonically regular nonsense words, and the child writes the word or the missing part.

Composite Scores

To enhance the clinical and diagnostic usefulness of the ITPA-3, the subtests can be combined to form 11 composites.

GLOBAL COMPOSITES

- *General Language Composite*—Formed by combining the results of all 12 subtests. For most children, this is the best single estimate of linguistic ability because it reflects status on the widest array of spoken and written language abilities.
- *Spoken Language Composite*—Formed by combining the results of the six subtests that measure aspects of oral language. The subtests assess oral language's semantical, grammatical, and phonological aspects.

- *Written Language Composite*—Formed by combining the results of the six subtests that measure different aspects of written language. The subtests assess written language's semantic, graphophonemic, and orthographic aspects. All subtests that involve graphemes (printed letters) to any degree in reading, writing, or spelling are assigned to this composite.

SPECIFIC COMPOSITES

- *Semantics Composite*—Formed using the results of the two subtests that measure the understanding and use of purposeful speech.
- *Grammar Composite*—Formed using the two subtests that measure grammar used in speech (one measures morphology, the other syntax).
- *Phonology Composite*—The two subtests that make up this composite measure competency with speech sounds, including phonemic awareness. One subtest involves deleting parts of words, and the other involves recalling strings of rhyming words.
- *Comprehension Composite*—The results of the two subtests that measure the ability to comprehend written messages (i.e., to read) and to express thoughts in graphic form (i.e., to write) make up this composite.
- *Spelling Composite*—The results of the two subtests that measure spelling form this composite.
- *SightSymbol Processing Composite*—The two subtests in this composite measure the pronunciation and spelling of irregular words. Parts of these words have to be mastered by sight because they do not conform to the most common English spelling rules or patterns (e.g., thumb).
- *SoundSymbol Processing Composite*—The two subtests in this composite measure the pronunciation and spelling of pseudowords (phonetically regular nonwords). These nonwords conform to the standard English phoneme-to-grapheme correspondence rules involved in pronouncing printed words or spelling spoken words.

Slingerland Screening Tests for Identifying Children with Specific Language Disability

Author: Beth H. Slingerland

Description of Test: The *Slingerland Screening Tests* do not test language but rather various auditory, visual, and motor skills related to specific academic areas. The multiple-item verbally presented paper-and-pencil examination contains eight subtests.

Administration Time: 60 to 80 minutes (Forms A, B, and C); 110 to 130 minutes (Form D)

Age/Grade Levels: Grades 1 through 6

Subtest Information: Each subtest focuses on curriculum-related skills.

- *Far-Point Copying*—This subtest requires the student to copy a printed paragraph from far points to probe visual perception and graphomotor responses. The subtest assesses visual–motor skills related to handwriting.
- *Near-Point Copying*—This subtest requires the student to copy a printed paragraph from nearby in order to probe visual perception and graphomotor responses. The subtest assesses visual–motor skills related to handwriting.

- *Visual Perception Memory*—This subtest requires the student to recall and match printed words, letters, and numbers presented in brief exposure with a delay before responding. This subtest assesses visual memory skills related to reading and spelling.
- *Visual Discrimination*—This subtest requires the student's immediate matching of printed words and eliminates the memory component of Visual Perception Memory. The subtest assesses basic visual discrimination without memory or written response.
- *Visual Kinesthetic Memory*—This subtest requires the student's delayed copying of words, phrases, letters, designs, and number groups presented with brief exposure. The subtest assesses the combination of visual memory and written response, which is necessary for written spelling.
- *Auditory Kinesthetic Memory*—This subtest requires the student to write groups of letters, numbers, and words to dictation after a brief delay with distraction. This subtest combines auditory perception and memory with written response.
- *Initial and Final Sounds*—This subtest requires the student to write the initial phoneme and later to write the final phoneme of groups of spoken words. This subtest assesses auditory discrimination and sequencing related to basic phonics with a written response.
- *Auditory/Visual Integration*—This subtest requires the student's delayed matching of spoken words, letters, or number groups. This subtest assesses visual discrimination related to word recognition. There are four different forms of this test (Forms A, B, C, and D). Some of the forms contain subtests other than those already mentioned:
- *Following Directions*—This subtest requires the student to give a written response from a series of directions given by the examiner. This subtest assesses auditory memory and attention with a written response.
- *Echolalia*—This subtest requires the student to listen to a word or phrase given by the examiner and to repeat it four or five times. This is an individual auditory test. This subtest assesses auditory kinesthetic confusion related to pronunciation.
- *Word Finding*—This subtest requires the child to fill in a missing word from a sentence read by the examiner. This is an individual auditory test; it assesses comprehension and the ability to produce a specific word on demand.
- *Storytelling*—This subtest requires the child to retell a story previously read by the examiner. This is an individual auditory test; it assesses auditory memory and verbal expression of content material.

CONCLUSION

Administering auditory and visual perception tests is very important in the special education process. Many children have great difficulties perceiving certain stimuli; yet a perception deficit often goes undetected. An evaluation is greatly enhanced when perceptual difficulties can be ruled out as factors contributing to a child's poor performance. Perceptual tests often take very little time to administer, so there should never be a concern about time factors when determining the battery of tests to use. In the end, using a perceptual measure can only increase the thoroughness and comprehensive nature of your assessment process and final report.

Vocabulary

Association or organization: Relating new information to other information and giving meaning to the information received.

Auditory association: The ability to organize and associate material presented auditorily.

Auditory discrimination: The ability to differentiate auditorily the sounds in one's environment.

Auditory long-term memory: The ability to retain and recall general and specific long-term auditory information.

Auditory modality: The delivery of information through sound.

Auditory motoric expression: The ability to reproduce motorically prior auditorily presented material or experiences.

Auditory sequential memory: The ability to recall in correct sequence and detail prior auditory information.

Auditory short-term memory: The ability to retain and recall general and specific short-term auditory information.

Auditory vocal expression: The ability to reproduce vocally prior auditorily presented material or experiences.

Expression: The output of information through vocal, motoric, or written responses.

Gustatory modality: The delivery of information through taste.

Kinesthetic modality: The delivery of information through movement.

Memory: The storage or retrieval process that facilitates the associational process to give meaning to information or help in relating new concepts to other information that might have already been learned. This process involves short-term, long-term, and sequential memory.

Multisensory approaches: The input of information through a variety of receptive mechanisms (i.e., seeing, hearing, touching, etc.).

Olfactory modality: The delivery of information through smell.

Perception: The initial organization of information.

Reception: The initial receiving of information.

Tactile modality: The delivery of information through touching.

Visual association: The ability to organize and associate visually presented material in a meaningful way.

Visual coordination: The ability to follow and track objects with coordinated eye movements.

Visual discrimination: The ability to differentiate visually the forms and symbols in one's environment.

Visual figure–ground discrimination: The ability to differentiate relevant stimuli (the figure) from irrelevant stimuli (the background).

Visual form perception (visual constancy): The ability to discern the size, shape, and position of visual stimuli.

Visual long-term memory: The ability to retain and recall general and specific long-term visual information.

Visual modality: The delivery of information through sight.

Visual motoric expression (visual motor integration): The ability to reproduce motorically prior visually presented material or experiences.

Visual sequential memory: The ability to recall in correct sequence and detail prior visual information.

Visual short-term memory: The ability to retain and recall general and specific short-term visual information.

Visual spatial relationships: The ability to perceive the relative positions of objects in space.

Visual vocal expression: The ability to reproduce vocally prior visually presented material or experiences.

13 | ASSESSMENT OF SPEECH AND LANGUAGE

Key Terms

Aphasia
Apraxia
Articulation
Broca's aphasia
Central auditory processing
    disorder (CAPD)
Cluttering
Content
Expressive language disorder
Fluency impairment

Form
Global aphasia
Language
Language disorder
Loudness
Morphology
Phonological process
Phonology
Pitch
Receptive language disorders

Sound quality
Speech
Speech disorder
Stuttering
Syntax
Use
Voice
Wernicke's aphasia

Chapter Objectives

This chapter focuses on the importance of speech and language assessment in the special education process. After reading this chapter, you should understand the following:

■ The difference between speech and language

■ Language processes

■ Educational implications of speech and language disorders

■ Types of speech disorders

■ Types of language disorders

■ Assessment of speech and language

■ Assessment measures of oral language

SPEECH AND LANGUAGE

Speech and language are related, but they are not the same thing. **Speech** is the physical process of making the sounds and sound combinations of a language. Language is much more complex than speech; however, speech production is one of its components. **Language** is essentially the system according to which people agree to talk about or represent environmental events. Once a group of people agree on a system for representing objects, events, and the relationships among objects and events, the system can be used to communicate all their experiences. The language system consists of words and word combinations.

Language is complex and involves multiple domains—nonverbal language, oral language (i.e., listening and speaking), written language (i.e., reading and writing), pragmatic language (e.g., using language for a specific purpose, such as asking for help), phonology, and audiology. How quickly a person can access words or ideas in memory further influences his or her use of language. A child who must struggle to find an appropriate term is at a great disadvantage in a learning and social environment. As he or she grapples to retrieve a word, others have moved on. The student may miss critical pieces of knowledge, connect incorrect bits of information in memory, or have an ineffective means of showing others all that he or she knows. Such problems can result in lowered levels of achievement and in feelings of confusion, helplessness, and frustration.

Whereas the meaning of language is contained in its words and word combinations, it is speech that permits the transmission of meaning. Speech sounds are not meaningful in themselves, of course. They acquire meaning only if the speaker or listener knows his or her relationship to real events. To state it very simply, speech sounds are a medium for carrying messages.

Language is an integral part of our everyday functioning. At a minimum, we use language for problem solving, communicating, and expressing knowledge. Therefore, when problems in language become evident, they can affect individuals in many different ways. In school, children need language in order to function in the classroom. Without language, a child would have serious disadvantages when compared to other students. Students with difficulties in language may not be able to express to teachers, parents, or peers all that they know. Such problems can result in lower levels of self-esteem, low achievement, confusion, helplessness, and frustration.

Because language plays such a critical role in a child's development, most schools have a speech or language pathologist to help students who are having difficulties with these areas. Speech and language pathologists are specially trained professionals who, working with other professionals throughout the school, gather data and assess the language functioning of individual students. Language processes can be broken down into three general categories:

1. **Form:** When special educators speak of form, they normally are speaking of three interconnected concepts:
   - **Phonology:** The knowledge a student has of sounds in language.
   - **Morphology:** The smallest meaningful unit of language, created by stringing together sounds.
   - **Syntax:** The rules used in combining words to make a sentence.
2. **Content:** The importance of meaning. It involves knowledge of vocabulary, relationships between words, and time and event relationships.
3. **Use:** The pragmatic functions of language in varying contexts. It sees the individual as an active communicator whose words and sentences are intentionally selected in relation to the effect the speaker wishes to have on a listener.

Assessment of Speech and Language

According to IDEA 2004, a speech and language impairment can be defined as a communication disorder such as stuttering, a language impairment, or a voice impairment that adversely affects a child's educational performance. Simply stated, a child with a **speech disorder** may have difficulties with any of the following:

- Producing sounds properly
- Speaking in a normal flow
- Speaking with a normal rhythm
- Using his or her voice in an effective way

Children with **language disorders** may exhibit the following:

- Difficulty in comprehending questions and following commands (receptive language)
- Difficulty in communicating ideas and thoughts (expressive language)

There are numerous tests one can give to assess speech and language disorders.

Speech and language evaluations are normally done by the speech and language pathologists in the school. However, teachers and parents play an instrumental role in these evaluations. Through interviews and observations, a student's teacher, with the parents, can gather and give valuable input to the overall assessment. As a result, both teachers and parents should become familiar with developmental language milestones.

Listed below are some important milestones for ages birth to 5:

BIRTH TO 6 MONTHS
- First form of communication—crying
- Sounds of comfort such as coos and gurgles
- Babbling soon follows as a form of communication
- Attaches no meaning to words heard from others

6 TO 12 MONTHS
- Voice begins to rise and fall while making sounds
- Begins to understand certain words
- May respond appropriately to the word *no* or own name
- May perform an action when asked
- May repeat words said by others

12 TO 18 MONTHS
- Has learned to say several words with appropriate meaning
- Is able to tell what he or she wants by pointing
- Responds to simple commands

18 TO 24 MONTHS
- Great spurt in the acquisition and use of speech at this stage
- Begins to combine words
- Begins to form words into short sentences

2 TO 3 YEARS
- Talks
- Asks questions
- Has vocabulary of about 900 words

- Participates in conversation
- Can identify colors
- Can use plurals
- Can tell simple stories

3 TO 4 YEARS

- Begins to speak more rapidly
- Begins to ask questions to obtain information
- Sentences longer and more varied
- Can complete simple analogies

4 TO 5 YEARS

- Average vocabulary of over 1,500 words
- Sentences average five words in length
- Able to modify speech
- Able to define words
- Can use conjunctions
- Can sing songs from memory

Educational Implications

Because all communication disorders carry the potential to isolate individuals from their social and educational surroundings, it is essential to find appropriate timely intervention. While many speech and language patterns can be called "baby talk" and are part of a young child's normal development, they can become problems if they are not outgrown as expected. In this way an initial delay in speech and language or an initial speech pattern can become a disorder that can cause difficulties in learning. Because of the way the brain develops, it is easier to learn language and communication skills before the age of 5. When children have muscular disorders, hearing problems, or developmental delays, their acquisition of speech, language, and related skills is often affected.

Speech–language pathologists assist children who have communication disorders in various ways. They provide individual therapy for the child, consult with the child's teacher about the most effective ways to facilitate the child's communication in the class setting, and work closely with the family to develop goals and techniques for effective therapy in class and at home. The speech–language pathologist may assist vocational teachers and counselors in establishing communication goals related to the work experiences of students and suggest strategies that are effective for the important transition from school to employment and adult life.

Technology can help children whose physical conditions make communication difficult. The use of electronic communication systems allows nonspeaking people and people with severe physical disabilities to engage in the give and take of shared thought.

Vocabulary and concept growth continues during the years children are in school. As students get older, reading and writing—understanding and using language—become more complex. Communication skills are at the heart of the education experience. Speech and language therapy may continue throughout a student's school years, either in the form of direct therapy or on a consultant basis.

Many speech problems are developmental rather than physiological, and as such they respond to remedial instruction. Language experiences are central to a young child's development.

In the past, children with communication disorders were routinely removed from the regular class for individual speech and language therapy. This is still the case in severe instances, but the trend is toward keeping the child in the mainstream as much as possible. To accomplish this goal, teamwork among the teacher, speech and language therapist, audiologist, and parents is essential. Speech improvement and correction are blended into the regular classroom curriculum and the child's natural environment.

TYPES OF SPEECH AND LANGUAGE DISORDERS

Common Speech Disorders

APRAXIA OF SPEECH. Apraxia is a motor disorder in which voluntary movement is impaired without muscle weakness. Rather, the ability to select and sequence movements is impaired. Apraxia is a problem in assembling the appropriate sequence of movements for speech production or executing the appropriate serial ordering of sounds for speech.

Oral apraxia affects one's ability to move the muscles of the mouth for nonspeech purposes, such as coughing, swallowing, wiggling the tongue, or blowing a kiss. Apraxia of speech, also known as *verbal apraxia* or *dyspraxia,* is a speech disorder in which a person has trouble saying what he or she wants to say correctly and consistently. It is not due to weakness or paralysis of the speech muscles (the muscles of the face, tongue, and lips).

ARTICULATION PROBLEMS. Articulation is the process by which sounds, syllables, and words are formed when the jaw, teeth, tongue, lips, and palate alter the airstream coming through the vocal folds; it is the production of speech sounds. Articulation disorders result from errors in the formation of individual speech sounds. Intelligibility is a measure of how well speech can be understood. Someone with an articulation disorder can be hard to understand because they say sounds incorrectly. Most errors fall into one of three categories: omissions, substitutions, or distortions. An *omission* might be "at" for "hat," whereas a substitution may be "wabbit" for "rabbit" or "thun" for "sun." When the sound is said inaccurately, but sounds something like the intended sound, it is called a *distortion*. The terms *articulation development* and *phonetic development* both refer to children's gradual acquisition of the ability to produce individual speech sounds.

PHONOLOGICAL PROCESSING PROBLEMS. Phonology is the science of speech sounds and sound patterns. The aims of phonology are to demonstrate the patterns of distinctive sound contrasts in a language and to explain the ways speech sounds are organized and represented in the mind. We have language rules about how sounds can be combined. If children do not use conventional rules for language but develop their own, they may have a phonological disorder.

A **phonological process** is a pattern a child develops to simplify articulation. Phonological processing disorders are characterized by failure to use speech sounds that are appropriate for the individual's age and dialect. Phonological disorders involve a difficulty in learning and organizing the sounds needed for clear speech, reading, and spelling. They are disorders that tend to run in families.

Children with a phonological disorder do not necessarily go on to experience literacy problems, but children who still have a phonological disorder in the form of speech errors (especially those at the severe end of the scale) when they start school are very much at risk for difficulties learning to read and spell.

Developmental phonological disorders affect children's ability to develop speech that can be easily understood. Children with phonological disorders have difficulty learning and organizing the sounds needed for clear speech. Two common phonological processes in children are *consonant sequence reduction* ("back" instead of "black," "sock" instead of "socks") and *velar deviation-fronting* ("dame" instead of "game," "take" instead of "cake"). Phonological disorders have been found to run in families. In some cases, these disorders may affect a child's reading and spelling abilities.

Speech Fluency Problems

A **fluency impairment** is characterized by speech broken with abnormal stoppages (no sound), repetition ("st-st-stopping"), or prolongations ("mmmmmmmmaking"). There may also be unusual facial and body movement associated with the effort to speak.

Cluttering occurs when speech becomes literally cluttered with faulty phrasing and unrelated words to the extent that it is unintelligible. Unlike stuttering, which involves hesitation and repetition of key words, cluttering usually includes effortless repetition of syllables and phrases. The affected person is often not aware of any communication difficulties.

Stuttering is a speech disorder in which the normal flow of speech is disrupted by frequent repetitions or prolongations of speech sounds, syllables, or words or by an individual's inability to start a word. The speech disruptions may be accompanied by rapid eye blinks, tremors of the lips and jaw, or other struggle behaviors of the face or upper body that a person who stutters may use in an attempt to speak. Certain situations, such as speaking before a group of people or talking on the telephone, tend to make stuttering more severe, whereas other situations, such as singing or speaking alone, often improve fluency.

Stuttering may also be referred to as *stammering,* especially in England, and by a broader term, *disfluent speech.* Stuttering is different from two additional speech fluency disorders, *cluttering,* characterized by a rapid, irregular speech, and *spasmodic dysphonia,* a voice disorder. It is estimated that in the United States, more than three million people stutter. Stuttering affects individuals of all ages, but occurs most frequently in young children between the ages of 2 and 6 who are developing language. Boys are three times more likely to stutter than girls. Most children, however, outgrow their stuttering, and it is estimated that less than 1 percent of adults stutter.

Scientists suspect a variety of causes. There is reason to believe that many forms of stuttering are genetically determined. The precise mechanisms causing stuttering are not understood. Many individuals who stutter have become successful in careers that require public speaking, including Winston Churchill, actress Marilyn Monroe, actors James Earl Jones, Bruce Willis, and Jimmy Stewart, and singers Carly Simon and Mel Tillis, to name only a few.

The most common form of stuttering is thought to be developmental, occurring in children who are in the process of developing speech and language. This relaxed type of stuttering is felt to occur when a child's speech and language abilities are unable to meet his or her verbal demands and happens when the child searches for the correct word. Developmental stuttering is usually outgrown.

VOICE PROBLEMS. **Voice** (or vocalization) is the sound produced by humans and other vertebrates using the lungs and the vocal folds in the larynx, or voice box. Voice is not always produced as speech, however. Infants babble and coo; animals bark, moo, whinny, growl, and meow; and adult humans laugh, sing, and cry. Voice is generated by airflow from the lungs as the vocal folds are brought close together. When air is pushed past the vocal folds with sufficient pressure, the vocal folds vibrate. If the vocal folds in the larynx did not vibrate normally, speech could only be produced as a whisper. Your voice is as unique as your fingerprint. It helps define your personality, mood, and health.

Approximately 7.5 million people in the United States have trouble using their voices. Voice disorders involve problems with pitch, loudness, and quality. **Pitch** is the highness or lowness of a sound based on the frequency of the sound waves. **Loudness** is the perceived volume (or amplitude) of the sound. **Sound quality** refers to the character or distinctive attributes of a sound. Many people who have normal speaking skills have great difficulty communicating when their vocal apparatus fails. This can occur if the nerves controlling the larynx are impaired because of an accident, a surgical procedure, a viral infection, or cancer.

Voice disorders can be divided into two categories, organic and functional. Organic disorders stem from disease or pathology, whereas functional voice disorders result from abuse or misuse of the voice. Organic disorders require medical intervention, whereas functional voice disorders can often be managed by voice therapy.

Common Language Disorders

APHASIA SYNDROMES. **Aphasia** is a language disorder caused by damage to portions of the brain responsible for language, which for most people is on the left side (hemisphere) of the brain. Aphasia usually occurs suddenly, often as the result of a stroke or head injury, but it may also develop slowly, as in the case of a brain tumor. The disorder impairs the expression and understanding of language as well as reading and writing.

Damage to one or more of the language areas of the brain can be caused by a stroke. A stroke occurs when, for some reason, blood is unable to reach a part of the brain. Brain cells die when they do not receive their normal supply of blood, which carries oxygen and important nutrients. Other causes of brain injury are severe blows to the head, brain tumors, brain infections, and other conditions of the brain.

Individuals with **Broca's aphasia** have damage to the frontal lobe of the brain. These individuals frequently speak in short, meaningful phrases that are produced with great effort. Broca's aphasia is thus characterized as a nonfluent aphasia. Affected people often omit small words such as *is, and,* and *the.* For example, a person with Broca's aphasia may say, "Walk dog" meaning, "I will take the dog for a walk." The same sentence could also mean "You take the dog for a walk," or "The dog walked out of the yard," depending on the circumstances. Individuals with Broca's aphasia are able to understand the speech of others to varying degrees. Because of this, they are often aware of their difficulties and can become easily frustrated by their speaking problems. Individuals with Broca's aphasia often have right-sided weakness or paralysis of the arm and leg because the frontal lobe is also important for body movement.

In contrast to Broca's aphasia, damage to the temporal lobe may result in a fluent aphasia that is called **Wernicke's aphasia**, in which individuals may speak in long sentences that have no meaning, add unnecessary words, and even create new words. For example, someone with Wernicke's aphasia may say, "You know that smoodle pinkered and that I want to get him round and take care of him like you want before," meaning "The dog needs to go out so I will take him for a walk." Individuals with Wernicke's aphasia usually have great difficulty understanding speech and are therefore often unaware of their mistakes. These individuals usually have no body weakness because their brain injury is not near the parts of the brain that control movement.

A third type of aphasia, **global aphasia**, results from damage to extensive portions of the language areas of the brain. Individuals with global aphasia have severe communication difficulties and may be extremely limited in their ability to speak or comprehend language.

Aphasia is usually first recognized by the physician who treats the individual for his or her brain injury. Frequently this is a neurologist. The physician typically performs tests that require the individual to follow commands, answer questions, name objects, and converse. If the physician suspects aphasia, the individual is often referred to a speech–language pathologist, who performs a comprehensive examination of the person's ability to understand, speak, read, and write.

CENTRAL AUDITORY PROCESSING DISORDERS (CAPD). **Central auditory processing disorder (CAPD)** is a term used to describe what happens when your brain recognizes and interprets the sounds around you. Humans hear when energy that we recognize as sound travels through the ear and is changed into electrical information that can be interpreted by the brain. The "disorder" part of auditory processing disorder means that something is adversely affecting the processing or interpretation of the information.

Children with CAPD often do not recognize subtle differences between sounds in words, even though the sounds themselves are loud and clear. For example, the request "Tell me how a chair and a couch are alike" may sound to a child with CAPD like "Tell me how a couch and a chair are alike." It can even be understood by the child as "Tell me how a cow and a hair are alike." These kinds of problems are more likely to occur when a person with CAPD is in a noisy environment or when he or she is listening to complex information.

What causes central auditory processing difficulty? We are not sure. Human communication relies on taking in complicated perceptual information from the outside world through the senses, such as hearing, and interpreting that information in a meaningful way. Human communication also requires certain mental abilities, such as attention and memory. Scientists still do not understand exactly how all of these processes work and interact or how they malfunction in cases of communication disorders. Even though a child seems to "hear normally," he or she may have difficulty using those sounds for speech and language.

The cause of CAPD is often unknown. In children, auditory processing difficulty may be associated with conditions such as dyslexia, attention deficit disorder, autism, autism spectrum disorder, specific language impairment, pervasive developmental disorder, or developmental delay. Sometimes this term has been misapplied to children who have no hearing or language disorder but have challenges in learning.

DEVELOPMENT OF LANGUAGE. The most intensive period of speech and language development for humans is during the first three years of life, a period when the brain is developing and maturing. These skills appear to develop best in a world that is rich with sounds, sights, and consistent exposure to the speech and language of others.

There is increasing evidence suggesting that there are critical periods for speech and language development in infants and young children. This means that the developing brain is best able to absorb a language, any language, during this period. The ability to learn a language will be more difficult, and perhaps less efficient or effective, if these critical periods are allowed to pass without early exposure to a language. The beginning signs of communication occur during the first few days of life when an infant learns that a cry will bring food, comfort, and companionship. The newborn also begins to recognize important sounds in his or her environment. The sound of a parent or voice can be one important sound. As they grow, infants begin to sort out the speech sounds (phonemes) or building blocks that compose the words of their language. Research has shown that by 6 months of age, most children recognize the basic sounds of their native language.

As the speech mechanism (jaw, lips, and tongue) and voice mature, an infant is able to make controlled sounds. This begins in the first few months of life with cooing, a quiet, pleasant, repetitive vocalization. By 6 months of age, an infant usually babbles or produces repetitive syllables such as "ba, ba, ba" or "da, da, da." Babbling soon turns into a type of nonsense speech (*jargon*) that often has the tone and cadence of human speech but does not contain real words. By the end of their first year, most children have mastered the ability to say a few simple words. Children are most likely unaware of the meaning of their first words, but soon learn the power of those words as others respond to them.

By 18 months of age, most children can say 8 to 10 words. By age 2, most are putting words together in crude sentences such as "More milk." During this period, children rapidly learn that words symbolize or represent objects, actions, and thoughts. At this age they also engage in representational or pretend play. At ages 3, 4, and 5, a child's vocabulary rapidly increases, and he or she begins to master the rules of language. Children vary in their development of speech and language. There is, however, a natural progression or timetable for mastery of these skills for each language. The milestones are identifiable skills that can serve as a guide to normal development. Typically, simple skills need to be reached before the more complex skills can be learned. There is a general age and time when most children pass through these periods. These milestones help doctors and other health professionals determine when a child may need extra help to learn to speak or to use language.

EXPRESSIVE LANGUAGE DISORDERS. A person with an **expressive language disorder** (as opposed to a *mixed receptive/expressive language disorder*) understands language better than he or she is able to communicate. In speech–language therapy terms, the person's receptive language (understanding of language) is better than his or her expressive language (use of language). This type of language disorder is often a component in developmental language delay (see next paragraph). Expressive language disorders can also be acquired (occurring as a result of brain damage or injury), as in aphasia (see previous section on aphasia). The developmental type is more common in children, whereas the acquired type is more common in the elderly. An expressive language disorder could occur in a child of normal intelligence, or it could be a component of a condition affecting mental functioning more broadly (i.e., mental retardation, autism).

Children with expressive language delays often do not talk much or often, although they generally understand language addressed to them. For example, a 2-year-old may be able to follow two-step commands but not name body parts. A 4-year-old may understand stories read aloud, but may not be able to describe the story even in a simple narrative. Imaginative play and social uses of language (i.e., manners, conversation) may also be impaired by expressive language limitations, causing difficulty in playing with peers. These are children who may have a lot to say but are unable to retrieve the words they need. Some children may have no problem in simple expression but have difficulties retrieving and organizing words and sentences when expressing more complicated thoughts and ideas. This may occur when they are trying to describe, define, or explain information or retell an event or activity.

RECEPTIVE LANGUAGE DISORDERS. **Receptive language disorders** involve difficulties in the ability to attend to, process, comprehend, retain, or integrate spoken language.

ASSESSMENT MEASURES OF SPEECH AND LANGUAGE

There are many tests that assess the strengths and weaknesses of a child's speech and language development. This section focuses on the most commonly used assessment measures for speech and language in school systems.

Peabody Picture Vocabulary Test–4th Edition (PPVT-4)

Authors: Lloyd M. Dunn and Douglas M. Dunn

Description of Test: The PPVT-4 is a measure of expressive vocabulary and word retrieval. It is a brief, easy-to-use individually administered norm-referenced assessment of listening comprehension for spoken words in Standard English.

Administration Time: 10–15 Minutes

Age/Grade Levels: Ages 2–6 to 90+ years

Subtest Information: This test is not divided into subtests.

Test of Auditory Comprehension of Language–3rd Edition (TACL-3)

Author: Elizabeth Carrow Woolfolk

Description of Test: The TACL-3 is designed to measure a child's auditory comprehension of language, determine the developmental level, and provide diagnostic information regarding those areas of language comprehension that present difficulty to the child. This is a multiple-item response test assessing auditory understanding of word classes and relations, grammatical morphemes, and elaborated sentence constructions.

Administration Time: 15 to 25 minutes

Age/Grade Levels: Ages 3 to 9

Subtest Information:

- *Vocabulary*—This subtest contains items composed of nouns, verbs, modifiers, and word relations. It measures mastery of vocabulary and concepts needed by children in preschool, kindergarten, and the elementary grades.
- *Grammatical Morphemes*—This subtest contains items composed of short simple sentences that measure grammatical morphemes, including prepositions, pronouns, noun inflections, verb inflections, noun–verb agreement, and derivational suffixes.
- *Elaborated Phrases and Sentences*—This subtest contains complex sentences that vary on a number of dimensions. It tests a student's competence on sentences with interrogatives, active and passive voice, direct and indirect objects, and coordination, subordination, and embedding of contextual elements.

Goldman-Fristoe Test of Articulation–2nd Edition (GFTA-2)

Authors: Ronald Goldman and Macalyne Fristoe

Description of Test: The GFTA-2 provides information about a child's articulation ability by sampling both spontaneous and imitative sound production. Examinees respond to picture plates and verbal cues from the examiner with single-word answers that demonstrate common speech sounds. Additional sections provide further measures of speech production.

Administration Time: 5 to 15 minutes for Sounds-in-Words Section, varied for other two sections.

Age/Grade Levels: Ages 2 to 21

Subtest Information:

- *Sounds in Words*—This subtest is a picture-naming task in which the child is shown pictures of familiar objects and asked to name or answer questions about them.
- *Sounds in Sentences*—This subtest assesses spontaneous sound production used in connected speech.
- *Stimulability Subtest*—This subtest assesses the child's ability to correctly produce a previously misarticulated sound when asked to watch and listen to the examiner's production of the sound.

Comprehensive Receptive and Expressive Vocabulary Test–2nd Edition (CREVT-2)

Authors: Gerald Wallace and Donald D. Hammill

Description of Test: *The Comprehensive Receptive and Expressive Vocabulary Test–2nd Edition* (CREVT-2) is an innovative, efficient measure of both receptive and expressive oral vocabulary. This test is a two-subtest measure based on current theories of vocabulary development. Two equivalent forms are available and full-color photos are used on the Receptive Vocabulary subtest. The kit includes examiner's manual, photo album picture book, and record forms.

Administration Time: 20 to 30 minutes

Age/Grade Levels: Ages 4 to Adult

Subtest Information:

- *Receptive Vocabulary*—The format for the 61-item Receptive Vocabulary Subtest is a variation of the familiar "Point to the picture of the word I say" technique, featuring the unique use of thematic full-color photographs. The subtest is made up of 10 plates, each of which comprises six pictures. All the pictures on a plate relate to a particular theme (animals, transportation, occupations, clothing, food, personal grooming, tools, household appliances, recreation, and clerical materials). The themes represent concepts with which most people are familiar. Five to eight words are associated with each plate and the words increase evenly in difficulty from young child through adult. The examiner begins with Item 1 on the first plate and asks the person being tested a series of words, one at a time. After each word, the examinee selects from six photographs the one that best goes with the stimulus word. When the person misses two words in a row, the examiner introduces the next plate. The pictures used to give the Receptive Vocabulary Subtest are spiral-bound in a Photo Album Picture Book featuring laminated covers for ease of use and durability. Each plate is printed in full color on heavy varnish-sealed cover stock designed for frequent use.
- *Expressive Vocabulary*—The Expressive Vocabulary Subtest uses the "Define the word I say" format—the most popular and precise way to measure expressive vocabulary. This format encourages and requires the individual to converse in detail about a particular stimulus word, making it ideal to measure expressive ability. The 25 items on this subtest pertain to the same 10 common themes used in the Receptive Vocabulary Subtest (i.e., animals, transportation, occupations, etc.), allowing for easy transition from subtest to subtest. The application of basals and ceilings (see Chapter 3) allows this test to be given quickly and makes it appropriate for a wide age range.

Test of Adolescent and Adult Language–4th Edition (TOAL-4)

Authors: Virginia Brown, Donald Hammill, Stephen Larson, and J. Lee Wiederholt

Description of Test: The *Test of Adolescent and Adult Language–4th edition* (TOAL-4) is designed to measure spoken and written language abilities of adolescents and young adults with varying degrees of knowledge of the English language.

Administration Time: 60 to 180 minutes

Age/Grade Levels: Ages 12-0 through 24-0

Subtest Information: The TOAL-4 has six subtests:

1. **Word Opposites**—examinee is asked for a spoken word of exact meaning of the word examiner says; the opposite of "Day" is "Night."
2. **Word Derivations**—examinee is asked for a missing word at the end of the second sentence the examiner says, deriving from a key word; "Laugh. The play was very funny. The people broke out laughing."
3. **Spoken Analogies**—examinee is asked to finish an examiner's partial analogous sentence with a word to complete the analogy; "Birds are to sing, as dogs are to bark."
4. **Word Similarities**—examinee is asked to write a synonym (correct spelling is irrelevant) for a printed stimulus word; "Pig" is written after seeing the word "Hog."
5. **Sentence Combining**—examinee is asked to write one grammatically correct sentence from the given two or more sentences; "We ate lunch," and "It was an hour ago" can be combined into, "We ate lunch an hour ago."
6. **Orthographic Usage**—examinee is asked to write down all the correct words and punctuation marks to all the sentences given; "I want to go home" can be corrected to "I want to go home."

Test of Early Language Development–3rd Edition (TELD-3)

Authors: Wayne P. Iliesko, D. Kim Reid, and Donald D. Hammill

Description of Test: The TELD-3 screens children for language deficiency. It is designed for normal children but can be administered to special populations after making proper adjustments in administering the test and establishing different norms.

Administration Time: 20 minutes

Age/Grade Levels: Ages 2 through 7

Subtest Information: The TELD-3 has two subtests: Receptive Language and Expressive Language.

Photo Articulation Test–3rd Edition (PAT-3)

Authors: Barbara Lipke, Stanley Dickey, John Selmar, and Anton Soder

Description of Test: The *Photo Articulation Test–3rd Edition* (PAT-3) is a completely revised edition of the popular *Photo Articulation Test*. It meets the nationally recognized need for a standardized way to document articulation errors. The PAT-3 enables the clinician to rapidly and accurately assess and interpret articulation errors.

Administration Time: 20 minutes

Age/Grade Levels: Ages 3–6 through 9

Subtest Information: The test consists of 72 color photographs (nine photos on each of eight sheets). The first 69 photos test consonants and all but one vowel and one diphthong. The remaining three pictures test connected speech and the remaining vowel and diphthong. A deck of the same 72 color photographs, each on a separate card, is provided for further diagnosis and may be used in speech–language remediation.

To administer the PAT-3, the examiner simply points to each consecutively numbered photograph and asks the child, "What is this?" The child's response is scored on the Summary/Response Form to indicate the presence or absence of errors. The elicited sounds are arranged by age of acquisition. The Summary/Response Form groups the sounds by the ages at which 90 percent of the sample correctly articulated the sounds. All sounds tested are written in the international phonetic alphabet. In addition, consonant sounds are differentiated into the initial, medial, and final positions within the stimulus words. The results from the PAT-3 provide the clinician with a straightforward, comprehensive view of each student's articulation errors.

Test of Language Development–4th Edition (TOLD-P:4)

Authors: Phyllis L. Newcomer and Donald D. Hammill

Description of Test: The Test of Language Development-Primary: Fourth Edition (TOLD-P:4) assesses spoken language in young children. Professionals can use the TOLD-P:4 to (1) identify children who are significantly below their peers in oral language proficiency, (2) determine their specific strengths and weaknesses in oral language skills, (3) document their progress in remedial programs, and (4) measure oral language in research studies.

Administration Time: 30 minutes to 1 hour

Age/Grade Levels: Ages 4–0 to 8–11

Subtest Information: The TOLD-P:4 has nine subtests which measure various aspects of oral language are described below. The results of these subtests can be combined to form composite scores for the major dimensions of language: semantics and grammar; listening, organizing, and speaking; and overall language ability.

1. *Picture Vocabulary*—measures a child's understanding of the meaning of spoken English words (semantics, listening)
2. *Relational Vocabulary*—measures a child's understanding and ability to orally express the relationships between two spoken stimulus words (semantics, organizing)
3. *Oral Vocabulary*—measures a child's ability to give oral directions to common English words that are spoken by the examiner (semantics, speaking)
4. *Syntactic Understanding*—measures a child's ability to comprehend the meaning of sentences (grammar, listening)
5. *Sentence Imitation*—measures a child's ability to imitate English sentences (grammar, organizing)
6. *Morphological Completion*—measures a child's ability to recognize, understand, and use common English morphological forms (grammar, speaking)
7. *Word Discrimination*—measures a child's ability to recognize the differences in significant speech sounds (phonology, listening)

8. *Word Analysis*—measures a child's ability to segment words into smaller phonemic units (phonology, organizing)
9. *Word Articulation*—measures a child's ability to utter important English speech sounds (phonology, speaking)

CONCLUSION

Of the many types of assessments that may be done when testing is mandated, those discussed in this chapter are very important to understand, even if you as a special educator may not have to actually administer them in your career. You should now understand that a thorough comprehension of speech and language is critical to developing appropriate hypotheses and theories about whether a specific disability exists in a child. The fact that a professional in the special education process may not be a speech and language clinician does not preclude him or her from knowing the various tests and assessment procedures that are used. When all team members have at least a general understanding of what the other members are doing, it makes the entire multidisciplinary evaluation stronger.

Vocabulary

Aphasia: A language disorder that results from damage to the portions of the brain that are responsible for language.

Apraxia: A motor disorder in which voluntary movement is impaired without muscle weakness.

Articulation: The process by which sounds, syllables, and words are formed when the jaw, teeth, tongue, lips, and palate alter the airstream coming through the vocal folds. It is the production of speech sounds.

Broca's aphasia: Individuals with damage to the frontal lobe of the brain frequently speak in short, meaningful phrases that are produced with great effort. Broca's aphasia is thus characterized as a nonfluent aphasia.

Central auditory processing disorder (CAPD):   A term used to describe brain impairments in recognizing and interpreting sounds. Humans hear when energy that we recognize as sound travels through the ear and is changed into electrical information that can be interpreted by the brain. The disorder part of auditory processing disorder means that something is adversely affecting the processing or interpretation of the information.

Cluttering: Speech becomes literally cluttered with faulty phrasing and unrelated words to the extent that it is unintelligible. Unlike stuttering, which involves hesitation and repetition over key words, cluttering usually includes effortless repetition of syllables and phrases. The affected person is often not aware of any communication difficulties.

Content: The importance of meaning. It involves knowledge of vocabulary, relationships between words, and time and event relationships.

Expressive language disorders: A person with an expressive language disorder (as opposed to a mixed receptive/expressive language disorder) understands language better than he or she is able to communicate. In speech–language therapy terms, the person's receptive language (understanding of language) is better than his or her expressive language (use of language).

Fluency impairment: A condition in which speech is broken by abnormal stoppages (no sound), repetition ("st-st-stopping"), or prolongations ("mmmmmmmmaking"). There may also be unusual facial and body movement associated with the effort to speak.

Form: The interconnected concepts of phonology, morphology, and syntax.

Global aphasia: Global aphasia results from damage to extensive portions of the language areas of the brain. Individuals with global aphasia have severe communication difficulties and may be extremely limited in their ability to speak or comprehend language.

Language: The system according to which a people agree to talk about or represent environmental events.

Language disorder: Difficulties in language that adversely affect a child's educational performance.

Loudness: The perceived volume (or amplitude) of the sound.

Morphology: The smallest meaningful unit of language, created by stringing together sounds.

Phonological process: Pattern a child develops in order to simplify articulation. Phonological processing disorders are characterized by failure to use speech sounds that are appropriate for the individual's age and dialect.

Phonology: The science of speech sounds and sound patterns.

Pitch: The highness or lowness of a sound based on the frequency of the sound waves.

Receptive language disorders: Involve difficulties in the ability to attend to, process, comprehend, retain, or integrate spoken language.

Sound quality: The character or distinctive attributes of a sound.

Speech: The physical process of making the sounds and sound combinations of a language.

Speech disorder: Difficulties in speech which adversely affect a child's educational performance.

Stuttering: A speech disorder in which the normal flow of speech is disrupted by frequent repetitions or prolongations of speech sounds, syllables, or words or by an individual's inability to start a word.

Syntax: The rules used in combining words to make a sentence.

Use: The pragmatic functions of language in varying contexts. It sees the individual as an active communicator whose words and sentences are intentionally selected in relation to the effect the speaker wishes to have on a listener.

Voice (or vocalization):   The sound produced by humans and other vertebrates using the lungs and the vocal folds in the larynx, or voice box.

Wernicke's aphasia: In contrast to Broca's aphasia, damage to the temporal lobe may result in a fluent aphasia called Wernicke's aphasia.

14 EARLY CHILDHOOD ASSESSMENT

Key Terms

Assessment for diagnosis and
    determination of eligibility
Authenticity
Case finding/child find
Collaboration
Congruence
Convergence
Developmental

Early childhood intervention
Equity
Facility or center-based visits
Family support groups
Group development intervention
Home and community-
    based visits
Home visits

Individualized family
    service plan (IFSP)
Parent–child groups
Program evaluation
Program planning
Qualified personnel
Screening
Sensitivity

Chapter Objectives

This chapter focuses on the importance of early intervention assessment and education in the birth to 5-year-old population. After reading this chapter, you should understand the following:

▪ The importance of early childhood assessment

▪ Legal foundations for assessment procedures

▪ The challenge of early childhood assessment

▪ Working with the family in early childhood assessment

▪ Early childhood assessment measures

EARLY CHILDHOOD ASSESSMENT

Early childhood intervention (often referred to as *early intervention*) is rapidly becoming an area of study for many special educators. Both undergraduate and graduate schools are beginning to stress the importance of early intervention assessment and education in the birth to 5-year-old population. Many states are becoming increasingly aware of the importance of early intervention for children. The idea of helping children before they get to elementary school with whatever concerns they may be facing has educational, social, and political implications. Whatever the reasons for the initiation of early intervention in a given state, it has become apparent that it is a very important part of the special education process.

It is important to keep in mind that the parents of very young children suspected of having a disability will be anxious and in search of answers from educational professionals. When potential problems occur at such an early age, parents need answers that will inform them as to the diagnosis of the problem, the prognosis or what the child will be like in later years, and remediation and intervention strategies that will help their child. Therefore, special educators need to be familiar with early childhood evaluation instruments that will begin the process of assessment by diagnosing the child's areas of strength and weakness. From this information, a team of professionals can then prepare intervention recommendations for the parents.

The goal of assessment in early childhood is the same as it is for an individual of any age— that is, to derive information to facilitate decision making with respect to that individual. Such decisions revolve around the potential existence, implications, and treatment needs of problems for the child and family.

One issue in early childhood assessment is that many special educators have limited, if any, training with the birth to 5-year-old population. Consequently, although there are a number of tests to measure intellectual development, speech and language delays, and behavioral norms, few educators are well versed in the use of these assessment instruments.

The assessment process in early childhood is an attempt to determine the strengths and weaknesses of a child so that a specific program of intervention can be planned and implemented. A good assessment program takes an ecological approach to the evaluation. By this, we mean that the assessment data accurately describe as many aspects of the child's functioning as possible (physical, social, and intellectual) in as many settings as possible (home, school, community) for the information necessary to plan an intervention program that will affect as much of the child's life as possible. To meet these objectives, an assessment program must be broad enough to include a fair sampling of the child's abilities, yet specific enough to provide useful information. It must include several instruments administered by specialists in various areas of development (e.g., language, motor development, cognition), as well as observational data concerning the child's daily environment.

Bagnato, Neisworth, and Munson (1997) list six standards of assessment materials for use with young children:

- **Authenticity:** Does the assessment focus on actual child behavior in real settings?
- **Convergence:** Does the assessment rely on more than one source of information?
- **Collaboration:** Does the assessment involve cooperation and sharing, especially with parents?
- **Equity:** Does the assessment accommodate special sensory, motor, cultural, or other needs rather than penalize children who have such needs?
- **Sensitivity:** Does the assessment include sufficient items for planning lessons and detecting changes?
- **Congruence:** Was the assessment developed and field-tested with children similar to those being assessed?

LEGAL FOUNDATIONS FOR ASSESSMENT PROCEDURES

The field of early childhood special education is relatively new. Laws that govern the assessment of young children with special needs have been passed, starting with Public Law 94-142, the Education of All Handicapped Children Act in 1975, which mandated services for all school-age children with disabilities and facilitated the provision of services for preschool children with disabilities in some states (see Chapter 2). P.L. 94-142 and its regulations provided guidelines for the assessment of children receiving special education services from state departments of education (McLean et al., 1996).

In 1986, Public Law 99-457 was passed, amending P.L. 94-142 and requiring the states to provide a free and appropriate public education to children with disabilities ages 3 through 5. The regulations that governed school-age children were then made applicable to the assessment of preschool children. In addition, a new part (Part H) was added to the law, establishing incentives for serving infants and toddlers with special needs.

In 1990, P.L. 99-457 was retitled the Individuals with Disabilities Education Act (IDEA)—P.L. 101-476. The IDEA amendment to P.L. 99-457 required a timely, comprehensive, multidisciplinary evaluation, including assessment activities related to the child and the child's play. For infants and toddlers (birth to 2 years of age), a new program (Part H was changed to Part C in the Amendments to IDEA '97) was established to help states develop and implement programs for early intervention services. Every U.S. state currently provides services for infants and toddlers with disabilities under IDEA 2004 (P.L. 108-446).

IDEA 2004 (sec. 636(a)(1)(2)) states that

a. the state shall provide at a minimum for each infant or toddler with a disability, and the infant's or toddler's family, to receive:
1. a multidisciplinary assessment of the unique strengths and needs of the infant or toddler and the identification of services appropriate to meet such needs;
2. a family-directed assessment of the resources, priorities, and concerns of the family and the identification of the supports and services necessary to enhance the family's capacity to meet the developmental needs of the infant or toddler (p. 62).

THE CHALLENGE OF EARLY CHILDHOOD ASSESSMENT

Environmental and cultural influences must be considered when testing young children. Special educators can expect much more variability in test performance due to environmental influences on infants and preschool children than on older school-age children. Measures of the home environment can be very helpful in understanding a child's **developmental** functioning. Such factors as the quality of the mother's or father's verbalization, the toys or variety of activities available in the environment, the restrictiveness of discipline, and the freedom from danger can influence the child's early developmental course. It was very appropriate that P.L. 99-457 included a focus on not only the child with disabilities, but also the family of the child.

Cultural influences also must be considered, as they may affect parenting style and the child's responsiveness to the examiner and the testing process. For instance, a young Native American child may make less eye contact, act more shy, and be less verbal with the examiner than a Caucasian child, but these differences may represent cultural influences rather than developmental delay. Reviewing the cross-cultural literature regarding the developmental performance of infants who are African American, Asian American, Hispanic, and other cultural groups would be helpful to the prospective examiner.

To effectively meet the challenges posed, the assessment process in early childhood should try to achieve eight fundamental goals (McLean, Wolery, & Bailey, 2004):

- Determine the eligibility for services and the appropriateness of alternative environments
- Identify developmentally appropriate and functional intervention goals
- Identify the unique styles, strengths, and coping strategies of each child
- Identify parents' goals for their children and their needs for themselves
- Build and reinforce parents' sense of competence and worth
- Develop a shared and integrated perspective on child and family needs and resources

- Create a shared commitment to intervention goals
- Evaluate the effectiveness of services for children and families

The assessment and evaluation process for early intervention normally consists of the following five stages:

- **Case finding/child find:** To alert parents, professionals, and the general public to children who may have special needs and to elicit their help in recruiting candidates for screening.
- **Screening:** To identify children who are not within normal ranges of development and who, based on further evaluation, may be candidates for early intervention programs.
- **Assessment for diagnosis and determination of eligibility:** To conduct an in-depth evaluation to verify if a problem exists, determine the nature and severity of the problem, and prescribe the treatment or type of intervention services needed.
- **Program planning:** To establish procedures used by the assessment team to develop the individualized family service plan (discussed later) and to revise these plans as necessary. The outcome of assessment for program planning is the identification of special services needed by the child and the family, the service delivery format that will be used (including location of services), and the delineation of intervention objectives as specified in the IFSP.
- **Program evaluation:** To evaluate the quality of the overall intervention program and to document its impact on the children or parents it serves. Information collected on an ongoing basis allows the team to determine to what extent progress is being made toward goals and objectives and, as a result, to identify changes that should be made in intervention strategies or objectives. When such data are collected across all of the children in a given program, it may be possible to measure overall program impact.

According to Hanson and Lynch (1995a), the following questions can be used to review and evaluate procedures used to assess young children and identify family concerns, priorities, and resources:

- Are diagnostic or eligibility assessment procedures clearly identified?
- Are child assessment and family procedures linked to programming?
- Are the staff members who are conducting child assessments trained in measurement, the particular strategies being used, and assessment of young children and infants?
- Are the assessment instruments used valid and reliable?
- Is the assessment being conducted by an interdisciplinary team that includes the parents or primary caregivers as equal partners?
- Is adequate time allocated for the team to plan assessments jointly with the family?
- Are assessments conducted in a setting that is familiar to the child, with the parents or primary caregivers present and assisting?
- Are assessment data collected in a variety of ways (observation, interview, etc.)?
- Are assessments of the child's strengths and needs and the family's concerns, priorities, and resources culturally and linguistically appropriate?
- Is there a standard procedure for writing reports and sharing the findings with all the members, including the parents?
- Are written and verbal reports free of judgment, stereotyping, and negative labeling?
- Is ample time allocated for discussing and sharing findings and making programming decisions?
- Is follow-up done soon after placement to determine the appropriateness of the program, the child's performance, and the family's and staff's satisfaction with the program?

- Is the identification of family concerns, priorities, and resources nonintrusive, nonjudgmental, and conducted with sensitivity?
- Does the information collected about the family's concerns, priorities, and resources assist in finding resources or developing programs? (p. 179)

THE INDIVIDUALIZED FAMILY SERVICE PLAN

After a child has been evaluated, it is mandated under federal law that an **individualized family service plan (IFSP)** be written. This plan sets forth critical information pertaining to both the child and the family's services. IFSP stands for

- *Individualized.* The plan will be specially designed for the child and the family.
- *Family.* The plan will focus on the family and the outcomes family members hope for the child and the family through early intervention.
- *Service.* The plan will include all the details about the services provided for both the child and the family.
- *Plan.* The plan is a written plan for services.

The IFSP is based on the premise that a child's home environment strongly influences that child's overall experiences and successes; therefore, it includes goals and objectives for the family as a unit, as well as goals and objectives for the individual child (Bigge & Stump, 1999, p. 15).

Under IDEA 2004, sec. 636(d), the components of an IFSP must include the following:

1. A statement of the infant's or toddler's present levels of physical development, cognitive development, communication development, social or emotional development, and adaptive development, based on objective criteria.
2. A statement of the family's resources, priorities, and concerns relating to enhancing the development of the family's infant or toddler with a disability.
3. A statement of the measurable results or outcomes expected to be achieved for the infant or toddler and the family, including preliteracy and language skills, as developmentally appropriate for the child, and the criteria, procedures, and time lines used to determine the degree to which progress toward achieving the results or outcomes is being made and whether modifications or revisions of the results or outcomes or services are necessary.
4. A statement of specific early intervention services based on peer-reviewed research, to the extent practicable, necessary to meet the unique needs of the infant or toddler and the family, including the frequency, intensity, and method of delivering services.
5. A statement of the natural environments in which early intervention services will appropriately be provided, including a justification of the extent, if any, to which the services will not be provided in the natural environment.
6. The projected dates for initiation of services and the anticipated length, duration, and frequency of the services.
7. The identification of the service coordinator from the profession most immediately relevant to the infant or toddler's family's needs (or who is otherwise qualified to carry out all applicable responsibilities under this part) who will be responsible for the implementation of the plan and coordination with other agencies and persons, including transition services.
8. The steps to be taken to support the transition of the toddler with a disability to preschool or other appropriate services.

The IFSP must be reviewed at 6-month intervals or more frequently as needed. Every 12 months, the child must be reevaluated. After assessment is completed, a program must be established for each child.

Under Part C of IDEA, the following services can be given to infants and toddlers in the IFSP:

- Family training, counseling, and home visits
- Special instruction
- Speech and language instruction
- Occupational and physical therapy
- Psychological testing and counseling
- Service coordination
- Medical services necessary for diagnostic and evaluation purposes
- Social work services
- Assistive technology
- Early identification, screening, and assessment services
- Health services, when necessary
- Transportation and related costs as necessary

Only **qualified personnel**—individuals who are licensed, certified, or registered in their discipline and approved by their state—can deliver early intervention services. All early intervention services can be given using any of the following service models (New York State Department of Health, 2000):

1. **Home and community-based visits:** In this model, services are given to a child and parent or other family member or caregiver at home or in the community.
2. **Facility or center-based visits:** In this model, services are given to a child and parent or other family member or caregiver where the service provider works (such as an office, hospital, clinic, etc.).
3. **Parent–child groups:** In this model, parents and children get services together in a group led by a service provider. A parent–child group can happen anywhere in the community.
4. **Family support groups:** In this model, parents, grandparents, or other relatives of the child get together in a group led by a service provider for help and support and to share concerns and information.
5. **Group development intervention:** In this model, children receive services in a group setting led by a service provider or providers without parents or caregivers. A group means two or more children who are eligible for early intervention services. The group can include children without disabilities and can happen anywhere in the community.

WORKING WITH THE FAMILY IN EARLY CHILDHOOD ASSESSMENT

Many times, when assessing children who may need early intervention, the special educator will have to interview the parents/caregivers. This is very often done during a **home visit** right in the home of these individuals. Often, this is a new experience for many special educators. With the more recent emphasis on ecological assessment, interviews have begun to examine the relationship of children to their environment. How parents are treated in initial contacts with professionals who will be working with their child shapes their current and future attitudes and behaviors. Thus, planning and conducting the interview thoughtfully and sensitively are important investments. Interviews should allow time for rapport building or "warm-up" for both the interviewer and the interviewee. The purpose of the interview and an overview of the kinds of questions provided should be reviewed. Listed here are some practical suggestions for special educators when conducting parent interviews in early intervention (cited in Hanson and Lynch's *Survival Guide for Interviewers,* 1995b):

- Write down the address, directions, and a phone number where you can reach or leave a message for the family that you are interviewing. It is easy to get lost when you are busy or nervous.
- There are different cultural rules related to being in someone's house. Do not be surprised if the father or elder does all of the talking in some situations or if a male interventionist cannot visit the home unless the husband is present.
- If you are conducting the interview through an interpreter, allow time to discuss the interview questions with the interpreter first. Give the family and the interpreter time to get acquainted and comfortable with one another, and be sure that you address your questions and comments to the family, not the interpreter.
- Dress professionally yet in keeping with the norms of the family and community.
- If you are taking toys or materials to the home, take something that can remain (picture books, crayons, animal crackers, etc.), remembering that there may be several brothers and sisters who will be very interested in what you are doing and what you have brought.
- Do not be afraid to admit if you are nervous. Parents always recognize bluffing.
- It is not appropriate to tell your own stories or say you know just how the family feels, but it is appropriate to laugh and cry with someone who is sharing joy or pain.
- Do not feel that you have to answer all of the family's concerns or questions. For some you may be able to find answers; for others you may be able to help them find answers; and for some there never will be an answer.
- If you do not feel safe in a neighborhood, take someone with you to the interview or arrange to conduct it outside the home.
- Remember the Golden Rule as you embark on any interview: Interview others as you would like to be interviewed (p. 161).

EARLY CHILDHOOD ASSESSMENT MEASURES

Bayley Scales of Infant Development–3rd Edition (Bayley-III)

Author: Nancy Bayley

Description of Test: The Bayley Scales of Infant Development (Bayley-III) are recognized internationally as one of the most comprehensive tools to assess children from as young as one month old. With Bayley-III, it is possible to obtain detailed information even from non-verbal children as to their functioning. Children are assessed in the five key developmental domains of cognition, language, social-emotional, motor, and adaptive behavior. Bayley-III identifies infant and toddler strengths and competencies, as well as their limitations

Administration Time: 1–3 months: 10 minutes
4 – 8 months: 15 minutes
9 + months: 20 minutes

Age/Grade Levels: Ages 1 through 42 months

Subtest Information: The Bayley–III has three major parts that are tested with the child: Cognitive, Language, and Motor. The questionnaire that parents complete measures the child's Social-Emotional and Adaptive Behavior development.

The *Cognitive Scale (Cog)* assesses at how the child thinks, reacts, and learns about the world around him or her.

The Language Scale (Lang) has two parts.

- The Receptive Communication (RC) part assesses how well the child recognizes sounds and how much the child understands spoken words and directions.
- The Expressive Communication (EC) part assesses how well the child communicates using sounds, gestures, or words.

The *Motor Scale (Mot)* has two parts.

- The Fine Motor (FM) part assesses how well the child can use his or her hands and fingers to make things happen.
- The Gross Motor (GM) part assesses how well the child can move his or her body.

The *Social-Emotional (SE)* section measures development in infants and young children by identifying social-emotional milestones that are normally achieved by certain ages.

The *Adaptive Behavior (GAC)* section asks caregivers to respond to items that assess their child's ability to adapt to various demands of normal daily living.

Preschool Language Scale–4th Edition (PLS-4)

Authors: Irla Lee Zimmerman, Violette G. Steiner, and Roberta L. Evatt

Description of Test: The PLS-4 provides an accurate picture of children's receptive and expressive language skills from birth to age 6, appropriate for children with and without disabilities. From birth to 3, the test includes items targeting interaction, attention, vocal and gestural behaviors to assess language skills.

Administration Time: 20 to 45 minutes

Age/Grade Levels: Birth through age 12

Subtest Information: The test includes two separate scales:

- *Auditory Comprehension Scale*—The scale requires nonverbal responses such as pointing to a picture that the examiner has named.
- *Expressive Communication Scale*—In this section, items are presented that require the child to name or explain the items. The difficulty varies depending on the child's developmental level during the time of testing.

The items on the test assess the following areas in both the receptive and expressive modes:

Vocabulary	Morphology
Concepts of quality	Syntax
Concepts of quantity	Integrative thinking skills
Space and time	

Metropolitan Readiness Test–6th Edition (MRT-6)

Authors: Joanne Ruth Nurss

Description of Test: The MRT-6 assesses literacy development in children from preschool to the first grade. It provides a measure for validating and expanding on what teachers know about the children in their classrooms.

Administration Time: 85 to 100 minutes in 4 sessions

Age/Grade Levels: Pre-K and kindergarten

Subtest Information: The MRT-6 assesses five different areas:

- Visual discrimination
- Beginning consonants
- Sound–letter correspondence
- Story comprehension
- Quantitative concepts and reasoning

Boehm Test of Basic Concepts–3rd Edition (BTBC-3)

Author: Ann E. Boehm

Description of Test: This new edition of an old favorite helps measure 50 basic concepts most frequently occurring in current kindergarten, first-, and second-grade curricula.

Administration Time: 30 to 40 minutes

Age/Grade Levels: Grades K to 2

Subtest Information: There are no subtests. The Boehm-3 is group-administered and designed to effectively identify concepts in areas children must master for success in school:

- Size (i.e., medium-sized)
- Direction (away)
- Quantity (as many)
- Time (first)
- Classification (all)
- General (other)

Bracken Basic Concept Scale–Revised (BBCS-R)

Author: Bruce A. Bracken

Description of Test: The BBCS-R measures 11 diagnostic subtest areas. Items are multiple-choice, and the child is shown four monochrome pictures and asked to identify the picture that depicts a particular concept. The test includes an examiner's manual, diagnostic stimulus manual, diagnostic record forms, one Screening Test Form A, and one Screening Test Form B.

Administration Time: 20 to 40 minutes

Age/Grade Levels: Ages 2-6 to 7-11

Subtest Information:

- Color/ Letter Identification—Children are tested on their knowledge of colors and letters.
- Numbers/Counting—Children are required to tell how many items and recognize numbers.
- Comparisons—Children are required to compare things.
- Shapes—Children are tested regarding their ability to recognize different shapes.
- Direction/Position—Children are tested on their ability to distinguish between different directions and positions.
- Social/ Emotional—This subtest determines children's social and emotional development.
- Size—This subtest determines children's ability to differentiate between sizes.
- Texture/Material—Children are given objects of different texture and must identify them.
- Quantity—Children are tested on their ability to distinguish amounts.
- Time/Sequence—Children are given numbers and asked to tell the missing number or the number that comes next.

The Preschool Evaluation Scales-Second Edition (PES-2)

Author: Stephen B. McCarney and Tamara J. Arthaud

Description of Test: The Preschool Evaluation Scale-Second Edition (PES-2) was developed to provide educators, diagnosticians, pediatricians, and psychologists with a measure of child development. The PES-2 may be used to contribute to the early identification of students with developmental delays for the purpose of implementing an intervention plan for remediation.

Administration Time: 20 to 25 minutes

Age/Grade Levels: Birth to 72 months

Subtest Information: The PES-2 is based on the most commonly recognized domains of child development identified in the federal definition of developmental delays. Each subscale is associated with one of the developmental domains. The PES-2 subscales are

- *Large Muscle Skills*
- *Small Muscle Skills*
- *Cognitive Thinking*
- *Expressive Language Skills*
- *Social/Emotional*
- *Self-Help Skills*

Developmental Indicators for the Assessment of Learning (DIAL-3)

Authors: Carol Mardell & Dorothea S. Goldenberg

Description of Test: The DIAL-3 is a global screener for assessing large groups of children quickly and efficiently. Children complete fun, age appropriate tasks using bright, appealing, child-friendly materials. Stimuli are presented one at a time using a dial, manipulatives, or other materials.

Administration Time: 20–30 minutes

Age/Grade Levels: Ages 3-0 through 6-11

Subtest Information: The DIAL-3 provides scores for *Motor, Concepts, Language*, totals an overall composite, and indicates behavioral observation cutoffs. The DIAL-3 also provides standardized scores for *Self-Help* and *Social Development*, assessed by a Parent Questionnaire.

- *Motor Area:* Gross Motor items include catching, jumping, hopping, and skipping. Fine Motor items include building with blocks, cutting, copying shapes and letters, and writing, and the popular finger-touching task from the DIAL-R.
- *Language Area:* Items include answering simple personal questions (name, age, sex), articulation, naming (expressive) or identifying (receptive) objects and actions, plus phonemic awareness tasks such as rhyming and I Spy.
- *Concepts Area:* Items include pointing to named body parts, naming or identifying colors, rote counting, counting blocks, placing a block in named positions relative to a little house, identifying concepts in a triad of pictures, and sorting shapes. The DIAL-3 includes an item that assesses automatic naming of colors. This skill has been shown to be associated with potential learning disabilities.
- *Self-Help Development:* Looks at the child's development of personal care skills related to dressing, eating, and grooming.
- *Social Development:* Looks at the child's development of social skills with other children and parents, including rule compliance, sharing, self-control, and empathy.

Kindergarten Readiness Test (KRT)

Authors: Sue L. Larson and Gary Vitali

Description of Test: The KRT assesses five general areas of readiness: awareness of one's environment, reasoning, numerical awareness, fine motor coordination, and auditory attention span.

Administration Time: 15 to 20 minutes

Age/Grade Levels: Ages 4 to 6

Subtest Information: The test has no subtests.

Early Screening Profiles (ESP)

Authors: Patti Harrison, Alan Kaufman, PhD, Nadeen Kaufman, EdD, Robert Bruininks, John Rynders, Steven Ilmer, Sara Sparrow, and Domenic Cicchetti

Description of Test: Early Screening Profiles uses multiple domains, settings, and sources to measure cognitive, language, motor, self-help, and social development. It also surveys the child's articulation, home environment, health history, and test behavior.

Administration Time: 15 to 40 minutes

Age/Grade Levels: Ages 2-0 through 6-11

Subtest Information: The three basic components, called Profiles, are supplemented by four Surveys. Examiners can administer all of the profiles and surveys—or just the ones needed. For most children, the Profiles can be administered in less than 30 minutes. The Surveys require an additional 15–20 minutes.

Three Profiles

Cognitive/Language Profile is administered individually to the child. Tasks assess reasoning skills, visual organization and discrimination, receptive and expressive vocabulary, and basic school skills. The profile can be separated into cognitive (nonverbal) and language (verbal) subscales, a useful feature for screening children with limited English proficiency, language difficulties, or hearing problems.

Motor Profile, also individually administered, assesses both gross and fine motor skills-such as walking a straight line, imitating arm and leg movements, tracing mazes, and drawing shapes.

Self-Help/Social Profile is a questionnaire completed by the child's parent, teacher, daycare provider, or a combination of them. It assesses the child's typical performance in the areas of communication, daily living skills, socialization, and motor skills.

Four Surveys

• *Articulation Survey* measures the child's ability to pronounce 20 words selected to test common articulation problems in the initial, medial, and final positions of words.
• *Home Survey* is completed by the parent and asks nonintrusive questions about the child's home environment.
• *Health History Survey*, also completed by the child's parent, is a brief checklist of any health problems the child has had.
• *Behavior Survey* is used by the examiner to rate the child's behavior during administration of the Cognitive/Language and Motor Profiles. The child is rated in categories such as attention span, frustration tolerance, and response style.

Battelle Developmental Inventory–2nd Edition (BDI-2)

Author(s): Jean Newborg

Description of Test: The BDI-2 is used for screening, diagnosis, and evaluation of early development. This instrument may be used by a team of professionals or by an individual service provider. The BDI-2 can be administered to children with various handicapping conditions by using stated modifications. This instrument is based on the concept of milestones. That is, a child typically develops by attaining critical skills or behaviors in a certain sequence, and the acquisition of each skill generally depends on the acquisition of the preceding skills.

Administration Time: Complete BDI: 1–2 hours, Screening Test: 10–30 minutes

Age/Grade Levels: Birth through age 7

Subtest Information:

• Personal–Social Domain—This subtest measures coping skills, self-concept, expressions of feelings, and adult interaction.
• Adaptive Domain—This subtest measures attention, eating skills, dressing skills, personal responsibility, and toileting.
• Motor Domain—This subtest measures muscle control, body coordination, locomotion, fine muscle skills, and perceptual–motor skills.
• Communication Domain—This subtest measures receptive and expressive communication.
• Cognitive Domain—This subtest measures memory, reasoning skills, perceptual discrimination, academic skills, and conceptual development.

Columbia Mental Maturity Scale (CMMS)

Authors: Bessie B. Burgemeister, Lucille Hollander Blurn, and Irving Lorge

Description of Test: The CMMS is an individual-type scale that requires perceptual discrimination involving color, shape, size, use, number, kind, missing parts, and symbolic material. Items are printed on 95 6-inch by 19-inch cards arranged in a series of eight overlapping levels. The subject responds by selecting the picture in each series that is different from, or unrelated to, the others.

Administration Time: 15 to 30 minutes

Age/Grade Levels: Ages 3.5 to 10

Subtest Information: There are no formal subtests on this scale; rather, it is a 92-item test of general reasoning abilities.

McCarthy Scales of Children's Abilities (MSCA)

Author: Dorothea McCarthy

Description of Test: The MSCA consists of 18 separate tests grouped into six scales: Verbal, Perceptual–Performance, Quantitative, Composite (General Cognitive), Memory, and Motor.

Administration Time: 45 to 60 minutes

Age/Grade Levels: Ages 2-4 to 8-7

Subtest Information: The MSCA consists of six scales comprising a variety of 18 subtests. Some subtests fall into more than one scale. Listed below is each scale and the corresponding subtests measuring that skill:

1. *Verbal Scale*—This scale consists of five subtests:
   - *Pictorial Memory*—The child is required to recall names of objects pictured on cards.
   - *Word Knowledge*—In Part 1, the child is required to point to pictures of common objects named by the examiner. In Part 2, the child is required to give oral definitions of words.
   - *Verbal Memory*—In Part 1, the child is required to repeat word series and sentences. In Part 2, the child is required to retell a story read by the examiner.
   - *Verbal Fluency*—The child is required to name as many articles as possible in a given category within 20 seconds.
   - *Opposite Analogies*—The child is required to complete sentences by providing opposites.

2. *Perceptual Performance Scale*—This scale consists of seven subtests:
   - *Block Building*—The child is required to copy block structures built by the examiner.
   - *Puzzle Solving*—The child is required to assemble picture puzzles of common animals or foods.
   - *Tapping Sequence*—The child is required to imitate sequences of notes on a xylophone, as demonstrated by the examiner.
   - *Right–Left Orientation*—The child is required to demonstrate knowledge of right and left.
   - *Draw-a-Design*—The child is required to draw geometrical designs as presented in a model.

- *Draw-a-Child*—The child is required to draw a picture of a child of the same sex.
- *Conceptual Grouping*—The child is required to classify blocks on the basis of size, color, and shape.

3. *Quantitative Scale*—This scale consists of three subtests:
   - *Number Questions*—The child is required to answer orally presented questions involving number information or basic arithmetical computation.
   - *Numerical Memory*—In Part 1, the child is required to repeat a series of digits exactly as presented by the examiner. In Part 2, the child is required to repeat a digit series in exact reverse order.
   - *Counting and Sorting*—The child is required to count blocks and sort them into equal groups.

4. *Motor Scale*—This scale consists of three subtests:
   - *Leg Coordination*—The child is required to perform motor tasks that involve lower extremities such as walking backward or standing on one foot.
   - *Arm Coordination*—In Part 1, the child is required to bounce a ball. In Part 2, the child is required to catch a beanbag, and in Part 3, the child is required to throw a beanbag at a target.
   - *Imitative Action*—The child is required to copy simple movements such as folding hands or looking through a tube.

5. *General Cognitive*—This scale consists of 17 subtests from many of the measures shown previously. Please refer to the four prior scales for a complete explanation of the subtests.

Pictorial Memory	*Draw-a-Design*
Word Knowledge	*Draw-a-Child*
Verbal Memory	*Conceptual Grouping*
Verbal Fluency	*Number Questions*
Opposite Analogies	*Numerical Memory*
Block Building	*Counting and Sorting*
Puzzle Solving	*Draw-a-Child*
Tapping Sequence	*Draw-a-Design*
Right–Left Orientation	

6. *Memory*—This scale consists of four subtests. Please refer to the first four scales for a complete explanation of these subtests.

Pictorial Memory	*Tapping Sequence*
Verbal Memory	*Numerical Memory*

CONCLUSION

The early years of a child's life are extremely important. During the infant and toddler years, children grow quickly and have much to learn. However, some children and families face special challenges and need extra help. Early help does make a difference. Young children present many challenges to the special educator, who is charged with evaluating their intellectual, language, motor, and adaptive functioning. Normal developmental transitions of infancy and early childhood influence motivation, interest, and cooperation with the testing process. The special educator experienced in testing school-age children may expect a young child to exhibit appropriate "testing behavior"—sitting quietly at a desk, attending to a task at hand, and being motivated to complete the tasks presented. Such characteristic testing behavior is not often present in this age group or, if present, is limited to a few brief moments. The special educator examining young children must be aware of the developmental influences affecting the young child and must be flexible enough to adapt the testing procedures accordingly.

Vocabulary

Assessment for diagnosis and determination of eligibility: Part of the assessment and evaluation process for early intervention that conducts an in-depth evaluation to verify if a problem exists, to determine the nature and severity of the problem, and to prescribe the treatment or types of intervention services needed.

Authenticity: Does the assessment focus on actual child behavior in real settings?

Case finding/child find: Part of the assessment and evaluation process for early intervention that alerts parents, professionals, and the general public to children who may have special needs and to elicit their help in recruiting candidates for screening.

Collaboration: Does the assessment involve cooperation and sharing, especially with parents?

Congruence: Was the assessment developed and field-tested with children similar to those being assessed?

Convergence: Does the assessment rely on more than one source of information?

Developmental: Having to do with the steps or stages in the growth of a child.

Early childhood intervention   (often referred to as *early intervention*): The early intervention through assessment and education in the birth to 5-year-old population.

Equity: Does the assessment accommodate special sensory, motor, cultural, or other needs rather than penalize children who have such needs?

Facility or center-based visits: In this early intervention services model, services are given to a child and parent or other family member or caregiver where the service provider works (office, hospital, clinic, etc.).

Family support groups: In this early intervention services model, parents, grandparents, or other

relatives of the child get together in a group led by a service provider for help and support and to share concerns and information.

Group development intervention: In this early intervention services model, children receive services in a group setting led by a service provider or providers without parents or caregivers.

Home and community-based visits: In this early intervention services model, services are given to a child, parent, or other family member or caregiver at home or in the community.

Home visits: Visits in the parents' home by a professional for the purpose of planning and providing early intervention services.

Individualized family service plan (IFSP):   After a child has been evaluated, it is mandated under Public Law 99-457 that an IFSP be written. This plan sets forth critical information pertaining to both the child and the family's services. The IFSP will be specially designed for the child and family. It will focus on the outcomes hoped for by the family. And it will include all the details about the services provided for both the child and the family.

Parent–child groups: In this early intervention services model, parents and children get services together in a group led by a service provider. A parent–child group can happen anywhere in the community.

Program evaluation: Part of the assessment and evaluation process for early intervention that evaluates the quality of the overall intervention program and documents its impact on the children or parents it serves.

Program planning: Part of the assessment and evaluation process for early intervention that refers to those procedures used by the assessment team to develop the IFSP (Individual Family Service Plan) and to revise these plans as necessary.

Qualified personnel: Those individuals who are approved to provide early intervention services within the limits of their licensure, certification, or registration.

Screening: Part of the assessment and evaluation process for early intervention that identifies children who are not within normal ranges of development, need further evaluation, and who may be candidates for early intervention programs.

Sensitivity: Does the assessment include sufficient items for planning lessons and detecting changes?

15 OTHER AREAS OF ASSESSMENT

Key Terms

Audiometric evaluation
measures
Behavioral play audiometry
Bilingual assessment
Central auditory disorders
Conductive hearing loss
Deafness
Dominant language

Evoked response
audiometry
Functional hearing loss
Hearing impairment
Impedance audiometry
Mixed hearing loss
Occupational therapy
Otosclerosis

Physical therapy
Pure tone audiometric
screening
Pure tone threshold
audiometry
Sensorineural hearing loss
Sound field audiometry
Speech audiometry

Chapter Objectives

The focus of this chapter will be to discuss three other areas of assessment: assessment of hearing, the roles and responsibilities of physical and occupational therapists, and bilingual assessment. After reading this chapter, you should understand the following:

▪ Assessment of hearing

▪ Assessment measures of hearing

▪ Occupational and physical therapy measures

▪ Multicultural assessment

ASSESSMENT OF HEARING

When people think of someone who is hearing impaired, they often think that the person is deaf. However, this is not true. Under IDEA 2004, **deafness** is a "hearing impairment that is so severe that the child is impaired in processing linguistic information through hearing, with or without amplification, that adversely affects a child's educational performance." Yet, under IDEA 2004, a **hearing impairment** is an "impairment in hearing, whether permanent or fluctuating, that adversely affects a child's educational performance but which is not included under the definition of deafness in this section."

In examining these two definitions, it is evident that being deaf means that hearing is disabled to an extent that precludes understanding speech through the ear alone, with or without a hearing aid. Being hearing impaired or hard of hearing makes hearing difficult, but does not preclude the understanding of speech through the ear alone, with or without a hearing aid.

Causes of Hearing Impairments

Hearing difficulties need to be identified as early as possible in order to plan an appropriate educational program. Some hearing problems occur from birth, whereas others occur at later stages in a child's development. There are several causes of hearing impairments.

- **Conductive hearing loss:** Problems with the structures in the outer or middle ear, generally attributed to a blockage in the mechanical conduction of sound. To overcome this blockage, the sounds must be amplified. These conditions are usually temporary. The leading causes of this type of hearing loss are:
  - Otitis media (middle ear infection)
  - Excessive ear wax
  - **Otosclerosis** (formation of a spongy-bony growth around the stapes, which impedes its movement)
- **Sensorineural hearing loss:** Damage to the cochlea or the auditory nerve caused by illness and disease and not medically or surgically treatable. Causes of this hearing loss include:
  - Viral diseases such as rubella (German measles) or meningitis
  - Rh incompatibility
  - Ototoxic medications (medicines that destroy or damage hair cells in the cochlea, such as streptomycin) taken by pregnant mothers or very young children
  - Hereditary factors
  - Exposure to noise
  - Aging
- **Mixed hearing loss:** This is a hearing loss caused by both sensorineural and conductive problems.
- **Functional hearing loss:** This results from those problems that are not organic in origin; examples include psychosomatic causes such as hysterical conversion, malingering, and emotional or psychological problems.
- **Central auditory disorders:** Despite no measurable peripheral hearing loss, children with these disorders have trouble learning and are often considered learning disabled. Causes include
  - Auditory comprehension problems
  - Auditory discrimination problems
  - Auditory learning difficulties
  - Language development delays

Whatever the cause, a parent or teacher may be the first individual to observe the symptoms of a hearing loss, such as

- Significant problems in expressive language
- Significant problems in receptive language
- Difficulties with speech development
- Problems in socialization
- Difficulty with alertness or speaking in class

Degrees of Hearing Impairment

Once the audiologist completes the assessment, a determination is made of the level of hearing loss. The following chart offers a comparison of the different levels of hearing loss.

Degree of Hearing Loss	Decibel Loss	Resulting Impairment
Slight	27–40 dB	Difficulty hearing faint noises or distant conversation. The individual with a slight hearing loss will usually not have difficulties in the regular school setting.
Mild	41–55 dB	This individual may miss as much as half of classroom conversations. The individual may also exhibit limited vocabulary and speech difficulties.
Moderate	56–70 dB	The individual will be able to hear only loud conversation, may exhibit defective speech, vocabulary, and language difficulties.
Severe	71–90 dB	Hearing may be limited to a radius of one foot. May be able to discriminate certain environmental sounds, shows defective speech and language ability, and has severe difficulty understanding consonant sounds.
Profound	91 dB or greater	The individual can sense but is unable to understand sounds and tones. Vision becomes the primary sense of communication, and speech and language are likely to deteriorate.

The diagnosis of a hearing loss is the initial step in the treatment and education of the child. Special education teachers need specialized assessment measures to conduct educational screenings and evaluations. These tests for the hearing-impaired child are crucial in the educational planning process.

ASSESSMENT MEASURES OF HEARING

When symptoms of hearing impairment are observed, the first step is usually a referral to an audiologist for a screening. Several assessment measures are utilized in the possible identification of a hearing loss. **Audiometric evaluation measures** are used by qualified audiologists who directly measure the level of hearing loss through the use of several techniques, including:

- **Pure tone audiometric screening**—Pure tone screening is often referred to as sweep testing, and is usually the child's first encounter with hearing testing. This type of testing, which is common in schools, presents the child with pure tones over a variety of frequency ranges. The child is then asked to respond if he or she hears a tone, usually by some gesture. If a child is unable to hear sounds at two or more frequencies, the child is usually referred for further evaluation.
- **Speech audiometry**—This type of evaluation is used to determine a child's present ability to hear and understand speech through the presentation of words in a variety of loudness levels.

- **Pure tone threshold audiometry**—In this procedure, the child is asked to make a gesture or push a button each time he or she hears a tone. The child is presented with a variety of frequencies through earphones. This type of ear conduction test reveals the presence of hearing loss.

Other special audiometric tests are more indirect and include:

- **Sound field audiometry**—This measure is used with very young children who cannot respond to manual responses or are unable or unwilling to wear headphones. The child is evaluated by observing the intensity levels at which he or she responds to different levels of sounds broadcast through speakers.
- **Evoked response audiometry**—This measure uses an electroencephalograph, and a computer measures changes in brain wave activity to a variety of sound levels. This measure can be used with infants who are suspected of being deaf.
- **Impedance audiometry**—There are two major impedance audiometry tests: Tympanometry measures the functioning level of the eardrum, and stapedial reflex testing measures the reflex response of the stapedial muscle to pure tone signals. Because these tests do not require a response on the part of the child, they can be used with very young children.
- **Behavioral play audiometry**—This technique involves placing the child in a series of activities that reward him or her for responding appropriately to tone or speech.

Listed next are some of the tests used most often to assess students for a possible hearing problem when being evaluated for special education services.

Auditory Perception Test for the Hearing Impaired (APT/HI)

Authors: Susan G. Allen and Thomas S. Serwatka

Description of Test: The APT/HI is designed to assess the building-block processes used to decode speech. It allows for specific analysis of the individual's ability to decode phonemes in isolation and in the context of words and sentences. It consists of a manual, plates, and record forms.

Administration Time: 30 minutes

Age/Grade Levels: Ages 5 and over

Subtest Information: The test has no subtests.

Carolina Picture Vocabulary Test for Deaf and Hearing Impaired (CPVT)

Authors: Thomas L. Layton and David W. Holmes

Description of Test: The CPVT is designed to measure the receptive sign vocabulary in individuals for whom manual signing is the primary mode of communication. The CPVT consists of a manual, record forms, and a picture book.

Administration Time: 10 to 30 minutes

Age/Grade Levels: Ages 4 to 11-5

Subtest Information: The test contains no subtests.

Hiskey-Nebraska Test of Learning Aptitude

Author: Marshall S. Hiskey

Description of Test: The test is designed as a nonverbal measure of mental ability that has been found helpful in the intellectual assessment of a variety of language-handicapped children and youth. The test is a performance scale that can be administered entirely via pantomimed instructions and requires no verbal response from the subject. The scale consists of a series of performance tasks that are organized in ascending order of difficulty within subscales.

Administration Time: Approximately 60 minutes

Age/Grade Levels: Ages 2 to 18

Subtest Information:

- *Memory for Colored Objects*—The child is required to perform memory tasks using colored objects.
- *Bead Stringing*—The child is required to put beads on a string.
- *Pictorial Associations*—The child has to decide what various pictures look like.
- *Block Building*—The child is required to build things with blocks.
- *Memory for Digits*—The child is given groups of numbers and asked to repeat them.
- *Completion of Drawings*—The child is required to finish a picture that is not completed.
- *Pictorial Identification*—The child is shown a picture and has to say what the picture is.
- *Visual Attention Span*—The child must focus on an object for a set period of time.
- *Puzzle Blocks*—The child is required to arrange the blocks into a picture that is shown.
- *Pictorial Analogies*—The child is required to compare two pictures and pick a picture that goes with the third picture.

Leiter International Performance Scale–Revised (LEITER-R)

Authors: Russel Graydon Leiter and Grace Arthur

Description of Test: The LEITER-R is designed as a totally nonverbal intelligence and cognitive abilities test; it does not require the child to read or write any materials or need any spoken words from the examiner or the child. It is presented in a gamelike administration by having the child match the full-color response cards with corresponding illustrations on the easel display.

Administration Time: 30 to 60 minutes

Age/Grade Levels: Ages 2 to 17

Subtest Information: The LEITER-R includes 20 subtests listed below, which are combined to create numerous composites that measure both general intelligence and discrete ability areas. The test consists of two batteries measuring a variety of skills:

1. **Visualization and Reasoning Battery**

   Reasoning skills measured in this battery include
Classification	*Repeated Patterns*
Sequential Order	*Design Analogies*

Visualization skills measured in this battery include

Matching	*Picture Context*
Figure–Ground	*Paper Folding*
Form Completion	*Figure Rotation*

2. Attention and Memory Battery

Memory skills measured in this battery include

Memory Span (Forward)	*Associative Memory*
Memory Span (Reversed)	*Associative Delayed Memory*
Spatial Memory	*Immediate Recognition*
Visual Coding	*Delayed Recognition*

Attention skills measured in this battery include

Attention Sustained	*Attention Divided*

Rhode Island Test of Language Structure (RITLS)

Authors: Elizabeth Engen and Trygg Engen

Description of Test: The *Rhode Island Test of Language Structure* (RITLS) provides a measure of English language development and assessment data. It is designed primarily for use with children who are hearing impaired but also is useful in other areas where language development is of concern, including mental retardation, learning disability, and bilingual programs. The RITLS focuses on syntax, unlike other tests that test morphology.

Administration Time: 25 to 35 minutes

Age/Grade Levels: Hearing-impaired children ages 3 to 20, hearing children ages 3 to 6

Subtest Information: This test measures syntax-response errors for 20 sentence types, both simple and complex. The sentence elements tests are

- *Relative and Adverbial Clauses*
- *Subject and Other Complements*
- *Reversible and Nonreversible Passives*
- *Datives*
- *Deletions*
- *Negations*
- *Conjunctives*
- *Embedded Imperatives*

Test of Early Reading Ability–2nd Edition: Deaf or Hard of Hearing (TERAD/HH-2)

Authors: D. Kim Reid, Wayne P. Jiresko, Donald D. Hammill, and Susan Wiltshire

Description of Test: The TERAD/HH-2 is designed to measure how well children with moderate to profound hearing loss attribute meaning to printed symbols, their knowledge of the alphabet and its functions, and their knowledge of the conventions of print. It isolates key components of early print experiences and assesses children's relative competence in deriving meaning from these print symbols. The test includes a sheet that allows the examiner to picture the student's "instructional target zone." By examining the student's item performance in the three components of early reading, the examiner can identify the types of concepts that might be profitably taught.

Administration Time: 15 to 30 minutes

Age/Grade Levels: Ages 8 and younger

Subtest Information: Three aspects of early reading behavior are specifically addressed:

- *Constructing meaning from print*—The construction of meaning encompasses a child's ability to read frequently encountered signs, logos, and words; relate words to one another; and understand the contextual nature of written discourse.
- *Knowledge of the alphabet*—Letter and word decoding (either orally or through sign).
- *Understanding print conventions*—Evaluation of the child's awareness of text orientation and organization (e.g., book handling, the spatial orientation of print on a page, and ability to uncover textual or print errors).

PHYSICAL AND OCCUPATIONAL THERAPY ASSESSMENT

Physical and occupational therapies are important components of the special education process. Many school districts now have physical and occupational therapists as part of their staff. These therapists may help students individually, in small groups, or as consultants. These two services are related therapies but specific in their function.

Physical therapy concentrates on lower-body and gross motor difficulties. **Occupational therapy** focuses mainly on fine motor and upper-body functions. The services are provided for students with disabilities who exhibit a range of difficulties such as learning disabilities (e.g., fine and gross motor problems, perceptual problems), developmental delays (e.g., mental retardation, vision or hearing impairment), respiratory problems (e.g., cystic fibrosis, asthma), neuromuscular problems (e.g., muscular dystrophy, cerebral palsy), muscle skeletal problems (e.g., arthritis, orthopedic problems, postural deviations), or traumatic accidents (e.g., amputations, brain injuries, burns). In addition to providing therapy for such students, physical and occupational therapists provide many other services including evaluations, screenings, consultations, education, and training.

Evaluations

Physical and occupational therapy evaluations may be referred to the multidisciplinary team (MDT) or eligibility committee by any number of school or medical professionals. Parents may also ask for a referral for physical and occupational therapy services for their child. In any case, written parental consent is required for an evaluation.

As with other evaluations, those of physical and occupational therapists need to be individualized, well-documented, and specific. Physical and occupational therapists play a significant role in regard to the service provided the student; the more thorough their documentation, the more appropriate the services will be. The evaluation will serve as a blueprint for the development of an IEP, should one be necessary, and will identify the child's current level of performance and his or her deficient areas of development in the physical realm. It will also suggest what he or she needs in order to achieve the next higher level of function. Parents need to be aware that the evaluation process is subjective and varies from district to district. In some districts, if a child can walk into a classroom, he or she would not be provided with physical therapy. In some districts, if a child can hold a pencil, he or she would not be provided with occupational therapy, whereas in other districts services are provided for problems others might consider marginal.

Assessment Areas

In general, both physical therapy and occupational therapy assess the following:

- Range of motion
- Sensory integration
- Activities for daily living
- Physical and mental development
- Muscular control
- Need for and uses of adaptive equipment

Certain assessments are unique to physical therapy:

- Posture
- Gait
- Endurance
- Personal independence
- Joint abnormalities
- Wheelchair management
- Transportation needs
- Architectural barriers
- Prosthetic and orthotic equipment checks

Other assessments are unique to occupational therapy:

- Neuromuscular functioning
- Sensory processing
- Manual dexterity
- Leisure time abilities
- Prevocational skills
- Oral motor and feeding problems

The Therapist's Many Roles

Occupational and physical therapists should meet with all of the professionals involved with a particular child as well as with the child's parents to fully explain the nature of the disability, to train them to work with the child in the areas of dysfunction, and to provide assistive devices or environmental aids that will help the child function in the least restrictive environment. The therapists should also model remedial techniques that can be duplicated by the parents and by other teaching professionals. Parents should be reminded that many of the school activities suggested by occupational and physical therapists can be duplicated in the home. Many of the exercises are really activities for daily living such as hopping, jumping, buttoning, and the like.

Occupational and physical therapists serve important roles as consultants. Some examples of their services are:

- Referring families to appropriate sources for assistance
- Helping families order adaptive or prosthetic equipment
- Coordinating with physical education programs

- Instructing families regarding methods used in physical therapy
- Formulating long-range developmental plans for children's education
- Training school professionals with special equipment
- Helping families and children learn how to deal with architectural barriers

Occupational and physical therapists should act as liaisons among the eligibility committee, the teaching staff, medical professionals, outside agencies, and parents. Many pupils in need of occupational and physical therapy have severe medical conditions. These conditions often require supervision of a family doctor. The therapist should help with the coordination between the school physician and the family doctor. The therapists play an important role in severe cases.

The following is a list of problems requiring occupational therapy:

- Perceptual problems (eye–hand coordination)
- Sensory problems (sensitive to sound, sensitive to visual changes, sensitive to odors, overly sensitive to touch)
- Gross motor difficulties (trouble with balance, coordination, moving)
- Fine motor problems (difficulty with coordination, handwriting, using scissors)
- Hardship with daily living activities (cannot dress, feed, or care for self)
- Organizational problems (difficulties with memory, time, spatial concepts)
- Attention span difficulties (difficulties focusing on task, short attention span)
- Interpersonal problems (difficulty with environmental and school-related social situations)

The following is a list of the kinds of evaluations an occupational therapist can conduct:

- Vision
- Abnormal movement patterns
- Range of motion
- Skeletal and joint conditions
- Behavior
- Skin and soft tissue
- Fine motor
- Perceptual
- Gross motor
- Balance and equilibrium
- Activities for daily living
- Equipment analysis

There are many different assessment measures used by occupational and physical therapists. Listed below are some of the most frequently used tests by these professionals.

First Step: Screening Test for Evaluating Preschoolers (FIRSTep)

Author: Lucy Jane Miller

Description of Test: FIRSTep is designed to identify children who exhibit moderate preacademic problems. It is a short but comprehensive preschool assessment instrument that evaluates children for mild to moderate developmental delays. The test includes an examiner's manual, item score sheets, and all materials needed for administration.

Administration Time: 15 minutes

Age/Grade Levels: Ages 2-9 to 6-2

Subtest Information: The test consists of five performance areas:

- *Foundations Index*—Assesses abilities involving basic motor tasks and the awareness of sensations, both of which are fundamental for the development of complex skills.
- *Coordination Index*—Assesses complex gross, fine, and oral motor abilities.
- *Verbal Index*—Assesses memory, sequencing, comprehension, association, and expression in a verbal context.
- *Nonverbal Index*—Assesses memory, sequencing, visualization, and the performance of mental manipulations not requiring spoken language.
- *Complex Tasks Index*—Measures sensory motor abilities in conjunction with cognitive abilities.

Quick Neurological Screening Test–II (QNST-II)

Authors: Margaret Motti, Harold M. Steling, Norma V. Spalding, and C. Slade Crawfold

Description of Test: The QNST-II is designed to assess neurological integration as it relates to learning. It is used for the early screening of learning disabilities. The QNST-II is a screening test that assesses 15 areas of neurological integration. It requires the examinee to perform a series of motor tasks adapted from neurological pediatric examinations and from neuropsychological and developmental scales. Each of the 15 areas tested involves a motor task similar to those observed in neurological pediatric examinations. The test includes recording forms, examiner's manual, reproduction sheets, remedial guidelines, and an administration and scoring flip card.

Administration Time: Untimed—takes approximately 20 minutes

Age/Grade Levels: Ages 5 to 18

- **Subtest Information:** The areas of neurological integration measured by the QNST-II include
- Motor development
- Fine/gross motor control
- Motor planning and sequencing and rhythm
- Visual/spatial perception
- Spatial organization
- Balance/vestibular function
- Attentional disorders

Sensory Integration and Praxis Tests (SIPT)

Author: Jean Ayres

Description of Test: The test is designed to measure the sensory integration processes that underlie learning and behavior. By showing how children organize and respond to sensory input, the SIPT helps pinpoint specific organic problems associated with learning disabilities, emotional disorders, and minimal brain dysfunction. The test measures visual, tactile, and kinesthetic perception as well as motor performance.

Administration Time: The entire battery can be administered in 2 hours. Any of the individual tests can be administered separately in about 10 minutes.

Age/Grade Levels: Ages 4 to 9

Subtest Information: The SIPT measures visual, tactile, and kinesthetic perception as well as motor performance. It is composed of 17 brief tests:

Bilateral Motor Coordination	*Motor Accuracy*
Constructional Praxis	*Oral Praxis*
Design Copying	*Postrotary Nystagmus*
Figure-Ground Perception	*Postural Praxis*
Finger Identification	*Praxis on Verbal Command*
Graphesthesia	*Sequencing Praxis*
Kinesthesia	*Space Visualization*
Localization of Tactile Stimuli	*Standing and Walking Balance*
Manual Form Perception	

MULTICULTURAL ASSESSMENT

It is a well-known fact that the demographics of American schools are changing. Many students come from ethnic, racial, or linguistic backgrounds that are different from the dominant culture, and this number is steadily increasing (National Center for Education Statistics, 2007). Much concern has been expressed in recent years about the overrepresentation of minority students in special education programs, particularly in programs for students with mild disabilities, and a great deal of research has been conducted to identify the reasons why. Many factors appear to contribute, including considerable bias against children from different cultural and linguistic backgrounds, particularly those who are poor (Sattler, 2001; Harry, 1992). The style and emphasis of the school may also be very different from those found in the cultures of students who are racially or linguistically diverse. Because culture and language affect learning and behavior (Sattler, 2001; Franklin, 1992), the school system may misinterpret what students know, how they behave, or how they learn. Students may appear less competent than they are, leading educators to refer them for assessment inappropriately. Once referred, inappropriate methods may then be used to assess the students, leading to inappropriate conclusions and placement into special education.

There is also a great deal of research and numerous court decisions (see Chapter 1, for example, *Larry P. v. Riles,* 1979; *Guadalupe Organization Inc. v. Tempe Elementary School District,* 1972) to support the fact that standardized tests (particularly intelligence and achievement tests) are often culturally and linguistically biased against students from backgrounds different from the majority culture. On many tests, being able to answer questions correctly too often depends on having specific culturally based information or knowledge. If students have not been exposed to that information through their cultures, or have not had the experiences that lead to gaining specific knowledge, then they will not be able to answer certain questions at all or will answer them in ways that are considered "incorrect" within the majority culture. This can lead to inappropriate conclusions about students' abilities to function within the school setting.

Under IDEA 2004, all children have the right to tests that are free of cultural bias. Furthermore, all tests must be conducted in the child's native language, and reports must be written in the parents' language. Given these mandates under federal law, it is evident that educators must be very aware of a child's native language. Consequently, it is critical that assessments done on children who are bilingual be done in a manner that is in compliance with all federal laws. Educators need to be aware of variables associated with the assessment of bilingual children, because the number of bilingual children with suspected disabilities is increasing.

The majority of tests used for assessment in special education are based on standards of the English-speaking culture. Given this fact, the use of these instruments on students who are bilingual may not be appropriate under federal law. Special educators must devise a way to assess children whose primary language may not be English. This is commonly referred to as *dynamic assessment* (see Chapter 02), which according to ASHA (2011), is a method of conducting a language assessment which seeks to identify the skills that an individual child possesses as well as their learning potential. The dynamic assessment procedure emphasizes the learning process and accounts for the amount and nature of examiner investment. It is highly interactive and process-oriented. Schools are moving toward requiring a prereferral process before any individualized evaluation is done (Chapter 07). The purpose of the prereferral process is "The purpose of the pre-referral process is to ensure your child tries reasonable accommodations and modifications before he/she's referred for special education assessment." (Stump, 2011). This allows the school to adjust instruction or make other classroom modifications to see if these changes address the problem being noted.

It is also important to interview people who are familiar with the student; these individuals can provide a wealth of information about the child's interests, adaptive behavior, how he or she processes information and approaches learning, language ability, and (in the case of students who are not native speakers of English) language dominance. Interviewers should be aware, however, that the differing culture or language of those being interviewed can seriously affect the nature and interpretation of information gathered. Some understanding of how individuals within that culture view disability, the educational system, and authority figures will be helpful in designing, conducting, and interpreting a culturally sensitive interview. It may be particularly useful to gather information from the home environment that will help the assessment team develop an understanding of the student within his or her own culture. To facilitate this, parents need to communicate openly with the school and share their insight into their child's behaviors, attitudes, successes, needs, and, when appropriate, information about the minority culture. Before conducting any formal testing of a student who is a nonnative speaker of English, it is vital to determine the student's preferred language and to conduct a comprehensive language assessment in both English and the native language.

Dominant Language

Examiners need to be aware that it is highly inappropriate to evaluate students in English when that is not their **dominant language** (unless the purpose of testing is to assess the student's English-language proficiency). Translating tests from English is not an acceptable practice either. IDEA 2004 (sec. 614[b][3][ii]) states that tests and other evaluation materials must be provided and administered in the language and form most likely to yield accurate information on what the child knows and can do academically, developmentally, and functionally, unless it is not feasible to so provide or administer. If possible, the evaluator in any testing situation or interview should be familiar to the child and speak the child's language. When tests or evaluation materials are not available in the student's native language, examiners may find it necessary to use English-language instruments. Because this is a practice fraught with the possibility of misinterpretation, examiners need to be cautious in how they administer the test and interpret results.

Alterations may need to be made to the standardized procedures used to administer tests for bilingual students. These can include paraphrasing instructions, providing a demonstration of how test tasks are to be performed, reading test items to the student rather than having him or her read them, allowing the student to respond verbally rather than in writing, or allowing the student to use a dictionary (Wallace et al., 1992). However, if any such alterations are made, it is important to recognize that standardization has been broken, limiting the usefulness and applicability of test norms. Results should be cautiously interpreted, and all alterations made to the testing procedures should be fully detailed in the report describing the student's test performance. As mentioned earlier, it is also essential that other assessment approaches be an integral part of collecting information about the student.

Ascher (1990) addresses options commonly used in testing limited-English speakers: nonverbal tests, translated tests, interpreters, and tests that are norm-referenced in the primary language. The following is a brief description of each of these options:

- Nonverbal tests are the most common procedure used with bilingual students. Unfortunately, nonverbal measures of intelligence predict less reliably than verbal measures and, despite appearances, may even be hypersensitive to language background.
- Translated tests are always different tests, unknown and unfair. Although it is not difficult to translate a test, it is extremely difficult, if not impossible, to translate psychometric properties from one language to another. A word in English is simply not the same word in terms of difficulty in Spanish, Hmong, Russian, or Chinese.
- Both trained and untrained interpreters are widely used in assessment. However, this practice remains risky. The research on interpreters is negligible. Although a number of commercial models exist for training and using interpreters, there is no empirical validation of their suggested procedures.
- Many testing specialists have become sensitive to the problems of testing bilingual individuals. However, because standardized tests in any language remain biased in favor of persons for whom that language is native, low test scores received by bilingual students often are interpreted as evidence of deficits or even disorders. This creates difficulties with every kind of assessment, from tests for English-language proficiency—used most often to place students in bilingual classes—to intelligence tests, the prime source of information for special education placement.

Multicultural Assessment

The materials and procedures required for a referral of culturally and linguistically diverse children to the eligibility committee (Chapter 18) may involve more than the normal packet of materials.

According to the North Carolina School Psychology Association (2004), as with any student experiencing learning difficulties, the intervention team is an appropriate vehicle for the teacher to get assistance in dealing with the difficulties. It is at this time that the committee members collect and analyze information in order to assist in determining whether an LEP student's problems are primarily related to his/her limited proficiency in English or whether a disability might be contributing to the student's school difficulties. It is particularly important to gather data about the student's background (including parental level of proficiency in L1 and L2), language acculturation level, sociolinguistic development, and response to the school and classroom environment. This should include information regarding the number of schools attended, interruptions in schooling, number of years in the U.S., language(s) used in former schools, school curricula, and methods of instruction in the regular classroom. The school psychologist should play an important role in completing this process due to the knowledge he/she has regarding data collection, data interpretation, and differences due to socioeconomic, cultural, and ethnic background. He/she should assist the teacher and/or team in employing a variety of intervention techniques within the general education classroom to accommodate the student's language and cultural background and to help resolve his/her learning and behavior problems. Suggestions include:

Observational data should be collected in a variety of settings, reflecting interactions with peers and adults. If possible, these observations should include comparisons with same-age culturally/linguistically similar and culturally/linguistically different peers.

Meetings should be held with parents, using a qualified interpreter when necessary, to determine their perceptions of the problem, to discuss suggestions for helping the student, and to obtain information regarding background. Parents sometimes may feel too intimidated to attend a conference at the school. Home visits may therefore be necessary.

Standardized screening instruments are generally not\ appropriate methods of obtaining academic functioning levels for LEP students due to the heavy reliance on language. Work samples and curriculum-based assessment are often more helpful in screening achievement levels and patterns.

A language proficiency assessment should be administered if it has not been given within the past six months. LEP students have usually had proficiency testing through the school district's LEP program. Consider the types of language skills being assessed, however, when interpreting those results. Oftentimes the assessment may only be assessing basic interpersonal communication skills.

Given the language difficulties, an LEP student generally is not referred to the special education referral committee unless he/she has been in an English speaking school for 2 years. This timeframe, of course, does not apply to those students who are exhibiting global developmental delays. This practice, however, should not be construed as a policy prohibiting the referral of an LEP student for a specific period of time as such a policy would be discriminatory.

Further, the evaluation team and hopefully the child study team prior to the referral for a comprehensive assessment may also have to look at the following:

- Identifying the reason for the referral and include any test results in both languages as appropriate.
- Including any records or reports on which the referral is based.
- Attaching a home language survey indicating the home language(s).
- Specifying the level of language proficiency.
- Describing the extent to which the LEP (limited English proficiency) student has received native language instruction and/or ESL (English as a second language) services prior to the referral.
- Describing experiential and/or enrichment services for students from diverse cultural and experiential backgrounds.
- Describing the school's efforts to involve parents prior to referral.
- Describing the amount of time and extent of services in an academic program for students who have had little or no formal schooling.
- Identifying length of residency of the referred student in the United States and prior school experience in the native country and in an English-language school system.
- Describing all attempts to remediate the pupil's performance prior to referral, including any supplemental aids or support services provided for this purpose.
- Holding parent interviews to elicit evidence of behaviors in the home and community settings.
- Measuring academic skills not dependent on English language (e.g., mathematics calculations, problem solving using visual-spatial reasoning).
- Using nonverbal cognitive screening tests.

- Testing nonverbal intelligence.
- Using curriculum-based assessment (if used with accommodations for heritage language).
- Student interviews.
- Reviewing prior school records and performance including scores on tests in heritage language.
- Gathering work samples in heritage language and English.
- Observing the student by school personnel, especially those who are proficient in the student's heritage language.
- Interviewing with teachers with special consideration of ESOL teachers, bilingual para-professionals, and other personnel who work with the student.
- Interviewing with other appropriate people with knowledge of the student/family (clergy, former teachers, pediatrician, etc.).
- Use of a test-educate-test paradigm to assess the modifiability of the student's cognitive processes.

CONCLUSION

In conclusion, it is necessary for those entering into or currently involved in the field of special education to be aware of the growing number of students designated as limited English proficient. Federal law mandates that minority students have rights for protection when being assessed. Consequently, knowledge of various tests, their limitations, and controversies surrounding the biases of **bilingual assessment** is imperative.

Vocabulary

Audiometric evaluation measures: Assessment measures used by qualified audiologists who measure the level of hearing loss through the use of several techniques.

Behavioral play audiometry: Placing the child in a series of activities that reward him or her for responding appropriately to tone or speech.

Bilingual assessment: An assessment whereby testing may be done in two or more languages based on the child's dominant language.

Central auditory disorders: Despite no measurable peripheral hearing loss, children with these disorders have trouble learning and are often considered learning disabled.

Conductive hearing loss: Problems with the structures in the outer or middle ear, generally attributed to a blockage in the mechanical conduction of sound.

Deafness: According to IDEA, "a hearing impairment that is so severe that the child is impaired

in processing linguistic information through hearing, with or without amplification, that adversely affects a child's educational performance."

Dominant language: The primary language spoken by an individual.

Evoked response audiometry: Using an electroencephalograph, a computer measures changes in brain wave activity to a variety of sound levels. This measure can be used with infants who are suspected of being deaf.

Functional hearing loss: Hearing loss from problems that are not organic in origin.

Hearing impairment: According to IDEA, "an impairment in hearing, whether permanent or fluctuating, that adversely affects a child's educational performance but which is not included under the definition of deafness in this section."

Impedance audiometry: There are two major impedance audiometry tests: Tympanometry measures the functioning level of the eardrum, and stapedial reflex testing measures the reflex response of the stapedial muscle to pure tone signals. Because these tests do not require a response on the part of the child, they can be used with very young children.

Mixed hearing loss: A hearing loss caused by both sensorineural and conductive problems.

Occupational therapy and physical therapy: Occupational therapy focuses mainly on fine motor and upper-body functions, whereas physical therapy concentrates on lower-body and gross motor difficulties. The services are provided for students with disabilities who exhibit a range of difficulties such as learning disabilities (e.g., fine and gross motor problems, perceptual problems), developmental delays (e.g., mental retardation, vision or hearing impairment), respiratory problems (e.g., cystic fibrosis, asthma), neuromuscular problems (e.g., muscular dystrophy, cerebral palsy), muscle skeletal problems (e.g., arthritis, orthopedic problems, postural deviations), or traumatic accidents (e.g., amputations, brain injuries, burns). In addition to providing therapy for such students, physical and occupational therapists provide many other services including evaluations, screenings, consultations, education, and training.

Otosclerosis: Formation of a spongy-bony growth around the stapes, which impedes its movement.

Pure tone audiometric screening: Pure tone screening is often referred to as sweep testing and is usually the child's first encounter with hearing testing. This type of testing, which is common in schools, presents the child with pure tones over a variety of frequency ranges. The child is then asked to respond if he or she hears a tone, usually by some gesture. If a child is unable to hear sounds at two or more frequencies, the child is usually referred for further evaluation.

Pure tone threshold audiometry: In this procedure, the child is asked to make a gesture or push a button each time he or she hears a tone. The child is presented with a variety of frequencies through earphones. This type of air conduction test reveals the presence of hearing loss.

Sensorineural hearing loss: Results from damage to the cochlea or the auditory nerve. This damage is caused by illness and disease and is not medically or surgically treatable.

Sound field audiometry: Used with very young children who cannot respond to manual responses or are unable or unwilling to wear headphones. The child is evaluated by observing the intensity levels at which he or she responds to different levels of sounds broadcast through speakers.

Speech audiometry: Used to determine a child's present ability to hear and understand speech through the presentation of words in a variety of loudness levels.

16 | DETERMINING WHETHER A DISABILITY EXISTS

Key Terms

Emotional disturbance
Higher-prevalence disabilities

Learning disabilities
Lower-prevalence disabilities

Mental retardation
Speech and language impairments

Chapter Objectives

In this chapter you learn about diagnosing a suspected disability. After reading this chapter, you should be able to understand the following:

- Higher- and lower-prevalence disabilities
- The process involved in diagnosing a suspected disability from the assessment materials gathered
- The definitions, the prevalence, the characteristics, an example assessment battery of, and the method to diagnose a learning disability
- The definitions, the prevalence, the characteristics, an example assessment battery of, and the method to diagnose a speech and language impairment
- The definitions, the prevalence, the characteristics, an example assessment battery of, and the method to diagnose mental retardation
- The definitions, the prevalence, the characteristics, an example assessment battery of, and the method to diagnose an emotional disturbance

---

DIAGNOSING A DISABILITY

A crucial part of assessment is the ability to take all the information, test results, observations, and so forth and put them together in a practical, informative, diagnostic, and professional manner. This process can be very difficult for evaluators because it requires the integration of many variables to determine the proper diagnosis and possible classification category. In reality, certain classifications under IDEA 2004 will be diagnosed by the local school-based team, some will be diagnosed by medical professionals, and others will be diagnosed by a combination of agencies. For example, the categories most likely to appear in the public school for initial diagnosis, if not previously identified by parents and medical professionals prior to school enrollment, are referred to as **higher-prevalence disabilities** and include

- Learning disabilities (LD)
- Emotional disturbance (ED)
- Mental retardation—higher-level functioning other than Down syndrome
- Speech and language impairments
- Other health impairment—ADHD-Prediagnosis

These diagnostic categories may first show up when the child enters formal schooling and is presented with educational and social demands that may prove to be too difficult. In these cases, the child study team (CST) will be directly involved in the identification, evaluation, diagnosis, and recommendation of classification, program, and services. It is not likely, in most of these cases, that outside agencies or medical personnel would need to be involved in this process unless the team needed further substantiation of the diagnosis (e.g., an audiology exam to rule out hearing impairment in the case of a child with a suspected language disorder).

The classification categories most likely diagnosed by medical professionals or early medical screening prior to formal schooling are referred to as **lower-prevalence disabilities** and include

- Autism
- Orthopedic impairments
- Visual impairments
- Hearing impairments
- Other health impairments
- Traumatic brain injury
- Deaf-blindness

These categories would most likely be diagnosed by doctors, early screening programs, or outside agencies involved in the early education (birth to age 5) of the child. The child with any of these conditions would most likely come to the school at age 5 with a classification from the district's eligibility committee on preschool special education. These conditions, if present prior to formal schooling, would not require diagnosis by the CST. However, occasionally some of these conditions might occur after entrance into school at age 5, such as, for example, traumatic brain injury, deafness, and the like. These would all be diagnosed by medical professionals, not the CST. However, the role of school professionals involves following the child's progress, determining educational levels, providing the triennial review, and so forth. (For definitions of all of the classifications under IDEA 2004, see Chapter 1).

The classification categories most likely diagnosed by a combination of professionals and agencies during school would be

- Visual impairments
- Hearing impairments
- Other health impairment—attention deficit disorder (ADD) or attention deficit/hyperactivity disorder (ADHD)

In such cases, there may be times when the school becomes the first level of awareness of a suspected medical problem. In these instances, the school would initially be involved in recommending outside evaluations for diagnosis and recommendations. To diagnose a suspected disability properly, you need to understand the necessary information gathered from the assessment process. This material will be quite comprehensive, and the key question becomes "What do I do with all this information?" In the following sections we describe examples of this process to determine a suspected learning disability, a suspected developmental disability, and a suspected emotional disturbance.

| Table 16.1 | Prevalence of Disabilities under IDEA 2004, Based on Number of Students Ages 3–21 Who Receive Special Education Services under the Federal Government's Disability Categories | |

Disability Category	Number of Children	Percentage of Total
Specific Learning Disabilities	2,573,000	39.0
Speech and Language Impairments	1,456,543	22.0
Other Health Impairments	641,000	9.7
Mental Retardation	500,000	7.6
Emotional Disturbance	442,000	6.7
Other Health Impairments	449,093	7.5
Developmental Delay	358,000	5.4
Autism	296,000	4.5
Multiple Disabilities	138,000	2.1
Hearing Impairments	79,000	1.2
Orthopedic Impairments	67,000	1.0
Visual Impairments	29,000	0.4
Traumatic Brain Injury	25,000	0.4
Deaf-Blindness	2,000	<0.1
All Disabilities	6,606,000	100.0

Source: U.S. Department of Education (2011). Digest of Education Statistics: 2009 (Table 50). Washington, DC.

LEARNING DISABILITIES

Definition under IDEA

 i. General. The term means a disorder in one or more of the basic psychological processes involved in understanding or in using language, spoken or written, that may manifest itself in an imperfect ability to listen, think, speak, read, write, spell, or to do mathematical calculations, including conditions such as perceptual disabilities, brain injury, minimal brain dysfunction, dyslexia, and developmental aphasia.

 ii. Disorders not included. The term does not include learning problems that are primarily the result of visual, hearing, or motor disabilities, of mental retardation, of emotional disturbance, or of environmental, cultural, or economic disadvantage (34 C.F.R. 300.7(c)(10)).

Important Point: The definition of "a specific learning disability" under IDEA 2004 remains unchanged from IDEA of 1997. However, under the new provisions of IDEA 2004:

a local educational agency is not required to take into consideration whether a child has a severe discrepancy between achievement and intellectual ability in oral expression, listening comprehension, written expression, basic reading skill, reading comprehension, mathematical calculation or mathematical reasoning. In determining whether a child has a specific learning disability, a local educational agency may use a process that determines if a child responds to scientific, research-based intervention as a part of the evaluation procedures (U.S.C. sec. 614(b)(2)(3)).

Overview

In general, **learning disabilities** refer to neurobiological disorders related to differences in how one's brain works and is structured. Further, *learning disability* is a general term that describes specific kinds of learning problems. A learning disability can cause a person to have trouble learning and using certain skills (Lerner, 2005). The skills most often affected are reading, writing, listening, speaking, reasoning, and doing math (Pierangelo and Giuliani, 2009; Heward, 2009; National Dissemination Center for Children with Disabilities, 2004).

The National Joint Committee on Learning Disabilities (NJCLD, 2005) discusses five constructs underlying the definition of learning disabilities.

1. Learning disabilities are heterogeneous, both within and across individuals. Intraindividual differences involve varied profiles of learning strength and need and/or shifts across the life span within individuals. Interindividual differences involve different manifestations of learning disabilities for different individuals.

2. Learning disabilities result in significant difficulties in the acquisition and use of listening, speaking, reading, writing, reasoning, and/or mathematical skills. Such difficulties are evident when an individual's appropriate levels of effort do not result in reasonable progress given the opportunity for effective educational instruction and with the recognition that all individuals learn at a different pace and with differing effort. Significant difficulty cannot be determined solely by a quantitative test score.

3. Learning disabilities are intrinsic to the individual. They are presumed to be related to differences in central nervous system development. They do not disappear over time, but may range in expression and severity at different life stages.

4. Learning disabilities may occur concomitantly with other disabilities that do not, by themselves, constitute a learning disability. For example, difficulty with self-regulatory behaviors, social perception, and social interactions may occur for many reasons. Some social interaction problems result from learning disabilities; others do not. Individuals with other disabilities, such as sensory impairments, attention deficit/hyperactivity disorders, mental retardation, and serious emotional disturbance, may also have learning disabilities, but such conditions do not cause or constitute learning disabilities.

5. Learning disabilities are not caused by extrinsic influences. Inconsistent or insufficient instruction or a lack of instructional experience cause learning difficulties but not learning disabilities. However, individuals who have had inconsistent or insufficient instruction may also have learning disabilities. The challenge is to document that inadequate or insufficient instruction is not the primary cause of a learning disability. Individuals from all cultural and linguistic backgrounds may also have learning disabilities; therefore, assessments must be designed acknowledging this diversity in culture and language, and examiners who test children from each background must be sensitive to such factors and use practices that are individualized and appropriate for each child.

Prevalence

According to the U.S. Department of Education (2011) *Digest of Education Statistics: 2009,* 2,573,000 students between the ages of 3 to 21 were identified as having specific learning disabilities. This represents approximately 39 percent of all students having a classification in special education.

DETERMINING THE PRESENCE OF A LEARNING DISABILITY STEP BY STEP

Step I. **Become Familiar with the Characteristics of Children with Specific Learning Disabilities**

There is no one sign that shows a person has a learning disability. Experts look for a noticeable difference between how well a child does in school and how well he or she *could* do, given his or her intelligence or ability. There are also certain clues that may mean a child has a learning disability. Most relate to elementary school tasks, because learning disabilities tend to be identified in elementary school. A child probably won't show all of these signs, or even most of them. However, if a child shows a number of these problems, then parents and the teacher should consider the possibility that the child has a learning disability.

When a child has a learning disability, he or she

- May have trouble learning the alphabet, rhyming words, or connecting letters to their sounds
- May make many mistakes when reading aloud, and repeat and pause often
- May not understand what he or she reads
- May have real trouble with spelling
- May have very messy handwriting or hold a pencil awkwardly
- May struggle to express ideas in writing
- May learn language late and have a limited vocabulary
- May have trouble remembering the sounds that letters make or hearing slight differences between words
- May have trouble understanding jokes, comic strips, and sarcasm
- May have trouble following directions
- May mispronounce words or use a wrong word that sounds similar
- May have trouble organizing what he or she wants to say or not be able to think of the word he or she needs for writing or conversation
- May not follow the social rules of conversation, such as taking turns, and may stand too close to the listener
- May confuse math symbols and misread numbers
- May not be able to retell a story in order (what happened first, second, third)
- May not know where to begin a task or how to go on from there

If a child has unexpected problems learning to read, write, listen, speak, or do math, then teachers and parents may want to investigate more. The same is true if the child is struggling to do any one of these skills. The child may need to be evaluated to see if he or she has a learning disability.

Step II. Determine the Procedures and Assessment Measures to Be Used

If a student is suspected of having a specific learning disability (SLD), the following evaluation should be considered:

A. An observation by a team member, other than the student's regular teacher, of the student's academic performance in a regular classroom setting; or in the case of a child less than school age or out of school, an observation by a team member conducted in an age-appropriate environment

B. A developmental history, if needed

C. An assessment of intellectual ability

D. Other assessments of the characteristics of learning disabilities if the student exhibits impairments in any one or more of the following areas: cognition, fine motor, perceptual motor, communication, social or emotional, and perception or memory; these assessments shall be completed by specialists knowledgeable in the specific characteristics being assessed

E. A review of cumulative records, previous individualized education programs, or individualized family service plans and teacher-collected work samples

F. If deemed necessary, a medical statement or health assessment statement indicating whether there are any physical factors that may be affecting the student's educational performance

G. Assessments to determine the impact of the suspected disability:
- On the student's educational performance when the student is at the age of eligibility for kindergarten through age 21
- On the child's developmental progress when the child is age 3 through the age of eligibility for kindergarten

H. Additional evaluations or assessments that are necessary to identify the student's educational needs; at least one observation is required as part of the evaluation for determining a specific learning disability, with minimal observation requirements as follows:
- At least one team member other than the student's regular teacher shall observe the student's academic performance in the regular classroom setting, and in the case of a child less than school age or out of school, a team member shall observe the child in an environment appropriate for a child of that age
- The relevant behavior noted during the observation of the child and the relationship of that behavior to the child's academic functioning

I. Documentation that the child's learning problems are not primarily due to
- Lack of appropriate instruction in reading and math
- Limited English proficiency
- Visual, hearing, or motor impairment
- Mental retardation
- Emotional disturbance
- Environmental, cultural, or economic disadvantage
- Motivational factors
- Situational traumas

Step III. Determination of Eligibility for a Diagnosis of a Specific Learning Disability

In general, states use three different methods to determine whether a child meets the eligibility criteria as a child with a specific learning disability under IDEA. We present a synopsis of these three options for an IEP team to consider.

Option 1. To be eligible for special education and related services as a child with a learning disability, all of the following four components must be addressed:

1. The IEP must determine that the child exhibits a disorder in one or more of the basic psychological processes involved in understanding or in using language, spoken or written, that may manifest itself in an imperfect ability to listen, think, speak, read, write, spell, or do mathematical calculations.

   The term *specific learning disability*

   • Includes such conditions as perceptual disabilities, brain injury, minimal brain dysfunction, dyslexia, and developmental aphasia.
   • Does not include learning problems that are primarily the result of a visual disability, motor disability, hearing disability, mental retardation, emotional disturbance, or environmental, cultural, or economic disadvantage.

2. The IEP team must show that
   • The child demonstrates limited academic achievement for his or her age and ability levels in one or more of the following areas when provided with learning experiences appropriate for the child's age and ability levels: oral expression, listening comprehension, written expression, basic reading skills, reading comprehension, mathematics calculation, or mathematical reasoning.
   • The child demonstrates a severe discrepancy between intellectual ability and academic achievement in one or more of the above-mentioned areas.

3. The team must also ensure the following:
   • At least one team member, other than the child's regular teacher, must observe the child's academic performance in the regular classroom setting
   • In the case of a child who is of less than school age or is out of school, a team member must observe the student in an environment appropriate for a child that age
   • The observation report must document the name and title of the observer, as well as the date and place of the observation

4. The group of qualified professionals and a parent of the child must prepare a written report of the evaluation results that includes statements of
   • Whether the child has a specific learning disability
   • The basis for making the determination
   • The relevant behavior(s) noted during the observation of the child
   • The relationship of the behavior(s) to the child's academic functioning
   • Medical information, if any, related to the child's educational functioning
   • The nature of the severe discrepancy between intellectual ability and academic achievement which is not correctable without special education and related services
   • The determination of the team regarding the effects of environmental, cultural, or economic factors on the child's academic performance

Option 2.   To identify and be determined as eligible for special education services as a child with a specific learning disability, the IEP team shall document that the following standards have been met. Based on the results of the assessment:

1. The child demonstrates a continued lack of progress when provided with appropriate instruction in the suspected area of disability.
2. Documented evidence exists which indicates that effective general education interventions and strategies have been attempted over a reasonable period of time.
3. The determining factor for identification of a learning disability is not due to a lack of appropriate instruction in reading and math.
4. Evidence exists that the child does not achieve commensurate with his or her age and ability in one or more of the following areas: listening comprehension, oral expression, basic reading skills, reading comprehension, written expression, mathematics calculation, and/or mathematics reasoning.
5. There is a severe discrepancy between educational performance and predicted achievement that is based on the best measure of cognitive ability. (This is an *optional consideration* under IDEA 2004.) Cognitive ability/achievement discrepancies should be used cautiously because a learning disability can exist when a numerical discrepancy does not. Such comparisons may assist in the diagnostic process. Careful diagnosticians examine all information and recognize developmental factors, including age and academic experience, in making a determination as to the value of such discrepancies.
6. There is evidence of a cognitive processing disorder that adversely affects the child's academic achievement. A cognitive processing disorder is defined as a deficit in the manner in which a child receives, stores, transforms, retrieves, and expresses information. Documented evidence exists that demonstrates or expresses the manifestation of the processing disorder in the identified achievement deficit.
7. Evidence exists that the child's learning problems are not due primarily to visual, hearing, or motor impairments; mental retardation; emotional disturbance; environmental, cultural, or economic disadvantage; limited English proficiency; motivational factors; or situational traumas.
8. There is evidence that characteristics as defined above are present and that the severity of the child's specific learning disability adversely affects his or her progress in the general education curriculum, demonstrating the need for special education and related services, and that children who perform in classroom academics in a manner commensurate with expected academic standards at the child's grade level cannot be considered as having a specific learning disability, even though they may show deficits on achievement tests in one or more of the seven academic areas.

Option 3.   The team shall determine that a pupil has a specific learning disability and is in need of special education and related services when the pupil meets the criteria described in Items A through C. Information about each item must be sought from the parent and included as part of the assessment data. The assessment data must confirm that the disabling effects of the pupil's disability occur in a variety of settings.

A. The pupil must demonstrate severe underachievement in response to usual classroom instruction. The performance measures used to verify this finding must be both representative of the pupil's curriculum and useful for developing instructional goals and objectives. The following assessment procedures are required at a minimum to verify this finding:

1. Evidence of low achievement from sources such as cumulative record reviews, classwork samples, anecdotal teacher records, formal and informal tests, curriculum-based assessment results.
2. At least one team member other than the pupil's regular teacher shall observe the pupil's academic performance in the regular classroom setting. In the case of a child served through an Early Childhood Special Education program or who is out of school, a team member shall observe the child in an environment appropriate for a child of that age.

B. The pupil must demonstrate a severe discrepancy between general intellectual ability and achievement in one or more of the following areas: oral expression, listening comprehension, written expression, basic reading skills, reading comprehension, mathematical calculation, or mathematical reasoning. The demonstration of a severe discrepancy shall not be based solely on the use of standardized tests. The team shall consider these standardized test results as only one component of the eligibility criteria.

1. The instruments used to assess the pupil's general intellectual ability and achievement must be individually administered and interpreted by an appropriately licensed person using standardized procedures.
2. For initial placement, the severe discrepancy must be equal to or greater than 1.75 standard deviations below the mean of the distribution of difference scores for the general population of individuals at the pupil's chronological age level.

C. The team must agree that it has sufficient assessment data that verify the following conclusions:

1. The pupil has an information processing condition that is manifested by such behaviors as inadequate or lack of organizational skills (such as in following written and oral directions, spatial arrangements, correct use of developmental order in relating events, transfer of information onto paper), memory (visual and auditory), expression (verbal and nonverbal), and motor control for written tasks such as pencil and paper assignments, drawing, and copying.
2. The disabling effects of the pupil's information processing condition occur in a variety of settings.
3. The pupil's underachievement is not primarily the result of vision, hearing, or motor impairment; mental impairment; emotional or behavioral disorders; environmental, cultural, economic influences; or a history of an inconsistent education program.

Final Thoughts

Ongoing assessment throughout the school years is critical to develop the educational potential of all children, especially those with learning disabilities. School personnel, parents, and students should proceed with as much information as possible, giving consideration to individual skills and academic needs.

The recent explosion in brain research is beginning to impact teaching practice and address the differences in brain anatomy and chemistry in students with SLD. Some current findings include insights on causation, hemispheric functioning, writing dysfunctions, dyslexia, and laterality. Overall, there is now scientific support for some LD characteristics that were previously identified mainly through observation and testing. Other information found in these studies suggests that LD teachers need to change some teaching practices based on brain research. As time goes on, there will be advances in identifying even more patterns of thinking in students with LD.

Given the enormous variability in the population of students with learning disabilities, the proliferation of tests on the market, and the problems cited above that are inherent in applying the definition, it has been extremely difficult to identify specific assessment instruments that consistently and appropriately identify these students. The problem of distinguishing students with LD from students without LD has become even more complicated by recent research suggesting that poor readers without disabilities and students who have been identified with mild learning disabilities may not differ significantly in the areas of information processing, genetic, or neurophysiological characteristics.

SPEECH AND LANGUAGE IMPAIRMENTS

Definition under IDEA

Under IDEA 2004, a speech or language impairment is defined as:

> a communication disorder, such as stuttering, impaired articulation, language impairment, or a voice impairment that adversely affects a child's educational performance.

Overview

Children with **speech and language impairments** have deficits in their ability to exchange information with others. A communication disorder may occur in the realm of language, speech, and/or hearing. Language difficulties include spoken language, reading, and/or writing difficulties. Speech encompasses such areas as articulation and phonology (the ability to speak clearly and be intelligible), fluency (stuttering), and voice. Hearing difficulties may also encompass speech problems (e.g., articulation or voice) and/or language problems. Hearing impairments include deafness and hearing loss, which can result from a conductive loss, a sensorineural loss, a mixed loss, or a central hearing loss.

Communication disorders may result from many different conditions. For example, language-based learning disabilities are the result of a difference in brain structure present at birth and may be genetically based. Other communication disorders stem from oral–motor difficulties (e.g., an apraxia or dysarthria of speech), aphasias (difficulties resulting from a stroke which may involve motor, speech, and/or language problems), traumatic brain injuries, and stuttering, which is now believed to be a neurological deficit. The most common conditions that affect children's communication include language-based learning disabilities, attention deficit disorder, attention deficit/hyperactivity disorder, cerebral palsy, mental disabilities, cleft lip or palate, and autism spectrum disorders.

The functions, skills, and abilities of voice, speech, and language are related. Some dictionaries and textbooks use the terms almost interchangeably. But for scientists and medical professionals, it is important to distinguish among them.

Prevalence

According to the U.S. Department of Education (2011) *Digest of Education Statistics: 2009,* there were 1,456,000 students between the ages of 3 to 21 were identified as having speech and language impairments. This represents approximately 22 percent of all students having a classification in special education.

This estimate does not include children who have speech/language problems secondary to other conditions such as mental retardation, traumatic brain injury, autism, cerebral palsy, and deafness (Friend, 2005).

DETERMINING THE PRESENCE OF A SPEECH AND LANGUAGE IMPAIRMENT STEP BY STEP

Step I. Become Familiar with the Characteristics of Children with Speech and Language Impairments

A child with a communication problem may present many different symptoms. These may include difficulty following directions, attending to a conversation, pronouncing words, perceiving what was said, expressing thoughts, or being understood because of a stutter or a hoarse voice. A child's communication is considered delayed when the child is noticeably behind his or her peers in the acquisition of speech and/ or language skills. Sometimes a child will have greater receptive (understanding) than expressive (speaking) language skills, but this is not always the case.

Speech disorders refer to difficulties producing speech sounds or problems with voice quality. They might be characterized by an interruption in the flow or rhythm of speech, such as stuttering, which is called dysfluency. Speech disorders may be problems with the way sounds are formed, called articulation or phonological disorders, or they may be difficulties with the pitch, volume, or quality of the voice. There may be a combination of several problems. People with speech disorders have trouble using some speech sounds, which can also be a symptom of a delay. They may say "see" when they mean "ski" or they may have trouble using other sounds like "l" or "r." Listeners may have trouble understanding what someone with a speech disorder is trying to say. People with voice disorders may have trouble with the way their voices sound.

A language disorder is an impairment in the ability to understand and/or use words in context, both verbally and nonverbally. Some characteristics of language disorders include improper use of words and their meanings, inability to express ideas, inappropriate grammatical patterns, reduced vocabulary, and inability to follow directions. One or a combination of these characteristics may occur in children who are affected by language learning disabilities or developmental language delay. Children may hear or see a word but not be able to understand its meaning. They may have trouble getting others to understand what they are trying to communicate.

Problems with language may involve difficulty expressing ideas coherently, learning new vocabulary, understanding questions, following directions, recalling information, understanding and remembering something that has just been said, reading at a satisfactory pace, comprehending spoken or read material, learning the alphabet, identifying sounds that correspond to letters, perceiving the correct order of letters in words, and possibly, spelling. Difficulties with speech may include being unintelligible due to a motor problem or due to poor learning. Sounding hoarse, breathy, or harsh may be due to a voice problem. Stuttering also affects speech intelligibility because the child's flow of speech is interrupted.

Step II. Determine the Procedures and Assessment Measures to Be Used

Speech/language impairments are determined through the demonstration of impairments in the areas of language, articulation, voice, and fluency:

Language Impairment—A significant deficiency that is not consistent with the student's chronological age in one or more of the following areas:

- A deficiency in receptive language skills to gain information
- A deficiency in expressive language skills to communicate information
- A deficiency in processing (auditory perception) skills to organize information

Articulation Impairment—A significant deficiency in ability to produce sounds in conversational speech that is not consistent with chronological age.
Voice Impairment—An excess or significant deficiency in pitch, intensity, or quality resulting from pathological conditions or inappropriate use of the vocal mechanism.
Fluency Impairment—Abnormal interruption in the flow of speech by repetitions or prolongations of a sound, syllable, or by avoidance and struggle behaviors.

If a child is suspected of having a speech and language impairment, the following procedures and assessment measures should be used.

LANGUAGE IMPAIRMENT.   A significant deficiency in language shall be determined by a minimum of two measures, including criterion and/or norm-referenced instruments, functional communication analyses, and language samples. At least one standardized comprehensive measure of language ability shall be included in the evaluation process.

Evaluation of language abilities shall include the following:

1. Hearing screening
2. Reception: vocabulary, syntax, morphology
3. Expression: mean length of utterance, syntax, semantics, pragmatics, morphology
4. Auditory perception: selective attention, discrimination, memory, sequencing, association, integration
5. Documentation and assessment of how a language impairment adversely affects educational performance in the classroom or learning environment

ARTICULATION IMPAIRMENT.   A significant deficiency in articulation shall be determined by an evaluation of articulation abilities that includes the following:

1. Appropriate formal/informal instrument(s)
2. Stimulability probes
3. Oral peripheral examination
4. Analysis of phoneme production in conversational speech
5. Documentation and assessment of how an articulation impairment adversely affects educational performance in the general education classroom or learning environment

VOICE IMPAIRMENT.   Evaluation of vocal characteristics shall include the following:

1. Hearing screening
2. Examination by an otolaryngologist
3. Oral peripheral examination
4. Documentation and assessment of how a voice impairment adversely affects educational performance in the general education classroom or learning environment

FLUENCY IMPAIRMENT. Evaluation of fluency shall include the following:

1. Hearing screening
2. Information obtained from parents, students, and teacher(s) regarding nonfluent behaviors/ attitudes across communication situations
3. Oral peripheral examination
4. Documentation and assessment of how a fluency impairment adversely affects educational performance in the general education classroom or learning environment

Other assessment measures should also be considered for a student suspected of having a speech and language impairment under the definition set forth in IDEA.

A. An observation by a team member other than the student's regular teacher of the student's academic performance in a regular classroom setting; or in the case of a child less than school age or out of school, an observation by a team member conducted in an age-appropriate environment
B. A developmental history, if needed
C. An assessment of intellectual ability
D. Other assessments of the characteristics of speech and language impairments if the student exhibits impairments in any one or more of the following areas: cognition, fine motor, perceptual motor, communication, social or emotional, and perception or memory. These assessments shall be completed by specialists knowledgeable in the specific characteristics being assessed
E. A review of cumulative records, previous individualized education programs or individualized family service plans, and teacher-collected work samples
F. If deemed necessary, a medical statement or health assessment statement indicating whether there are any physical factors that may be affecting the student's educational performance
G. Assessments to determine the impact of the suspected disability:
   • On the student's educational performance when the student is at the age of eligibility for kindergarten through age 21
   • On the child's developmental progress when the child is age 3 through the age of eligibility for kindergarten

H. Additional evaluations or assessments necessary to identify the student's educational needs.

Step III. Determination of Eligibility for a Diagnosis of Speech and Language Impairment.

Four types of speech or language impairments are generally recognized:

1. A fluency disorder is the intrusion or repetition of sounds, syllables, and words; prolongations of sounds; avoidance of words; silent blocks; or inappropriate inhalation, exhalation, or phonation patterns. These patterns may also be accompanied by facial and body movements associated with the effort to speak.
2. A voice disorder is the absence of voice or presence of abnormal quality, pitch, resonance, loudness, or duration.
3. An articulation disorder is the absence of or incorrect production of speech sounds or phonological processes that are developmentally appropriate (e.g., lisp, difficulty articulating certain sounds, such as *l* or *r*).

4. A language disorder is a breakdown in communication characterized by problems in expressing needs, ideas, or information that may be accompanied by problems in understanding.

Many states identify students with speech and language impairments using one of the following two methods.

Determination of Eligibility—Method 1

To identify and be determined as eligible for special education services as a child with a speech and language impairment, the IEP team shall document that the following standards have been met. Based on the results of the assessment:

1. **Determine that the student meets one or more of the following criteria (a–d):**

    a. For a voice impairment, determine whether
    - the student demonstrates chronic vocal characteristics that deviate in at least one of the areas of pitch, quality, intensity, or resonance; AND
    - the student's voice disorder impairs communication or intelligibility; AND
    - the student's voice disorder is rated as moderate to severe on a voice assessment scale.

    b. For a fluency impairment, determine whether
    - the student demonstrates an interruption in the rhythm or rate of speech characterized by hesitations, repetitions, or prolongations of sounds, syllables, words, or phrases; AND
    - the student's fluency disorder interferes with communication and calls attention to itself across two or more settings; AND
    - the student demonstrates moderate to severe vocal dysfluencies or the student evidences associated secondary behaviors such as struggling or avoidance, as measured by a standardized measure.

    c. For a phonological or articulation impairment, determine whether
    - the student's phonology or articulation is rated significantly discrepant as measured by a standardized test; AND
    - the disorder is substantiated by a language sample or other evaluation(s).

    d. For a syntax, morphology, pragmatic, or semantic impairment, determine whether
    - the student's language in the area of syntax, morphology, pragmatics, or semantics is significantly discrepant as measured by standardized test(s); AND
    - the disorder is substantiated by a language sample or other evaluation(s); AND
    - the disorder is not the result of another disability.

2. **Determine whether the student's disability has an adverse impact on educational performance.**
    The student's disability must have an adverse impact on educational performance when the student is at the age of eligibility for kindergarten through age 21, or has an adverse impact on the child's developmental progress when the child is age 3 through 5 (kindergarten); and

3. **Determine that the eligibility is not due to a lack of instruction in reading or math or due to limited English proficiency.**

4. **Determine whether the student needs special education services.**

Determination of Eligibility—Method 2

A speech or language impairment shall be demonstrated by significant deficits in listening comprehension or oral expression. The IEP team shall obtain an opinion from a licensed speech–language pathologist as to the existence of a speech or language impairment and its effect on the student's ability to function. The determination of a speech or language impairment shall be based on the following criteria:

1. **Determine whether a deficit exists in listening comprehension.**
   A significant deficit in listening comprehension exists when a student demonstrates a significant deficit from the test mean on one or more measures of auditory processing or comprehension of connected speech. Auditory processing or comprehension includes:

   - Semantics
   - Syntax
   - Phonology
   - Recalling information
   - Following directions
   - Pragmatics

2. **Determine whether a deficit exists in oral expression.**
   For purposes of determination of a speech and language impairment, a significant deficit in oral expression exists when a child demonstrates one or more of the following conditions:

   i. *Voice.* A significant deficit in voice exists when both of the following are present:
      - Documentation by an otolaryngologist that treatment is indicated for a vocal pathology or speech-related medical condition
      - Abnormal vocal characteristics in pitch, quality, nasality, volume, or breath support, which persist for at least one month.

   ii. *Fluency.* A significant deficit in fluency exists when the student exhibits one or more of the following behaviors:
      - Part word repetitions or sound prolongations occur on at least 5 percent of the words spoken in two or more speech samples
      - Sound or silent prolongations exceed one second in two or more speech samples
      - Secondary symptoms or signs of tension or struggle during speech so severe as to interfere with the flow of communication

   iii. *Articulation.* A significant deficit in articulation attributed to an organic or functional disorder exists when a student is unable to articulate two or more of the unrelated phonemes in connected speech, and it is not attributed to dialect or second-language difficulties.

   iv. *Oral Discourse.* A significant deficit exists when a student demonstrates a deficit of at least two standard deviations from the test mean on one or more measures of oral discourse. Oral discourse includes:
      - Syntax
      - Semantics
      - Phonology
      - Pragmatics

3. **Determine whether the student's disability has an adverse impact on educational performance.**
   The student's disability must have an adverse impact on educational performance when the student is at the age of eligibility for kindergarten through age 21, or has an adverse impact on the child's developmental progress when the child is age 3 through 5 (kindergarten).
4. **Determine that the eligibility is not due to a lack of instruction in reading or math or due to limited English proficiency.**
5. **Determine whether the student needs special education services.**

Final Thoughts

It is important to note that the IEP team may not identify a child who exhibits any of the following as having a speech or language impairment:

- Mild, transitory, or developmentally appropriate speech or language difficulties that children experience at various times and to various degrees
- Speech or language performance that is consistent with developmental levels as documented by formal and informal assessment data unless the child requires speech or language services in order to benefit from his or her educational programs in school, home, and community environments
- Speech or language difficulties resulting from dialectical differences or from learning English as a second language, unless the child has a language impairment in his or her native language
- Difficulties with auditory processing without a concomitant documented oral speech or language impairment
- A tongue thrust which exists in the absence of a concomitant impairment in speech sound production
- Elective or selective mutism or school phobia without a documented oral speech or language impairment

Finally, a strong relationship exists between communication and academic achievement. Language and communication proficiency, along with academic success, depend on whether students can match their communications to the learning/ teaching style of the classroom. Students with communication disorders are capable of high academic success if they learn the classroom's social, language, and learning patterns. Teachers and speech–language pathologists should focus their attention on classroom interactions and the language and communications used within the school in order to help students learn to communicate in these environments. Explicit language and communication planning as well as nondeliberate language use (e.g., unconscious choice of language) are important features of the school and class environments that provide opportunities for teaching and learning.

MENTAL RETARDATION

Definition under IDEA

According to IDEA, **mental retardation** is defined as

> significantly subaverage general intellectual functioning, existing concurrently with deficits in adaptive behavior and manifested during the developmental period, that adversely affects a child's educational performance.

Overview

Mental retardation is a term describing the condition in a person who has certain limitations in mental functioning, in taking care of him- or herself, and in social skills such as communicating. These limitations will cause a child to learn and develop more slowly than a typical child. Children with mental retardation may take longer to learn to speak, walk, and take care of their personal needs such as dressing or eating. They are likely to have trouble learning in school, or they will learn, but it will take them longer. For those with mental retardation, there may be some concepts that cannot be learned (National Dissemination Center for Children and Youth with Disabilities, 2004b). The field of mental retardation continues to evolve (Baroff, 2000), with an emphasis on inclusive practices, recommended strategies, and decreasing the stigma for those diagnosed with mental retardation.

Over the past decade, several efforts have been made to describe mental retardation in terms of needed levels of support rather than to define it in terms of deficits. There have also been efforts to shift from the term *mental retardation* to *intellectual disability*, which more accurately connotes the cognitive underpinning of the disability.

Intellectual disability (ID) can be viewed as a disorder in three distinct areas: thinking (conceptual), learning (practical), and social competence. Children with ID show more limitations in the spontaneous use of thinking skills that will enable them to learn effectively.

Difficulty is encountered when the student has to make decisions about how to approach the problem. In order for learning to occur, the student has to make decisions about the nature of the information and the steps needed to process the information.

Intellectual disability has traditionally been seen as a deficiency in the area of learning. However, research shows that students with mild to moderate ID can, and do, learn academic and adaptive skills, if appropriate learning strategies and explicit instructions are provided. The research presented in the guidelines provides stronger support for intellectual disability as a thinking disorder, rather than a learning disorder, since thinking appears to be a prerequisite for learning as well as part of the learning process.

The poorly developed social skills of students with ID are a major factor in drawing the attention of school and community personnel to their disability. One of the factors that limits self-determination and quality of life of individuals with intellectual disability is limited social and cognitive problem-solving skills. However, social problem-solving strategies can be learned and used when instructions are explicit.

Prevalence

According to the U.S. Department of Education (2011) *Digest of Education Statistics: 2009,* there were 500,000 students between the ages of 3 to 21 were identified as having specific learning disabilities. This represents approximately 7.6 percent of all students having a classification in special education. The American Association on Mental Retardation estimates that 2.5 percent of the population has this disability (Luckasson, 2002).

DETERMINING THE PRESENCE OF MENTAL RETARDATION STEP BY STEP

Step I. Become Familiar with the Characteristics of Children with Mental Retardation
Children with mental retardation may

- Sit up, crawl, or walk later than other children
- Learn to talk later, or have trouble speaking

- Find it hard to remember things
- Not understand how to pay for things
- Have trouble understanding social rules
- Have trouble seeing the consequences of their actions
- Have trouble solving problems
- Have trouble thinking logically
- Exhibit failure to meet intellectual developmental markers
- Exhibit persistence of infantile behavior
- Lack curiosity
- Have decreased learning ability
- Have an inability to meet educational demands of school (National Library of Congress, 2005)

Among individuals with mental retardation, there is a wide range of abilities, disabilities, strengths, and needs for support. It is common to find language delay and motor development significantly below norms of peers who do not have mental retardation. More seriously affected children will experience delays in such areas of motor skill development as mobility, body image, and control of body actions. Compared to their nondisabled peers, children with mental retardation may generally be below norms in height and weight, may experience more speech problems, and may have a higher prevalence of vision and hearing impairment.

In contrast to their classmates, students with mental retardation often have problems with attention, perception, memory, problem solving, and logical thought. They are slower in learning how to learn and find it harder to apply what they have learned to new situations or problems. Some professionals explain these patterns by asserting that children with mental retardation have qualitatively different deficits in cognition or memory. Others believe that persons with mental retardation move through the same stages of development as those without retardation, although at a slower rate, reaching lower levels of functioning overall. Many persons with retardation are affected only minimally, and will function only somewhat slower than average in learning new skills and information.

Step II. Determine the Procedures and Assessment Measures to Be Used

When a student has been referred for assessment to determine the presence of a disability, the IEP team reviews the documentation of the general education interventions used with the student. The team also collects and reviews a variety of readily available information about the student to determine whether additional formal information gathering is needed. Sources of information include, but are not limited to, the following:

- Information from school records
- Information from the teacher
- Grades
- Instructional levels based on daily attendance pattern
- Classroom behavior
- Health record
- General education interventions
- Screening records
- Vision
- Peer relationships
- Hearing

- Information from parent conferences
- Speech/language interviews
- Discipline records
- Home behavior
- Hobbies and interests
- Neighborhood friendships

The following high-risk factors may indicate the presence of mental retardation:
Academic skill development and adaptive behavior is below that of most, if not all, of the children in the class.

- Work samples evidence delay across all academic areas.
- Low performance level cannot be attributed to factors other than mental retardation (i.e., social/emotional, visual, or hearing problem).
- It is difficult for the student to retain information taught from one day to the next.
- There is a delay in development of gross and fine motor coordination.

The IEP team gathers all pertinent data (e.g., documentation of general education interventions, written records, observations, tests, and interviews) to identify the presence of factors indicative of mental retardation. The assessment for the diagnosis of mental retardation needs to include

- An individually administered standardized intelligence test administered by a qualified professional
- An adaptive behavior scale
- A developmental history of the student
- A medical statement or a health assessment indicating whether there are any sensory or physical factors that may be affecting the student's educational performance
- Assessments to determine the impact of the suspected disability

Besides these assessment measures, the following assessment measures should also be considered if a student is suspected of having a speech and language impairment under the definition set forth in IDEA.

A. An observation by a team member other than the student's regular teacher of the student's academic performance in a regular classroom setting; or in the case of a child less than school age or out of school, an observation by a team member conducted in an age-appropriate environment
B. A developmental history, if needed
C. An assessment of intellectual ability
D. Other assessments of the characteristics of speech and language impairments if the student exhibits impairments in any one or more of the following areas: cognition, fine motor, perceptual motor, communication, social or emotional, and perception or memory. These assessments shall be completed by specialists knowledgeable in the specific characteristics being assessed
E. A review of cumulative records, previous individualized education programs or individualized family service plans, and teacher-collected work samples
F. If deemed necessary, a medical statement or health assessment statement indicating whether there are any physical factors that may be affecting the student's educational performance

G. Assessments to determine the impact of the suspected disability
   • On the student's educational performance when the student is at the age of eligibility for kindergarten through age 21
   • On the child's developmental progress when the child is age 3 through the age of eligibility for kindergarten

H. Additional evaluations or assessments necessary to identify the student's educational needs.

Step III. Detwermination of Eligibility for a Diagnosis of Mental Retardation
Based on the results of assessment, in order to meet eligibility standards for the diagnosis of mental retardation, a child has to meet all of the following:

1. **Determine whether the student exhibits "significantly impaired intellectual functioning."**
Significantly impaired intellectual functioning, which is two or more standard deviations below the mean, with consideration given to the standard error of measurement for the test at the 68 percent confidence level, on an individually administered, standardized measure of intelligence.

   Interpretation of evaluation results shall take into account factors that may affect test performance, including

   • Limited English proficiency
   • Cultural background and differences
   • Medical conditions that impact school performance
   • Socioeconomic status
   • Communication, sensory, or motor disabilities
   • Difficulties in these areas cannot be the primary reason for significantly impaired scores on measures of intellectual functioning

2. **Determine whether the student exhibits "significantly impaired adaptive behavior in the home or community."**
Significantly impaired adaptive behavior can be determined by:

   a. A composite score on an individual standardized instrument to be completed with or by the child's principal caretaker which measures two standard deviations or more below the mean. Standard scores shall be used. A composite age equivalent score that represents a 50 percent delay based on chronological age can be used only if the instrument fails to provide a composite standard score. A composite score two or more standard deviations below the mean cannot be primarily the result of

   • Limited English proficiency
   • Cultural background and differences
   • Medical conditions that impact school performance
   • Socioeconomic status
   • Communication, sensory, or motor disabilities

   b. Additional documentation which may be obtained from systematic documented observations, impressions, developmental history by an appropriate specialist in conjunction with the principal caretaker in the home, community, residential program, or institutional setting

c. Significantly impaired adaptive behavior in the school, daycare center, residence, or program as determined by

i. Systematic documented observations by an appropriate specialist, which compare the child with other children of his or her chronological age group.

Observations shall address age-appropriate adaptive behaviors. Adaptive behaviors to be observed in each age range are to include:

- birth–6 years—communication, self-care, social skills, and physical development
- 6–13 years—communication, self-care, social skills, home living, community use, self-direction, health and safety, functional academics, and leisure
- 14–21 years—communication, self-care, social skills, home living, community use, self-direction, health and safety, functional academics, leisure, and work

ii. When appropriate, an individual standardized instrument may be completed with the principal teacher of the child. A composite score on this instrument shall measure two standard deviations or more below the mean. Standard scores shall be used. A composite age equivalent score that represents a 50 percent delay based on chronological age can be used only if the instrument fails to provide a composite standard score. A composite score two or more standard deviations below the mean cannot be primarily the result of

- Limited English proficiency
- Cultural background and differences
- Medical conditions that impact school performance
- Socioeconomic status
- Communication, sensory, or motor disabilities

iii. Developmental history (birth to age 18) indicates delays in cognitive/ intellectual abilities and delays are currently demonstrated in the child's natural (home and school) environment.

iv. The characteristics as defined above are present and cause an adverse affect on educational performance in the general education classroom or learning environment.

Final Thoughts

Historically, mental retardation has either been described in controversial terms or presented as a clear-cut disability category. At various times, subcategories of mental retardation have been identified based on degree of severity, with concomitant labels such as "educable" versus "trainable," "moderate," "severe," and "profound." Systemic changes in education emphasize that "special education is a set of services brought to natural environments rather than a set of places where services are provided" (Iowa Department of Education, 1997). In such a system, all subcategories have disappeared.

Over the past decade, various groups (American Association on Mental Retardation, American Psychological Association) have made several efforts to shift the model for describing mental retardation from one based on deficits in the individual to one based on levels of support needed by the individual with the disability. There have also been efforts to shift from the label *mental retardation* to *intellectual disability,* a term that more accurately connotes the cognitive underpinning of the disability.

EMOTIONAL DISTURBANCE

Definition under IDEA

Under IDEA, an **emotional disturbance** is defined as:

> a condition exhibiting one or more of the following characteristics over a long period of time and to a marked degree that adversely affects a child's educational performance:
>
> **a.** An inability to learn that cannot be explained by intellectual, sensory, or health factors.
> **b.** An inability to build or maintain satisfactory interpersonal relationships with peers and teachers.
> **c.** Inappropriate types of behavior or feelings under normal circumstances.
> **d.** A general pervasive mood of unhappiness or depression.
> **e.** A tendency to develop physical symptoms or fears associated with personal or school problems.

The term includes schizophrenia. The term does not apply to children who are socially maladjusted, unless it is determined that they have an emotional disturbance.

Overview

The term *emotional disturbance* is often used interchangeably with the terms *emotional disorder/problem, behavior disorder/disturbance, psychiatric illness,* and *mental illness/ disorder.* An emotional disturbance refers to social, emotional, or behavioral functioning that so departs from generally accepted, age-appropriate ethnic or cultural norms that it adversely affects a child's academic progress, social relationships, personal adjustment, classroom adjustment, self-care, or vocational skills.

According to the National Mental Health Information Center (2003, p. 1), "emotional disturbances are mental health problems that severely disrupt a child's or adolescent's daily life and functioning at home, at school or in the community. Tragically, an estimated two-thirds of the young people who need mental health services are not getting them. Without help, these problems can lead to school failure, alcohol and other drug abuse, family discord, violence or even suicide."

The causes of emotional disturbance have not been adequately determined. Biology, environment, or a mix of both can cause mental health problems in youth. Examples of biological causes are genetics, chemical imbalances in the body and damage to the central nervous system, such as head injury. There are many environmental factors that can put children at risk of developing mental health problems. Examples include exposure to violence, stress-related chronic poverty, discrimination and other hardships, or loss of important people in the lives of the youth through death, divorce, or broken relationships. Although various factors such as heredity, brain disorder, diet, stress, and family functioning have been suggested as possible causes, research has not shown any of these factors to be the direct cause of behavior or emotional problems (Jensen, 2005).

Children with the most serious emotional disturbances may exhibit distorted thinking, excessive anxiety, bizarre motor acts, and abnormal mood swings. Some are identified as children who have a severe psychosis or schizophrenia (Jensen, 2005).

Many children who do not have emotional disturbances may display some of these same behaviors at various times during their development. However, when children have an emotional disturbance, these behaviors continue over long periods of time. Their behavior thus signals that they are not coping with their environment or peers (Turnbull et al., 2004).

Possibly more than any other group of children with disabilities, children with emotional or behavior disorders present social problems to themselves, their families, their peers, and their teachers (Gresham, Lane, MacMillan, & Bocian, 1999).

Prevalence

According to the U.S. Department of Education (2011) *Digest of Education Statistics: 2009,* 442,000 students between the ages of 3 to 21 were identified as having speech and language impairments. This represents approximately 6.7 percent of all students having a classification in special education.

DETERMINING THE PRESENCE OF AN EMOTIONAL DISTURBANCE STEP BY STEP

Step I. Become Familiar with the Characteristics of Children with Emotional/Behavioral Disorders

Characteristics often associated with students having emotional and or behavioral disorders include:

An inability to build or maintain satisfactory interpersonal relationships with peers and teachers

- Physical or verbal aggression when others approach him or her
- Lack of affect or disorganized/distorted emotions toward others
- Demands for constant attention from others
- Withdrawal from all social interactions

Inappropriate types of behavior or feelings under normal circumstances

- Limited or excessive self-control
- Low frustration tolerance, emotional overreactions, and impulsivity
- Limited premeditation or planning
- Limited ability to predict consequences of behavior
- Rapid changes in behavior or mood
- Antisocial behaviors
- Excessive dependence and overcloseness, and/or inappropriate rebellion and defiance, and low self-esteem and/or distorted self-concept

A general pervasive mood of unhappiness or depression

- Depressed or irritable mood most of the time (e.g., feeling sad, appearing tearful)
- Diminished interest or pleasure in daily activities
- Significant and unexpected changes in weight or appetite
- Insomnia or hypersomnia nearly every day
- Fatigue or diminished energy nearly every day
- Feelings of worthlessness or excessive or inappropriate guilt
- Diminished ability to think or concentrate or indecisiveness nearly every day
- Recurrent thoughts of death or suicidal ideation

Physical symptoms or fears associated with the child's personal or school life. Examples of these characteristics include:

- Headaches
- Gastrointestinal problems

- Cardiopulmonary symptoms
- Incapacitating feelings of anxiety often accompanied by trembling, hyperventilating, and/or dizziness
- Panic attacks characterized by physical symptoms, for example, when an object, activity, individual, or situation cannot be avoided or is confronted
- Persistent and irrational fears of particular objects or situations
- Intense fears or irrational thoughts related to separation from parent(s)

Other Characteristics of Students with Emotional Disorders

- A lack of understanding about consequences of actions
- Problems with reasoning characterized by confused thoughts about and perceptions of social situations
- Highly unusual and bizarre behaviors
- A lack of understanding or misinterpretations of social conventions and behavioral expectations
- Excessive anxiety, pervasive depression, and/or excessive guilt

Finally, it should be noted that an emotional disturbance exists only when the traits are considered to have been exhibited over a long period of time and to a marked degree. This means the characteristic(s) are persistent, generalized, and extended over time and situations. The marked degree standard is met when the characteristic(s) are significantly deviant from expectations for age-level peers and have a low frequency of occurrence in the peer group.

Step II. Determine the Procedures and Assessment Measures to Be Used

Each child shall have a multidisciplinary evaluation for the initial assessment of a suspected disability (emotional disturbance) that includes, but is not limited to, the following:
- Comprehensive social history collected directly from the child's parent/ guardian, custodial guardian, or if necessary, from an individual with intimate knowledge of the child's circumstances, history, or current behaviors. A comprehensive social assessment shall include family history, family– social interactions, developmental history, medical history (including mental health), and school history (including attendance and discipline records)
- Direct and anecdotal observations over time and across various settings by three or more licensed professionals
- Documentation and assessment of how emotional disturbance adversely affects educational performance in the learning environment
- Individual assessment of psychoeducational strengths and weaknesses, including intelligence, behavior, and personality factors, taking into account any exceptionality of the individual in the choice of assessment procedures
- Individual educational assessment (criterion- or norm-referenced) including direct measures of classroom performance to determine the student's strengths and weaknesses
- Physical conditions ruled out as the primary cause of atypical behavior(s)
- Review of past educational performance
- Specific behavioral data, including documentation of previous interventions and an evaluation of the locus of control of behavior to include internal and external factors
- Visual or auditory deficits ruled out as the primary cause of atypical behavior(s)

Besides these assessment measures, the following assessment measures should also be considered if a student is suspected of having a speech and language impairment under the definition set forth in IDEA.

A. An observation by a team member other than the student's regular teacher of the student's academic performance in a regular classroom setting; or in the case of a child less than school age or out of school, an observation by a team member conducted in an age-appropriate environment

B. A developmental history, if needed

C. An assessment of intellectual ability

D. Other assessments of the characteristics of speech and language impairments if the student exhibits impairments in any one or more of the following areas: cognition, fine motor, perceptual motor, communication, social or emotional, and perception or memory. These assessments shall be completed by specialists knowledgeable in the specific characteristics being assessed

E. A review of cumulative records, previous individualized education programs or individualized family service plans, and teacher-collected work samples

F. If deemed necessary, a medical statement or health assessment statement indicating whether there are any physical factors that may be affecting the student's educational performance

G. Assessments to determine the impact of the suspected disability:
  • On the student's educational performance when the student is at the age of eligibility for kindergarten through age 21
  • On the child's developmental progress when the child is age 3 through the age of eligibility for kindergarten

H. Additional evaluations or assessments necessary to identify the student's educational needs

Step III. Determination of Eligibility for a Diagnosis of an Emotional Disturbance

To be eligible for a classification as a student with an emotional disturbance under IDEA, the following standards should be met:

1. **Determine whether the student exhibits one or more of the following (a–e):**

   a. An inability to learn at a rate commensurate with the student's intellectual, sensory motor, and physical development

   This characteristic requires documentation that a student is not able to learn, despite appropriate instructional strategies and/or support services. A comprehensive and differential assessment is performed to establish an "inability to learn." The assessment should rule out any other primary reasons for the suspected disability, such as mental retardation, speech and language disorders, autism, learning disability, hearing/vision impairment, multihandicapping conditions, traumatic brain injury, neurological impairment, or other medical conditions. If any of these other conditions is the primary cause, then the student may be deemed eligible for special education under that category of disability.

   b. An inability to build or maintain satisfactory interpersonal relationships with peers and teachers

   This characteristic requires documentation that the student is unable to initiate or to maintain satisfactory interpersonal relationships with peers and teachers. Satisfactory interpersonal relationships include the ability to demonstrate sympathy, warmth, and empathy toward others; establish and maintain friendships; be constructively assertive; and work and play independently. These abilities should be considered when observing the student's interactions with both peers and teachers. This characteristic does not refer to the student who has conflict with only one teacher or with certain peers. Rather it is a pervasive inability to develop relationships with others across settings and situations.

c. Inappropriate types of behavior or feelings under normal circumstances

This characteristic requires documentation that the student's inappropriate behavior or feelings deviate significantly from expectations for the student's age, gender, and culture across different environments. The IEP team must determine whether the student's inappropriate responses are occurring "under normal circumstances." When considering "normal circumstances," the IEP team should take into account whether a student's home or school situation is disrupted by stress, recent changes, or unexpected events.

d. A general pervasive mood of unhappiness or depression

This characteristic requires documentation that the student's unhappiness or depression is occurring across most, if not all, of the student's life situations. The student must demonstrate a consistent pattern of depression or unhappiness in keeping with the criterion "long period of time" (i.e., several months). In other words, this pattern is not a temporary response to situational factors or to a medical condition. The characteristics should not be a secondary manifestation attributable to substance abuse, medication, or a general medical condition (e.g., hypothyroidism). The characteristics cannot be the effect of normal bereavement.

e. Physical symptoms or fears associated with the child's personal or school life

Physical symptoms that qualify under the emotional disturbance characteristic should adhere to the following four conditions:

i. Symptoms suggesting physical disorders are present with no demonstrable medical findings

ii. Positive evidence or strong presumption exists that these symptoms are linked to psychological factors/conflict

iii. The person is not conscious of intentionally producing the symptoms

iv. The symptoms are not a culturally sanctioned response pattern

2. **Determine whether the student's educational performance is adversely affected.**

Indicators of educational performance include present and past grades, achievement test scores, and measures of ongoing classroom performance (e.g., curriculum-based assessment and work samples). Adverse effect on educational performance implies a marked difference between the student's academic performance and reasonable (not optimal) expectations of performance. The appropriateness of the school district's educational goals, as reflected in the curriculum and in the formal grading report, should be considered in determining whether the student's performance meets reasonable expectations.

3. **Determine that the student does not meet the criteria for a "socially maladjusted" student.**

A social maladjustment is a persistent pattern of violating societal norms, such as multiple acts of truancy, or substance or sex abuse, and is marked by struggle with authority, low frustration threshold, impulsivity, or manipulative behaviors.

A social maladjustment unaccompanied by an emotional disturbance is often indicated by some or all of the following:

a. Unhappiness or depression that is not pervasive

b. Problem behaviors that are goal-directed, self-serving, and manipulative

c. Actions that are based on perceived self-interest even though others may consider the behavior to be self-defeating

d. General social conventions and behavioral standards that are understood but not accepted

e. Negative countercultural standards or peers that are accepted and followed

f. roblem behaviors that have escalated duringpreadolescence or adolescence

g. Inappropriate behaviors that are displayed in selected settings or situations (e g , only at home, in school, or in selected classes), while other behavior is appropriately controlled

h. Problem behaviors that are frequently the result of encouragement by a peer group, are intentional, with the student understanding the consequences of such behaviors

Final Thoughts

Assessment information collected or generated during the eligibility determination phase should contribute to developing the plan that eventually becomes the individualized education program. These assessments by the multidisciplinary evaluation team should yield a profile of the student's needs and strengths as well as the student's characteristic pattern of response to environmental and internal influences. Assessment for serious emotional disturbance will include not only information about the student's aptitude and academic achievement levels, but also information regarding (1) social and personal competence needed to maximize independence and (2) when appropriate, the student's vocational aptitudes and interests. Social and personal information should lead to the identification of affective skills to be targeted in the IEP. Examples include (1) managing anger, frustration, and other emotions that tend to exacerbate conflict with peers, teachers and school administrators, and (2) coping effectively with withdrawal or depression.

The IEP team may not identify or refuse to identify a child as a child with an emotional behavioral disability solely on the basis that the child has another disability, or is socially maladjusted, adjudged delinquent, a dropout, chemically dependent, or a child whose behavior is primarily due to cultural deprivation, familial instability, suspected child abuse, or socioeconomic circumstances, or when medical or psychiatric diagnostic statements have been used to describe the child's behavior.

CONCLUSION

The diagnosis of any suspected disability is without any doubt the most important part of the assessment process. Having all the data and relevant information available and not knowing what to do with it is a disservice to both the parent and the child with a suspected disability. Therefore, it is your professional responsibility to stay abreast of any changes in the federal and state laws as well as local policies involving the assessment of children with suspected disabilities.

Vocabulary

Emotional disturbance: Social, emotional, or behavioral functioning that so differs from generally accepted norms for a child's age, ethnicity, and culture that it adversely affects their academic progress, social relationships, adjustment, self-care, or vocational skills.

Higher-prevalence disabilities: Classifications of disabilities that are frequently first diagnosed at public school, including learning disabilities, emotional disturbances, mental retardation, speech and language impairments, and other health impairment—ADHD prediagnosis.

Learning disabilities: A general term describing specific kinds of learning problems, and neurobiological disorders related to differences in how one's brain works and is structured.

Lower-prevalence disabilities: Classifications of disabilities that are frequently first diagnosed by a medical professional before the child enters school, including autism; traumatic brain injury; deaf-blindness; and orthopedic, visual, hearing, or other health impairments.

Mental retardation: A condition in a person who has certain limitations in mental functioning, taking care of him or herself, and in social skills such as communicating. Mental retardation may cause a child to learn and develop more slowly than a typical child.

Speech and language impairments: Deficits in the ability to exchange information with others; a communication disorder occurring in the realms of language, speech, and/or hearing.

17 | WRITING A COMPREHENSIVE REPORT IN SPECIAL EDUCATION

Key Terms

Academic history
Background History
Behavioral Observations
Chronological age
Conclusions
Content area by content area
   approach

Developmental History
Family history
Identifying Data
Reason for Referral
Recommendations
Social history
Test-by-test approach

Test Results
Tests and Procedures
   Administered

Chapter Objectives

Writing a report is not a simple task. It takes knowledge and skill because it is being written for parents, teachers, and administrators. After reading this chapter, you should be able to understand why reports need to be written, general guidelines when writing a report, and all sections of a comprehensive report. These sections include:

- Identifying data
- Reason for Referral
- Background History
- Behavioral Observations
- Tests and Procedures Administered
- Test Results
  - Test-by-test analysis
  - Content area by content area analysis
- Conclusions
- Recommendations

REPORT WRITING

Many different professionals may provide input in the assessment of a child with a suspected disability. From this input, a comprehensive report based on the findings must be written. The purpose of this report is to communicate results in such a way that the reader will understand the rationale behind the recommendations and will be able to use the recommendations as practical guidelines for intervention. This report may be presented to the parent, sent to an outside doctor or agency, or presented to the eligibility committee. In any case, the report needs to be professional, comprehensive, and practical.

Writing a good report is a real skill. The fact is, all the wonderful data collection becomes useless if it cannot be interpreted and explained in a clear and concise manner. Being too general or explaining results poorly creates many problems and confusion for readers. Also, citing numerous general recommendations will not be practical for the school, teacher, or parents. Writing a report that contains jargon that no one other than you understands is also useless. Completing an extremely lengthy report in an attempt to be too comprehensive will result only in losing your reader. As you review each section in this chapter, you may wish to refer to the example report extracts we have provided.

PRACTICAL GUIDELINES FOR REPORT WRITING

When writing a report, the key is to be as comprehensive as possible while being clear and concise. To do this effectively, it is important to understand some very practical guidelines, including those listed below.

WRITE THE REPORT IN THE THIRD PERSON. Never write "I think" or "If it were up to me." This is not a term paper, but rather a legal document. As such, the professional approach is to remain in the third person. Use phrases such as

- According to the examiner
- It was felt that
- There seems to be
- It is the professional opinion of this evaluator that

SINGLE-SPACE YOUR REPORT TO CONDENSE THE LENGTH. A report of three to five pages is not overwhelming. There are several suggestions throughout this chapter on how to break up the report so that the format is easy on the reader.

In general, try to separate your recommendation section into three parts to make it easy for a reader to follow the recommendations. To allow interested parties to see their responsibilities, the three parts should be addressed to

- The school
- The teacher
- The parents

USE THE PAST TENSE AS OFTEN AS POSSIBLE. Because the data are already collected and you have done the assessment, the use of the past tense is most appropriate.

- On the Reading subtest, Jared *scored* in the 95th percentile.
- During testing, Tamika *exhibited* shyness.
- Throughout the interview, David *showed* no signs of hyperactivity.
- Sonya *appeared* to lack confidence when doing tasks that *required* hand–eye coordination.

UNDERLINE, BOLD, OR ITALICIZE PARAGRAPH HEADINGS SO THEY STAND OUT AND ARE EASY TO LOCATE. When you create a new section in your report, format it so that the reader knows that this starts a different area of the report. Separate sections (e.g., Reason for Referral and Background History) with extra "white space."

WRITE REPORTS USING COMPLETE SENTENCES. A report should never read like a telegram. Be sure all sentences make sense. Always check spelling and grammar to make sure there are no errors. Nothing is more unprofessional than a report that looks sloppy and has many mistakes.

CRITERIA FOR WRITING A COMPREHENSIVE REPORT

Now that you have some practical guidelines to follow, take a comprehensive look at each specific section. Reports can be written in many ways, and report format is decided by the personal choice of the examiner, the supervisor, or the district. However, it is important not to overlook certain information. What follows is one suggested outline and sections that would meet all the criteria for a professional and comprehensive report. We will now look at each section of a report following along with a fifth grade student who was evaluated. The final report at the end will contain all the sections discussed in this chapter.

Section I: Identifying Data

The first section is called **Identifying Data** and contains all the necessary basic information about the child. This section is important to the reader, especially if further contact is required. It allows the reader to have all the basic information in one place. The parts of this section include:

Name of Student:	**School:**
Address:	**Teacher:**
Phone:	**Referred by:**
Date of Birth:	**Date of Testing:**
Grade:	**Date of Report:**
Parent's Names:	**Chronological Age:**
	Examiner:

For example, in a model report, the first section might be completed as follows:

Name of Student: Jessica Willow	**School:** Meadow Lane
Address: 31 Apple Tree Rd., Mineola, N.Y.	**Teacher:** Mrs.Gaines
Phone: (516) 742-1097	**Referred by:** Child Study Team
Date of Birth: 1/9/2000	**Date of Testing:** March 22, 23, 2011
Grade: 5	**Date of Report:** April 1, 2011
Parent's Names: John/Patricia	**Chronological Age:** 11-2
	Examiner: Ms. Tracy Doe

Although most of this information is usually found in school records, having it all in one place will save time. Make sure that the date/s of testing and the date of the report are always included for comparisons. Some evaluations are finished several months before the report is typed, and the scores can be misleading if the reader assumes that they represent the child's present levels on the date of the report when they may really be reflective of ability levels in prior months. It is always more acceptable when the two dates are within one month of each other. Also keep in mind that the **chronological age** (CA) is at the time of initial testing and is presented in years and months, for example, 11-2 (see Chapter 5).

Section II: Reason for Referral

The second section is called **Reason for Referral** and explains to the reader the specific reasons the evaluation is taking place. It should not be longer than two to three sentences, but should be comprehensive enough to clarify the purpose. The following are some examples of this section:

Reason for Referral

- Jessica was referred for a comprehensive assessment as the result of a suspected disability.

  Other examples may include:

- Jarmel was referred by his teacher for an evaluation as a result of inconsistent academic performance and poor social skills.
- Mary was referred by her parents for an evaluation in order to determine if a learning disability was interfering with her ability to learn.
- Benjamin is being tested as part of the triennial evaluation.
- Peter was referred by the child study team in order to determine his present intellectual, academic, and perceptual levels.

This section should not contain a great deal of parent or teacher information. There may be a tendency here to bring in other information to substantiate the reason for the evaluation. Avoid this, and keep it short and to the point. Substantiation for this referral is part of another section that offers a more detailed explanation of the child.

Section III: Background History

The next section is called **Background History**, and it contains a very thorough description of the child's family history, developmental history, academic history, and social history (refer to the parent intake form in Chapter 8).

This general section is very comprehensive and establishes a foundation for what will follow. If you suspect a disability that may have historical features, then you need to present the development of this disability and its interfering factors in depth. The reader should come away from the section seeing the substantiation for a suspected disability. Certain areas should always be covered in the Background History section, as shown in the following paragraphs.

A. **Family History.** A **family history** provides the reader with a general understanding of the family structure, siblings, parental perceptions, and so on. Examples of sentences that would appear in this section include the following:

- Jessica and her family are living on the first floor of Mrs. Willow's mother's house, and her mother occupies the upstairs space. Jessica has two sisters who both live with her named Margaret and Mary.

Other examples may include:

- Jacob lives at home with his mother and a younger brother, Jon. His parents are divorced and Jacob has no contact with his father.
- Rosa lives at home with her father, mother, and two older sisters.
- Julie is an only child who was adopted at the age of six months by her parents, Ted and Jane. She knows that she is adopted and has never had any contact with her biological parents.

B. **Developmental History.** The purpose of a **developmental history** is to give the reader any relevant background history pertaining to developmental milestones. This section need not read like a hospital report but should contain the basic developmental history. Examples of sentences that would appear in this section include the following:

- Mrs. Willow indicated that Jessica was the result of a full-term pregnancy. However, it was a difficult birth because she needed a forceps delivery due to the umbilical cord complications.

Other examples may include:

- All of Julio's developmental milestones were reached in the normal limits.
- Yolanda started to talk only at 2 years of age and received early intervention to help her with language ability.
- Mike had many ear infections during the first year of life and needed tubes put in when he was 13 months of age.
- Emily started to walk later than the norm, as she started at 21 months of age.

C. **Academic History.** An **academic history** section provides the reader with relevant academic performance during the child's school years. If you suspect a learning disability, then the academic section must be extensive. Trace the child's educational performance as far back as possible and establish the consistency of the pattern to the reader. Include all pertinent academic information such as past teacher comments, grades, attendance, group scores, and the like. Lead the reader grade by grade in establishing a pattern of concern or a pattern that may rule out a specific type of suspected disability. Example sentences used in this section might read as follows:

- Jessica has always done poorly in math and has never received a grade of higher than C in this subject throughout her educational career.
- Laura's first-grade teacher reported that she had great difficulty in the area of spelling.
- Justin's reading scores on the ABC National Standardized Test were well below the norm (8th percentile) when he took it two years ago in the fourth grade.

D. **Social History.** A **social history** provides the reader with an understanding of the child in his social world. Group participation, organizations, hobbies, interests, interaction with peers, social style, and so forth should all be discussed. Examples of sentences that would appear in this section include the following:

- Mrs. Linus, Jessica's kindergarten teacher, indicated that socially Jessica got along well with the other children in the class. Although she was not a very active participant, she was well liked by the other children who reached out to her a great deal.

Other examples may include:

- According to Tomas, he enjoys playing baseball and hanging out with his friends at the mall.
- Karen reported that she has no friends and does not participate in any extracurricular activities.
- Ted is the eleventh-grade class president of his school and plays on the junior varsity basketball and varsity baseball teams.

E. **Parent's Perception of the Problem.** The parent's will need to be asked their perception of the problems their child is having in school. For example:

According to Mrs. Willow, she too struggled when she was younger with learning but grew out of it over time. It did however affect her self esteem. She thinks that Jessica has learning problems like she had, but isn't classified yet.

When the Background History section is complete, it should provide the reader with a clear understanding of the child and his or her world at the present time.

Section IV: Behavioral Observations

The fourth section is called **Behavioral Observations** and may include the write up from several types of meeting you may have with the child. For instance there may be three possible times when you interact or observe the child:

1. **Classroom observation:** If you do the classroom observation you will need to write up a short summary of the findings in this section.
2. **Initial interview with the student:** You should have a brief interview with the student prior to starting the assessment. This will allow you to see the child in a different manner and may provide some valuable information. During this time you should also note any areas of anxiety, resistance, opposition, etc. This will also have to be written up and would be another paragraph in this section.
3. **Behavior during testing:** The third possible time is when you test the child and write up a description of the child's behavior during the testing sessions. This can be a very important section because it may reinforce what is seen in the class or be very different, in which case the structure of the testing environment should be explored for clues to learning style. Here, for the first time, you are providing the reader with your professional and firsthand observation of this child in a controlled setting. This type of structure provides a great deal of valuable information that may be later transferred to recommendations about the way the child learns best. Examples of sentences that would appear in this section include the following:

- Jamal approached the testing situation in a reluctant and hesitant manner.
- During testing, it was evident that Hannah was frustrated with many of the reading tasks.
- Throughout the assessment, Keith appeared anxious and nervous, as he was biting his nails and always asking whether his answers were correct.

Section V: Tests and Procedures Administered

The next section is called **Tests and Procedures Administered**. This includes a simple list of the individual tests included in the test battery and any procedures used to enhance the report, such as classroom observation, review of records, and parent intake. Do not use abbreviations when referring to test names except to add them after the name of each specific test—for example, Wide Range Achievement Test–4th Edition (WRAT-4). No further explanation is required here other than a list. This section will vary depending on the professional doing the evaluation. For example, the educational evaluator's list of tests and procedures administered may look like this:

- Classroom observation
- Interview with child
- Parent interview
- Review of records
- Wechsler Individualized Achievement Test–3rd Edition (WIAT-III)

Section VI: Test Results

The sixth section, **Test Results**, is crucial because it analyzes the results of each test and looks at the child's individual performance on each measure. There are several approaches to this section, but the two most widely used are test-by-test analysis and content area by content area analysis. The approach chosen is the personal choice and preference of the examiner.

A **test-by-test approach** separately analyzes the child's performance on each test. It analyzes the results of the different subtests and provides indications of strengths and weaknesses, manner of approach, and indications of whether the scores on the specific test should be considered valid. In this section, the first paragraph of each test analyzed usually contains all the basic score information provided by that specific test: grade levels, age levels, percentiles, stanines, and ranges. It should not contain raw scores or other statistical information not meaningful to the reader. The next several paragraphs under each test normally describe the subtest performance, patterns, strengths and weaknesses, and child's style in handling the task. Information on whether the scores should be considered a valid indicator is provided. For example, if a child refuses to do more than two problems and receives a low score due to giving up or an unwillingness to venture a guess, it is important to inform the reader that the score may be misleading and may not reflect the child's true ability.

A **content area by content area approach** takes all the reading, math, spelling, writing, visual, auditory, and motor tests from each evaluation measure and analyzes the results separately by content area. The examiner analyzes each content area in hopes of establishing patterns of strengths and weaknesses. For example, deficient scores on all tests of reading comprehension may establish a pattern of disability, especially if they are discrepant from the child's ability levels. However, extremely high scores on some tests of comprehension and low scores on others need to be explained to the reader. Here are the key steps to follow in the Test Results section. *Italicized* writing indicates the information you might type in a particular step.

However, there may be times when you are asked to provide detailed academic levels and may only need to use a comprehensive test like the Wechsler Individual Achievement Test–3rd edition. In our example, we will use the WIAT-III to show how the results may be written.

WRITING TEST RESULTS

Step 1. Write out the name of the test.

Wechsler Individualized Achievement Test, 3rd Edition

Step 2.   Create a table (Standard Score, Classification, and Percentile).

Name of Subtest	Standard Score	Classification/Range	Nat. Percentile Rank
Listening Comp.	114	Average	82
Reading Comp.	118	Above Average	88
Math Prob. Solving	76	Low Average	14
Sentence Composition	77	Low Average	11
Word Reading	118	Above Average	83
Essay Composition	70	Low Average	10
Pseudoword Decoding	113	Average	81
Numerical Operations	77	Low Average	13
Oral Expression	111	Average	77
Oral Reading Fluency	118	Above Average	82
Spelling	80	Low Average	12
Math Fluency-Add.	77	Low Average	13
Math Fluency-Sub.	76	Low Average	12
Math Fluency-Multip.	77	Low Average	13

Note: The WIAT-III uses a new standard score classification system. This differs from all previous versions of Wechsler scales. The new table is as follows:

Standard Score	Classification
Above 145	Very Superior
131–145	Superior
116–130	Above Average
85–115	Average
70–84	Low Average
55–69	Low
Below 55	Very Low

Step 3.   Write a brief 1– or 2-sentence statement about what each subtest measures, the student's standard score, classification, and percentile for each subtest. You are reiterating what is stated on the table. An example write-up of this section for the WIAT-III may look like this (This can is obtained through the Examiner's Manual.)

The Listening Comprehension subtest of the WIAT-III measures the student's ability to listen for details. On this subtest Jessica performed in the Average range, earning her a standard score of 114. As indicated by her percentile rank of 82, Jessica performed as well or better than 82 percent of all students when compared to the norms for her age.

On the Reading Comprehension subtest of the WIAT-III students must read a sentence or passage and then answer questions orally to measure their comprehension. On this subtest Jessica's performance was in the Above average range, earning her a standard score of 118. As indicated by her percentile rank of 88, Jessica performed as well or better than 88 percent of all students when compared to the norms for her age. Her scores represent a significant strength.

The Math Problem Solving asks students to solve math word problems, involving areas such as the basic operations of time, money, and interpreting graphs. On this subtest Jessica's performance was in the Low Average range, earning her a standard score of 76. As indicated by her percentile rank of 14, Jessica performed as well or better than 14 percent of all students when compared to the norms for her age. Her scores represent a significant weakness.

On the Sentence Composition subtest the student is asked to take two or more separate sentences and write one good sentence that means the same thing. On this subtest Jessica performed in the Low Average range earning her a standard scorer or 77. As indicated by her percentile rank of 11, Jessica performed as well or better than 11 percent of all students when compared to the norms for her age.

The Word Reading subtest of the WIAT-III assesses the student's ability to read familiar words aloud from a list. Both accuracy and speed of response are measured. On this subtest Jessica performed in the Above Average range, earning her a standard score of 118. As indicated by her percentile rank of 83, Jessica performed as well or better than 83 percent of all students when compared to the norms of her age.

On the Essay Composition subtest the student is asked to write an essay about his or her favorite game, including three reasons why. On this subtest Jessica performed in the Low Average range earning her a standard score of 70. As indicated by her percentile rank of 10, Jessica performed as well or better than 10 percent of all students when compared to the norms of her age.

The Pseudoword Decoding subtest of the WIAT-III assesses the student's ability to apply phonetic decoding skills. On this subtest Jessica performed in the Average range, earning her a standard score of 113. As indicated by her percentile rank of 81, Jessica performed as well or better than 81 percent of all students when compared to the norms for her age.

The Numerical Operations subtest of the WIAT-III evaluates the student's ability to identify and write dictated numerals and solve written calculation problems and equations involving all basic operations. On this subtest Jessica performed in the Low Average range earning her a standard score of 77. As indicate by her percentile rank of 13, Jessica performed as well or better than 13 percent of all students when compared to the norms for her age.

The Oral Expression of the WIAT-III subtest measures the student's ability to repeat sentences, generate lists of specific kinds of words, describe pictured scenes, and describe pictured activities. Content of answers is scored, but quality of spoken language is not. On this subtest Jessica performed in the Average earning her a standard score of 111. As indicated by her percentile rank of 77, Jessica performed as well or better than 77 percent of all students when compared to the norms for her age.

The Oral Reading Fluency subtest measures the accuracy, rate, ease, and rhythm with which a person reads. On this subtest Jessica performed in the Above Average range earning her a standard score of 118. As indicated by her percentile rank of 82, Jessica performed as well or better than 82 percent of all students when compared to the norms for her age.

The Spelling subtest of the WIAT-III measures the student's ability to spell by a word by its meaning in a sentence. On this subtest Jessica performed in the Low Average range earning her a standard score of 80. As indicated by her percentile rank of 12, Jessica performed as well or better than 12 percent of all students when compared to the norms for her age.

On the Math Fluency-Addition subtest, the student solves as many simple addition problems as he/she can in one minute. On this subtest Jessica performed in the Low Average range earning her a standard score of 77. As indicated by her percentile rank of 13, Jessica performed as well or better than 13 percent of all students when compared to the norms fro her age.

On the Math Fluency-Subtraction subtest, the student solves as many simple subtraction problems as he/she can in one minute. On this subtest Jessica performed in the Low Average range earning her a standard score of 76. As indicated by her percentile rank of 12, Jessica performed as well or better than 12 percent of all students when compared to the norms for her age.

On the Math Fluency-Multiplication subtest, the student solves as many simple multiplication problems as he/she can in one minute. On this subtest Jessica performed in the Low Average range earning her a standard score of 77. As indicated by her percentile rank of 13, Jessica performed as well or better than 13 percent of all students when compared to the norms for her age.

Section VII: Conclusions

The **Conclusions** section is probably the essence of the report. Here the examiner explains in very simple terms to the reader the trends in the child's testing results that may indicate academic strengths and weaknesses, modality strengths and weaknesses, process strengths and weaknesses, and overall diagnosis and level of severity of the problem areas indicated. It is not a restatement of the test results section but a summary of overall performance.

1. **State the name of the student, age, grade, and the reason for referral.**
   Jessica Willow is an 11 year fifth grade girl who was administered the WIAT-III for the purposes of assessing her academic achievement.

2. **In the next sentence, discuss strengths.**
   Jessica Willow is an 11-year fifth-grade girl who was administered the WIAT-III for the purposes of assessing her academic achievement. *Results of the WIAT-III indicated that Jessica obtained above average scores in Word Reading (83rd percentile), Reading Comprehension (88th percentile), and Oral Reading Fluency (82nd percentile)*

3. **The next few sentences discuss weaknesses.**
   Results of the WIAT-III indicated that Jessica's deficit areas indicated that she obtained scores within the low average range in Math Problem Solving (14th percentile), Sentence Completion (11th percentile), Essay Composition (10th percentile), Numerical Operations (13th percentile), Spelling (12th percentile), Math Fluency Addition (13th percentile), Math Fluency Subtraction (12th percentile), and Math Fluency Multiplication (13th percentile).

4. **Add a sentence about the level of severity of the student's profile:**
   Results of testing, observation, history and interviews all seem to indicate that Jessica's pattern is similar to children with moderate to severe learning disabilities.

Section VIII: Recommendations

The last section of the report is probably the most valuable section for the reader— **Recommendations**. It should contain practical recommendations that will bring some hope and direction for the identified problem areas. Keep in mind that the recommendations should be practical enough and explained in such a way that the reader will have no problem following through. The most important aspect of a recommendation is that it will need to answer the question "Why" and "How." For example, a recommendation to a parent of "Try to spend more time with Jessica" is useless. It provides the reader with no direction or specifics. Instead, a recommendation such as "It is suggested that Mr. and Mrs. Willow read at home with Jessica in unison. By this, we mean that both the parent and Jessica have the same book and read aloud together so that she receives constant auditory feedback." This recommendation answers why we are suggesting it and how to do it. This more detailed recommendation provides the reader with specific direction.

Try to separate the recommendations into the following three sections:

1. **Recommendations to the school:** This section might contain suggestions such as further testing from other professionals on staff, vision or hearing tests by the school nurse, recommendation for a review by the eligibility committee, remedial reading assistance, or an ESL evaluation.

2. **Recommendations to the teacher:** This section should contain useful information for the teacher including an indication of the conditions under which the child learns best. The teacher is probably mainly interested in "What do I do to help the child learn?" Keep in mind that even before you begin the evaluation process, you should ask the teacher what he or she has already tried in an attempt to alleviate the problems. This should be done so that your recommendations do not include suggestions already attempted by the teacher. Doing this will avoid having your recommendations being viewed as "nothing I haven't already tried before."

3. **Recommendations to the parent:** This part should be very practical, direct, and diplomatic. The suggestions should also be inclusive enough to answer the questions "why" and "how" so that parents do not have to interpret them. Finally, each subsection should contain recommendations in priority order. Try to number each recommendation separately for purposes of clarity. For examples of recommendations to the school, parents, and teachers, see the following model report.

MODEL REPORT

Manassa Public Schools
Manassa, NY
Privileged and Confidential Information

Name of Student: Jessica Willow	**School:** Meadow Lane
Address: 31 Apple Tree Rd Manassa, N.Y.	**Teacher:** Mrs. Gaines
Phone: 742–1097	**Referred by:** Child Study Team
Date of Birth: 1/9/2000	**Date of Testing:** March 22, 23, 2011
Grade: 5	**Date of Report:** April 1, 2011
Parent's Names: John/Patricia	**Chronological Age:** 11–2
	Examiner: Ms. Tracy Doe

Reason for Referral

Jessica was referred for a comprehensive assessment as the result of a suspected disability.

Background History

Family History: Jessica and her family are living on the first floor of Mrs. Willow's mother's house, and her mother occupies the upstairs space. Jessica has two sisters who both live with her named Margaret and Mary. Margaret is 16 years old, and Mary is 13 years old. Jessica is currently sharing a bedroom with her sister, Mary. Mrs. Willow is currently 42, and Mr. Willow is 46 years old. Mrs. Willow has an Associates Degree from Nassau Community College and works part-time at a grocery store. Mr. Willow has a Bachelor's Degree from Hofstra University and is currently a middle manager at a Sears Department Store. Jessica seems to have a limited amount of hobbies. She loves to read and is currently reading Animal Farm. Mrs. Willow noticed that she doesn't have good eye hand coordination when she plays videogames, and also noticed that she is uncoordinated when she tried to play soccer. She has tried Brownies, but couldn't keep up with all of the projects, some of which were "made fun of" by other members. Mrs. Willow says that Jessica is very responsible when it comes to caring for her dog, Pedro. She feeds him, walks him, and plays with him. Mrs. Willow stated that Jessica's past teachers noticed how responsible she was and let her take home the classroom pets for a couple of days as well.

Developmental History: Mrs. Willow indicated that Jessica was the result of a full-term pregnancy. However, it was a difficult birth because she needed a forceps delivery due to the umbilical cord complications. Mrs. Willow stated that the doctor said the was no anoxia that resulted from the situation. Jessica did not have to spend a long time in the hospital, and there were no complications from the forceps delivery. She also had an Apgar scale of 8 at the hospital, which is in good health range. Mrs. Willow stated that Jessica had no childhood illnesses. She was healthy and was on no medications. She also had food allergies when she was younger, but they seem to have gone away with age. In terms of development, Mrs. Willow stated that Jessica walked a little later than usual, and talked very late. However, when she did talk, she was talking in full sentences with good articulation and good vocabulary.

According to Mrs. Willow, Jessica was a picky eater growing up. She would eat a little bit, leave, and then come back later and eat a little more. Jessica seemed to have difficulty falling asleep at night, and it was also difficult for her to wake up in the morning. Mrs. Willow stated that it wasn't impossible for her to wake up, but definitely challenging. She started developing somatic difficulties such as stomach aches and fevers, so Mrs. Willow kept her home. According to Mrs. Willow, Jessica's doctor said these symptoms were due to anxiety, and they were causing her to get sick. Mrs. Willow said that Jessica has had no traumatic experiences growing up. She also said that she was border line with her vision, so the eye doctor gave her glasses to try. However, the doctor said not to force her to wear them if she didn't want to. She often left them at home and did not use them for school.

Academic History: Mrs. Linus, Jessica's kindergarten teacher indicated that Jessica was a very sweet little girl. At first, she seemed to have some anxiety about being in school. She talked about wanting to go home but after a few weeks that behavior subsided. Jessica seemed to be somewhat slower than her peers in cutting, coloring, writing and other fine and gross motor areas.

When Mrs. Linus started getting into reading sounds and so on Jessica seemed to be more involved. On math tasks she seemed to have a short attention span and seemed confused.

Jessica seemed to need things repeated when it came to directions. Mrs. Linus was concerned so she had Jessica hearing tested by the school nurse and that seemed to be fine. Jessica's desk was always filled with papers even though Mrs. Linus asked her several times to clean it. She always seemed to misplace things especially her math work.

Jessica strengths were in reading, sound recognition, and verbal participation. Mrs. Linus looked back on her Kindergarten screening results again and noticed several high risk issues which she felt needed special attention. She thought she made some progress and hoped that she would continue the progress the next year.

Ms. Padula, Jessica's first grade teacher indicated that Jessica had a somewhat inconsistent year. She seemed to like reading and participated in that activity. She was in the top reading group and seemed to enjoy the status. However, Jessica seemed to avoid written work and math work. She told Ms. Padula that she just forgot to do her assignments. Ms. Padula spoke with Mrs. Willow and she said she would work with Jessica. She thought about referring Jessica but thought that her issues were based in maturity and considering how bright she was she would grow out of them. She suggested to Mrs. Willow that she should work with Jessica over the summer in the areas of writing and spelling which she hoped would help a great deal for the next year.

The physical education teacher had also noted that he saw Jessica as a child with coordination issues but felt that it is was developmental and she would mature with age.

Jessica was also administered the Stanford Achievement Test which resulted in the following national percentiles:

Subtest	Reading Comp.	Vocabulary	Math Applications	Math Computation	Math Operations	Total Reading	Total Math
National Percentile	87	85	15	14	12	86	15

Mrs. Bellow, Jessica's second grade teacher indicated that Jessica had struggled in her class except in reading. She seemed to begin having social and academic problems as the year progressed. She was going to refer her for testing but it was late in the year. She spoke with Mrs. Willow who said she had been working with Jessica but would increase it. She told her that she needed a great deal of math help and hoped Jessica would mature and grow out of her resistance to school. She indicated that Jessica was a likable child with a great deal of potential.

Jessica seemed to shine in reading, which was her favorite area. She was far ahead of the other children so Mrs. Bellows had her read to the Kindergarten children which she loved. She also had her work in the library with Mrs. Carson who enjoyed her company very much.

In class Jessica seemed to often daydream and wander off and Mrs. Bellow had to bring her back to the reality of the situation rather often.

Mrs. Bellow stated that Mrs. Willow was very cooperative and they had several meetings that year to discuss Jessica's issues. She did not get the opportunity to meet Mr. Willow.

Mrs. Kapson, Jessica's third grade teacher indicated that Jessica seemed to have a difficult year in third grade. Her attendance was a serious problem and she seemed overwhelmed by the work. Mrs. Kapson spoke to Mrs. Willow several times about her attendance and she indicated that Jessica was sick in the mornings so she kept her home.

She stated that Jessica was an avid reader, but her skills in writing and spelling held her back from handing in work. She seemed bright and contributed to class discussions. Mrs. Kapson had several conferences with Mrs., Willow although she never had the opportunity to meet with Jessica's father. Jessica often did not finish work in class and had to frequently take it home to finish.

Jessica was also administered the Stanford Achievement Test which resulted in the following national percentiles:

Subtest	Reading Comp.	Vocabulary	Math Applications	Math Computations	Math Operations	Total Reading	Total Math
National Percentile	87	86	13	15	12	86	14

Jessica was also administered the Otis-Lennon School Abilities Test which resulted in the following school abilities index (SAI) and national percentiles:

	Total	Verbal	Nonverbal
SAI	112	119	96
National Percentile	76	79	45

Mrs. Garcia, Jessica's fourth grade teacher indicated that Jessica had a very inconsistent year. She was very concerned about her lateness's and absence patterns and spoke at length with the mother. Mrs. Willow indicated that she would work on it. Mrs. Garcia indicated that Jessica's reading was exceptional and so was her language and vocabulary. She had definite problems in math, spelling, and writing. She expressed her ideas very nicely but could not seem to place her ideas coherently on paper. Mrs. Garcia was concerned about her work and considered referring her but felt she might grow out of it. She spoke with her mother and gave her suggestions on helping her at home. Mrs. Garcia tried to help her in school but the techniques she used did not seem to work. She thought that she will grow out of it since she was such a bright girl. She judged her reading to be above average, spelling and writing below average, and math below average.

Mrs. Gaines, Jessica's fifth grade teacher indicated that Jessica was new to this school this year. Her parents moved within the district but she was attending another school in the district. Jessica was being referred because she was not performing in school up to her ability. In math she was below level and frequently omitted key steps when performing mathematical operations. Mrs. Gaines was not sure if she understood what she was doing. Jessica also did not know her basic math facts and seemed unable to memorize them. When she did do her math she had poorly controlled handwriting and confused arrangement of numerals and signs on the page. Jessica's handwriting was poor and often illegible. As a result it affected her class work and essays on tests. Jessica's spelling was also a major problem in that she often added unrelated letters, reversed syllables, omitted letters and had trouble with spacing and letter formation.

Jessica was an excellent reader and was in the top reading group. She participated in this area but not too many others. However, Mrs. Gaines said that Jessica was also very disorganized and had serious difficulties being neat, structured, and organized in school. As a result her work was often messy. Mrs. Gaines indicated that while a very caring child Jessica often had serious difficulties with time management and the organization of time needed for the completion of tasks in school. Jessica also had trouble copying from a book to her paper, copying from the board to her notebook, and was very awkward, frequently bumping into things around the room.

According to Mrs. Gaines observations, academic skills also seemed poor in computational math, written spelling, art and physical activities. Her reading seemed on grade level but no formal tests had been given. Mrs. Gaines often saw her squinting but Jessica did not wear glasses. Mrs. Gaines sometimes became frustrated because Jessica was very "stubborn" in finishing her class work.

Mrs. Gaines had tried working with her individually and at times she seemed to respond but did not seem as if she can be consistent. She gave up easily and Mrs. Gaines felt that there was more there than he she was able to see.

Mrs. Gaines had spoken to Jessica's parents and had expressed her concerns. They were cooperative and were also looking for answers.

Jessica was also administered the Stanford Achievement Test which resulted in the following national percentiles:

Subtest	Reading Comp.	Vocabulary	Math Applications	Math Computation	Math Operations	Total Reading	Total Math
National Percentile	88	88	12	14	13	86	13

Jessica was also administered the Otis-Lennon School Abilities Test which resulted in the following school abilities index (SAI) and national percentiles:

	Total	Verbal	Nonverbal
SAI	110	115	93
National Percentile	75	77	44

Jessica was also rated on her behaviors as seen in the classroom by Mrs. Gaines. According to this rating scale, Jessica exhibited the following behaviors most to all of the time in the classroom; being anxious, being withdrawn, being moody, being easily distractible, having a short attention span, not completing work, daydreaming, being disorganized, being easily confused, being a poor speller, having poor fine motor skills, being slow in her completion of tasks, having poor number concepts, being painfully shy, being a slow starter, being inconsistent, being fearful of new situations, procrastinating, rarely taking chances, problems with writing, problems with math, poor balance and coordination, poor gross motor skills, and racing/drawing difficulties.

The areas that Jessica did not seem to have trouble in were being disruptive, frequent fighting, being impulsive, being argumentative, being a poor reader, having limited reading comprehension, having faulty articulation, having problems judging time, having poor logical reasoning and thinking skills, defying authority, being critical to others, being controlling, having hyperactivity, being over reactive, having poor vocabulary usage, having poor expressive language ability, having inadequate work attack skills, and having difficulty with abstract concepts.

Social History: Mrs. Linus, Jessica's kindergarten teacher indicated that socially Jessica got along well with the other children in the class. Although she was not a very active participant, she was well liked by the other children who reached out to her a great deal.

Ms. Padula, Jessica's first grade teacher stated that Jessica did not seem to be part of any particular group of students, although the other children never mistreated her. On the playground she said Jessica would sometimes wander off by herself.

Mrs. Bellows, Jessica's second grade teacher indicated that when she was on the playground Jessica seemed to be a loner. While the other children tried to get her involved she seemed to prefer being by herself.

Mrs. Kapson, Jessica's third-grade teacher indicated that Jessica was tolerated by her peers but had very few real friends. She also indicated that although she was a very articulate girl with an excellent vocabulary, she did not seem to interact with her peers even in small groups. She did however participate regularly in reading discussions and social studies. Mrs. Kapson had her help other children with reading and she seemed very patient and caring toward the other children.

Mrs. Garcia, Jessica's fourth-grade teacher indicated that socially Jessica had definite problems and seemed to be isolated despite attempts by others to engage her. She was not mean to other children, just withdrawn. She frequently became lost in her readings during recess and free time. Mrs. Garcia also stated that Jessica was a sweet girl with a big heart. She took care of all the animals during the year and was very responsible.

Mrs. Gaines, Jessica's fifth-grade teacher indicated that socially, Jessica was not very popular. The other children accepted her but they would rarely seek her out. She was also not very socially assertive and as a result spent a great deal of the day by herself. She did eat lunch with some girls, but she never seemed to interact with them.

Parent's perception of the problems: According to Mrs. Willow, she too struggled when she was younger with learning but grew out of it over time. It did however affect her self esteem. She thinks that Jessica has learning problems like she had, but isn't classified yet.

Behavioral Observation

Interview with student: Jessica was brought to the examiner's office for an interview in order to gather more information on her perception of school and life. Jessica drew a picture of her family that consisted of her dad, middle sister, older sister, mom, herself, her grandmother, and her dog, Pedro. Jessica stated that she loves talking and learning to cook with her grandmother. She also eats dinner with her grandmother and mother a lot of the time because her dad works late and her sisters are busy. Jessica said that she takes care of her dog Pedro and likes the fact that he seems to know that she is the one that feeds him and plays with him. Jessica also recalled an enjoyable time with her father when he explained the history and background of the book she was reading called "Animal Farm."

According to Jessica, her favorite subject is reading, which also seems to be her only hobby and interest other than spending time with her grandmother and dog, Pedro. Jessica said that her teacher, Mrs. Gaines allows her to read to a kindergarten class, which she really enjoys because she can act out the story and entertain the children. She also likes her teacher Mrs. Gaines, especially because she allows her to do her book reports on video tape because she has trouble with writing.

When asked what her least favorite subject is in school, she replied "Only one?" indicating that she has difficulties in more than one area. She stated that mathematics was her least favorite because she doesn't understand it, gets the signs mixed up, and doesn't know her basic facts. She can read word problems but then doesn't know what do next, which makes her nervous. Her teacher Mrs. Gaines gives her math tables to use during math because she doesn't know the basic facts. Jessica stated that she also has trouble writing essays and using bubble sheets to record her answers. Instead, she was allowed to record her answers in the test book, and that helped her a lot. Jessica also has trouble typing on the computer, and usually resorts to using one finger, but it takes her too long. Jessica stated that a teacher had recommended she use voice recognition software because she is not good with writing. Jessica also stated that she had a bad experience in third grade and said she was out sick a lot during that year.

When asked about her friends at school, Jessica stated that she has a lot of friends, and that she sits with all of the popular girls at lunch. She stated that she doesn't need other friends outside of school because she likes to spend time with her grandmother, and she really doesn't have time to hang out with anyone. She did have a best friend who moved in third grade that she keeps in touch with through email, and she will be visiting Jessica next spring, which she seemed pretty excited about.

Observation during testing: Jessica entered the testing situation in a relatively relaxed and calm manner. She intersected well with the examiner and appeared involved and animated. She asked several questions which may have been a result of some anxiety but this soon subsided. Jessica was very involved and responsive to the sections dealing with reading which was administered first to allow her a foundation of success. However, her attitude and demeanor changed completely when she was asked to do spelling, math and writing. She seemed visually upset and struggled throughout all the tasks. He kept getting angry at herself, calling herself an idiot and stupid when she did not understand a math problem. As the frustration increased the test was stopped to speak with her and try to comfort her. She responded well but tried to explain that this was so very hard and all she does is fail. She was encouraged to do her best and when the test was over her tome again seemed to change back to a more relaxed state.

Tests and Procedures Administered

- Review of Records
- Parent Intake
- Student Interview
- Wechsler Individual Achievement Test 3rd Edition (WIAT-III)

Test Results

Jessica was administered the Wechsler Individual Achievement Test-3rd ed. which resulted in the following results:

Name of Subtest	Standard Score	Classification/Range	Nat. Percentile Rank
Listening Comp.	114	Average	82
Reading Comp.	18	Above Average	88
Math Prob. Solving	76	Low Average	14
Sentence Composition	77	Low Average	11
Word Reading	118	Above Average	83
Essay Composition	70	Low Average	10
Pseudoword Decoding	113	Average	81
Numerical Operations	77	Low Average	13
Oral Expression	111	Average	77
Oral Reading Fluency	118	Above Average	82
Spelling	80	Low Average	12
Math Fluency-Add.	77	Low Average	13
Math Fluency-Sub.	76	Low Average	12
Math Fluency-Multip.	77	Low Average	13

The Listening Comprehension subtest of the WIAT-III measures the student's ability to listen for details. On this subtest Jessica performed in the Average range, earning her a standard score of 114. As indicated by her percentile rank of 82, Jessica performed as well or better than 82 percent of all students when compared to the norms for her age.

On the Reading Comprehension subtest of the WIAT-III students must read a sentence or passage and then answer questions orally to measure their comprehension. On this subtest Jessica's performance was in the Above Average range, earning her a standard score of 118. As indicated by her percentile rank of 88, Jessica performed as well or better than 88 percent of all students when compared to the norms for her age. Her scores represent a significant strength.

The Math Problem Solving asks students to solve math word problems, involving areas such as the basic operations of time, money, and interpreting graphs. On this subtest Jessica's performance was in the Low Average range, earning her a standard score of 76. As indicated by her percentile rank of 14, Jessica performed as well or better than 14 percent of all students when compared to the norms for her age. Her scores represent a significant weakness.

On the Sentence Composition subtest the student is asked to take two or more separate sentences and write one good sentence that means the same thing. On this subtest Jessica performed in the Low Average range earning her a standard score or 77. As indicated by her percentile rank of 11, Jessica performed as well or better than 11 percent of all students when compared to the norms for her age.

The Word Reading subtest of the WIAT-III assesses the student's ability to read familiar words aloud from a list. Both accuracy and speed of response are measured. On this subtest Jessica performed in the Above Average range, earning her a standard score of 118. As indicated by her percentile rank of 83, Jessica performed as well or better than 83 percent of all students when compared to the norms of her age.

On the Essay Composition subtest the student is asked to write an essay about his or her favorite game, including 3 reasons why. On this subtest Jessica performed in the Low Average range earning her a standard score of 70. As indicated by her percentile rank of 10, Jessica performed as well or better than 10 percent of all students when compared to the norms of her age.

The Pseudoword Decoding subtest of the WIAT-III assesses the student's ability to apply phonetic decoding skills. On this subtest Jessica performed in the Average range, earning her a standard score of 113. As indicated by her percentile rank of 81, Jessica performed as well or better than 81 percent of all students when compared to the norms for her age.

The Numerical Operations subtest of the WIAT-III evaluates the student's ability to identify and write dictated numerals and solve written calculation problems and equations involving all basic operations. On this subtest Jessica performed in the Low Average range earning her a standard score of 77. As indicate by her percentile rank of 13, Jessica performed as well or better than 13 percent of all students when compared to the norms for her age.

The Oral Expression of the WIAT-III subtest measures the student's ability to repeat sentences, generate lists of specific kinds of words, describe pictured scenes, and describe pictured activities. Content of answers is scored, but quality of spoken language is not. On this subtest Jessica performed in the Average earning her a standard score of 111. As indicated by her percentile rank of 77, Jessica performed as well or better than 77 percent of all students when compared to the norms for her age.

The Oral Reading Fluency subtest measures the accuracy, rate, ease, and rhythm with which a person reads. On this subtest Jessica performed in the Above Average range earning her a standard score of 118. As indicated by her percentile rank of 82, Jessica performed as well or better than 82 percent of all students when compared to the norms for her age.

The Spelling subtest of the WIAT-III measures the student's ability to spell by a word by its meaning in a sentence. On this subtest Jessica performed in the Low Average range earning her a standard score of 80. As indicated by her percentile rank of 12, Jessica performed as well or better than 12 percent of all students when compared to the norms for her age.

On the Math Fluency-Addition subtest, the student solves as many simple addition problems as he/she can in one minute. On this subtest Jessica performed in the Low Average range earning her a standard score of 77. As indicated by her percentile rank of 13, Jessica performed as well or better than 13 percent of all students when compared to the norms for her age.

On the Math Fluency-Subtraction subtest, the student solves as many simple subtraction problems as he/she can in one minute. On this subtest Jessica performed in the Low Average range earning her a standard score of 76. As indicated by her percentile rank of 12, Jessica performed as well or better than 12 percent of all students when compared to the norms for her age.

On the Math Fluency-Multiplication subtest, the student solves as many simple multiplication problems as he/she can in one minute. On this subtest Jessica performed in the Low Average range earning her a standard score of 77. As indicated by her percentile rank of 13, Jessica performed as well or better than 13 percent of all students when compared to the norms for her age.

Conclusions

Jessica Willow is an 11-year-old fifth-grade girl who was administered the WIAT-III for the purposes of assessing her academic achievement. *Results of the WIAT-III indicated that Jessica obtained Above Average scores in Word Reading (83rd percentile), Reading Comprehension (88th percentile), and Oral Reading Fluency (82nd percentile)* Further, Jessica obtained scores within the Average range on Listening Comprehension (82nd percentile), Pseudoword Decoding (81st percentile), and Oral Expression (77th percentile).

Jessica's deficit areas indicated that she obtained scores within the Low Average range in Math Problem Solving (14th percentile), Sentence Completion (11th percentile), Essay Composition (10th percentile), Numerical Operations (13th percentile), Spelling (12th percentile), Math Fluency Addition (13th percentile), Math Fluency Subtraction (12th percentile), and Math Fluency Multiplication (13th percentile).

Results of testing, observation, history and interviews all seem to indicate that Jessica's pattern is similar to children with moderate to severe learning disabilities.

Recommendations

To The School

1. It is suggested that Jessica be referred for a review by the CSE based on the results of testing, observation, review of records and interviews. This recommendation is based on the findings of a documented educational disability.

To The Teacher

1. It is suggested that Jessica's teacher give fewer spelling words to Jessica each week. Instead of giving her twenty words, she should get ten and have words that she got incorrect the previous week on her new list of words. This will help Jessica stay on task and focused because she will have fewer words to worry about. It will also help her master words she has gotten wrong previous weeks through repetition.
2. Jessica's teacher may want to explore the use of manipulatives, basic fact tables and calculators during math to help give Jessica hands on learning experiences. This will help Jessica with her basic math facts because she will be able to use these resources for harder math problems, instead of having her get confused with the basics.
3. Jessica's teacher may want to set up a positive behavior reward plan, where she can earn reading time when she completes her work and stays on task. This will help Jessica work towards something she enjoys and will hopefully motivate her to finish the work that she starts in class. She can also have this plan set up for Jessica's homework to help Jessica want to complete her homework at home. That way, she can finish the work she needs to and gain time doing something that she loves.
4. It is suggested that Jessica's teacher use a lot of group activities for different subjects to help Jessica interact with other students in the class. This will allow her to be more social in class and will hopefully help her communication skills. A good time to use it would be during reading because Jessica seems to really love it and could help other students if they are struggling. This will give Jessica a sense of pride and leadership, which may help increase her self esteem as well.

5. It is recommended that Jessica's teacher use approaches to help with sentence and essay composition. Ways to do this include having cut outs of words (nouns, verbs, pronouns, etc.) that Jessica has to put together to make a sentence. She can do this on her free time or during any learning centers. This will help her learn the different parts of a sentence and help her later in forming paragraphs and essays. She can have peers partner up with her to explain the process to her, and this will also help promote social interaction.

To The Parent(s):

1. It is crucial for Jessica's parent(s) to structure her day after school. She needs to have a specific time for homework put aside each day so she gets it done. For example, they can set aside 4:00–5:00 every day to complete homework. This will give Jessica a routine to work with so that it becomes a habit. She is more likely to do her homework if she knows that she has to get it done at a certain time.
2. It is very important for Jessica's parent(s) to increase her self esteem by giving her praise constantly throughout the day. There needs to be at least four positive reinforcements each day by means of verbal praise. For example, Jessica's parent(s) could provide her with jobs or activities that would result in a positive outcome. Jessica's self-esteem will increase when she hears these encouraging words from her family because it will allow her to feel good about herself.
3. It is crucial for Jessica's parent(s) to check her math homework. They need to have Jessica complete a couple of problems (4-5) and then stop so they can check her work. They need to check the correct problems first and be positive about anything she gets wrong. This will give Jessica positive feedback to help build her confidence level and sense of accomplishment, which can ultimately lead to an increased feeling of self esteem.
4. It is very important for Jessica's parent(s) to help her with spelling. They can do this by making flash cards of her words for the week and going over them during her homework time every day. Her parent(s) can focus on certain rules that these words might have to help increase her spelling ability. Repetition is very important, and that is why they should go over the words everyday with Jessica. It will help her learn the rules and recognize the words so that she will know them for her spelling test at the end of the week.
5. It is very important for Jessica's parent(s) to encourage her to write and increase her sentence and essay compositions. They can do this by having Jessica write in a journal about her feelings, her day at school, etc. Her parent(s) and teacher can come up with a checklist of things to look for when reading over her entries. When she is done writing, Jessica and her parent(s) can go over what she wrote using the checklist. This will not only help her get her feelings out, but will also help her writing ability through practice. It will give her a sense of ownership because she will be helping her parent(s) correct it and fix it.

Tracy Doe, M.S.
Educational Examiner

CONCLUSION

When all is said and done, the comprehensive report is perhaps the most important part of the special education process. All of the data collection, hard work, statistical analyses, and relevant information now need to be expressed to all those involved. When a report is well written, it explains everything that was found along with appropriate recommendations. As special educators, writing is a critical part of your job. Being able to express yourself clearly helps all those with whom you work. In the end, the comprehensive report should be clear, cogent, and concise. When written professionally, the reader should walk away with a complete and thorough understanding of the testing done, what was found, and recommendations for the future.

Vocabulary

Academic History: This section provides the reader with relevant academic performance during the child's school years.

Background History: The section of the comprehensive report that contains a very thorough description of the child's family history, developmental history, academic history, and social history.

Behavioral Observations: The fourth section of the comprehensive report that includes a description of the child's behavior during the testing sessions. This can be a very important section because it may reinforce what is seen in the class or be very different, in which case the structure of the testing environment should be explored for clues to learning style.

Chronological age: The age of the child at the time of testing.

Conclusions: In this section of the comprehensive report, the examiner indicates in very simple terms to the reader the trends in the child's testing results that may indicate academic strengths and weaknesses, modality strengths and weaknesses, process strengths and weaknesses, and overall diagnosis and level of severity of the problem areas indicated.

Content area by content area approach: In the test results section, results from all the reading, math, spelling, writing, visual, auditory, and motor tests from each evaluation measure are analyzed separately by content area. The examiner hopes to establish patterns of strengths and weaknesses.

Developmental history: The purpose of this information is to give the reader any

relevant background history pertaining to developmental milestones. This section need not read like a hospital report but should contain the basic developmental history.

Family history: This information provides the reader with a general understanding of the family structure, siblings, parental perceptions, and so on.

Identifying Data: The first section of a comprehensive report, which contains all the necessary basic information about the child. This section is important to the reader, especially if further contact is required. It allows the reader to have all the basic information in one place.

Reason for Referral: The second section of the comprehensive report, which explains to the reader the specific reasons for this evaluation. It should not be more than two to three sentences, but should be comprehensive enough to clarify the purpose.

Recommendations: The last section of the comprehensive report and probably the most valuable section for the reader. It should contain practical recommendations that will bring some hope and direction for the identified problem areas.

Social history: This section should provide the reader with an understanding of the child in his or her social world. Group participation, organizations, hobbies, interests, interaction with peers, social style, and so forth should all be discussed.

Test-by-test approach: The test results section analyzes the child's performance on each test separately. It analyzes the results of the different subtests and provides indications of strengths and weaknesses, manner of approach, and indications of whether the scores on the specific test should be considered valid.

Test Results: The section of the comprehensive report that analyzes the results of each test and looks at the child's individual performance on each measure.

Tests and Procedures Administered: The section of the comprehensive report that includes a simple list of the individual tests included in the test battery and any procedures used to enhance the report, such as classroom observation, review of records, parent intake.

18 | ELIGIBILITY PROCEDURES FOR SPECIAL EDUCATION SERVICES

Key Terms

Adaptive physical education
Annual review
Case manager
Change in placement
Cooperative educational services
Declassification
Due process rights
Eligibility committee (EC)
Eligibility committee packet
Evaluation summary sheet
Extended school year

Full-time special class in a general
    education school
General education placement
Home/hospital settings
Homebound instruction
Hospital or institution
Impartial hearing officer
Inclusion classroom
Independent evaluation
Itinerant services
Least restrictive education (LRE)

Local school district
Neighboring school district
Pendency
Private approved schools
Residential school
Resource room program
Special class
Special day school
State operated schools
Triennial review

Chapter Objectives

This chapter focuses on the preparation for presenting the case to the eligibility committee, classification, and placement. After reading this chapter, you should be able to understand the following:

- Overview of the eligibility committee
- Members of the eligibility committee
- Responsibilities of the eligibility committee
- IDEA 2004 and eligibility committee meetings
- Development of the information packet for presentation to the eligibility committee
- Presentation at the eligibility committee by the special education teacher as educational evaluator
- Recommendations for classification
- Specific placement considerations according to IDEA 2004
- Developing the individualized education plan (IEP)
- Appealing the decision of the eligibility committee
- Special meetings of the eligibility committee
- Presentation at the eligibility committee by the special education teacher as classroom teacher
- The annual review
- Suggestions for the special educator's participation in the annual review
- The triennial review
- Declassification of a child in special education

THE ELIGIBILITY COMMITTEE (IEP TEAM)

Once the evaluation process is completed by the MDT, the **eligibility committee** will meet to discuss the results of the evaluations and the school's recommendations. Normally, the individuals who have completed each evaluation discuss the results of the evaluations with the parents prior to the eligibility committee meeting. However, this is an informal process, and recommendations for classification and placement usually are not discussed because that is the responsibility of the eligibility committee. Formally, parents will receive a notice indicating the time and date of an eligibility meeting.

According to IDEA 2004, every public school district is required to have an eligibility committee, which, as previously mentioned, may be referred to as the *IEP committee, committee on special education,* and so forth. If the population of special education students reaches a certain level, then more than one eligibility committee may be formed. Eligibility committees are responsible for the identification of children with disabilities within the district and recommending appropriate education at public expense for students identified as having disabilities.

Members of the Eligibility Committee

The eligibility committee is usually made up of members mandated by IDEA 2004 and assigned members whom the board of education deems necessary. Most states require that certain professionals and individuals be core members. Consistent with IDEA 2004 regulations, these members must include

1. The parents of a child with a disability
2. Not less than one regular education teacher of such child (if the child is or may be participating in the regular education environment)
3. Not less than one special education teacher of the child or, where appropriate, not less than one special education provider of such child
4. A representative of the school district who is qualified to provide or supervise the provision of special education and is knowledgeable about the general curriculum and the availability of resources in the district (this individual can also be the special education teacher, the special education provider, or the school psychologist, provided he or she meets the other qualifications)
5. An individual who can interpret the instructional implications of evaluation results (this individual can also be the regular education teacher, the special education teacher, the special education provider, the school psychologist, a direct representative, or a person having knowledge or special expertise regarding the student if that person is determined by the district to have knowledge and expertise to fulfill this role) ‾
6. The child, where appropriate
7. A school physician, if requested in writing by the student's parent or the district at least 72 hours prior to the meeting
8. An additional parent member who is a parent of a student with a disability residing in the district or a neighboring district; however, the participation of this member is not required if the student's parents request that this additional parent member not participate in the meeting
9. At the discretion of the parent or the district, other individuals who have knowledge and special expertise regarding the student, including related services personnel, as appropriate

Responsibilities of the Eligibility Committee

The eligibility committee is charged with many important responsibilities both before and after a child is classified in special education. Some of the responsibilities of the eligibility committee are discussed in the following sections.

During the Initial Eligibility Meeting

1. Following appropriate procedures and taking appropriate action for a child referred as having a suspected disability
2. Determining the suitable classification for a child with a suspected disability (see Chapter 1 for a detailed explanation of the possible choices for a suspected disability)
3. Reviewing and evaluating all relevant information that may appear for each student with a disability
4. Determining the least restrictive educational (LRE) setting for any child having been classified as having a disability
5. Finalizing the child's IEP

After the Child Is Classified

1. Reviewing, at least annually, the status of the child, known as an annual review
2. Evaluating the adequacy of programs, services, and facilities for the child
3. Maintaining ongoing communication in writing to parents in regard to planning, modifying, changing, reviewing, placing, or evaluating the program, classification, or educational plan of the child
4. Advising the board of education as to the status of and recommendations for the child
5. Making sure that every three years the child is retested with a full educational and psychological battery, known as a triennial review

Most eligibility committees try to remain as informal as possible to reduce the anxiety of the situation. This is a crucial issue because a parent may enter a room with numerous professionals and feel overwhelmed or intimidated. The parent member usually serves as a liaison and advocate for the parent(s), establishing contact prior to the meeting to reduce anxiety and alleviate any concerns that the parent(s) may have. School personnel should also be in contact with the parent(s) prior to the meeting to go over the process, their rights, and what may take place at the meeting. At no time should anyone in contact with the parent(s) prior to the meeting give them false hope, make promises, or second guess the eligibility committee. What needs to be communicated are procedural issues and options, and the awareness that it is the eligibility committee that will make the recommendation, not one individual. Further, the parent(s) must be made aware of their rights, and you should make sure they understand their right to due process if they do not agree with the eligibility committee's recommendations. Making sure parents understand their rights before the meeting may reduce the possibility of conflict.

IDEA 2004 AND ELIGIBILITY COMMITTEE MEETINGS

1. IDEA 2004 makes it clear that parents have a right to participate in eligibility committee meetings with respect to the identification, evaluation, educational placement, and provision of FAPE (free and appropriate public education) for their child.

2. IDEA 2004 regulations provide that a meeting not include informal or unscheduled conversations involving school district personnel and conversations on issues such as teaching methodology, lesson plans, or coordination of service provision if those issues are not addressed in the child's IEP.

3. IDEA 2004 regulations also provide that if neither parent can participate in a meeting in which a decision is to be made relating to the educational placement of their child, the school district must either use other methods to ensure their participation, including individual conference calls or videoconferencing. The eligibility committee may make a placement decision without parental participation in the decision, but in such an instance the school district must have a record of its attempt to ensure parental involvement, including

   • Detailed records of telephone calls made or attempted and the results of those calls
   • Copies of correspondence sent to the parents and any responses received
   • Detailed records of visits made to the parents' home or place of employment and the results of those visits.

4. IDEA 2004 regulations further require that school districts inform parents of the purpose of an eligibility meeting and those who will be in attendance in addition to the time and location of the meeting.

5. IDEA 2004 regulations indicate that it may be appropriate for a school district to ask the parents to inform it of any individuals the parents will be bringing to an eligibility meeting and encourage parents to do so.

DEVELOPING THE INFORMATION PACKET FOR THE ELIGIBILITY COMMITTEE

Once the MDT has considered all the information and completed the evaluations, intakes, assessments, and so on, team members need to prepare the necessary information packet that will be presented to the district's eligibility committee for review of the case for possible classification and special education programs and services. This information will be viewed by all the members of the eligibility committee along with the parents and other individuals so designated, such as an advocate or lawyer. This **eligibility committee packet** is a crucial part of the special education process because most of the committee members will not be familiar with the child. Because the information gathered and forwarded will be used to determine the child's educational future, it is imperative that the MDT present the most thorough and practical information to the committee.

To facilitate the process of preparing the required documentation for presentation, the team usually designates a **case manager,** the specific individual whose responsibility it will be to gather, organize, and forward the packet to the eligibility committee. The case manager can be anyone, but in many cases it will be either the special education teacher or the psychologist. All districts will have their own specific forms and guidelines for presentation to the committee. However, in most of these cases the information presented, regardless of the forms, will be somewhat the same.

This section of the chapter presents an example of what the case manager may need to forward to the eligibility committee. It is a typical list of materials included in the eligibility packet that might be required by the committee for a review of a student for classification. These materials may vary from district to district and from state to state.

Required Forms

1. **Initial referral to the MDT from school staff:** The child study team fills out this form when the team suspects that the child being reviewed may have an educational disability. This type of referral occurs when a child is being assessed for special education by the MDT for the very first time and usually involves children previously in the mainstream who have had no prior services. (See Chapter 8 for further explanation and an example of this form.)

2. **Initial referral to MDT from parent/guardian:** This form is filled out if the parent makes the initial referral for assessment to the MDT for a suspected disability, which is part of the parent's **due process rights** (See Chapter 8 for further explanation and an example of this form.)

3. **Assessment plan and parent consent:** This plan and form must be signed and dated by a parent prior to evaluation and is part of the parent's due process rights. (See Chapter 8 for further explanation.)

4. **Social history form:** This form is the result of a recent parent intake and provides the most recent pertinent background information on the child. (See Chapter 8 for further explanation and an example of this form.)

5. **Medical report form:** This is usually filled out by the teacher or school nurse and includes the latest medical information on the child within the last year that may be related to the child's learning problems.

6. **Classroom observation form:** This form is the result of an on-site visit observation by some member of the child study team.

Evaluations (Initial Referral)

1. **Psychological:** A full psychological evaluation is required, including all identifying data, reason for referral, background and developmental history, prior testing results, observations, tests administered, test results (including a breakdown of scaled scores), conclusions, and recommendations. This evaluation must be conducted within one year of the eligibility committee meeting. It may also be helpful to include any prior evaluations done over the years.

2. **Educational:** An educational evaluation is required, including identifying data, reason for referral, academic history, prior testing results, observations, tests administered, test results, conclusions, and recommendations. This report should identify achievement strengths and weaknesses.

3. **Speech/language:** A speech/language evaluation including identifying data, reason for referral, observations, tests administered, test results, conclusions, and recommendations should be included if applicable. A description of the severity of the language deficit should also be included and, if possible, the prognosis.

4. **Vocational (secondary level only):** A copy of the child's Differential Aptitude Test results or other measures of vocational aptitude should be included, if applicable.

5. **Other (e.g., occupational therapist, physical therapist, ESL, reading):** From time to time, parents or the school will have a variety of reports from outside agencies, such as medical, neurological, psychiatric, occupational therapy screening, physical therapy screening, psychological, audiological, visual training, and so forth. These reports should be included only when they are relevant to the possible disability. If outside reports are to be used in lieu of the district's own evaluations, they should be fairly recent, within the past 6 months to 1 year.

Guidance and School Materials (Initial Referral)

1. **Child's schedule:** A copy of the student's daily school schedule.
2. **Transcript of past grades:** All the child's report card grades should be attached as far back as possible, or a report indicating the patterns of grades throughout the child's school career should be included.
3. **Latest report card:** The most up-to-date report card should be included.
4. **Teacher's reports:** Teacher reports in behavioral terms should be included from all the child's teachers.
5. **Standardized achievement test scores:** Many schools require standardized achievement testing in certain grades. Any and all scores should be provided to reinforce historical patterns or levels of ability.
6. **Discipline information:** Any referrals to the principal, dean, and so on should be included as well as descriptions of incidents and disposition.
7. **CST related documents (i.e., minutes):** This provides the eligibility committee with pertinent information regarding prior intervention strategies and procedures followed prior to the referral.
8. **Attendance records:** Attendance patterns and records should be provided, especially if this is a recurring issue and a serious symptom.

Other Materials

Some schools also may include the following materials in a draft form. This draft becomes a working model at the eligibility committee meeting between the committee and the parent, and the final version is mailed to the parent after the meeting.
These may include:

1. **SPAM Needs (Social, Physical, Academic, and Management):** In some states and school districts, a working draft copy of the child's needs should be included in the eligibility packet. These needs will provide the committee with an idea of the environmental, educational, social, and physical requirements under which the child may learn best.
2. **Draft IEP including goals and objectives:** In some states and school districts, a working draft copy of the IEP is prepared prior to the eligibility meeting. This is a basic working draft of the IEP, not the final draft, because no IEP can be finalized without parental involvement (for a more extensive explanation, see Chapter 20).
3. **Testing modifications worksheet:** This worksheet outlines the suggested test and classroom modifications being suggested and the supporting data for such recommendations. As will be discussed in Chapter 20, testing modifications are a component of the child's IEP. The modifications must be consistent with the criteria established. The worksheet may be completed by a member of the MDT or school staff to be processed as a draft recommendation for discussion at the eligibility committee meeting.

Depending on the state, there are usually four circumstances in which students with disabilities may be eligible to receive test modifications:

- Students with disabilities whose individualized education program includes test modifications
- Students who are declassified by the eligibility committee
- Students with disabilities whose Section 504 Accommodation Plan includes test modifications
- Students who acquire disabilities shortly before test administration

In making its decision regarding the need for test modifications, the EC reviews all available information regarding the student's individual needs. Such information might include recent evaluations, previous school records and IEPs, classroom observations, and the student's experience on previous tests. Information and suggestions from the student's teachers, related service providers, and parents should also be sought. Testing modifications are to be limited to specific needs of the student.

If such a determination is made by the EC and documented in the recommendation for declassification, the test modification(s) must continue to be consistently provided to the student for the balance of his or her public school education. The continuation of test modifications upon declassification, however, is not automatic. During subsequent school years, if it is felt that such modification(s) is no longer appropriate, the school staff is to meet with the student's parent to review and document the discontinuation or revision of the test modification(s).

The school principal may modify testing procedures for general education students who experience temporary (e.g., broken arm) or long-term (e.g., paraplegic) disabilities shortly before the administration of state exams. In such cases when sufficient time is not available for the development of an IEP or 504 plan, principals may authorize testing modifications. Also, if the student is expected to continue to need test modifications, the principal should make the appropriate referral for the development of an IEP or 504 plan.

4. **Extended school year worksheet:** This worksheet provides the eligibility committee with the information and criteria necessary to make a recommendation for extended school services in July and August. At annual review meetings, parents of students with disabilities may ask for special education services during the summer (**extended school year**).

5. **Extended school year criteria:** Depending on the state, the law may indicate the extended school year service be considered by the eligibility committee when a student experiences substantial regression. Substantial regression means a student's inability to maintain developmental levels due to a loss of skill or knowledge during the months of July and August of such severity as to require an inordinate period of review at the beginning of the school year to reestablish and maintain IEP goals and objectives mastered at the end of the previous school year. For example, a teacher would project November 1 of the upcoming school year as the target date for the student to reacquire skills demonstrated at the end of the previous school year (a typical period of review or reteaching is up to 40 school days). Classroom teachers and/or service providers are expected to provide documentation (qualitative and/or quantitative) as to the evidence of regression discussion at the eligibility committee meeting.

An analysis of students' substantial regression, if any, may be monitored during school vacation periods (winter, spring, summer). Note the above definition includes not only regression but also an inordinate period of time to reestablish and maintain IEP goals/objectives.

Extended school year services are not provided in order for students to improve their skills. Such instruction is a parent responsibility. Extended year services may differ from services provided during the school year. The eligibility committee will determine the type, amount, and duration of services to be provided. Extended school year services may be provided at a different location than provided during the school year.

6. **Adaptive physical education worksheet:** If a child's disability prevents him or her from participating in a regular, mainstreamed physical education program, then the district must provide adaptive alternatives that capitalize on the student's abilities. This worksheet outlines the criteria exhibited by the child for possible **adaptive physical education**. The

behaviors, supporting reports, and data are included for the EC in order to make a recommendation. The physical education teacher in consultation with other EC staff members usually completes this. This worksheet then becomes a draft recommendation for discussion at the EC.

7. **Other:** This includes any other information not noted in the above categories. In conclusion, the above forms and information will represent a picture of the child with a disability including strengths, weaknesses, recommendations, and any other information that will assist the eligibility committee in making the most educationally sound decision.

PRESENTATION TO THE EC BY THE SPECIAL EDUCATION TEACHER AS EDUCATIONAL EVALUATOR

After meeting with the parents to discuss the results, the individuals who evaluated the student must now focus on the presentation of test results at the eligibility meeting. If your role on the MDT has resulted from your evaluation of the child, then you need to keep the following in mind:

1. Prior to the meeting, many school districts will ask that you meet with the parents and go over your results.
2. Make sure that you have your report complete and typed at least one week to ten days prior to the eligibility meeting. In some districts, the eligibility committee requires that the entire packet be forwarded a week in advance.
3. Prior to the meeting, outline the important points of the report that you wish to make. Do not go through the report at the eligibility meeting looking for the issues that you feel need to be discussed. Preparation will make you look more professional.
4. Make sure you report strengths as well as weaknesses.
5. Even though everyone should have copies of your report in front of them, the length of the report may make it impossible for them to filter out the crucial sections in the time allotted for the meeting. Therefore, you may want to develop a one-page **evaluation summary sheet** that clearly outlines what you will be presenting, to be handed out as you begin your presentation.
6. Remember that this is not a parent conference to review the entire report. You may have done that earlier and, if so, keep it brief and highlight the important issues. Several individuals may need to report results or speak, and the committee may have several meetings that day.
7. If you feel that the nature of the case may require more time than that normally set aside by the eligibility committee for a review, then call the chairperson and make a request for a longer meeting time. It is very uncomfortable when crucial meetings have to be ended because of time constraints.
8. Prepare to answer questions about your findings or some aspect of the report by either a parent, committee member, lawyer (sometimes brought by the parent), and others. Even though this may not happen, you should be ready to answer without being defensive or anxious. Carefully looking over your report and being prepared is the best advice.

CLASSIFICATION RECOMMENDATIONS OF THE EC

In developing recommendations, all the members of the EC present will discuss the evaluations presented and any other pertinent information on the child. The first issue decided will be whether the child has an educational disability that adversely affects his or her educational performance. The EC will review the EC packet prepared by the school and ask any sitting member pertinent questions necessary to clarify the information. If an educational disability is found, the child will be classified according to the categories outlined in IDEA 2004. There are a number of classifications from which the committee can draw, such as learning disabled or emotion ally disturbed (see Chapter 1 for a complete description of these classifications).

The concept of **least restrictive education (LRE)** applies to the placement of students with disabilities in the most advantageous educational placement suitable for their needs. Contrary to the belief of many teachers and parents, LRE does not mean every student with a disability should be placed in a general education classroom.

LRE PLACEMENT CONSIDERATIONS ACCORDING TO IDEA 2004

A placement is the location where the special educational program will be provided. According to IDEA 2004, the requirements involving least restrictive environment are as follows:

1. In selecting the LRE for a student with a disability, school districts must consider any potential harmful effect on the child or on the quality of services that he or she needs.
2. School districts may not remove a student with a disability from education in age-appropriate general education classrooms solely because of needed modifications in the general curriculum.
3. LRE requirements apply to both nonacademic and extracurricular activities, including meals and recess periods, athletics, transportation, health services, recreational activities, special interest groups or school sponsored clubs, referral to agencies that provide assistance to individuals with disabilities and employment of students, including both employment by the public agency and assistance in making outside employment available.

IDEA 2004 regulations also indicate that

a. The determination of an appropriate placement for a child whose behavior is interfering with the education of others requires careful consideration of whether the child can appropriately function in the general education classroom if provided appropriate behavioral supports, strategies and interventions.
b. If a student's behavior in the general education classroom, even with the provision of appropriate behavioral supports, strategies and interventions, would significantly impair the learning of others, that placement would not meet her needs and would not be appropriate for that child.

The placement of students with disabilities is the responsibility of the eligibility committee with the input of staff and parents and final consent by the parents. This committee must analyze all the available information and determine the best "starting placement" for the child that will ensure success and provide the child with the highest level of stimulation and experience for his or her specific disability and profile of strengths and weaknesses.

To accomplish this task, the eligibility committee chooses from a variety of placements that range in levels of restriction, including class size, student–teacher ratio, length of program, and degree of mainstreaming. In the normal course of events, it is hoped that children should be placed in a more restrictive environment only if it is to their educational advantage. However, they should be moved to a less restrictive setting as soon as they are capable of being educated in that environment. The placements below follow a path from least restrictive to most restrictive.

GENERAL EDUCATION PLACEMENT. **General education placement** is the least restrictive placement for all children. This placement alone, without some type of special education supportive services, is not suitable for a child with a disability and is usually considered unsuitable by the eligibility committee.

INCLUSION CLASSROOM. **Inclusion classroom** placement involves the maintenance of the child in a general education classroom assisted by the presence of a second teacher who is certified in special education.

GENERAL EDUCATION PLACEMENT WITH CONSULTING TEACHER ASSISTANCE. A consultant teacher model is used when supportive special education services are required, but the eligibility committee feels that the child will be better served while remaining in the classroom rather than being pulled out for services. Because the child remains within the class, even though he or she is receiving services, this placement is considered the next LRE setting.

GENERAL EDUCATION PLACEMENT WITH SOME SUPPORTIVE SERVICES. General education placement with supportive services may be used for students with mild disabilities who require supportive services but can remain in the general education class for the majority of the day. The services that may be applied to this level include adaptive physical education, speech and language therapy, in-school individual or group counseling, physical therapy, and occupational therapy.

GENERAL EDUCATION PLACEMENT WITH ITINERANT SPECIALIST ASSISTANCE. **Itinerant services** are services subcontracted by the district and provided by outside agencies. These services are usually provided for students when the disability is such that the district wishes to maintain the child in the district, but there are not a sufficient number of students with that disability to warrant hiring a teacher. An example of this may be a hard-of-hearing child who can maintain a general education class placement as long as supportive itinerant services by a teacher specializing in hearing impairments are provided.

GENERAL EDUCATION PLACEMENT WITH RESOURCE ROOM ASSISTANCE. A **resource room program** is usually provided for students who need supportive services but can successfully remain within the general education classroom for the majority of the day. This type of program is a "pullout" program, and the services are usually provided in a separate room. The student–teacher ratio with this type of service is usually 5:1, and the amount of time spent within the resource room cannot exceed 50 percent of the child's day.

SPECIAL CLASS PLACEMENT WITH PART TIME IN THE GENERAL EDUCATION CLASS. Part-time placement is for students who need a more restrictive setting for learning, behavioral, or intellectual reasons and cannot be successful in a full-time general education class or with a pullout supportive service, but can be successfully mainstreamed (part-time participation in a general education classroom setting) for a part of the school day. The special education teacher determines the nature of the mainstream experience.

FULL-TIME SPECIAL CLASS IN A GENERAL EDUCATION SCHOOL. A **full-time special class in a general education school** placement is viewed as the LRE setting for students whose disability does not permit successful participation in any type of general education class setting, even for part of the day. The students in a special class usually require a very structured, closely monitored program on a daily basis but not so restrictive as to warrant an out-of-district placement. These students can handle the rules and structure of a general education school building but not the freedom or style of a less restrictive setting within the school.

SPECIAL DAY SCHOOL OUTSIDE THE SCHOOL DISTRICT.   A **special day school** is a type of restrictive educational setting that is a desirable placement for students whose disability is so severe that they may require a more therapeutic environment and closer monitoring by specially trained special education teachers or staff members. The child is transported at district expense to the placement, and many state policies try to limit travel time on the bus to no more than one hour.

These types of programs may have student–teacher–aide ratios of 6:1:1, 6:1:2, 9:1:1, 9:1:2, 12:1:1, or 15:1:1, depending on the severity of the child's disability. The more severe the disability, the lower the student–teacher ratio. These programs can run 10 or 12 months, again depending on the severity of the disability and the individual needs of the child.

RESIDENTIAL SCHOOL.   **Residential school** placements are considered the next most restrictive placement. Not only does the student with a disability receive education within this setting but also usually resides there for the school term. The nature and length of home visits depend on several factors that are usually determined by the residential school staff after evaluation and observation. For some students, home visits may not take place at all, whereas others may go home every weekend.

Some students are placed in residential placements by the court. In this case, the child's local school district is only responsible to provide the costs of the educational portion, including related services if needed.

HOMEBOUND INSTRUCTION.   **Homebound instruction** provides a very restrictive setting that is usually for students who are in the process of transition between programs and have yet to be placed. It should never be used as a long-term placement because of the social restriction and limitations. This option is also used when a child is restricted to his or her house because of an illness, injury, and so on, and this option remains the only realistic educational service until the child recovers. Homebound instruction requires an adult at home when the teacher arrives or can be held at a community center, library, or some other site deemed appropriate by the eligibility committee.

HOSPITAL OR INSTITUTION.   The most restrictive setting used is a **hospital or institution**. Although this is the most restrictive setting, it may be the LRE setting for certain students, such as situations of attempted suicide by an adolescent, pervasive clinical depression, or severe or profound retardation.

In conclusion, the least restrictive educational setting is not something that is etched in concrete. It is normally reviewed every year at the annual review, and changes are made in either direction should the situation warrant it.

Once the EC determines the most suitable LRE, committee members will need to determine the facility or program that best fits their decision. The following examples are types of placements that the eligibility committee may consider for the LRE and are listed in order of educational restriction.

LOCAL SCHOOL DISTRICT.   The child's home school in the **local school district**, depending on the severity of the disability, will generally provide the types of services he or she requires. This is preferential for the many reasons previously discussed. Maintaining the child in his or her home school should be the parents' and the district's goal. This, of course, is not always possible. If not, the next step is another school in the district.

NEIGHBORING SCHOOL DISTRICT.   Due to the nature of special education programs, all special education services are not offered within every district. The child's local school may arrange for participation in necessary programs and services in **neighboring school districts** if they cannot be provided within the child's home district.

COOPERATIVE EDUCATIONAL SERVICES.   **Cooperative educational service** agencies are usually set up by your state to assist local districts with the student population or specific services one or more districts cannot provide them.

HOME/HOSPITAL SETTINGS.   There may be times when a child needs temporary instruction at home or in a **hospital setting** due to severe illness or special circumstances indicated on the IEP. The key term here is *temporary*. The instruction should approximate what is offered in school within reasonable limits. Home and hospital instruction is highly restrictive; the continuing need for such services should be assessed frequently, and this service should be seen as temporary. State laws may vary on the minimum amount of educational time allotted to children involved in these services. A general guide should be two hours per day of individual instruction for a secondary student and one hour per day for an elementary-grade student.

PRIVATE APPROVED SCHOOLS.   School districts may place students in private schools, special act schools (schools set up by the state to provide services for a child with a disability), or residential placements approved by the State Education Department. These **private approved schools** may be located in or out of state. Students placed in such facilities have such diverse needs that the home school district may not be able to service them due to the severity of their medical, physical, mental, or emotional needs.

STATE OPERATED SCHOOLS FOR THE DEAF, BLIND, AND SEVERELY EMOTIONALLY DISTURBED.   These state operated schools are examples of educational programs that are available for students with educational needs who require a school with a special focus.

It is the responsibility of the eligibility committee to provide programs based on the least restrictive environment concept. Remember, it is important to provide programs that are in close proximity to the child's home (some states limit this to one hour on the bus). The child should have involvement with his or her peers without disabilities. Finally, the program must be based on the student's needs.

When considering any of the above placements, everyone works toward providing the best possible placement for the child in the least restrictive environment. However, the school district, on the other hand, needs to provide only an appropriate placement, not the best placement, in a program that is appropriate to the child's needs, as close to home as possible.

DEVELOPING THE IEP

During the meeting, the eligibility committee, along with the parent(s), should finalize the various components of the child's IEP. This final draft document will then be mailed home along with the minutes of the meeting, the parents' rights, and other necessary forms for their approval. (See Chapter 20 for an extensive discussion of IEP development.)

Appealing the Decision of the Eligibility Committee

The process of identifying and finding an appropriate educational placement for a child with a disability should be a joint process between the district and the family. Assuming that the parents agree with the eligibility committee's decisions, the parents will sign off on the IEP, and the child's program will begin as of the start date mandated in the IEP. When both the parents and the eligibility committee work in the best interests of the child, the process can be very positive and rewarding. However, there can be times when the family and the district disagree. When this occurs, each party has the right to due process. This procedure protects the rights of both the school and the family and allows another avenue for resolution. An **impartial hearing officer** may be requested to intervene when there is a difference of opinion. This is an independent individual assigned by the district's board of education or commissioner of education to hear an appeal and render a decision. Impartial hearing officers can in no way be connected to the school district, may have to be certified (depending on state regulations), are trained, and usually must keep their skills updated. Although due process rights of parents allow this appeal to continue to the state department of education if they disagree with the impartial hearing officer's decision, it is hoped that through a thorough understanding of the needs of the parent and the child, conflict resolution, and a positive working relationship, a solution that is acceptable to both sides can be established at the local level.

Special Meetings of the Eligibility Committee

Sometimes, the parents or eligibility committee will call a special meeting. This type of review can occur for several reasons and is always held for a child who has been previously classified. Among the reasons for such a meeting are:

- Change in a child's IEP
- Change in a child's program
- Declassification request
- Addition or deletion of a modification
- Parental request for an eligibility committee meeting
- Disciplinary concerns
- New student to district previously identified as disabled
- Referral from the building administrator

PRESENTATION TO THE EC: THE SPECIAL EDUCATION TEACHER AS CLASSROOM TEACHER

There may be times when you will be called upon to attend an eligibility committee meeting that has been called for one of the reasons listed previously. If you are the child's classroom or special education teacher, then you should consider the following:

1. The first thing you should do when you receive a request to participate at a meeting is to find out the reason for the meeting. The material required may vary, but your preparation prior to the meeting is crucial. If the parents called the meeting, you may want to have them in for a conference to discuss their concerns.

2. Once you know why the meeting will be held, organize yourself so that you will have information in front of you in the following areas:
   - The child's present academic levels in reading, math, spelling, and writing. These may be available as a result of recent individual or group achievement tests, informal evaluations that you may have administered, observation (although try to be more objective), class tests, and so on. Determine grade levels if possible and where the child falls in comparison to others in the class.
   - The child's present pattern of classroom behavior written up in behavioral terms (factual, observable, and descriptive notes of behavior that do not include analysis or judgment).
   - The child's present levels of social interaction and social skills.
   - The child's interest areas and areas of strength.
   - The child's present schedule.
   - Samples of the child's work.
   - Outline of parent conferences, phone conversations, or meetings and the purpose and outcome of each. These notes should be kept on an ongoing basis.
   - Your opinion as to whether the child is benefiting from his or her present placement.
   - Any physical limitations noted and their implication on the learning process.
   - Your opinion of the child's self-esteem.
   - Any pertinent comments made by the child that may have a bearing on his or her present situation.

3. You should be well prepared to answer any questions with the above information at hand. When it is your turn to present, do so in an organized manner. You may want to provide the participants with an outline of what you will be covering.

4. Try not to be defensive, even if the reason for the meeting is the parents' concern over the child's placement in your class, the work load, or some such matter. Try to listen carefully for what the parents are saying or really asking for. It may not be as big of a problem as you may think, and therefore, try to be solution oriented, even if the parents may be blame oriented.

THE ANNUAL REVIEW

Each year the eligibility committee is required to review the existing program of a child with a disability. **Annual review** meetings are required for all students receiving special instruction or related services. The required eligibility committee participants of an annual review meeting may include the eligibility committee chairperson, psychologist, special education teacher, general education teacher (if student is in general education or will receive general education services), parent of child, parent representative, and student (if over 16 years of age). During this process, the eligibility committee will make recommendations upon review of records that will continue, change, revise, or end the child's special education program. Based on these findings, the eligibility committee will make adjustments to the IEP and recommendations to the board of education.

The annual review occurs within a year of initial placement and yearly thereafter. The date of the annual review should be part of the child's IEP. A parent, the child's teacher, or a school administrator may request an eligibility committee review at any time to determine if a **change in placement** is needed. If this occurs, the next review must be conducted within one year.

The parents are notified of the date, time, location, and individuals expected to attend their child's meeting. They will also be given a statement about their right to bring other people to the meeting. As earlier stated, parents have the same rights as at the initial eligibility committee meeting. They will also be notified that if they cannot attend the meeting, they will have the opportunity to participate in other ways such as through telephone calls or written reports of the annual review meeting. If necessary, they will be able to have an interpreter provided at no cost. The parents' notice of their child's annual review will include their right to have information about the planned review. They may at any time inspect their child's school files, records, and reports and make copies at a reasonable cost. If medication or a physical condition is part of the child's disability, the parent may request that a physician attend the meeting. The parent may request an **independent evaluation**, an impartial hearing, or appeal the decision from the impartial hearing to the state review office of the state education department.

In some cases, the parent may be entitled to receive free or low-cost legal services and a listing of where those services can be obtained. They also are entitled to **pendency**, having the child stay in the current educational placement during formal due process proceedings, unless both parties agree otherwise.

After the annual review, the parents will receive another notice regarding the recommendation that has been made to the board of education. A copy of their child's IEP will be sent to them indicating that their child has been recommended to continue to receive special education. The notice will also explain all factors used to make the recommendation. Again, the notice will describe the parents' due process rights.

Suggestions for the Special Educator's Participation in the Annual Review

When you attend an annual review meeting as a special educator, there are some key points that you should follow.

- Suggest ways to meet the child's proposed goals and objectives as specified in the IEP.
- Discuss changes or additions for the child's upcoming program and services. Talk about what worked and what needs adjustment from your point of view.
- Present the areas in which the child showed success and significant progress.
- Discuss high school diploma and credential options, if applicable.
- Discuss need for a referral to an adult service provider—that is, state vocational rehabilitation coordinator—for services the child may need as an adult, if applicable.
- Review problems that the child has experienced or encountered throughout the year with the eligibility committee and parent.
- When the child is 13, you should begin to consider plans for occupational education and transition services and become very familiar with the transitional process and all the factors involved.

THE TRIENNIAL REVIEW

A child in special education will have a **triennial review** (evaluation) every three years to provide current assessment information to help determine his or her continued placement in special education. At this triennial evaluation, updated information is provided through reexamining many of the areas previously tested in the initial evaluation. The results of this evaluation, usually conducted by school officials, must be discussed at an eligibility committee meeting.

DECLASSIFYING A CHILD IN SPECIAL EDUCATION

It is the responsibility of the eligibility committee to declassify students previously classified with a disability who no longer meet the requirements for special education. The rationale for **declassification** is as follows:

- The child demonstrates effective compensatory skills.
- The student no longer exhibits difficulty in the classroom (no classroom impact on performance) despite a process deficit and discrepancy.
- The student no longer exhibits difficulty in the classroom (performance) or a discrepancy between ability and achievement (no classroom impact) despite a process deficit.
- The student no longer exhibits difficulty in the classroom (performance) or a process deficit (no classroom impact) despite a discrepancy between ability and achievement.

Depending on the state regulations, the child who is declassified may be entitled to transition services that offer up to one year of support following the declassification. However, testing modifications can continue after the student is declassified when the student graduates from high school or receives an IEP diploma (a diploma offered to children with disabilities who meet the criteria of their IEP but do not meet district or state standards for graduation).

CONCLUSION

The eligibility committee packet is a crucial piece of the special education process because it represents the culmination of gathering information, evaluations, observations, intakes, professional opinions, and recommendations necessary for the proper educational direction of a child with a suspected disability. This information will be viewed by all the members of the eligibility committee along with the parents and other individuals so designated, such as an advocate or lawyer. This packet is also crucial because most of the eligibility committee members will not be familiar with the child, and they will use the information gathered and forwarded to determine the child's educational future. Therefore, it is imperative that the MDT present the most thorough and practical information to the eligibility committee.

If a child is classified with a disability, several other procedures will occur in the special education process. Some of these may occur during the year, at the end of the year, or every three years. These procedures are also part of due process rights for students with disabilities and their parents. The eligibility committee handles many types of issues, but the three more common ones are special meetings, annual reviews, and triennial reviews. All of these meetings are for the sole purpose of protecting the rights of both the children and the parents. In the end, the eligibility committee plays a very significant role within the school district. An effective eligibility committee, working as an interdisciplinary team, can make a tremendous difference in the lives of children with disabilities. It is truly the link between the child and his or her educational future.

Vocabulary

Adaptive physical education: Services provided to a child with a disability who is unable to perform the required tasks of a regular mainstreamed physical education class.

Annual review: Reviewing, at least annually, the status of a child in special education.

Case manager: The individual designated to collect, organize, and forward the eligibility committee packet to the administrator of the eligibility committee.

Change in placement: Any change of educational setting from or to a public school, local special school, or state approved school.

Cooperative educational services: Cooperative service agencies are usually set up by your state to assist local districts with the student population or specific services one or more districts could not provide themselves.

Declassification: The process of taking a child who is currently in special education and removing his or her classification so that he or she is no longer a part of the special education program.

Due process rights: The rights of a child and parent in the special education process.

Eligibility committee: The team that oversees the identification, monitoring, review, and status of all children with disabilities residing within the school district.

Eligibility committee packet: An organized, thorough packet of required forms and information necessary for a presentation to the eligibility committee of a child with a suspected disability.

Evaluation summary sheet: A summary of all scores and tests administered that becomes part of the eligibility committee packet.

Extended school year: The determination by the eligibility committee of continued services through the summer to avoid regression of learning on the part of a child with a disability.

Full-time special class in a general education school: This placement is viewed as the LRE setting for students whose disability does not permit successful participation in any type of general education class setting, even for part of the day. These are students who usually require a very structured, closely monitored program on a daily basis but not so restrictive as to warrant an out-of-district placement.

General education class placement: Placement in a general education class is the least restrictive placement for all children without a disability. This placement alone, without some type of special education supportive services, is not suitable for a child with a disability and is usually considered unsuitable by the eligibility committee.

Home/hospital settings: There may be times when a child needs temporary instruction at home or in a hospital setting due to severe illness or special circumstances indicated on the IEP. Home and hospital instruction is highly restrictive; the continuing need for such services should be assessed frequently, and this service should be seen as temporary.

Homebound instruction: This very restrictive setting is usually provided for students who are in the process of transition between programs and have yet to be placed.

Hospital or institution: The most restrictive setting used is a hospital or institutional setting. Although this is the most restrictive setting, it may be the LRE setting for certain students, such as situations of attempted suicide by an adolescent, pervasive clinical depression, or severe or profound retardation.

Impartial hearing officer: An independent individual assigned by the district's board of education or commissioner of education to hear an appeal and render a decision. These individuals can in no way be connected to the school district, may have to be certified (depending upon state regulations), are trained, and usually must update their skills.

Inclusion classroom: This placement involves the main tenance of the child in a regular mainstreamed classroom assisted by the presence of a second teacher who is certified in special education.

Independent evaluation: A full and comprehensive individual evaluation conducted by an outside professional or agency not involved in the education of the child.

Itinerant services: Services subcontracted by the district and provided by outside agencies.

Least restrictive education (LRE): Applies to the placement of students with disabilities in the most advantageous educational placement suitable for their needs.

Local school district: The child's home school, depending on the severity of the disability, will generally provide the types of services he or she requires.

Neighboring school district: Due to the nature of special education programs, not all special education services are offered within every district. The child's local school may arrange for participation in necessary programs and services in surrounding districts if they cannot be provided within the child's home district.

Pendency: Having the child stay in the current educational placement during formal due process proceedings.

Private approved schools: School districts may place students in private schools, special act schools (schools set up by the state to provide services for child with a disability), or residential placements approved by the state education department. These schools may be located in or out of state. Students placed in such facilities have such diverse needs that the home school district may not be able to service them due to the severity of their mental, physical, or emotional needs.

Residential school: Residential placements are settings where students reside and receive their education for the school term. The nature and length of home visits depend on several factors that are usually determined by the residential school staff after evaluation and observation. For some students home visits may not take place at all, whereas others may go home every weekend.

Resource room program: Part-time supplementary instruction on an individual or small-group basis outside the general education classroom for a child with a disability.

Special class: A placement for students with disabilities who attend a general education school but do not participate in any type of general education class.

Special day school: A special day school is a restrictive educational setting that is a desirable placement for students whose disability is so severe that they may require a more totally therapeutic environment and closer monitoring by specially trained special education teachers or staff members.

State operated schools: These schools have educational programs available for students whose educational needs require a special focus.

Triennial review: Under federal law, the mandated assessment battery that must be given to a child in special education every 3 years.

19 | DEVELOPMENT OF THE IEP

Key Terms

Academic/educational
achievement and learning
characteristics
Annual goals
Assistive technology devices
Benchmarks
Classification
Committee on special education
Community experiences

Dominant language of parent/
guardian
Dominant language of student
Extended school year program
Management needs
Medical alerts/prescriptive devices
Participating agency
Physical development
Postschool adult living objectives

Related services
Short-term objectives
Social development
Supplementary aids
Vocational and Educational
Services for Individuals with
Disabilities (VESID)

Chapter Objectives

This chapter focuses on the individualized education plan (IEP). After reading this chapter, you should be able to understand the following:

- The purpose of an IEP
- The components of an IEP
- How to read a sample IEP
- How to interpret all parts of an IEP

IEP DEVELOPMENT

All students in special education are expected to leave school prepared to

- Live independently
- Enjoy self-determination
- Make choices
- Contribute to society
- Pursue meaningful careers
- Enjoy integration in the economic, political, social, cultural, and educational mainstream of American society

As discussed in Chapter 18, the school district's committee on eligibility for special education services (eligibility committee) is charged with ensuring that each student with a disability is educated to the maximum extent appropriate in classes and programs with his or her peers who do not have disabilities. For school-age students with disabilities, this committee must consider the supports, services, and program modifications necessary for a student to participate in general education classes and extracurricular and nonacademic activities. To better ensure that this occurs, the Individuals with Disabilities Education Improvement Act (IDEA 2004) requires that all students in special education have an individualized education program (IEP).

The IEP is the blueprint for attaining improved educational results for students with disabilities. It is used to strengthen the connection between special education programs and services and the general education curriculum. The IEP serves two major purposes:

- *It is a written plan for a student in special education:* Simply stated, the IEP explains the specific educational objectives and placement for a particular student.
- *It is a management tool for the entire assessment process:* The IEP becomes the critical link between the student in special education and the special teaching that the student requires.

Components to Be Included in the IEP

IDEA 2004 is very specific about the contents of an IEP. An IEP must include [34 C.F.R. 300.320; 20 U.S.C. 1414(d)(1)(A) and (d)(6)]:

1. A statement of the child's present levels of academic achievement and functional performance, including:
   - How the child's disability affects the child's involvement and progress in the general education curriculum (i.e., the same curriculum as for nondisabled children); or
   - For preschool children, as appropriate, how the disability affects the child's participation in appropriate activities;
2. A statement of measurable annual goals, including academic and functional goals designed to:
   - Meet the child's needs that result from the child's disability to enable the child to be involved in and make progress in the general education curriculum; and
   - Meet each of the child's other educational needs that result from the child's disability;

   Note: For children with disabilities who take alternate assessments aligned to alternate academic achievement standards, a description of benchmarks or short-term objectives;
3. A description of:
   - How the child's progress toward meeting the annual goals will be measured; and
   - When periodic reports on the progress the child is making toward meeting the annual goals (such as through the use of quarterly or other periodic reports, concurrent with the issuance of report cards) will be provided;
4. A statement of the special education and related services and supplementary aids and services, based on peer-reviewed research to the extent practicable, to be provided to the child, or on behalf of the child, and a statement of the program modifications or supports for school personnel that will be provided to enable the child—
   - To advance appropriately toward attaining the annual goals;
   - To be involved in and make progress in the general education curriculum and to participate in extracurricular and other nonacademic activities; and

- To be educated and participate with other children with disabilities and nondisabled children in the activities described in this section;

5. An explanation of the extent, if any, to which the child will not participate with nondisabled children in the regular class and in the activities described above (see #4);

6. A statement of any individual appropriate accommodations that are necessary to measure the academic achievement and functional performance of the child on State and district wide assessments consistent; and if the IEP Team determines that the child must take an alternate assessment instead of a particular regular State or district wide assessment of student achievement, a statement of why—
   - The child cannot participate in the regular assessment; and
   - The particular alternate assessment selected is appropriate for the child; and

7. The projected date for the beginning of the services and modifications, and the anticipated frequency, location, and duration of those services and modifications.

8. Transition services. Beginning not later than the first IEP to be in effect when the child turns 16, or younger if determined appropriate by the IEP Team, and updated annually, thereafter, the IEP must include:
   - Appropriate measurable postsecondary goals based upon age appropriate transition assessments related to training, education, employment, and, where appropriate, independent living skills; and
   - The transition services (including courses of study) needed to assist the child in reaching those goals.

9. Transfer of rights at age of majority. Beginning not later than one year before the child reaches the age of majority under State law, the IEP must include a statement that the child has been informed of the child's rights under Part B of the Act, if any, that will transfer to the child on reaching the age of majority.

IEP Requirements under IDEA

The initial draft of the IEP should be developed at the eligibility meeting by the committee members, the parent(s), and, when appropriate, the student (see Chapter 18 for a review of this material). Each student's IEP is a vital document, because it spells out the special education and related services that he or she will receive. A team that includes parents and school professionals and, when appropriate, the student develops the IEP. IDEA 2004 maintains the IEP as a document of central importance and, in the hope of improving compliance, moves all provisions related to the IEP to one place in the law—Section 614(d).

Since 1990, several key changes have been made as to what information the IEP must contain and the way in which the IEP is developed. The IEP retains many familiar components from previous legislation, such as statements regarding the student's present levels of educational performance, annual goals, special education and related services to be provided, projected dates for the beginning and end of services, and transition services for youth. However, some modifications have been made to these familiar components to place more emphasis within the law on involving students with disabilities in the general curriculum and in the general education classroom, with supplementary aids and services as appropriate.

For example, "present levels of academic achievement and functional performance" must now include a statement of how the child's disability affects his or her involvement and progress in the general curriculum. Similarly, the IEP must contain a statement of special education and related services, as well as the supplementary aids and services, that the child or youth needs in order to "be involved and progress in the general curriculum and to participate in extracurricular and other nonacademic activities; and to be educated and participate with other children with disabilities and non-disabled children."

With these new IEP requirements, there is a clear intent to strengthen the connection between special education and the general education curriculum. As the Committee on Labor and Human Resources' Report (to accompany S. 717) stated:

> The new emphasis on participation in the general education curriculum is intended to produce attention to the accommodations and adjustments necessary for disabled children to access the general education curriculum and the special services which may be necessary for appropriate participation in particular areas of the curriculum (IDEA Amendments of 1997, p. 20).

Along the same line, it is required that the IEP include an explanation of the extent to which the student will not be participating with children without disabilities in the general education class and in extracurricular and nonacademic activities. This explanation of the extent to which the child will be educated separately is a new component of the IEP, yet it is clearly in keeping with the changes noted earlier.

Other aspects of the IEP have changed over the past 15 years. For example, each student's IEP must now include a statement of how the administration of state or districtwide assessments will be modified for the student so that he or she can participate. If the IEP team determines that the student cannot participate in such assessments, then the IEP must include a statement of (1) why the assessment is not appropriate for the child and (2) how the child will be assessed. These changes work in tandem with changes elsewhere in IDEA 2004, requiring that students with disabilities be included in state and districtwide assessments of student achievement.

Other IEP requirements include the following:

1. Informing the student about the transfer of rights as he or she approaches the age of majority
2. How parents will be regularly informed of their child's progress toward meeting the annual goals in the IEP
3. Where services will be delivered to the student
4. Transition service needs of the student beginning at age 14

IDEA 2004 maintains essentially the same process for developing the IEP— namely, that the document is developed by a multidisciplinary team, including the parents. However, the new legislation increases the role of the general educator on the IEP team to include, when appropriate, helping to determine positive behavioral interventions and appropriate supplementary aids and services for the student.

Also added to the IEP process are "special factors" that the IEP team must consider. These factors include

- Behavior strategies and supports, if the child's behavior impedes his or her learning or that of others
- The child's language needs (as they relate to the IEP) if the child has limited English proficiency
- Providing for instruction in Braille and the use of Braille (unless not appropriate) if a child is blind or visually impaired
- The communication needs of the child, with a list of specific factors to be considered if a child is deaf or hard of hearing
- Whether the child requires assistive devices and services

The language in the new IDEA 2004 emphasizes periodic review of the IEP (at least annually, as previously required) and revision as needed. A new separate requirement exists that schools must report to parents on the progress of their child with disabilities at least as frequently as progress of nondisabled children is reported, which seems likely to affect the revision process for IEPs. If it becomes evident that a child is not making "expected progress toward the annual goals and in the general curriculum," the IEP team must meet and revise the IEP.

The new legislation specifically lists a variety of other circumstances under which the IEP team would also need to review and revise the IEP, including the child's anticipated needs, the results of any reevaluation conducted, or information provided by the parents. The requirements for providing transition services for youth with disabilities have been modified in IDEA 2004 (see later in this chapter for a detailed discussion on transition services).

Understanding the IEP

When writing an IEP, it is very important to remember that it is being written for both administrators and parents. Therefore, be sure that it is

- Clear and concise
- User-friendly
- A working document
- A reflection of the abilities of the student
- A document that involves the parents and school personnel in the student's education

Now we take you through a sample IEP. Each section will be a model of what an IEP can look like, and we then explain that section in detail. IEPs differ from state to state and even from district to district. Therefore, the sample IEP used here may be a little different in format than that used in your school district. However, the areas covered will be similar, if not exactly the same. Regarding the sample IEP, it is important to realize a few important points:

- Some sections of the sample IEP apply only to students who are age 14 and older. These sections will be designated as we go along.
- The term *committee* is used to designate the state's committees for special education eligibility (i.e., EC, **committee on special education**, multidisciplinary team, eligibility team, multifactor team). These teams are responsible for children age 3 to 21 years.
- Some districts separate responsibilities by having separate teams for ages 3 to 5 (i.e., committee on preschool special education, or CPSE) and 5 to 21 (those listed above).
- Additional space may be added to any section of the sample IEP to meet the needs of the student. Because the number of goals is determined by the needs of the student, space for additional goals may be added.

SAMPLE IEP

Section 1—Background Information

School District/Agency: _____

Name and Address: _____

Individualized Education Program

Date of Eligibility Committee/CPSE Meeting: _____

Purpose of Meeting: _____

Student Name: _____

Date of Birth: _____ Age: _____

Street: _____ County of Residence: _____

City: _____ Zip: _____ Telephone: _____

Male _____ Female _____ Student ID#: _____ Current Grade: _____

Dominant Language of Student: _____

Interpreter Needed: Yes _____ No _____

Racial/Ethnic Group of Student:
(optional information)

     American Indian or Alaskan Native _____

     Black (not of Hispanic origin) _____

     White (not of Hispanic origin) _____

     Asian or Pacific Islander _____

     Hispanic _____

Date of Initiation of Services: _____ Projected Date of Review: _____

Date of Eligibility: _____ Date for Reevaluation: _____

Medical Alerts: _____

Mother's Name/Guardian's Name: _____

Street: _____ County of Residence: _____

City: _____ Zip: _____ Telephone: _____

Dominant Language of Mother/Guardian: _____

Interpreter Needed: Yes _____ No _____

Father's Name/Guardian's Name: _____

Street: _____ County of Residence: _____

City: _____ Zip: _____ Telephone: _____

Dominant Language of Mother/Guardian: _____

Interpreter Needed: Yes _____ No _____

Explanation of Section 1—Background Information

Date of the Eligibility Committee/CPSE Meeting: The date the committee meeting occurred.

Purpose of Meeting: The eligibility committee, subcommittee on special education, or committee on preschool education (eligibility committee/committee on preschool special education) meeting may be conducted to address several purposes. The meeting may be an initial review, an annual review, a review of reevaluation results, or a request for review by the student's parent or teacher, and should be noted accordingly.

Student Name: The full name of the student should be noted.

Date of Birth: Student's birth date.

Age: The age of the student on the date of the meeting.

Address of Student: Legal address and phone number of the student.

County of Residence: The county in which the parent(s) and student reside.

Gender: Male or female.

Student Identification Number (ID): The ID number may be the student's social security number or a number assigned by the school.

Current Grade: For school-age students, the current grade is designated as of the date of the committee meeting. Students with disabilities who are participating in instruction based on the general education curriculum should have a grade designation, which generally is the grade in which the student would be enrolled if the student did not have a disability. For all other students, the term *ungraded* should be noted.

Dominant Language of Student: For a student who is deaf or hearing impaired or whose native language is other than English, specify the language or mode of communication used with the student. The committee must arrange for an interpreter if needed for the student to participate meaningfully in developing the IEP.

Race/Ethnic Group of Student: Listing the race/ethnicity of the student is optional.

Date of Initiation of Services: The date when this IEP is to be implemented.

Projected Date of Review: The date when review of this IEP is expected.

Date of Eligibility: The date when the student was first identified as a student with a disability and eligible for special education programs and services.

Date for Reevaluation: The date when the next reevaluation of the student is expected to occur. Reevaluations must occur at least every three years.

Medical Alerts/Prescriptive Devices: Any information that should be readily available to all teachers and other appropriate school personnel, such as medications or specific health-related conditions requiring either constant or intermittent care by a qualified individual (e.g., eyeglasses, hearing aids, and allergic reactions).

Parent(s)/Guardian's Name: The names of the parent(s) or the name of a guardian, if appropriate.

Street, City, and Zip: If the address of a parent(s)/guardian is different from the student's address, both addresses should be indicated, when appropriate.

Telephone: If appropriate, the telephone numbers of parent(s)/guardian should be indicated.

County of Residence: The county(ies) in which the parent(s) resides.

Dominant Language of Parent(s)/Guardian: For parent(s)/guardians who are deaf or hearing impaired or whose native language is other than English, specify the language or mode of communication used by the parent(s). The committee must ensure that the parent(s)/guardian understands the proceedings of the committee meeting and must arrange for an interpreter if needed for the parent(s)/guardian to participate meaningfully in developing the IEP.

Section 2—Present Levels of Performance and Individual Needs

1. **Academic/Educational Achievement and Learning Characteristics:** Address current levels of knowledge and development in subject and skill areas, including activities of daily living, level of intellectual functioning, adaptive behavior, expected rate of progress in acquiring skills and information, and learning style.

Present Levels: Academic development
> Desmond is currently functioning below his chronological age in the area of academic ability.

Present Levels: Cognitive ability
> Desmond is currently functioning at his chronological age in the area of cognitive ability.

Present Levels: Language ability
> Desmond is currently functioning below his chronological age in the area of language development.
> Desmond is currently functioning below his chronological age in the area of receptive development.
> Desmond is currently functioning below his chronological age in the area of pragmatic/social speech development. *(continued)*

Abilities: Desmond understands multistep directions.
Needs: None

Present Levels: Learning style
> Desmond has a multisensory learning style.

Present Levels: General
> Given Desmond's functional level, his disability affects his involvement and progress in the general education program.
> Desmond models math/goal skills only with teacher support. Desmond is able to perform language arts goals/skills independently with minimal support.

Present Levels: Rate of Progress
> Desmond's rate of progress is below average.
> Desmond reads on or above grade level.
> Desmond's computational skills impact the ability to perform general education at his grade level.

Abilities: Desmond is able to read and follow written directions.
Needs: Desmond requires an individualized and/or small group for instruction in math.
> Desmond needs to develop self-monitoring skills as a means of avoiding carelessness and of focusing attention to detail (copying homework assignment, completing classwork).

2. **Social Development:** Describe the quality of the student's relationships with peers and adults, feelings about self, social adjustment to school and community environments, and behaviors that may impede learning.

Present Levels: Social Interaction with Peers
> Desmond is presently functioning below his chronological age in the area of social development.
Abilities: Desmond has developed some friendships.

Needs: Desmond needs to relate appropriately to peers in the classroom.
                      Desmond needs to relate appropriately to adults in the classroom.
                      Desmond needs to relate appropriately to adults outside the classroom.
                      Desmond needs to learn how to communicate effectively in social situations.

Present Levels: Feelings about Self
                      Desmond is currently functioning below his chronological age level with
                      regard to feelings about himself.
Abilities: Desmond identifies himself as an individual.
Needs: Desmond needs to develop positive self-concept.

Present Levels: School/Community
                      Desmond is currently functioning below his chronological age level with
                      regard to school and community.
Abilities: Desmond initiates social interactions with adults.
Needs: Desmond needs to respond to adult intervention.
                      Desmond needs to respond to adult praise.

Present Levels: Adjustment to School/Community
                      Desmond does not display appropriate social adjustment to school, fam-
                      ily, and/or community environment skills.
Abilities: Desmond can adapt to changes in routine.
Needs: Desmond needs guidance to participate in small groups.
                      Desmond needs to take initiative in social situations.

3. **Physical Development:** Describe the student's motor and sensory development, health,
   vitality, and physical skills or limitations that pertain to the learning process.

   Present Levels: Desmond has ADHD medical diagnosis, which impacts learning—see
   health file.
   Abilities: Desmond may participate in all school activities.
   Needs: Desmond needs to develop skills required to sit independently. Desmond
                      needs to improve attending skills when visual distractions are present.

4. **Management Needs:** Describe the nature of and degree to which environmental modifications
   and human or material resources are required to address academic, social, and physical needs.
   A functional behavioral assessment should be completed for any student who demonstrates
   behaviors that impede learning. A functional behavioral assessment becomes the basis for
   positive behavioral interventions, strategies, and supports for the student.

   Present Levels: Desmond has moderate management needs to address academic goals.
                      Desmond has moderate needs to address social goals.
                      Desmond has no management needs to address physical goals.
   Abilities: Desmond is able to perform effectively and complete tasks in the class-
                      room environment with the assistance of additional personnel.

   Needs: Desmond needs full-time general education placement with moderate
                      support through special education.

Explanation of Section 2—Present Levels of Performance and Individual Needs

The IEP must describe the student's present levels of educational performance, including the
student's abilities and needs, based on relevant functional and developmental evaluation infor-

mation, including information provided by the parent. Many tests and assessment procedures are used to obtain information about a student's present performance.

Present levels of performance must include a statement that explains how the student's disability affects his or her involvement and progress in the general education curriculum. The committee uses this information to determine a student's eligibility for special education, the specific classification, annual goals and objectives, and the specific type and extent of special education programs and services. The committee must assess present levels of performance and individual needs in the following areas:

Academic/Educational Achievement and Learning Characteristics: Levels of knowledge and development in subject and skill areas, including activities of daily living, level of intellectual functioning, adaptive behavior, expected rate of progress in acquiring skills and information, and learning style are addressed. Performance in subject areas should be based on the student's ability in relation to the learning standards and performance indicators established for all students.

Social Development: The degree and quality of the student's relationships with peers and adults, feelings about self, and social adjustment to school and community environments are explained.

Physical Development: The degree or quality of the student's motor and sensory development, health, vitality, and physical skills or limitations that pertain to the learning process, including pertinent information from the student's physical examination, are noted.

Management Needs: The nature of and degree to which environmental modifications and human or material resources are required to enable the student to benefit from instruction are discussed.

Section 3—Long-Term Adult Outcome Statement

Long-Term Adult Outcomes: Beginning at age 14, or younger if appropriate, long-term adult outcomes are anticipated, reflecting student's needs, preferences, and interests.

Postsecondary Education/Training:

Desmond anticipates receiving the following postsecondary education/ training:

Desmond will attend college.

The transition service needs of Desmond to meet long-term adult outcomes are:

Desmond will receive guidance/career counseling.

Desmond will take college entrance courses.

Desmond will take Regents courses.

Employment: *NA*

Community Living: *NA*

Explanation of Section 3—Long-Term Adult Outcome Statement

The IEP must include a long-term adult outcome statement related to the student's individual needs, preferences, and interests for adult employment, postsecondary education, and community living. At age 14, federal law requires that the IEP include a statement of the transition services needs of the student that focuses on the student's courses of study, such as advanced-placement courses or an occupational education program. The IEP must reflect the full array of transition service needs in instruction, related services, community experiences, development of employment, and other **postschool adult living objectives**, including, as appropriate, acquisition of daily living skills and a functional vocational evaluation.

The long-term adult outcome statements establish clear expectations for the school, the student, the student's family, and any agencies participating in planning and implementing the transition programs and services in the IEP. These statements are the basis for planning the student's movement from school to post-school activities and for discussion with appropriate public and private community agencies regarding their contributions to the student's transition process.

Once the statements are established, annual goals and objectives and other activities can be developed to help the student incrementally develop skills, experiences, and contacts with resources, as needed, to work toward these desired adult outcomes. Vocational rehabilitation counselors from the federal agency, **Vocational and Educational Services for Individuals with Disabilities (VESID)**, in consultation with the student, parents, and school personnel, can provide advice on long-term adult outcomes, including appropriate vocational assessments, postsecondary services, and selection of employment goals for students who meet vocational rehabilitation eligibility criteria.

Section 4—Measurable Annual Goals and Short-Term Instructional Objectives

Annual Goal: *Desmond will maintain and improve study skill levels.*

Short-Term Instructional Objective	Evaluation Procedures	Evaluation Schedule
1. *Improve work habits and study skills*	*Classroom teacher contact*	*Quarterly*
2. *Organize material including classwork, major assignments, and homework*		

Annual Goal: *Desmond will successfully complete academic course requirements.*

Short-Term Instructional Objective	Evaluation Procedures	Evaluation Schedule
1. *Incorporate writing process strategies*		
2. *Improve math computation*	*Quizzes, tests*	*Quarterly*

Annual Goal: Desmond will increase attentiveness and concentration skills.

Short-Term Instructional Objective	Evaluation Procedures	Evaluation Schedule
1. *Develop necessary behaviors, attitudes, and expectations that will lead to self-growth*	*Teacher contact*	*Quarterly*
2. *Learn to express feelings, both positive and negative*		

Explanation of Section 4—Measurable Annual Goals and Short-Term Instructional Objectives

Annual goals are statements, in measurable terms, that describe what the student can reasonably be expected to accomplish within a 12-month period. There must be a direct relationship between the annual goals and the present levels of performance. Annual goals focus on addressing needs resulting from the disability so that the student can appropriately participate in the general curriculum. The committee should consider goals from all areas of the student's individual needs, including those associated with behavior and long-term adult outcomes, where appropriate. Annual goals should be developed using the following criteria:

- Should be determined from the abilities and needs of the student as described in the present levels of performance
- Should focus on offsetting or reducing the learning or behavioral problems resulting from the student's disability
- Should focus on meeting the special education needs of the student
- Must be written in measurable terms

In a manner of speaking, annual goals are like a road map. Where is the child heading this year? What will he or she work on, both academically and in terms of functional development? What does the IEP team feel the child can achieve by the end of the year—again, academically and functionally?

Annual goals should be related to meeting the child's needs that result from the disability and, to the extent possible, enable the child to be involved in and make progress in the general curriculum.

In the past, annual goals were paired with short-term objectives or benchmarks of progress. With the 2004 Amendments to IDEA 2004, this requirement has been removed. Now, benchmarks or short-term objectives are required only for children with disabilities who take alternate assessments aligned to alternate achievement standards [34 C.F.R. 300.320(a)(2)(ii)].

Section 5—Special Education Programs and Related Services/Program Modifications

1. **Special Education Programs/Related Services**

	Initiation Date	Frequency	Duration
In-school counseling	*September 2007*	*1 × a week*	*45 min.*

2. **Extended School Year Programs/Services**   Yes _____ No _____
3. **Supplementary Aids and Modifications or Supports For the Student**

	Initiation Date
Modification of curriculum	*September 2007*
Extra time between classes	*September 2007*
Calculator	*September 2007*

4. **Describe any assistive technology devices or services needed**: *Given Desmond's functional level, he does not need assistive technology services and devices in order to have an equal opportunity to succeed academically.*
5. **Describe the program modifications or supports for school personnel that will be provided on behalf of the students to address the annual goals and participation in general education curriculum and activities:** *School staff will be provided with information on a specific disability and implications for instruction for Desmond.*

6. A. **Individual Testing Modification(s):**

> *Desmond requires time and a half to complete standardized tests.*
> *Desmond requires double time to complete classroom tests.*
> *Desmond requires tests to be administered in a small group in a separate location.*
> *Desmond will have tests administered in a location with minimal distractions.*

B. **State why the student will not participate in a state or districtwide assessment:**

_____

C. **Explain how the student will be assessed:**

_____

Explanation of Section 5—Special Education Programs and Related Services/Program Modifications

The IEP must indicate the special education programs and related services, supplementary aids and services, assistive technology devices, and program supports or modifications that are to be provided to the student or on behalf of the student. Special education means specially designed individualized or group instruction or special programs or services to meet the individual needs of students with disabilities. Specially designed instruction ensures access of the student to the general curriculum so the student can meet the educational standards that apply to all students.

The IEP must indicate the type of program or service (e.g., special class, consultant teacher, resource room, related service), the initiation date, frequency (the number of times per week a service will be provided), duration (number of minutes per session), and location (e.g., general education class, separate location) for each special education program and service. The IEP must describe the special class size, if appropriate. If the student needs direct and/or indirect consultant teacher services, the IEP should indicate the general education classes, including occupational education, in which the student will receive such service. The location where special education and related services will be provided to a student may influence decisions about the nature and amount of these services and when they should be provided. For example, the appropriate location for the related service to be provided may be the regular classroom or a separate location.

RELATED SERVICES. These are school-based services that the child with a disability will be receiving that provide support for him or her and enhance educational performance. Examples of related services include but are not limited to:

> **In-school individual counseling:** When this service is recommended on an IEP, it usually means that the child would benefit from a more intimate therapeutic situation with emphasis on control, insight, cause and effect awareness, special attention, and developing a trusting relationship with an authority figure. Although some children need only individual counseling, others might move from individual to group to try out the insights and experiences learned from the individual experience.

> **In-school group counseling:** When this service is recommended on an IEP, it means that the child would benefit from a group situation that emphasizes interpersonal relations, social skills, cooperative play and interaction, interdependence, social delay of gratification, peer feedback, and social connections. The group usually meets once or twice a week and many times may be combined with individual in-school counseling.

Resource room: This service is recommended when the eligibility committee feels that the child would benefit from extra academic assistance depending on the recommendations of the diagnostic evaluation, IEP recommendation, and teacher observation. This assistance might involve remediation, compensation, or survival skills depending on the age and grade of the child. Most children will be recommended for a minimum of three hours per week (divided as needed) to a maximum of 50 percent of the child's school day.

Speech/language therapy: This service is recommended when the eligibility committee feels that the child's poor performance is directly related to disabilities in language or speech development. This service might emphasize remediation in expressive or receptive language, articulation, voice disorders, fluency disorders, and so on. These services may be administered in small-group or individual settings. This recommendation can also be made in conjunction with some other service such as resource room, if indicated.

Physical therapy and occupational therapy: The eligibility committee usually makes this recommendation when the child is suffering from some physical or motor impairment. Physical therapists usually provide exercise therapy and special devices to improve the total physical functioning and strength of a student with a disability. Generally, occupational therapists focus more on fine motor skills such as hand control, using the mouth to chew, and any other factor involved in daily living skills.

Art therapy: This recommendation, although not as common as some other services, is usually recommended when the eligibility committee feels that the production of art in its various forms would have beneficial qualities for exceptional students. Major factors involved in this recommendation include the opportunity for the child with a disability to express creativity, to improve fine motor skills, and to develop appropriate leisure-time activities.

Adaptive physical education: This service is usually recommended when the eligibility committee feels that the general physical development of a child with a disability is impaired or delayed. When these programs are instituted, they tend to have a therapeutic orientation. The teachers utilized for this service must have special training in the use of specialized equipment to improve muscle development and coordination.

Music therapy: This recommendation may be made by the eligibility committee when it feels that music can be used to prompt the development of various functional behaviors for students with disabilities such as motivation or improvement of speech, language, and communication skills through singing.

EXTENDED SCHOOL YEAR PROGRAMS AND SERVICES. Some students may require special education services during the months of July and August to prevent substantial regression. Substantial regression means a student's inability to maintain developmental levels due to a loss of skill or knowledge during the months of July and August of such severity as to require an inordinate period of review at the beginning of the school year to reestablish and maintain IEP goals and objectives mastered at the end of the previous school year. The committee should consider **extended school year programs** for those students

- Whose management needs are determined to be highly intensive, who require a high degree of individualized attention and intervention, and who are placed in special classes
- With severe multiple disabilities, whose programs consist primarily of rehabilitation and treatment, and who are placed in special classes

- Who are recommended for home and hospital instruction, whose special education needs are determined to be highly intensive, who require a high degree of individualized attention and intervention, or who have severe multiple disabilities and require primarily rehabilitation and treatment
- Whose needs are so severe that they can be met only in a seven-day residential program
- Who are receiving other special education services and, because of their disabilities, exhibit the need for a special service and/or program provided in a structured learning environment for up to 12 months in order to prevent substantial regression

The committee must specifically state the initiation date, frequency, duration, and location of services the student is to receive during July and August. In addition, the IEP must indicate the provider of such services.

An IEP developed for an extended school year program may differ from the IEP developed for the school year program. The eligibility committee determines the type and amount of services that a student needs for an appropriate extended school year program. The IEP developed for the extended school year program should focus on the areas in which the student is expected to experience substantial regression. The eligibility committee must determine the least restrictive environment required for the student to benefit from special education services during July and August. Extended school year programs or services may be provided in a location that differs from the one the student attends during the school year, provided the eligibility committee determines that the setting is appropriate for the student to benefit from the special education services and to meet the IEP goals.

SUPPLEMENTARY AIDS AND SERVICES AND PROGRAM MODIFICATIONS OR SUPPORTS.
Supplementary aids and services and/or program modifications or supports means aids, services, and other supports that are provided in general education classes or other education-related settings to enable students with disabilities to be educated with students without disabilities to the maximum extent appropriate in the least restrictive environment. Examples of supplementary aids and services include

- A note taker
- Written materials in Braille format
- Extra time to go between classes
- Modification of curriculum
- Special seating arrangements

Providing modifications to students with suspected disabilities must be substantiated and documented by evidence within the testing results. Although these criteria may vary from district to district, examples that may be used to determine the type of modification recommended are listed below:

Flexible Scheduling. Usually applied to students who may have problems in the rate in which they process information (e.g., physical disabilities such as motor or visual impairments). Examples of flexible scheduling modifications include

- Time extensions on tests
- Administration of a test in several sessions during the course of the day
- Administration of a test in several sessions over several days

The documentation required to make this recommendation should include evidence of at least one of the following:

1. Slow processing speed
2. Slow psychomotor speed
3. Severe anxiety

Flexible Setting. A modification that allows students with disabilities to take a test in a setting other than a regular classroom. This flexible setting may become necessary for a child whose health impairments prevent him or her from leaving home or the hospital, for a child whose disability interferes with his or her remaining on task, or for a child who is easily distracted. In other cases, a student with a disability may require special lighting or acoustics or a specially equipped room. Examples of flexible setting include

- Individual administration of a test in a separate location
- Small-group administration of a test in a separate location
- Provisions for special lighting
- Provisions for special acoustics
- Provision for adaptive or special furniture
- Administration of test in a location with minimal distractions

The documentation required to make this recommendation should include evidence of one of the following:

1. Students with serious attentional difficulties
2. Students who are easily distracted and have difficulty remaining on task due to processing difficulties, anxiety, and so on.

Revised Test Format. Appropriate for students whose disability may interfere with taking a test using the standard test format, such as students with visual or perceptual disabilities who may not be able to read regular-size print, revised test formats include the following examples:

- Use of a large-print edition
- Increased spacing between items
- Reduction in the number of items per page
- Use of a Braille edition
- Increased size of answer bubbles on test answer forms
- Rearrangement of multiple-choice items with answer bubble right next to each choice

The documentation required to make this recommendation should include evidence of visual–perceptual processing deficits that would cause difficulty transferring answers onto a machine scorable booklet or sheet.

Revised Test Directions. To allow students with certain disabilities a greater chance of understanding directions and thereby successfully completing a test, revised test directions include the following examples:

- Have directions read to child
- Reread the directions for each page of questions
- Simplify the language in the directions
- Provide additional examples

The documentation required to make this recommendation should include evidence of at least one of the following:

1. Students who have documented reading comprehension skills below the 25th percentile on standardized tests
2. Documented language-processing deficits
3. Significant receptive language weaknesses

Use of Aids. Some students with disabilities—for example, children with hearing impairments—require the use of aids in order to interpret test items, such as the following:

- Auditory amplification devices
- Visual magnification devices
- Auditory tape of questions
- Masks or markers to maintain the student's place on a page
- Having questions read to the student
- Having questions signed to the student

The documentation required to make the recommendation for use of a word processor or a scribe (individual who copies notes for the child) should include evidence of one of the following:

1. Documented graphomotor deficits
2. Documented written language deficits significantly below current grade level

The documentation required to make the recommendation to permit recording answers in any manner should include evidence of one of the following:

1. Documented graphomotor deficits
2. Documented written language deficits significantly below current grade level

The documentation required to make the recommendation of not penalizing spelling errors should show evidence of one of the following:

1. Below 25th percentile on standardized tests
2. A 50 percent discrepancy between aptitude and spelling achievement score on standardized tests

Revised Format. Some students with disabilities may be unable to record their responses to test questions on conventional answer forms and as a result may require a change in the test format, such as the following:

- Recording answers directly in the test booklet
- Increasing the spacing between questions or problems
- Increasing the size of the answer blocks
- Providing cues (stop sign, arrows) directly on the answer form

The documentation required to make format revisions should show evidence of visual–perceptual processing deficits that would cause difficulty transferring answers onto a machine scorable booklet or sheet or with other tasks involving visual discrimination or spatial difficulties.

Testing Modifications. When making testing modification recommendations for a student, remember the following:

- Testing modifications are to give students the same opportunities as their peers. They are not designed to achieve the identical result or give an unfair advantage to students with disabilities.
- Testing modifications should *not* be excessive. They should alter standard administration to the least extent possible.

- Testing modifications may allow a student access to higher-level classes.
- Higher scores are *not* reasons for giving test modifications.
- Testing modifications are to be specific.
- Students should have to take state exams and the IEP must indicate why a student is exempted from them, if necessary. Only IEP-diploma-bound students may be exempted from certain tests.
- It is the building principal's responsibility to ensure that test modifications are correctly implemented.
- Diagnostic evaluations (newly referred students) do not require test modifications. Administration of test modifications is at the discretion of the examiner.
- If a student refuses to utilize a test modification, it should be documented and if necessary eliminated from the IEP.
- The principal, as well as all teachers of appropriate students, should receive information on test modifications.
- Students should not be counseled toward more restrictive career objectives because they have disabilities.
- The general education teacher *must* administer test modifications as described in the IEP.

THE ONLY STUDENTS ALLOWED TO HAVE MODIFICATIONS

1. Students with disabilities
2. Declassified students (until graduation or before if no longer appropriate)
3. Students (same as classified) with accommodation plans
4. Students who acquire short-term disabilities shortly before the test

SPECIALIZED EQUIPMENT OR ASSISTIVE TECHNOLOGY DEVICES AND/OR SERVICES. The IEP must describe any specialized equipment and adaptive devices needed for the student to benefit from education. IDEA 2004 requires each school district to ensure that assistive technology devices and/or services are made available to a preschool or school-age student with a disability as part of the student's special education, related services, or supplementary aids or services as described in the IEP. **Assistive technology devices** are any item, piece of equipment, or product system—whether acquired commercially off the shelf, modified, or customized—used to increase, maintain, or improve the functional capabilities of a child with a disability.

A school district is not responsible to make available, through purchase or rental, devices that a student would require only for nonschool settings or activities. In addition, the district would not, unless specifically stated in the IEP, have to provide items that a student routinely would require for daily life functions regardless of the setting (e.g., wheelchair, hearing aid, or some prosthetic or orthotic devices) that are prescribed by a licensed physician. If a student requires assistive technology to meet the IEP goals and objectives or to participate in the general education curriculum or classes, the committee must consider who will be responsible for day-to-day maintenance as well as developing a contingency plan to provide repairs, replacements, or backup equipment.

PROGRAM MODIFICATIONS OR SUPPORTS FOR SCHOOL PERSONNEL ON BEHALF OF THE STUDENT. The IEP must describe the program modifications or supports for school personnel that will be provided on behalf of the student to address annual goals and participation in general education curriculum and activities. Examples of modifications or supports that may be provided for school personnel are

- Information on a specific disability and implications for instruction
- Training in use of specific positive behavioral interventions
- Information on the need for special placement of the student within the classroom
- Training in the use of American Sign Language

Individual Testing Modifications Required, Nonparticipation in a State or Districtwide Assessment, and How the Student Will Be Assessed

1. **Individual testing modifications:** The IEP must clearly state testing modifications to ensure a consistent understanding by the committee, the principal, the teacher(s), the student, and the parents. Specific test modifications (e.g., "use of word processor with a spell-check function") should be indicated rather than generic test modification categories (e.g., "answers recorded in another manner"). It is appropriate to indicate the conditions or nature of tests that will require test modifications (e.g., "use of a note taker for tests having answer sheets requiring answers to be blackened"); however, qualifying terms such as *as appropriate* or *when necessary* should not be used on the IEP.

2. **Statement of nonparticipation in a state or districtwide assessment and how the student will be assessed:** The committee must consider the far-reaching effects of nonparticipation in a particular state or districtwide assessment of student achievement (or part of such an assessment) before determining that a student will not participate in the assessment. If the committee determines that the student will not participate in a particular state or districtwide assessment, the IEP must contain a statement of why that assessment is not appropriate for the student. In addition, the IEP must indicate how the student will be assessed.

Section 6—Participation in General Education Classes and Nonacademic and Extracurricular Activities

Explain the extent of participation in general education programs and extracurricular and other nonacademic activities including physical education or adaptive (adapted) physical education and occupational education (if appropriate). Explain the extent, if any, to which the student will not participate with students without disabilities in the regular class and in other activities.

Desmond will participate in all general education classes with support personnel.

If the student is exempt from the second-language requirement, explain why.

Desmond will be exempt from foreign language requirements due to the following reasons: Desmond exhibits a significant discrepancy between verbal and performance areas on IQ testing, and the profile suggests significant verbal difficulties, which exempts Desmond from participation in a required second language course.

Explanation of Section 6—Participation in General Education Classes and Nonacademic and Extracurricular Activities

IDEA 2004 presumes that all students with disabilities are to be educated in general education classes. The IEP must explain both how the student will participate in general education classes, programs, and activities and the extent, if any, to which the student will not participate in such classes, programs, and activities with peers without disabilities. For preschool students, the committee must explain why the student will not participate in age-appropriate activities with peers without disabilities.

The IEP must specifically indicate how the school-age student will participate in general education programs, including

- Physical education or adaptive (adapted) physical education
- Occupational education, if appropriate
- Second-language instruction
- Nonacademic activities
- Extracurricular activities

Because all students are expected to participate in the second-language requirement unless specifically exempted by the committee, the committee must explain why the student is exempt.

Students with severe disabilities can also benefit from participation in general education classes and activities with appropriate supports to them and their teachers. In determining the placement of a student with severe disabilities, the committee must determine whether to require the assistance of supplementary aids and services. Only upon determining that such goals and objectives cannot be achieved in a general education classroom, with supports and services, should the student be educated in an alternative placement. Moreover, the committee should also consider the nonacademic benefits to the student (e.g., language development and role modeling) that will result from interaction with students without disabilities.

Section 7—Participating Agencies for Students Who Require Transition Services

Participating agencies that have agreed to provide transition services/supports (before the student leaves the secondary school program):

Agency Name: _____ **Telephone Number:** _____

Service: _____

Implementation date if different from IEP implementation date:_____

Agency Name: _____ **Telephone Number:** _____

Service: _____

Implementation date if different from IEP implementation date:_____

Agency Name: _____ **Telephone Number:** _____

Service: _____

Implementation date if different from IEP implementation date: _____

Agency Name: _____ **Telephone Number:** _____

Service: _____

Implementation date if different from IEP implementation date: _____

Explanation of Section 7—Participating Agencies for Students Who Require Transition Services

Beginning at age 16 or younger, if appropriate, the IEP must reflect the full array of transition programs and services designed to develop postsecondary education, employment, and community living skills. The committee is responsible for identifying appropriate and necessary participating agencies that will be a part of the student's transition to postschool opportunities.

A **participating agency** is defined as a state or local agency, other than the school district responsible for a student's education, that may have financial and/ or legal responsibility for providing transition services to the student. Prior to the eligibility committee meeting to determine needed transition services, eligibility committee members should have knowledge of both the eligibility criteria and the services provided by agencies that could be expected to send a representative. This will enable the eligibility committee to invite appropriate agencies to participate in discussions regarding the provision of transition services for each student. When an agency agrees to provide a service, the IEP must include that service and the implementation date of the service if it is different from the implementation date of the IEP. The eligibility committee must document these contacts on the IEP and the services and supports to be provided to the student as he or she transitions from school. The eligibility committee must reconvene as soon as possible to consider other strategies to meet the transition objectives should the participating agency fail to deliver agreed-on services stated in the IEP.

Section 8—Coordinated Set of Activities Leading to Long-Term Adult Outcomes

If any of the following areas are not addressed, explain why.

1. Instruction
2. Related Services
3. Employment/Postsecondary Education
4. Community Experience
5. Activities of Daily Living
6. Functional Vocational Assessment

Explanation of Section 8—Coordinated Set of Activities Leading to Long-Term Adult Outcomes

For a student age 14 and older, the IEP, as a whole, must demonstrate the use of a coordinated set of activities that the student can use to achieve long-term adult outcomes. Beginning at age 14, the focus of activity is on instruction. At age 15 and older, the coordinated set of activities must address instruction, related services, community experiences, and the development of employment or other postschool adult living objectives. If one of these activities is not included in the IEP in a particular year, then the IEP must explain why that activity is not reflected in any part of the student's program. Activities of daily living and functional vocational evaluation activities should also be included when appropriate to the student's needs. The coordinated set of activities shown below, in conjunction with special education programs and services, should incrementally provide the student with skills and experiences to prepare him or her to attain long-term adult outcomes:

1. **Instruction:** Educational instruction will be provided to the student to achieve the stated outcome(s) (e.g., general and/or special education course instruction, occupational education, and advanced placement courses).
2. **Related services:** These are specific related services, such as rehabilitation counseling services, that will support the student in attaining the stated outcome(s).

3. **Employment and other postschool adult living objectives:** These are educational services provided to the student to prepare for employment or other postschool activity. Postschool activities determine what other skills or supports will be necessary for the student to succeed as independently as possible. Examples include participation in a work experience program, information about colleges in which the student has an interest, and travel training.

4. **Community experiences:** These are community-based experiences that will be offered, or community resources utilized, as part of the student's school program, whether utilized during school hours or after school hours, to achieve the stated outcome(s) (e.g., local employers, public library, local stores).

5. **Activities of daily living (ADL) skills, if appropriate:** These are ADL skills necessary to be worked on to achieve the stated outcome(s) (e.g., dressing, hygiene, self-care skills, self-medication).

6. **Functional vocational assessment (if appropriate):** If the vocational assessment has not provided enough information to make a vocational program decision, additional assessment activities can be performed to obtain more information about the student's needs, preferences, and interests.

Section 9—Graduation Information for Secondary Students

Credential/Diploma Sought: _____

Expected Date of High School Completion: _____

Credits Earned to Date: _____

Explanation of Section 9—Graduation Information for Secondary Students

CREDENTIAL/DIPLOMA SOUGHT. Students with disabilities must be afforded the opportunity to earn a local high school diploma, if appropriate. Access must be provided to required courses, electives, and tests for all students, regardless of placement. Not all students with disabilities will pursue a high school diploma. Some students with disabilities will earn an IEP diploma, which are accepted as a minimum requirement by the Armed Forces to take the Armed Services Vocational Aptitude Battery and by some colleges to take college entrance examinations. However, all of these examinations have set passing scores. Additionally, each college sets its own admission requirements and, therefore, may or may not accept students with disabilities with IEP diplomas.

EXPECTED DATE OF HIGH SCHOOL COMPLETION. This is the expected date of high school completion.

CREDITS EARNED TO DATE. This indicates the number of high school units of credit earned.

Section 10—Summary of Selected Recommendations

Classification of the Disability: _____

Recommended Placement: September to June: _____

Extended School Year (ESL) Services? Yes _____ No _____

Recommended Placement, July and August: _____

Transportation Needs: _____

Explanation of Section 10—Summary of Selected Recommendations

The summary of selected recommendations is completed after the committee has reviewed the student's present levels of performance and individual needs and has finalized all other components of the IEP.

CLASSIFICATION OF THE DISABILITY. In **classification**, the committee determines a specific disability category based on the definitions of these categories for school-age students or preschool students.

RECOMMENDED PLACEMENT. After the completion of all other components of the student's IEP, the committee determines the recommended placement. The placement of a student with a disability in a special class, special school, or other removal from the general educational environment should occur only when the nature of the disability is such that the student cannot be educated, even with the use of supplementary aids and services, in the general education setting.

EXTENDED SCHOOL YEAR PROGRAM/SERVICES. The necessity of a July and August program, and where such services will be made available, may be documented in the Summary of Selected Recommendations for convenience in locating this information.

TRANSPORTATION. The IEP must document any special transportation to be provided to and from school and/or extracurricular activities. In determining whether to include transportation on a student's IEP, the committee must consider how the student's disability affects the student's need for transportation, including determining whether the student's disability prevents him or her from using the same transportation provided to those without disabilities or from getting to school in the same manner.

Section 11—Reporting Progress to Parents

State the manner and frequency in which progress will be reported: Parents/guardians or students over 18 will be informed of the student progress toward meeting academic goals and objectives with the same frequency as students without disabilities using the following criteria:

- Textbook tests, quizzes, and standardized tests
- Review of report card grades
- Contact with classroom teachers on an ongoing basis

Explanation of Section 11—Reporting Progress to Parents

The IEP must contain a statement of how parents will be regularly informed of their child's progress, at least as often as parents of children without disabilities are informed of their child's progress. Specifically, the parents must be informed of progress toward annual goals and the extent to which this progress is sufficient to achieve the child's goals by the end of the year.

CONCLUSION

Unless the student's IEP requires some other arrangement, the student with a disability must be educated in the school he or she would have attended if the student did not have a disability. The determination of the recommended placement is the final step in developing an IEP. The placement decision must address the full range of the student's cognitive, social, physical, linguistic, and communication needs. According to the least restrictive environment (LRE) requirements of federal and state law and regulations, a student may be removed from the general education environment only when the nature or severity of the disability is such that the student's education cannot be satisfactorily achieved even with the use of supplementary supports and services in the general education setting.

Vocabulary

Academic/educational achievement and learning characteristics: The current levels of knowledge and development in subject and skill areas, including activities of daily living, level of intellectual functioning, adaptive behavior, expected rate of progress in acquiring skills and information, and learning style.

Annual goals: Statements, in measurable terms, that describe what the student can reasonably be expected to accomplish within a 12-month period. There must be a direct relationship between the annual goals and the present levels of performance.

Assistive technology devices: Any item, piece of equipment, or product system—whether acquired commercially off the shelf, modified, or customized—that is used to increase, maintain, or improve the functional capabilities of a child with a disability.

Benchmarks: Major milestones between present levels of performance and annual goals.

Classification: The committee determination of a specific disability category based on the definitions of these categories for school-age students or preschool students.

Committee on special education: The committee charged with ensuring that each student with a disability is educated to the maximum extent appropriate in classes and programs with their peers who do not have disabilities.

Community experiences: Community-based experiences that will be offered, or community resources utilized as part of the student's school program, whether during school hours or after school hours, to achieve the stated outcome(s).

CPSE: Committee on preschool special education.

Credits earned to date: The number of high school units of credit earned.

Current grade: For school-age students, the current grade is designated as of the date of the committee meeting.

Date for reevaluation: The date when the next reevaluation of the student is expected to occur. Reevaluations must occur at least every 3 years.

Date of eligibility: The date when the student was first identified as a student with a disability and eligible for special education programs and services.

Date of initiation of services: The date when this IEP is to be implemented.

Dominant language of parent/guardian: For parents/guardians who are deaf or hearing impaired or whose native language is other than English, the language or mode of communication used by the parents.

Dominant language of student: For a student who is deaf or hearing impaired or whose native language is other than English, the language or mode of communication used with the student.

Extended school year programs and services: The necessity of a program during July and August.

Instruction: Educational instruction that will be provided to the student to achieve the stated outcome(s) (e.g., general and/or special education course instruction, occupational education, and advanced placement courses).

Management needs: The nature of and degree to which environmental modifications and human or material resources are required to address academic, social, and physical needs.

Medical alerts/prescriptive devices: Any information that should be readily available to all teachers and other appropriate school personnel, such as medications or specific health-related conditions requiring either constant or intermittent care by a qualified individual (e.g., eyeglasses, hearing aids, and allergic reactions).

Participating agency: A state or local agency, other than the school district responsible for a student's education, that may have financial and/or legal responsibility for providing transition services to the student.

Physical development: The student's motor and sensory development, health, vitality, and physical skills or limitations that pertain to the learning process.

Postschool adult living objectives: Educational services that will be provided to the student to prepare for employment or other postschool activity. Postschool activities determine what other skills or supports will be necessary for the student to succeed as independently as possible. Examples include participation in a work experience program, information about colleges in which the student has an interest, and travel training.

Projected date of review: The date when review of this IEP is expected.

Related services: These are specific related services, as defined in Section 200.1 of the Regulations of the Commissioner of Education, such as rehabilitation counseling services, which will support the student in attaining the stated outcome(s).

Short-term objectives: Measurable intermediate steps between present levels of performance and annual goals.

Social development: The quality of the student's relationships with peers and adults, feelings about self, social adjustment to school and community environments, and behaviors that may impede learning.

Student identification number (ID): The ID number may be the student's social security number or a number assigned by the school.

Supplementary aids: Aids, services, and other supports that are provided in general education classes or other education-related settings to enable students with disabilities to be educated with nondisabled students to the maximum extent appropriate in the least restrictive environment.

Vocational and Educational Services for Individuals with Disabilities (VESID): Federal agency concerned with providing services to individuals with disabilities.

REFERENCES

Adkins, W. D. (2010). How to calculate percentiles. Retrieved January 4, 2011, from http://www.ehow. com/how_2310404_calculate-percentiles.html.

American Psychological Association. (1999). *Standards for educational and psychological testing.* Washington, DC: Author.

Ascher, M. (1990, February). A river-crossing problem in cross-cultural perspectives. *Mathematics Magazine, 63*(1), 26–29.

ASHA (American Speech-Language Hearing Association, 2011). Dynamic assessment. Retrieved on January 12, 2011, from http://www.asha.org/practice/ multicultural/issues/Dynamic-Assessment.htm.

Bagnato, S. J., Neisworth, J. T., & Munson, S. M. (1997). *Sensible strategies for assessment in early intervention* (3rd ed.). New York: Guilford Press.

Bank, C. (2011). Pros & cons of IQ testing. Retrieved on January 12, 2011, from http://www.ehow.com/ about_5372456_pro-cons-iq-testing.html.

Baroff, G. S. (2000). *Mental retardation: Nature, cause and management* (3rd ed.). Philadelphia: Brunner/ Mazel.

Batzle, J. (1992). *Portfolio assessment and evaluation: Developing and using portfolios in the classroom.* Cypress: Creative Teaching Press.

Berk, L. E. (2007). *Development through the lifespan* (4th ed.). Boston: Allyn & Bacon.

Bigge, J., & Stump, C. (1999). *Curriculum, assessment, and instruction for students with disabilities.* Belmont, CA: Wadsworth.

Bigge, J., & Stump, C. (1999). *Curriculum, assessment, and instruction for students with disabilities.* Belmont: Wadsworth.

Center for Collaboration and Effective Practice (2011). *Functional behavioral assessment.* Retrieved on February 4, 2011, from http://cecp.air.org/fba/default.asp.

Cohen, L. G., & Spenciner, L. J. (2007). *Assessment of children and youth with special needs* (3rd ed.). Boston: Allyn & Bacon.

Cohen, L. G., & Spenciner, L. J. (2011). *Assessment of children and youth with special needs* (4th ed.). Upper Saddle River: Merrill/Pearson Education.

Council of Educators for Students with Disabilities. (2007). *Overview of Section 504.* Retrieved on January 2, 2011, from http://www.504idea.org.

Diana v. State Board of Education. (1970, February). No. C-70 37 RFP, District Court of Northern California.

Division for Learning Disabilities of the Council for Exceptional Children. (2006). *Teaching students with learning disabilities.* Retrieved on August 30, 2007, from http://www.teachingld.org.

Encyclopedia of Mental Disorders. (2011). *Intelligence tests.* Retrieved on January 12, 2011, from http://www. minddisorders.com/Flu-Inv/Intelligence-tests.html.

Feuerstein, R. (1979, May). Cognitive modifiability in retarded adolescents: Effects of instrumental enrichment. *American Journal of Mental Deficiency, 83*(6), 539–550.

Fletcher, J. M., Francis, D. J., Shaywitz, S. E., Lyon, G. R., Foorman, B. R., Steubing, K. K., et al. (1998). Intelligent testing and the discrepancy model for children with learning disabilities. *Learning Disabilities Research and Practice, 13*(4), 186–203.

Fletcher, J., Francis, D., Moris, R., & Lyon, M. (2005). Evidence-based assessment of learning disabilities in children and adolescents. *Journal of Clinical and Adolescent Psychology, 34*(3), 506–522.

Franklin, M. E. (1992, October/November). Culturally sensitive instructional practices for African-American learners with disabilities. *Exceptional Children, 59* (2), 115–122.

Friend, M. (2005). *Special education: Contemporary perspectives for school professionals.* Needham Heights, MA: Allyn & Bacon.

Friend, M. (2008). *Special education: Contemporary perspectives for school professionals* (2nd ed.). Boston: Allyn & Bacon.

Fuchs, D., Mock, D., Morgan, P. L., & Young, C. L. (2003). Responsiveness-to-intervention: Definitions, evidence, and implications for the learning disabilities construct. *Learning Disabilities Research & Practice, 18*(3), 157–171.

Gargiulo, R. (2008). *Special education in contemporary society: Introduction to exceptionality* (3rd ed.). Thousand Oaks, CA: Sage Publications, Inc.

Glascoe, F.P. (2011). *CIBS–R: Standardization and validation manual.* Retrieved on January 9, 2011, from http://www.casamples.com/downloads/BrigCIBS-R-research.pdf.

Goodman, Y., & Burke, C. (1972). *Reading miscue inventory manual: Procedure for diagnosis and evaluation.* New York: Macmillan.

Gresham, F. M. (2002). Responsiveness to intervention: An alternative approach to the identification of learning disabilities. In R. Bradley, L. Danielson, & D. P. Hallahan (Eds.), *Identification of learning disabilities: Research to practice.* Mahwah, NJ: Lawrence Erlbaum.

Gresham, F. M., Lane, K. L., MacMillan, D. L., & Bocian, K. M. (1999). Social and academic profiles of externalizing and internalizing groups: Risk factors for emotional and behavioral disorders. *Behavioral Disorders, 24,* 231–245.

Hager, R. (1999). *Funding of assistive technology.* Assistive technology funding and systems change project. Retrieved January 14, 2011, from http://www.springerlink.com/content/r3x1014426275883/.

Hall, T., & Mengel, M. (2002). *Curriculum-based evaluations.* Retrieved on January 2, 2011, from http://www.cast.org/publications/ncac/ncac_ curriculumbe.html.

Hanson, M. J., & Lynch, E. W. (1995b). Survival guide for interviewers. Austin, TX: PRO-ED. Harcourt Brace Educational Measurement. (1996). *Stanford-Diagnostic Mathematical Test–4th edition.* San Antonio, TX: Harcourt Brace.

Hanson, M., & Lynch, E. (1995a). *Early intervention: Implementing child and family services for infants and toddlers who are at risk or disabled* (2nd ed.). Austin, TX: PRO-ED.

Harry, B. (1992). *Cultural diversity, families, and the special education system: Communication and empowerment.* New York: Teachers College Press.

Hart, D. (1994). *Authentic assessment: A handbook for educators.* Menlo Park, CA: Addison-Wesley.

Heiman, G. (2002). *Research methods in psychology* (3rd ed.). Boston: Houghton Mifflin.

Herman, J., Aschbacher, P., & Winters, L. (1992). *A practical guide to alternative assessment.* Alexandria: Association for Supervision and Curriculum Development.

Heward, W. L. (2009). *Exceptional children: An introduction to special education* (9th ed.). Upper Saddle River: Merrill/Pearson Education.

Hoy, C., & Gregg, N. (1994). *Assessment: The special educator's role.* Pacific Grove, CA: Brookes/Cole.

Iowa Department of Education. (1997). *Assessment and decision making for special education entitlement: Technical assistance guide for mental disability.* Des Moines, IA: Bureau of Special Education.

Ireland, J. (2010). *The disadvantages of IQ tests.* Retrieved on January 12, 2011, from http://www.livestrong.com/article/127284-disadvantages-iq-tests/.

Jensen, M. (2005). *Introduction to emotional and behavioral disorders: Recognizing and managing*

problems in the classroom. Upper Saddle River, NJ: Merrill/Prentice Hall.

John, J. L. (1985). *Basic reading inventory* (3rd ed.). Boise, IA: Kendall-Hunt.

Lane, D. M. (2011). *Measurement Scales.* Retrieved on January 8, 2011, from http://davidmlane.com/hyperstat/A30028.html.

Learning Disabilities Roundtable. (2002, July). Specific learning disabilities: Finding common ground. A report by the ten organizations participating in the Learning Disabilities Roundtable, Sponsored by the Division of Research, Office of Special Education Programs, Department of Education, Washington, DC. Retrieved April 11, 2006, from http://www.ncld.org/ content/view/280.

Learning Disabilities Roundtable. (2005, February). *Comments and recommendations on regulatory issues under the Individuals with Disabilities Education Improvement Act of 2004.* Public Law 108–446.

Lerner, J. W. (2005). *Learning disabilities: Theories, diagnosis, and teaching strategies* (10th ed.). Boston: Houghton Mifflin. Lezak, M. D. (1995). *Neuropsychological assessment* (4th ed.). New York: Oxford University Press.

Luckasson, R. (2002). *Mental retardation: Definition, classification, and systems of supports* (10th ed.). Washington, DC: American Association on Mental Retardation.

Lyon, G. R., Fletcher, J. M., Shaywitz, S. E., Shaywitz, B. A., Torgeson, J. K., Wood, F. B., et al. (2001). Rethinking learning disabilities. In C. E. Finn, Jr., A. J. Rotherham, & C. R. Hokanson, Jr. (Eds.), *Rethinking special education for a new century* (pp. 259–287). Washington, DC: Progressive Policy Institute & The Thomas B. Fordham Foundation.

Marston, D. (2001, August). *A functional and intervention-based assessment approach to establishing discrepancy for students with learning disabilities.* Paper presented at the LD Summit, Washington, DC.

McLane (2011). *What is curriculum-based measurement and what does it mean to my child?* Retrieved on January 13, 2011, from http://www.studentprogress.org/families.asp.

McLean, M., Wolery, M., & Bailey, Jr., D. B. (2004). *Assessing infants and preschoolers with special needs* (3rd ed.). Upper Saddle River, NJ: Merrill.

McLoughlin, J. A., & Lewis, R. B. (2008). *Assessing students with special needs* (7th ed.). Upper Saddle River, NJ: Merrill/Pearson.

Mellard D. (2003). *Understanding responsiveness to intervention in learning disabilities determination.* Retrieved August 2007, from http://www.nrcld.org/publications/papers/mellard.shtml.

Mills v. Board of Education. (1972). DC, 348 F.Supp. 866 (D. DC 1972). United States District Court, District of Columbia.

Morris, G. (2001). *Psychology: An introduction* (11th ed.). Upper Saddle River, NJ: Prentice Hall.

Multi-Health Systems (2011). *Conners 3rd edition™.* Retrieved on January 14, 2011, from http://www.mhs.com/product.aspx?gr=cli&prod=conners3&id=overview.

Myers, A., & Hansen, C. (2002). *Experimental psychology* (6th ed.). Belmont, CA: Brooks/Cole.

National Association of State Directors of Special Education (NASDSE), Inc. (2005). *Response to intervention: Policy considerations and implementation.* Alexandria, VA: Author.

National Center for Education Statistics. (2007). *American education at a glance.* Washington, DC: Author.

National Council of Supervisors of Mathematics. (1978). Position statement on basic skills. *Mathematics Teacher, 71,* 147–152.

National Dissemination Center for Children with Disabilities. (2004a). *Learning disabilities: A fact sheet.* Retrieved September 10, 2006, from http://www.nichcy.org/pubs/factshe/fs7txt.htm.

National Dissemination Center for Children with Disabilities. (2004b). *Mental retardation.* Retrieved July 13, 2005, from http://www.nichcy.org/pubs/factshe/fs8txt.htm.

National Information Center for Children and Youths with Disabilities (2000). *Questions and answers about IDEA.* Retrieved January 14, 2011, from http://www.nichcy.org/InformationResources/Documents/NICHCY%20PUBS/nd21.pdf.

National Information Center for Children and Youths with Disabilities (1996). *The education of children and youth with special needs: What do the laws say?* Retrieved January 14, 2011, from http://www.nichcy.org/InformationResources/Documents/NICHCY%20PUBS/nd15.pdf.

National Joint Committee on Learning Disabilities (NJCLD). (2005). *Responsiveness to intervention and learning disabilities.* Retrieved on January 20, 2011, from http://www.ncld.org/content/view/497.

National Joint Committee on Learning Disabilities (NJCLD). (2005). *Responsiveness to intervention and learning disabilities.* Retrieved on February 20, 2007, from http://www.ncld.org/content/view/497.

National Library of Congress. (2005). *Mental retardation.* Retrieved October 20, 2007, from http://www.nlm.gov/medlineplus/ency/article/001523.htm.

National Mental Health Information Center. (2003). *Child and adolescent mental health.* Retrieved on March 23, 2008, from http://mentalhealth.samhsa.gov/publications/allpubs/CA-0004/default.asp.

National Research Center on Learning Disabilities. (2007). *Responsiveness to intervention in conjunction with learning disability determination.* [Brochure]. Lawrence, KS: Author.

National Research Council. (2002). *Scientific research in education.* Washington, DC: National Academy Press.

Navarete, C., Wilde, J., Nelson, C., Martinez, R. & Hergett, G. (1990). *Informal assessment in educational evaluation: Implications for bilingual programs.* Retrieved on July 29, 2010, from http://www.finchpark.com/courses/assess/informal.htm.

New York State Department of Health. (2000). *Early intervention program: A parent's guide.* Albany, NY: Author.

North Carolina School Psychology Association (2004). Referring and evaluating limited English proficient (LEP) students for programs and services for children with special needs. Retrieved on January 12, 2011, from http://ncschoolpsy.org/NCSPALEPProfessionalPracticePaper.pdf.

O'Connor, R., Tilly, D., Vaughn, S., & Marston, D. (2003). *How many tiers are needed within RTI to achieve acceptable prevention outcomes and to achieve acceptable patterns of LD identification?* Individual papers presented at NRCLD Symposium, Response to Intervention, Kansas City, MO. Retrieved on January 21, 2011, from http://www.nrcld.org/symposium2003/ index.html.

Office for Civil Rights. (2006). *Americans with Disabilities Act (ADA).* Retrieved on February 2, 2011, from http://www.ed.gov/about/offices/list/ocr/docs/hq9805.html.

Overton, T. (2009). *Assessment in special education: An applied approach* (6th ed.). Upper Saddle River, NJ: Merrill.

PARC v. Commonwealth of Pennsylvania. (1972). 343 F. Supp. 279, E.D. PA.

PASE v. Hannon. (1980). No. 74 C 3586 N.D. Ill.

Pierangelo, R., & Giuliani, G. (2007). *The special educator's comprehensive guide to 301 diagnostic tests.* San Francisco: Jossey Bass.

Pierangelo, R., & Giuliani, G. (2009). *Assessment in special education: A practical approach* (3rd ed.). Boston: Allyn & Bacon.

Plake, T., & Impara, B. (2001). *Fourteenth mental measurement yearbook.* Lincoln: University of Nebraska Press.

President's Commission on Excellence in Special Education. (2002). *A new era: Revitalizing special education for children and their families.* Washington, DC: U.S. Department of Education.

Reschly, D. J., Hosp, J. L., & Schmied, C. M. (2003). *And miles to go . . . : State SLD requirements and authoritative recommendations.* Retrieved July 21, 2005, from Vanderbilt University, National Research Center on Learning Disabilities web site http://www.nrcld.org/research/states.

Rutter, M., & Yule, W. (1975). The concept of specific reading retardation. *Journal of Child Psychology and Psychiatry, 16,* 181–197.

Salvia, J., & Ysseldyke, J. (2007). *Assessment: In special and inclusive education* (10th ed.). Boston: Houghton Mifflin.

Sattler, J. (2001). *Assessment of children* (5th ed.). San Diego: Sattler.

Sattler, J. (2008). *Assessment of children: Cognitive foundations* (5th ed.). La Mesa: Jerome M. Sattler Publisher Inc.

Stanovich, K. (2005). The future of a mistake: Will discrepancy measurement continue to make the learning disabilities field a pseudoscience? *Learning Disability Quarterly, 28,* 103–105.

Steubing, K. K., Fletcher, J. M., LeDoux, J. M., Lyon, G. R., Shaywitz, S. E., & Shaywitz, B. A. (2002). Validity of IQ-discrepancy classification of learning disabilities: A meta-analysis. *American Educational Research Journal, 39*(2), 469–518.

Stump, C. (2011). Before special ed: How pre-referral works. Retrieved on January 12, 2011, from http://www.greatschools.org/special-education/LD-ADHD/pre-referral.gs?content=517.

Tabachnick, B.G., & Fidell, L.S. (2007). *Using multivariate statistics* (5th ed.). Boston: Allyn & Bacon.

Tallal, P., Miller, S. L., Bedi, G., Byma, G., Wang, X., Nagarjan, S. S., et al. (1996). Language comprehension in language-learning impaired children improved with acoustically modified speech. *Science, 271,* 81–84.

Taylor, R. (2009). *Assessment of exceptional students: Educational and psychological procedures* (8th ed.). Upper Saddle River: Merrill/Pearson.

Turnbull, A., Turnbull, R., Shank, M., & Smith, S. J. (2004). *Exceptional lives: Special education in today's schools* (4th ed.). Upper Saddle River, NJ: Merrill/Pearson.

U.S. Department of Education (2011). *Digest of Education Statistics: 2009* (Table 50). Washington, DC.

U.S. Department of Education (2011). *The Carl D. Perkins Vocational and Technical Education Act, Public Law 105–332.* Retrieved on July 3, 2007, from http://www2.ed.gov/policy/sectech/leg/perkins/index.html.

U.S. Department of Health and Human Services (2006). *Your rights under section 504: Fact sheet.* Retrieved on July 6, 2007, from http://www.hhs.gov/ocr/civilrights/resources/factsheets/504.pdf.

U.S. Department of Labor Employment and Training Administration. (1999). *Understanding test quality-concepts of reliability and validity.* Retrieved on January 13, 2011, from http://www.hr-guide.com/data/G362.htm.

Vacca, J., Vacca, R., & Grove, M. (1986). *Reading and learning to read.* Boston: Little, Brown.

Venn, J. J. (1999). *Assessing students with special needs* (2nd ed.). Upper Saddle River, NJ: Merrill/Pearson.

Venn, J. J. (2007). *Assessing students with special needs* (4th ed.). Upper Saddle River, NJ: Merrill/Pearson.

Virginia Department of Education Office of Student Services (2009). *RTI and the special education eligibility process*: Frequently asked questions. Retrieved on January 12, 2011, from http://www.doe.virginia.gov/instruction/response_intervention/guidance/special_ed_eligibility_faq.pdf.

Wallace, G., Larsen, S. C., & Elksnin, L. K. (1992). *Educational assessment of learning problems: Testing for teaching* (2nd ed.). Boston: Allyn & Bacon.

Waterman, B. (1994). Assessing children for the presence of a disability. *NICHCY News Digest, 4*(1), 1–15.

Wright, J. (2007). *Curriculum-based measurement: A manual for teachers.* Retrieved on July 2, 2007, from http://www.jimwrightonline.com/pdfdocs/cbaManual.pdf.

Wyatt v. Stickney. (1972). 344 F. Supp. 387 M.D. Ala.

Zisko, D. (2010). The advantages of IQ testing. Retrieved on January 12, 2011, from http://www.livestrong.com/article/129676-advantages-iq-tests/.

NAME INDEX

SUBJECT INDEX

TEST NAME INDEX